CREATING THE NATION IN PROVINCIAL FRANCE

CREATING THE NATION
IN PROVINCIAL FRANCE

RELIGION AND POLITICAL IDENTITY
IN BRITTANY

Caroline Ford

PRINCETON UNIVERSITY PRESS   PRINCETON, NEW JERSEY

Copyright © 1993 by Princeton University Press
Published by Princeton University Press, 41 William Street,
Princeton, New Jersey 08540
In the United Kingdom: Princeton University Press, Chichester, West Sussex

Library of Congress Cataloging-in-Publication Data

Ford, Caroline C., 1956–
    Creating the nation in provincial France : religion and political identity in Brittany /
Caroline Ford.
        p.   cm.
    Includes bibliographical references and index.
    ISBN 0-691-05667-6
    1. Finistère (France)—Politics and government.   2. France—Politics and
government—1789–.   3. Acculturation—France—Finistère—Political
aspects.   4. Politics and culture—France—Finistère.   5. Nationalism—France—
Finistère.   6. Revolutions—France—Finistère—Religious aspects—Catholic
Church.   I. Title.
DC611.F498F67   1993
944'.11—dc20   92-20828   CIP

This book has been composed in Linotron Sabon

Princeton University Press books are printed
on acid-free paper, and meet the guidelines
for permanence and durability of the Committee
on Production Guidelines for Book Longevity
of the Council on Library Resources

Printed in the United States of America

10 9 8 7 6 5 4 3 2 1

In memory of my Father

_____

Contents

List of Maps and Tables _____

Maps

Tables

Acknowledgments

THIS BOOK began as a doctoral dissertation at the University of Chicago, where I benefited from the sound judgment and counsel of Jan Goldstein, Keith Baker, and John Boyer. Through the years Jan Goldstein's incisive criticism, warm support, and enthusiasm have been a continuing source of inspiration. Keith Baker brought his very useful insights to bear on this book's conceptual framework, and his own study of French political culture stimulated me to think about my work from new perspectives.

I owe a debt to many librarians and archivists in France and the United States, but I would particularly like to acknowledge the help of Daniel Collet in identifying sources and ensuring that various microfilms were sent expeditiously from the Archives Départementales du Finistère to the United States. On my numerous visits to the Archives de l'Eveché de Quimper, chanoine Le Floc'h was always a welcoming host and generously shared his immense knowledge of Lower Brittany with me. Many people made my stay in Finistère both enjoyable and memorable. In particular, Roseline Manière's kind hospitality made the splendid *manoir* of Tulgoat a home away from home, and Jacques and Hélène Guias's marvelous dinners enlivened the long winter months.

Closer to home, many colleagues, friends, and institutions have been of immeasurable intellectual and material assistance to me. I wrote much of this book at Harvard's Minda de Gunzburg Center for European Studies. Stanley Hoffmann, Patrice Higonnet, Olwen Hufton, Simon Schama, Charlie Maier, Susan Pedersen, Laura Frader, Peter Hall, and Tom Ertman, among many others, make the Center a highly congenial and enormously stimulating environment in which to work. My friend and colleague Olwen Hufton generously read the entire manuscript and made excellent suggestions for revision. I will always be grateful for her steadfast support and indispensable advice at a particularly critical moment. I deeply appreciate Patrice Higonnet's kind encouragement in commenting on the manuscript, and I learned much from conversations with my neighbor at the Center, Simon Schama.

Suzanne Desan shared her own work on lay religion and popular politics and graciously read the entire manuscript. Dena Goodman helped me to improve the introduction and chapter 5. Margot Finn, James Johnson, Don Sutherland, and Gene Lebovics all commented on portions of the manuscript. I am very grateful to Ted Margadant and Peter Jones for their close and careful reading of the text. Their suggestions for revision (almost all of which I eventually adopted) were invaluable to me.

I gratefully acknowledge the financial support provided by the Social Science Research Council, American Council of Learned Societies, Georges Lurcy Educational Trust, and Fribourg Foundation, which made the original research for my dissertation possible. The Norman Foundation and Harvard University's Clark Fund enabled me to spend two summers in France undertaking additional research. A Georges Lurcy Foundation Faculty Fellowship has once again provided me with valuable leave time in which to finish the manuscript and underwrote the cost of the maps. I thank Rick Belsky for his helpful research assistance and Eliza McLennan for executing the maps in record time. I am grateful to the editors of the *Journal of Modern History* and the University of Chicago Press for allowing me to reprint parts of a previously published article. At Princeton University Press, Joanna Hitchcock showed unflagging enthusiasm for this project. Lauren Osborne and Colin Barr shepherded the manuscript through the publication process with remarkable efficiency and good cheer.

Finally, Joe Wagstaff's editorial advice, humor, and unfailing support contributed in no small measure to the successful completion of this book.

Cambridge, Massachusetts
December 1991

CREATING THE NATION IN PROVINCIAL FRANCE

Introduction ────────────────────────────

THIS BOOK explores the relationship between religion and the formation of national identity in provincial France in the two centuries following the French Revolution. It is both a study of the construction of national identity by elite groups in Paris and an analysis of nation building from the perspective of the periphery. It examines local expressions of identity and the creation of national attachments by focusing more particularly on the political acculturation of the inhabitants of the lower Breton department of Finistère through the agency of a social Catholic political movement that emerged in the far reaches of the Breton peninsula at the end of the nineteenth century.

The pace and extent of the integration of provincial France into a common national political culture have recently been subjects of heated debate among historians on both sides of the Atlantic. The French Revolution has long been considered the great political watershed marking the advent of new political labels and the participation of a large proportion of the French population in national politics for the first time.[1] Historians of nineteenth-century France, however, have long seen that this was true only to a limited extent. The Revolution did galvanize the country as a whole and create a new political language, but it did not foster a shared understanding of national community, particularly in provincial France. Many men and women continued to identify more with their locality than with the nation state.[2]

Some scholars have argued that the experience of 1848 led to the political and cultural integration of important areas of rural France in the post-revolutionary period,[3] while others have claimed that not until the Third Republic did roads, railways, market expansion, and military conscription successfully sweep away old commitments, instill a "national view in re-

---

[1] Nonetheless, historians have argued that it is possible to find expressions of patriotism in the borderlands of the French kingdom before the revolutionary moment. Godechot, "Nation, patrie, nationalisme et patriotisme en France"; and Conor Cruise O'Brien, "Nationalism and the French Revolution," in *The Permanent Revolution: The French Revolution and Its Legacy, 1789–1989*, ed. Geoffrey Best (London, 1988), pp. 17–48. For a view from the periphery, see Peter Sahlins's excellent *Boundaries*, and "The Nation in the Village." Also see J. Armstrong, *Nations Before Nationalism* (Chapel Hill, 1982).

[2] This is a position taken by both Jones, *Politics and Rural Society*, and Karnoouh, "La démocratie impossible."

[3] Charles Tilly, "How Protest Modernized in France, 1845–1955," in *The Dimensions of Quantitative Research in History*, ed., William O. Aydelotte et al. (Princeton, 1972); Margadant, *French Peasants in Revolt*.

gional minds," and confirm "the power of that view by offering advancement to those who adopted it."[4] Still others have argued that provincial France will forever be incompletely integrated into a common political culture.[5]

The timing of the process by which the borderlands of France came to participate in the larger national community in the postrevolutionary period has thus been subject to sharp debate and can by no means be fixed decisively at any moment in time.[6] Opposing views of this process can in part be attributed to regional disparities within France and to differences in how national integration has been defined. It has, for example, been associated with the advance of a progressive, enlightened Left in electoral politics.[7] It has implied the perception that there is a direct and clear link between national politics and local social, economic, and cultural concerns.[8] Moreover, the process of national integration has quite simply meant the degree to which men and women imagined themselves to be a part of a community whose boundaries extended beyond the household, village, or region.[9]

If the timing and nature of the integration of provincial France has been subject to dispute, since the Revolution the conceptual boundaries of national community have also been contested and politicized. In repudiating many institutions associated with the Bourbon monarchy and in attempting to erase the memory of the ancien régime, the Revolution left France with an understanding of the "nation" that was grounded in both the principles of the revolution and a shared prerevolutionary cultural past. Indeed, the nineteenth and twentieth centuries have proven to be a battleground for a people who attempted to come to terms with their contested history and with the claims to a largely disputed national idea.[10]

Although there has been sharp disagreement over the nature of French national identity, there has been surprising consensus regarding the general process of national and political integration in France. Influenced by modernization theory borrowed from the social sciences, as the subtitle of one of the most important of these works suggests,[11] historians have generally

---

[4] Weber, *Peasants Into Frenchmen*, p. 486.

[5] See, e.g., Karnoouh in "La démocratie impossible."

[6] See ibid.; Tilly, "Did the Cake of Custom Break?" pp. 17–41; Margadant, *French Peasants in Revolt*; Agulhon, "Vues nouvelles sur la France rurale"; Margadant, "Tradition and Modernity in Rural France," pp. 668–97; Jones, *Politics and Rural Society*; Sahlins, *Boundaries* and "The Nation in the Village."

[7] See, e.g., Maurice Agulhon, *La république au village: les populations du Var de la révolution à la Seconde République* (Paris, 1970).

[8] Berger, *Peasants Against Politics*.

[9] Anderson, *Imagined Communities*.

[10] See Nora, "Nation," pp. 742–52.

[11] Weber, *Peasants Into Frenchmen*.

distinguished between local and national politics and between "archaic" and "modern" forms of political behavior. According to this view, a national consciousness emerges and politicization occurs when a local *politique du clocher* (petty power struggles shaped by local loyalties and enmities and kinship) are undermined by the forces of cultural and economic modernization. This center-based typology—resting as it does on the binary oppositions of urban/rural, elite/popular, traditional/modern—has dominated current historical approaches to the phenomenon of politicization and nation formation.[12] The political integration of rural France has primarily been analyzed in terms of how urban values were disseminated in the countryside and how large-scale social and economic change—industrialization, new modes of production, and technologies—ultimately broke down local cultural attitudes and political practices. In this view, national identity, defined as a curiously reified object, is something imposed by the center on the periphery: Provincial France became integrated into the political life of the French nation as national political issues and urban values replaced those at the borders of France.

This study of politics, religion, and the creation of the nation in the lower Breton department of Finistère from 1890 to 1926 challenges this center-based analysis of political acculturation and reconceptualizes the problem of nation formation in postrevolutionary France. It shows that the creation of national identity is a process continually in the making rather than the imposition of a fixed set of values and beliefs. Indeed, this study understands the formation of national identity as a process by which individuals and social groups define and redefine themselves, and it examines how "people actually represented themselves to themselves and to each other."[13] As the way in which the nation was created in Lower Brittany was largely shaped by religious conflicts that occurred in the context of the state's attempts to impose a secular, republican conception of the nation at the periphery and by a social Catholic movement that emerged in response to these conflicts, religion is an important interpretive key to understanding nation formation in this work.

In France, however, religion has generally been regarded as an impediment to national integration, in contrast to other parts of Europe where religion has been pressed into the service of defining ethnic and national claims.[14] The nineteenth-century historian Jules Michelet began his great

---

[12] See, for example, Bendix, *Nation-Building and Citizenship*; Karl Deutsch, *Nationalism and Social Communication: An Inquiry Into the Foundations of Nationality* (Cambridge, Mass., 1953); Deutsch, "Some Problems in the Study of Nation-Building," in *Nation-Building*, ed. K. Deutsch and W. Folz (New York, 1963). There are some persuasive exceptions to this rule. See Sahlins, *Boundaries*, and Jones, *Politics and Rural Society*.

[13] Clifford Geertz, "'From the Native's Point of View': On the Nature of Anthropological Understanding," in *Local Knowledge*, p. 58.

[14] See, for example, the essays in *Religion and Nationalism in Soviet and East European Politics*, ed. Ramet.

history of the French Revolution with the question of whether Christianity could be reconciled with the revolutionary nation: he concluded that he could see only "two principles, two actors and two persons, Christianity and the Revolution."[15] Indeed, historians have continued to view religion more as a divisive element in French society than as an integrative force and have tended to regard popular religiosity less as an expression of social cohesion than as a vehicle of elite domination.[16] Throughout much of the nineteenth century the French Catholic Church and popular religiosity were tarred with the brush of political reaction, obscurantism, and traditionalism. The historical record provides many examples to justify the blackened picture. More often than not—during the revolution of 1848 and the Commune of 1871—an ultramontane Church and clergy sided with the Pope, the Right, and a monarchist nobility against the Republic. The emergence of a social Catholic movement in Lower Brittany at the end of the nineteenth century has also been seen as a reactionary movement, as a reflection of attempts by local elites to shield the peasantry from the state's effort to integrate the diverse regions of France into the larger republican nation.[17] I argue that religious institutions did serve as avenues of resistance to the state at the periphery, but they often also played an integrative role by mediating the cultural conflicts between center and periphery thereby reconciling the nation with the region. I argue that the political crisis following the growing intrusion by the state in local affairs during the early Third Republic resulted in the selective appropriation of republican articulations of national identity and in attempts by social Catholic groups, who became the dominant political forces in the region, to bridge the political claims of the republican nation with the cultural claims of the region. This book examines, then, how religious institutions and ideologies expressed as well as shaped social norms and how those norms were reassessed as well as criticized. At both the center and the periphery the meaning with which the nation was invested was continually redefined: the nation as an "imagined community"[18] was a fluid ideological construction governed by political exigency, historical memory, and competing interests.

[15] Jules Michelet, *History of the French Revolution*, trans. Charles Cocks (Chicago, 1967), p. 18.

[16] Emile Durkheim's social analysis of religion as "collective representations that express collective realities" has not, in general, guided studies of religion in nineteenth-century France. It is rather Max Weber's perspective on the uses of religion in legitimizing elite rule that has tended to shape postrevolutionary historiography. Emile Durkheim, *The Elementary Forms of Religious Life*, trans. Joseph Ward Swain (New York, 1915; reprint 1965), p. 22, and Max Weber, *The Sociology of Religion*, trans. E. Fischoff (1922; reprint, Boston, 1963).

[17] Berger, *Peasants Against Politics*, pp. 1, 10, 49–54.

[18] Anderson, *Imagined Communities*, and Pierre Nora's multivolumed *Lieux de mémoire* (Paris, 1984–) have recently suggested some fruitful ways in which to examine the "imagined" or symbolic dimension of nation building.

The lower Breton department of Finistère might appear to be an unlikely locus to explore the formation of national identity because of the region's continued reputed difference. Finistère—end of the earth—lies at the extreme westerly tip of the French hexagon. Brought into existence during a Revolution that attempted to efface the memory of the province and *pays*, the department unites the southern region of Cornouaille and portions of the Vannetais to the south with the Léon to the north. Finistère, France's westernmost department whose rocky coast to the north and west jut out into the waters of the Channel and the Atlantic, has long fascinated scholars, government administrators, and intrepid travelers because of its history of insubordination, its cultural and linguistic distinctiveness, in short, its "otherness." Since the early observations of Emile Souvestre in *Les derniers bretons* at the beginning of the nineteenth century, the province has long been a central site of folkloric and anthropological study in France. Lower Brittany became the principal site of my research precisely because it was one of the last regions to become incorporated into the French state: it retained its indigenous cultural traditions, including a marked attachment to the Catholic faith. It became, moreover, an important stronghold of a social Catholic political movement that played a vital role in shaping the way in which local populations confronted the French state and reconciled their identities as Bretons and Catholics within a larger nation. For this reason the emergence and development of a democratic variety of social Catholicism in Finistère stand at the center of this book. Social Catholicism does not, however, easily fit into standard interpretations of French political alignments or into standard theories of political modernization. The intellectual origins and complexities of this form of republicanism, which shared elements of right- and left-wing ideology, have been ably studied.[19] But its grassroots political, cultural, and social history has largely been ignored, or it has been argued that the movement consistently worked against national integration. This book calls such assessments of the movement into question and demonstrates the ways in which it played a vital role in creating a national consciousness at the periphery even as it defended local attachments and allegiances.

As the political acculturation of Finistère and the emergence of social Catholicism occurred within the context of attempts by an anticlerical republican government to secularize and republicanize the French countryside in the twenty-five years before World War I, chapter 1 examines the ways in which the nation was defined by the Left and the Right during the nineteenth century. Whereas many prevailing views of French nationalism and the formation of national identity posit the nation as a given, as a

---

[19] Emile Poulat, *Catholicisme, démocratie et socialisme* (Paris, 1977); Poulat, *Eglise contre bourgeoisie*; Mayeur, "Catholicisme intransigeant," pp. 483–99.

product of state building,[20] I emphasize the symbolic, imagined components in the construction of national and political identities. This chapter
traces the political articulation of national belonging in the postrevolutionary period and, in particular, examines why republican groups at the center
came to express a notion of nationhood at the end of the nineteenth century
that was predicated on linguistic, cultural, and political unity. This republican conception of nationality underpinned centrally coordinated policies
aimed at national integration as they came to be the object of bitter contesta-
tion at the periphery. Subsequent chapters explore a continuing negotiation
between center and periphery and the ways in which identity defined at the
center was resisted, redefined, and transformed in the provinces.

Chapter 2 moves from Paris to the provinces. This chapter examines the
nature of the society that the republican state sought to replace, while
reassessing the economic and social foundations on which interpretations
of Breton social Catholicism have rested. As some historians and social
scientists have suggested that social Catholicism blocked the integration of
Finistère into the nation and have posited the existence of a "traditional"
rural society without forms of organization or links to the outside world,
chapter 2 examines the nature and extent of economic and social change in
Finistère. It demonstrates that "traditional" society in Finistère underwent
significant transformation during the first half of the nineteenth century,
but retained distinctive cultural characteristics that set it apart from the
rest of France.

Chapters 3 and 4 describe how the social Catholic movement emerged in
Finistère and served as a bridge between center and periphery. They argue
that Finistère's cultural characteristics provide a prism through which to
understand political change and the formation of a national consciousness.
They explain how the local clergy became the political brokers of the
movement and, in contrast to their counterparts elsewhere, repudiated
royalism.

Chapters 5 and 6 explore the ideological basis of Breton social Catholicism, how the social Catholic movement garnered broad-based support,
and why Finistère was particularly receptive to "Catholic republicanism."
The state's anticlerical policies of the turn-of-the-century did much to
heighten awareness of the impact of national policy in local affairs, driving
many into the arms of the social Catholic cause. Moreover, mass resistance
to the secular and linguistic policies of the French state revealed the central
role assumed by women in articulating local demands and defending local
institutions. An analysis of this resistance explores the ways in which gen-

---

[20] Peter Sahlins's *Boundaries* and Gérard Noiriel's *Le creuset français* argue against this
perspective. Noiriel, in particular, critiques the ways in which Pierre Chaunu, Fernand
Braudel, and Pierre Nora,—to name a few of the most noted French historians—have presented the nation and national identity as a given, a *toujours déjà là*, by the French Revolution.

der and popular religious institutions shaped local claims and allegiances in response to attempts to impose a secular, unitary conception of national community on Lower Brittany.

Chapter 7 examines how this social Catholic political movement dominated local politics in the 1920s and played a central role in the formation of the first national Christian Democratic party in France in 1924, which formed a *troisième voie*, mediating between the parties of Left and Right. Indeed, it was an important precursor of one of the largest political parties in France after World War II, the Mouvement Républicain Populaire.

The social Catholic movement and religion more generally did not serve as a vehicle to express mass-based claims to an alternative "nation" predicated on ethnic or religious ties in Lower Brittany. Chapter 8 evaluates the significance of the social Catholic movement by explaining patterns of nation formation at the periphery and suggests hypotheses for the absence of mass-based support for an alternative ethnic minority nationalist movement in the region before the Second World War.

The lower Breton case and others like it in France and western Europe have led some observers to conclude that certain areas never became integrated into the political life of the nation because of the persistence of regional and religious identities. To arrive at such a conclusion is to fail to confront local articulations of the national identity. In Finistère, these articulations must be understood in terms of the ways in which cultural and national identity came to be separately defined in the context of a structural process of democratization that marked *la fin des notables*. The history of the lower Breton department of Finistère shows that political change and national awareness were effected not through the wholesale importation of urban values, Parisian political movements, and the assimilation of the periphery into the center, but through an indigenous movement that emerged in the countryside and ultimately came to represent the periphery at the center.

This study finally suggests a new framework for understanding the acculturation of a society far from the capital and examines the nature of national, cultural, and local identifications. Indeed, my task has been to see why these identities often collided and how they came to be contested and politicized. This is not, then, another regional or local study that explains why a region voted Left or Right. Nor is it a work that further emphasizes the endless diversity of the French landscape and celebrates or laments rites of passage into the present. As a study of nation building and acculturation, this work shows how and why regions both resisted and appropriated policies of national integration while voicing new political ideologies fashioned from local understanding.

1

Which Nation? Language, Identity, and Republican Politics in Postrevolutionary France

IN 1882, Ernest Renan devoted a public lecture at the Sorbonne to the question, "What Is a Nation?" He affirmed that the nation was a spiritual principle, a personality, shaped by a common will and memory as well as by a process of historical forgetting: "Man is a slave neither of his race nor of his language, nor of his religion, nor of the course of rivers, nor of the direction of mountain chains. A great aggregate of men, healthy in spirit and warm of heart, creates the kind of moral conscience which we call a nation."[1] For Renan, common ideas, a common will, consent, and shared memory were more important components of nationality than birth, lineage, or language. This political conception of the nation, which was predicated on consent and a shared historical past within the spatial grid of a territorial, centralized state, shaped republican conceptions of French national identity and the historiography of French nationalism since the French Revolution. A long tradition in the historiography of French nationalism has posited a static, unitary conception of the French nation. Indeed, one central and ostensible difference between French and German nationalisms of the nineteenth century is the emphasis that the former placed on consent and contract and that the latter assigned to a common culture in defining the identity of the nation. France's "political" nationalism, defined in terms of a collective social contract and given currency by Jean-Jacques Rousseau, and Germany's "cultural" nationalism, so clearly articulated by J. G. Herder, are frequently compared and contrasted with one another.[2]

Although political nationalism was an important component of France's revolutionary republican legacy, French nationalism was by no means as unchanging as such a typology implies. The French Revolution left France with a fundamentally contested conception of who and what constituted the nation. In replacing the public person of the sovereign with the "nation," the Revolution ultimately spawned differing and shifting understandings of the nation among the Right and the Left in the postrevolution-

---

[1] Renan, "What Is a Nation?" p. 20. See Ernest Renan, *Qu'est-ce qu'une nation?*.
[2] See, e.g., Barnard, "National Culture and Political Legitimacy," 231–53.

ary period.[3] Conflicting claims to the nation and the national past were deeply rooted in the political divisions created by the Revolution, and these divisions dominated the postrevolutionary public arena of politics. Throughout much of the nineteenth century the republican Left, issuing from the Revolution, tended to define the nation in terms of a common sovereign will and contract; it repudiated language, race, or ethnicity as criteria for national belonging. The postrevolutionary Right, however, laid claim to a conception of France rooted in France's monarchical and prerevolutionary past.[4]

By 1900, however, both the republican Left and a nationalist Right paradoxically began to define the nation in similar terms by placing a new emphasis on culture as a central component of French national identity. This new emphasis came to underpin state-centered policies designed to create national consensus and to integrate the disparate regions of provincial France into a common political culture. In no domain is this process of national redefinition clearer than in the way in which the French language became an essential defining feature of French national identity. Despite the publication of a number of important studies on state formation and national identity in postrevolutionary France, the question of why language became a vital part of the cultural system out of which French "nationness" was constructed by the beginning of the twentieth century remains obscure.[5] This development, in turn, raises questions concerning the conditions under which language became a necessary constituent element of French national identity, and the extent to which the insistence on a common language was reconciled with democratic, consensual understandings of national belonging, which ostensibly eschewed criteria of ethnicity or culture for national belonging. In exploring the process of nation formation in Brittany toward the end of the nineteenth century, this chapter

[3] This suggests that historical assessments of the construction of French national identity must be problematized to a greater extent than they have. For a theroretical perspective on this problem, see Schlesinger, "On National Identity: Some Conceptions and Misconceptions Criticized," and Herman Lebovics, *True France: The Wars of Cultural Identity in France, 1900–1945* (Ithaca, N.Y., 1992).

[4] Pierre Nora has argued in an important essay that the French Revolution created a right- and left-wing nation; however, he appears to suggest that the boundaries between two conceptions of the French nation remained fixed from the Revolution onward. See Nora, "Nation," p. 749. For a critique of this immutable conception of the nation, see Noiriel, *Le creuset français*, pp. 13–67.

[5] See, however, David Laitin's comments in this regard in "Linguistic Revival: Politics and Culture in Catalonia," *Comparative Studies in Society and History* (1989): 297–317, esp. 297–301. For perspectives on this problem, see Fishman, ed., *Language Problems in Developing Nations*, and Jonathan Steinberg, "The Historian and the *questione della lingua*," in *The Social History of Language* (Cambridge, 1987), pp. 198–209. E. J. Hobsbawm has noted that attempts to eradicate minority languages and cultures in states outside of France were rare. Hobsbawm, *Nations and Nationalism since 1780*, p. 36.

begins by examining the question of why cultural uniformity and the complete renunciation of regional allegiance ultimately became essential components of French conceptions of nationality among republican elites by the early twentieth century. It suggests that the turn-of-the-century republican nation was a fluid ideological construction shaped by three phenomena: the revolutionary memory, the paradoxical appropriation of both nationalism and regionalism by the New Right in the 1890s, and the preeminence of religious conflict as the central fact of French political and cultural life.

Language, Revolution, and National Memory

The centrality of language to definitions of the French political community was quite foreign to the Old Regime. Despite efforts by the French monarchy to encourage the use of the French language as early as 1539, when the Villers-Cotterêts decree made French the language of official documents, there was no implicit relationship between language and patriotism.[6] The sporadic attempts by the French crown to encourage the use of the French language served strategic purposes. Policies were implemented to propagate French among elites in borderland communities in order to facilitate governmental administration.[7] At key moments military considerations governed linguistic measures designed to insure the loyalty of royal administrators, as in 1682 when the sovereign council of Roussillon issued an edict that allowed only francophones to enter its administrative offices and liberal professions.[8] The monarchy, however, made no attempt to impose the French language on the masses.

Although policies created to promote the use of a national language among elites had been an inherent part of French state building since at least the sixteenth century, not until the French Revolution did language become a necessary feature of fundamentally new notions of national identity in France. From 1789 to 1794 the revolutionary leadership, like the Bourbon monarchy, tolerated linguistic plurality. The revolutionary government of 1789, translating government decrees and directives into regional tongues, appeared even more solicitous than the crown had been toward the use of languages other than French.

Linguistic uniformity did not become a political and cultural goal until

[6] Georges Mounin, *Histoire de la linguistique des origines au XX siècle* (Paris, 1985), p. 120.

[7] Febvre, "Langue et nationalité en France au XVIII siècle," 19–40, and Peyre, *La royauté et les langues provinciales*. Also see Sahlins, *Boundaries*, pp. 166–67.

[8] Sahlins, *Boundaries*, p. 116. Sahlins argues that before the Revolution state policies of gallicization remained "limited to administrative and political contexts" (p. 118).

the Revolution and, more specifically, the establishment of the first French Republic. Soon after the overthrow of the French monarchy in 1792 linguistic unity was introduced as a major subject of political debate, and in 1794 the French revolutionary leaders articulated a program that would promote linguistic uniformity.[9] In short, during the course of the revolutionary decade, the sovereign nation *une et indivisible* came to supplant the public person of the monarch, and for some revolutionary leaders, this nation was predicated on a unitary social body bound by a single common language.[10]

In 1794, year II of the Republic, a republican priest, abbé Grégoire, and the fiery orator Barère submitted independent reports on the necessity and means through which to abolish regional tongues and universalize the use of the French language,[11] as the knowledge of the French language became an essential indicator of national loyalty under the Republic. When Urbain Domergue declared, "let us efface [local] jargons as we have effaced the provinces,"[12] he voiced the sentiment of many members of the Committee of Public Safety and the leaders of the Republic in 1794. It soon became clear that Grégoire and other revolutionary leaders associated patois— local variations of French—and regional languages, such as Flemish, Basque, Breton, and Provençal, with religious fanaticism and therefore with counterrevolution; they thus specifically recommended enacting policies to eradicate completely their use.[13]

Why did language become a public political issue in 1794 when revolutionary leaders had not seen it as such in 1789? The politicization and nationalization of language after the establishment of the First French Republic in 1792 has been variously explained in terms of the internal dynamic of revolutionary politics and a logical extension of certain linguistic and political theories of the Old Regime.[14] Some historians, more-

[9] For the linguistic policies of the revolution, see De Certeau, *Une politique de la langue*, Higonnet, "The Politics of Linguistic Terrorism," 41–69, and Roger, "Le débat sur la 'langue révolutionnaire,'" pp. 157–84.

[10] Jacques Godechot treats prerevolutionary articulations of nationality in France in "Nation, patrie, nationalisme et patriotisme en France au XVIIIe siècle," in *Regards sur l'Epoque révolutionnaire* (Toulouse, 1980), pp. 53–68. For a discussion of competing notions of "nation" during the French Revolution, see Guiomar, *L'idéologie nationale*, and Wolfgang Geiger, "L'Etat-Nation: un concept révolutionnaire," *Dalc'homp Sonj!* no. 25 (1989): 14–26.

[11] Barère, "Rapport du Comité de Salut Public sur les idiomes"; Grégoire, "Rapport sur la nécessité et les moyens d'anéantir les patois et d'universaliser l'usage de la langue française," reprinted in De Certeau, *Une politique de la langue*, pp. 291–317.

[12] Cited in Michel Brunet, *Le Roussillon: Une société contre l'état 1780–1820* (Toulouse, 1986), p. 521.

[13] De Certeau, *Une politique de la langue*, and Higonnet, "The Politics of Linguisitic Terrorism."

[14] Ibid.; Achard, "History and the Politics of Language in France, " 175–83.

over, have concluded that the republican nation issuing from the French Revolution by definition represented the juridical expression of popular sovereignty and that this sovereignty implied "linguistic unity."[15] In short, the politicization of language has been viewed, first, as an outgrowth of the changing nature of French domestic and foreign politics, and, second, as a product of the ideological articulation of national identity during the First Republic.

By 1794 the leaders of the newly created French Republic had executed France's king and had embarked on an internal crusade to purge the country of its internal and external enemies. Revolutionary attempts to impose linguistic uniformity can be considered a component of this effort to rid the country of its enemies and to forge a new national consensus in the midst of war. Patrice Higonnet has also persuasively argued that it can be viewed as a kind of politics of diversion, which turned attention away from more fundamental social and political tensions.[16] The Committee on Public Safety's language policy was an outgrowth of a domestic political crisis, the perceived threat of secession and subversion by the enemies of the Republic: the priest and the noble. The federalist crisis of 1793 revealed the extent to which the centrifugal forces at the periphery could threaten the stability of the nation. Movements of counterrevolutionary insurrection in the Vendée led by renegade priests and nobles reinforced the revolutionary association of regional idioms with disunity. According to Barère, the continued use of Basque, Breton, Italian, and German merely perpetuated "the reign of fanaticism and superstition";[17] regional languages thus assured the domination of priests and nobles hostile to the Revolution and prevented revolutionary ideas from penetrating the nine departments where the idioms were spoken: "You have taken the saints away from these erring fanatics through the calendar of the republic, take from them the empire of priests through the teaching of the French language."[18] By 1796 regional languages were invested with a new political and cultural significance as they were intimately associated with federalism, clericalism, religious fanaticism, and counterrevolution.

The importance of language in defining the new French nation must,

---

[15] "Tant que l'Etat français sera défini comme la seule traduction juridique de la souveraineté nationale et populaire, qui n'a d'expression légitime que dans la loi, il faudra bien que la loi soit la même pour tous et qu'elle soit souveraine. . . . Il faut qu'elle soit exprimée dans un seul langage, ce qui implique bien évidemment, à ce niveau étatique, l'unité linguistique. La loi française doit parler français. Il est grave d'avoir à le rappeler aujourd'hui, où fleurissent tant de sottises sur 'l'impérialisme' linguistique." Nicolet, *L'idée républicaine en France*, p. 461.

[16] Higonnet, "The Politics of Linguistic Terrorism."

[17] Cited in De Certeau, *Une politique de la langue*, p. 292.

[18] Ibid., p. 293.

finally, be located in the First Republic's larger utopian, democratic blue-print. It must be regarded as an essential component of the republican agenda, which insisted on political unity and conformity that would be predicated on a common language. In other words, the eradication of local languages was a logical extension of a democratic project designed to erase the historical memory of monarchy and oppression with a new calendar, revolutionary festivals, a new religion, new administrative units, and a single language. Language policy, like the revolutionary festivals that Mona Ozouf has so skillfully analyzed, worked for an enlightened citizenry and the "homogenization of mankind."[19] As Citizen Barère declared before the convention in 1794, "It is necessary . . . to destroy this aristocracy of language which seems to establish a refined nation in the middle of a barbarous nation. We have revolutionized government, laws, customs, dress, commerce and thought even; let us then revolutionize language."[20] Language had become an essential litmus test to define the unitary social body that was to comprise the Republic. A politics of reason made linguistic plurality unacceptable precisely because a multiplicity of languages reinforced the superstitions and historical memory that the Revolution wished to efface. Language became a defining feature of a distinctly republican conception of national identity, and the language policies of the First Republic came to express the Revolution's obsession with unity as well as its negation of its monarchical past.

Ultimately, revolutionary measures to promote the use of the French language had little widespread support and failed along with many dreams of the republican moment. What was then the importance of the largely unsuccessful language measures of the First Republic for republican articulations of the nation and the nation's identity? Did they represent the aberrations of the political moment? Policies enacted to obliterate the use of local tongues in 1794 ultimately failed along with many utopian dreams of the republican moment, but they left an indelible mark on public memory by linking support for the preservation of regional tongues with counterrevolution and the insistence on the use of a single language—French—with the nation.

From the end of the French Revolution to the 1890s six different political regimes succeeded each other in turn. Each regime—First Empire, the Restoration, July Monarchy, Second Republic, Second Empire, and Third Republic—made the diffusion of French a national and practical objective. None of these regimes insisted, however, on linguistic uniformity. Even though language became a political concern during the First Republic, which rested on universal manhood suffrage, language was not defined as

---

[19] Mona Ozouf, *Festivals and the French Revolution* (Cambridge, 1988), p. 279. Also see Hunt, *Politics, Culture, and Class in the French Revolution*, pp. 19–28.

[20] Barère, "Rapport," cited in De Certeau, *Une politique de la langue*, p. 295.

an essential feature of the republican nation in 1848 or during the early years of the Third Republic. To a large extent this may be explained by the fact that during the early part of the nineteenth century the republican left was more populist than nationalist in orientation, as the démocrate-socialiste alliance of the Second Republic suggests. Nonetheless, where writers and politicians with republican sympathies articulated conceptions of the nation, they tended to be predicated on consent rather than culture. For the historian Michelet, unity and personality elevated individuals as well as nations. In *Tableau de la France*, he observed that "esprit local has disappeared each day; the influence of soil, climate, race has ceded to social and political action . . . society, liberty have overcome nature, history has effaced geography."[21] Similarly, Léon Gambetta, who dominated republican politics in the 1870s and 1880s stressed such contractual, consensual conceptions of nationality that were nonetheless invested with a spiritual and sovereign force. Gambetta informed a group of ardent republicans in 1872 at Annecy that the French Republic was not the "meeting of associated provinces. . . . It is not the Touraine united with Provence, nor Picardy joined to Languedoc, nor Burgundy attached to Brittany. . . . No! this whole, this unity, it is the French Republic."[22] Gambetta's eloquent language recalled Jules Michelet's evocative celebration of the French nation as a living personality. Michelet and Renan ultimately embraced a conception of nationhood that emphasized the contractual nature of the republican nation and clearly rejected racial or ethnic definitions of the nation. Indeed, the rejection of ethnic components of French identity had been reflected in the work of a series of republican theorists from Rousseau and the abbé Sieyès to Emile Littré. Littré defined nation in his 1881 *Dictionnaire de la langue française*: "The assembly of men living in the same territory, subject or not to the same government, having for a long time interests more or less in common."[23] As Claude Nicolet has argued, although nation, in etymological terms, has a genetic, organic, racist connotation, Littré posited that since the ancien régime this racial component had been superseded by definitions that privileged the common will and common interest.[24] Nowhere is this more clearly expressed than in Sieyès's 1789 "What Is the Third Estate": "Is there a prior authority which could have told a multitude of individuals: 'I put you together under such and such laws; you will form a nation on the conditions I prescribe.' We are not speaking here of brigandage or domination, but of a legitimate, that is to say voluntary and free, association. . . . Where is the nation to be found:

---

[21] Jules Michelet, *Tableau de la France* (Paris, 1934), p. 94.

[22] "Discours prononcés à Annecy, 1 Octobre 1872," *Discours et plaidoyers politiques de M. Gambetta*, 3 (Paris, 1881): 169.

[23] Cited in Nicolet, *L'idée républicaine en France*, pp. 400–401.

[24] Ibid.

Where it is: in the 40,000 parishes which embrace the whole territory, all
its inhabitants and every element of the commonwealth; indisputably, the
nation lies there."[25]

Nationalism and the Politics of Regionalism

Historians have generally identified a renewed concern for linguistic uniformity toward the end of the nineteenth century with the establishment of
the Third Republic. It has been suggested that the drive for linguistic unity
was part of the larger republican *mission civilisatrice*, its quest to civilize
and assimilate the far reaches of the Republic that only incompletely accepted and supported French republican rule.[26] Indeed, during the 1870s
and 1880s a new positivist generation of French republicans who came to
power in the aftermath of the Franco-Prussian war launched a full-scale
campaign to tame "unenlightened," "savage," and "backward" France.

These efforts and methods were clearly politically motivated. Local in-
stitutions and primary education in France were largely in the hands of the
Church and antirepublican elites until the advent of the Third Republic.
The failure of the Second Republic and the initial success of the authoritar-
ian Second Empire revealed to many republicans that the Church and
clericalism were major obstacles to the creation of a democratic republic.
After the springtime of the people in 1848, the Church and the clergy in
France increasingly lent support to the forces of order and appeared to
contribute to the demise of the democratic and social Republic. Republicans had "two means of taking action," in the words of Roger Martin du
Gard's turn-of-the-century hero Jean Barois, "by our personal attitude and
the education of our children. . . . Only think! the Church inveighs against
us. It launches anathemas at all that constitutes the most vital part of our
being, and yet, fools that we are, we hand our children over to the priest!"[27]
Exactly this sentiment spawned the free, compulsory, secular educational

---

[25] Abbé Sieyès, "What Is the Third Estate?" in *The Old Regime and the French Revolution*,
ed. Keith Baker (Chicago, 1987), pp. 172–73.

[26] One scholar has argued that since the beginning of the nineteenth century the French
state played a major role in the construction of national identity and that "ideologically, then,
political community is, in France, identical to cultural community." This conflation of cultural and national identity only came to be articulated in explicit terms toward the end of the
nineteenth century. David Beriss, "Scarves, Schools, and Segregation: The Foulard Affair,"
French Politics and Society 8 (Winter 1990): 2, 1–13. Sahlins has made a convincing case for a
continued separation of cultural and national identity in the Catalan Cerdagne at least into
the 1860s; see Sahlins, *Boundaries*.

[27] Roger Martin du Gard, *Jean Barois*, trans. Stuart Gilbert (Indianapolis, 1969), pp. 248–
49. See Auspitz, *The Radical Bourgeoisie*, for a subtle discussion of republican secular
ideology and the educational reforms of the early Third Republic.

system in the early 1880s that made the primary schoolteachers who staffed it into "black hussars" of the Republic.

The founders of the Third Republic did not, however, make linguistic or cultural unity essential to republican efforts to integrate the country's diverse social groups. Republicans who included Jules Ferry and Léon Gambetta openly acknowledged the vitality of regional differences, but both were silent about how these differences might be reconciled with a unitary, secular conception of the nation and the problems that these differences might pose for the Republic.

During the early years of the Third Republic, educators with impeccable republican credentials also showed open toleration for the use of regional languages. Michel Bréal, professor at the Collège de France, recommended that local dialects be respected and the schoolteacher take an interest in the languages and local history of the region to which he was assigned.[28] Moreover, Jules Ferry, the chief architect of the universal primary educational system in France in the 1880s, remained quiet on the necessity of linguisitic uniformity and never explicitly made it a part of his educational reforms.[29]

This benign attitude toward local languages was predicated on republican conceptions of the nation stemming from the revolutionary period. Ernest Renan, who profoundly influenced the generation of republicans who came to power in 1877, declared in his 1882 "What Is a Nation?" speech: "A fact that is honorable for France is that she has never sought to attain unity of language by coercive measures. Can one not have the same feelings and thoughts, love of the same things in different languages?"[30] A native of the Lower Breton episcopal town of Tréguier, Renan clearly had no difficulty separating his emotional attachment to his pays natal with a commitment to the French nation because the bonds of the nation were principally created by a common will and consent. Renan's abstract, contractual notion of the nation, which explicitly repudiated race and language as defining features of nationality, was essentially political in character.

This understanding of the nation was embodied in the new civic morality

---

[28] "Au lieu d'être un étranger parmi les paysans, au lieu de représenter une culture officielle toujours suspecte, il deviendra le vrai représentant de la commune, celui qui en saura le mieux l'histoire, et qui, sans les contestations de mots ou de choses, sera consulté comme le dépositaire de la tradition et comme le savant du canton." Michel Bréal, *Quelques mots sur l'instruction publique en France* (Paris, 1872), p. 66. Mona Ozouf's comments on Bréal, however, suggest that he assumed contradictory positions on the subject. He explicitly argued, for example, that local languages were instruments of political reaction. Ozouf, "Unité nationale et unité dans la pensée de Jules Ferry," in *Jules Ferry: Fondateur de la République*, ed. F. Furet (Paris, 1985), p. 65.

[29] Ibid.

[30] Renan, "Qu'est ce qu' une nation?" p. 20.

that was at the heart of the compulsory primary school system designed by Jules Ferry and shaped by Ferdinand Buisson, Ernest Lavisse, and Paul Bert. Although government officials continued to encourage the popular diffusion of French in the classroom and playground, the Ministry of Education often used gentle means of persuasion and tolerated bilingual methods of language instruction. These methods included, for example, the establishment of savings accounts for young schoolchildren learning French, monetary indemnities for schoolteachers, and French language societies.[31] In short, until the early 1890s, government officials stopped short of banning local languages completely in schools.

While the republican leadership adopted relatively tolerant attitudes toward regional difference, its far-reaching campaign to secularize and republicanize the countryside through an ambitious system of universal, compulsory primary education was justified in terms of a unitary nation. The campaign had a clear strategic purpose: it was intended to destroy the political influence of the Church and antirepublican social elites in the disparate regions of France.

Between the Boulangist Affair of 1889 and the Dreyfus Affair of the late 1890s, a new, nationalist Right challenged the legitimacy of the Republic and its enterprise by justifying its assault in terms that called the Republican leadership's abstract, consensual, national community into question. This challenge was achieved through a gradual and, one might argue, paradoxical appropriation of both nationalism and regionalism by the Right. Whereas the republican leadership of the 1880s spoke of the nation in terms of unity, *laicité*, and contract, the *droite révolutionnaire* came to embrace a nation defined in ethnic, racial, and cultural terms. The virulent right-wing nationalism that characterized the 1890s is frequently regarded as evidence of the transfer of nationalism from the Left to the Right that occurred in the years between the Commune and the First World War.[32] It might, however, best be seen as less of a transfer than as a new articulation of national identity.

The New Right, as represented primarily by Maurice Barrès and Charles Maurras, ironically arrived at a new formulation of nationality by way of regionalism and *revanchisme* between the Boulangist and Dreyfus affairs. And this "strange relationship between dynamic (pre-)fascist nationalism and desperate regionalism"[33] ultimately resulted in the repoliticization of

---

[31] Archives Départementales du Finistère [hereafter A.D. Finistère], 1T68, letter from Jules Ferry to the prefect of Finistère, 22 October 1882.

[32] Rémond argues that an entire set of nationalist "sentiments and values heretofore considered the birthright of radicalism" were transferred to the Right. René Rémond, *The Right in France from 1815 to de Gaulle*, trans. James Laux (Philadelphia, 1966), p. 208.

[33] Ernst Nolte, *Three Faces of Fascism*, trans. L. Vennewitz (New York, 1969), p. 601.

language and of regional culture for the first time since the French Revolution.

The Right's new articulation of French national identity was a logical extension of their appropriation of the regionalist cause. Maurras's and Barrès's interest in regionalism grew out of their involvement in provincial literary movements and philosophical concerns expressed in their literary work in the 1880s and early 1890s. Their regionalist ideas came to be placed in distinctly pragmatic terms after 1895 when they launched attacks on republican efforts to laicize and republicanize France. Both Maurras and Barrès increasingly attributed the moral degeneration of the French nation to efforts to impose cultural and political uniformity on the diverse regions of the country. Both viewed regionalism as a means to regenerate the French nation, but the two had very different ends in mind, a reflection of their commitment to divergent social and political ideals.

Barrès's interest in regionalism, or in what he termed federalism, dated from the completion of his novelistic *Culte de Moi* trilogy and grew out of a philosophical problem of reconciling the individual with society. Although his secretary, Albert Tharaud, claimed that Barrés's interest was more apparent than real and that he continued to reside in Paris,[34] he devoted seven years of his life, from 1888 to 1895, to the federalist campaign, as deputy of Nancy, contributor to the *Quinzaine*, and editor of *La Cocarde*, a newspaper whose professed aim was to reconcile "individualism" and "social solidarity."[35] Barrès proclaimed in none too ambiguous terms that *La Cocarde* advocated administrative decentralization and liberty of association in order to resuscitate "our faculties of cohesion."[36] Citing the Provençal poet Frédéric Mistral, he claimed that every region had its own temperament, its own raison d'être, and that the individual could only acquire a sense of social solidarity by affirming his relationship to his native soil.[37] However, he emphasized that regionalism was a necessary consequence of the democratic tradition by claiming that the French Revolution, in principle, was a reaction against administrative centralization, uniformity, and the corporate society of the ancien régime defined in terms of privilege. Indeed, in the 1880s, Barrès never failed to insist on the value and legitimacy of the democratic tradition and argued that decentralization by no means contradicted the principles of the Revolution.[38]

His support for regionalism in the 1880s and 1890s was also a conse-

---

[34] Tharaud, *Mes années chez Barrès* (Paris, 1928), pp. 208–209.

[35] *La Cocarde*, 17 October 1894, p. 1. In the last issue of *La Cocarde*, which was published on 7 March 1895, Barrès wrote: "Individualisme et solidarité. Tel a été la formule constante de *La Cocarde* pour affirmer qu'entre ces deux termes, l'individu et collectivité, il n'y a pas une antinomie irréductible" (p. 1).

[36] "Les bénéfices de la décentralisation," *La Cocarde*, 10 November 1894, p. 1.

[37] "La glorification de l'énergie," *La Cocarde*, 19 December 1894, p. 1.

[38] "Partisans de la décentralisation," *La Cocarde*, 10 November 1894, p. 1.

quence of his growing concern with the social question, the conflict between capital and labor, and the plight of the French worker. In "Le socialisme sera décentralisation," Barrès argued that decentralization would not necessarily provide a solution to the social problem but that it would facilitate a solution.[39] According to Barrès, each particular region was a "social laboratory," with its own needs and economic resources. He perceived that the intense conflict between capital and labor, unemployment and the terrible poverty of the French worker were aggravated by the growth of centralized industrial enterprises based in Paris and supported by foreign capital. Urban industrialists felt no qualms about importing cheap labor from Belgium, Italy, and Spain, which destroyed the independence and security of the French worker.

Regionalism was also an argument, in effect, against international collectivism. He suggested that one great danger of international socialism was that the worker would again be forced to follow the dictates of a central decision-making authority that would ultimately fail to respond to the needs of different national and regional economies. He railed against the way in which international socialism suppressed the legitimate and concrete basis of national allegiance; it substituted the abstract principles of equality stressed by republicans in the tradition of Renan for an allegedly more natural attachment to kin and soil. In short, in the early 1890s, Barrès worked out an eclectic brand of what he called "national socialism." He actively supported freedom of association, the cooperative movement, and labor policies discriminating against foreign immigrants.

Although Barrès never wholly repudiated the principles of the Revolution of 1789, his nationalism and his concern for national unity came to be articulated in a new way as a result of the Dreyfus Affair and his conversion to the doctrine of *la terre et les morts* (blood and soil). As Zeev Sternhell has pointed out, Barrès's conceptions of nationality in the 1880s and 1890s were jacobin—a far cry from the notion of "organic nationalism," which he came to espouse in the *Roman de l'énergie nationale*, published in the wake of the Dreyfus Affair.[40]

Barrès's conversion to "rootedness," to "organic nationalism," occurred between 1895 and 1902, during the course of his work on the *Roman de l'énergie nationale*, his penultimate novel, which concerned itself with several major themes: the moral degeneration of France, the problem of national unity, and, finally, the cult of Alsace-Lorraine. On the political level, it was an indictment of republican attempts to laicize and republicanize the French countryside. More specifically, it was a condemnation of the French educational system. Thibaudet, Maurras, and Charles Brun claimed that, in essence, Barrès's novel popularized the regionalist cause;

[39] *La Cocarde*, 10 November 1894, p. 1.
[40] Sternhell, *Maurice Barrès*, p. 221

déraciné, the uprooted, became a part of the political language of administrative reform in the early twentieth century. More important, perhaps, Barrès forged the link between fin-de-siècle nationalism and regionalism.[41]

The *Roman de l'énergie nationale* was an explicit attack on both the republican regime and the political corruption of parliamentary politics. It provided a solution to the national degeneration of the country by spelling out the basis of a regionalism, to which the concept of organic nationalism was intimately linked. This attack is embodied in the figure of the schoolmaster Bouteiller. Described as a "pedagogical product, a son of reason, alien to our traditional, local, and familial customs, completely abstract, and truly suspended in the void," he is entrusted by Gambetta with the task of instilling republican ideals and patriotic fervor in his students.[42]

Bouteiller teaches the central characters in the novel notions of abstract liberty, patriotism, and a universal Kantian morality summed up in the maxim: "I must always act in such a way that I can wish to have my action serve as a universal rule."[43] One of main characters in the book, Saint-Phlin, a native of Lorraine, finds such prescriptions to be "half Parisian, half German," dreamt up by the Ministry of Education to serve political objectives.[44] Barrès condemns the republican regime for making citizens scorn their localities, their *petite patrie* without providing them a basis on which to identify themselves with the French nation: "To uproot these children, to detach them from soil and social group where all is joined, in order to place them beyond their prejudices in abstract reason, how that will trouble him, he who has neither roots nor social ties?"[45] Bouteillier, in Barrès's view, fails to give his students a sense of social cohesion.

In essence, Barrès attempted to show how regionalism and nationalism, two sides of the same coin, were a means to achieve his aim of national regeneration. At the international federalist congress in 1895, he proclaimed that Paris had given France an abstract notion of liberty, which had no real concrete basis. He argued that the French nation was composed of regional *patries* and that in order for the citizens to have a sense of national identity, they had to have precise and tangible reasons to love their country: "That the word 'country' not only be a metaphysical expression used by orators at agricultural fairs, at banquets. . . . One will never love one's country as much as when one touches it, when one belongs to a region."[46]

[41] Albert Thibaudet, *La vie de Maurice Barrès* (Paris, 1921), p. 276. Maurras wrote that after 1898 *déracinés* became a household word: "Déracinés, déracineurs, déracinement, la même image, plus ou moins modifiée, a passé dans la langue du journalisme et de la conversation." Maurras, *L'idée de la décentralisation*, p. 26. J. Charles-Brun, *Le régionalisme* (Paris: Bloud, n.d.), p. 225.

[42] *L'oeuvre de Maurice Barrès*, vol. 3: *Les déracinés* (Paris, 1965), p. 24.

[43] *L'oeuvre de Maurice Barrès*, vol. 4: *Leurs figures*, p. 393.

[44] Ibid.

[45] Barrès, *Les déracinés*, pp. 24, 181.

[46] Barrès, *Scènes et doctrines du nationalisme*, p. 235.

By the late 1890s he believed that French national identity was not derived from the revolutionary principles, as he had claimed in the 1880s; rather, national allegiance rested on the individual's consciousness of the historical, climatic, cultural, and racial forces that shaped his development.[47]

Maurice Barrès's new formulation of the basis of French patriotism in the 1890s was clearly embraced by his monarchist compatriot, Charles Maurras, founder of the right-wing political organization Action Française. In 1895, Maurras wrote in *La Cocarde*: "Country is a certain place in the world where one has flesh-and-bones ancestors."[48] He contrasted a "real France," defined in terms of provincial variations with an artificial France defined in terms of uniform, rational administrative units. He praised Barrès for being the first to emphasize the important distinction between nationalism and federalism. Barrès's book, *Déracinés*, he argued, helped to publicize the federalist cause and to indicate the ways in which metaphysical nationalism, espoused by republicans, must be replaced by a territorial and ethnic conception.[49] Maurras derived his conception of nationality from not only Barrès, but also Auguste Comte, Le Play, and Hippolyte Taine. Comte's "elementary axiom of sociology" was that "human society is composed of families, not of individuals."[50] The family, which was the natural vehicle of tradition and the least artificial form of association, necessarily provided the basis of a tangible, concrete patriotism.[51]

In the words of Marcel Prélot, whereas efforts to decentralize governmental institutions prior to the 1890s might be viewed as a "technique," regionalism became a sentimental "mystique."[52] As representatives of the New Right, Charles Maurras and Maurice Barrès played crucial roles in popularizing the mystique of both nationalism and regionalism. Maurras, in fact, argued that Barrès was the first to reconcile nationalism with regionalism, to show that it was necessary to substitute "administrative patriotism" with "territorial patriotism," to replace the republican notion of "ideal France" with a new notion of "real France."[53] In this sense Barrès was largely responsible for politicizing the term regionalism by linking it to a national past rooted in the Old Regime.

Not surprisingly, proponents of the New Right became ardent and vocal defenders of the use of patois and regional languages. Barrès met with Charles Le Goffic, the Breton patriot, in Brittany in August 1886, where they decided to form a regionalist review, *Chroniques*. The project proved a

[47] Ibid., pp. 3–21.
[48] "Quelle France," *La Cocarde*, 4 January 1895, p. 1.
[49] Maurras, *L'idée de la décentralisation*, p. 24.
[50] Quoted in Maurras, *Enquête sur la monarchie* (Paris, 1924), p. 108.
[51] Ibid., p. 96.
[52] Marcel Prélot, *Institutions politiques* (Paris, 1963), p. 231.
[53] Maurras, *L'idée de la décentralisation*, p. 16.

failure, but Le Goffic and Barrès continued to correspond with one another for some time.[54] He also had a number of ties with local literary societies that included the Félibrige, which was devoted to the preservation of Provençal culture, to local languages, and to the poet Mistral, who served as an inspiration for the group. Barrès, in fact, made pilgrimages to Provence to visit Mistral in the autumn of 1895 with Maurras and again in October 1898.[55] Regional literary societies formed during these years, and specifically those dedicated to the preservation of local languages were composed of notables of the Old and the New Right, which, for republicans, further emphasized the Right's appropriation of regional culture for political purposes.

In the 1890s regionalism and the defense of local languages and culture came to be associated with the New Right in the popular mind. Indeed, many believed that Barrès had coined the term *regionalism*.[56] Barrès's "politicization" of the term ultimately gave the movement a reactionary association.

The Right's articulation of national identity in terms of linguistic, ethnic, and emotional attachments to blood and soil was a powerful reaction against the agencies of the state's mission civilisatrice, which ostensibly served to create new allegiances and undermine the "natural" and historical division of provincial France. The Right was quick to exploit the contradictions inherent in republican conceptions of national identity and its civilizing mission. The republican government ostensibly remained committed to a nation based on consent, contract, and a shared revolutionary past, but, at the same time, it needed the political support of even the most remote antirepublican constituencies. The new nationalist Right made the republican leadership confront the problem of cultural diversity head on: How could the republican government tolerate linguistic and cultural pluralism and, at the same time, retain control of reactionary regions such as Brittany where an allegedly antiparliamentary notability successfully controlled a non-French-speaking electorate?

Regionalism and Clericalism

Competing claims to the nation and the challenge of the republican project came from not only political groupings on the Right but also the Catholic Church. The use of regional languages was intimately linked to maintaining the Catholic faith in postrevolutionary France. Throughout the nine-

[54] Léon Dubreuil, "Lettres de Maurice Barrès à Charles Le Goffic," *Annales de Bretagne* 58 (1951): 19–88.

[55] Charles Maurras, *Oeuvres capitales*, vol. 3: *Maurice Barrès* (Paris, 1954), p. 437.

[56] Charles-Brun, *Le régionalisme*, p. 225.

teenth century, the clergy were generally regarded as ardent defenders of popular tradition and opponents of the centralizing power of the French state. Toward the end of the nineteenth century, the parish priest more often than not defended local culture and saw the maintenance of regional tongues as a means of preserving the Catholic faith. In 1863, for example, a school inspector in the department of Finistère put it this way: "we cannot bar the use of Breton in an absolute manner, even in public schools. Two reasons oppose it: first, the teacher really must use this idiom so as to be understood. . . . In the second place, the teacher owes his pupils an instruction in religion."[57] He went on to explain that all religious instruction was given in Breton. "From the day that one would . . . impose the exclusive study of the French catechism in classrooms, one would see the welling up of opposition that would soon render them completely deserted. For right or for wrong, most of the members of the clergy think that with[out] Breton, one would see the disappearance of faith and religious customs of our peasantry."[58] The link between local idioms and popular religiosity, first articulated during the French Revolution, was reiterated by the state and the ecclesiastical establishment in France, which often refused, when requested, to propagate the French language in religious instruction.[59]

For a positivist generation of French republicans, the theological age necessarily had to give way to the democratic and positive age enshrined in the Republic, which was both "laic" and anticlerical. Its mission was to "found a new spiritual power, solidly based in science, destined to assure the profound unity of the social body."[60] By the early Third Republic the nation was expicitly defined in opposition to the Catholic Church. Indeed, Jules Barni's 1871 *Manuel républicain* saw the Republic as a secular *chose publique* that could not be separated from the nation itself.[61] For this reason, the separation of Church and state and the "transfer of sacrality" to the nation were implicit parts of the republican program. Like much of the revolutionary, republican project, this symbolic transfer of the sacred was not so easily achieved. Religion and politics remained "deeply, inextricably intermingled."[62]

[57] A.D. Finistère, 1T68, report, inspection de l'instruction primaire, December 1863.
[58] Ibid.
[59] When the bishop of the diocese of Quimper in Brittany was sent a deliberation on the utility of propagating the French language in religious instruction, the bishop informed the prefect that he would not authorize any of his curés to recite the catechism in French. A.D. Finistère, 1T68, letter from the bishop of Quimper to the prefect, 14 March 1838. For the close connection between Catholic instruction and regional languages in other regions of France, see Cholvy, "Enseignement religieux," and Coornaert, "Flamand et français."
[60] Nicolet, *L'idée républicaine*, p. 268.
[61] Jules Barni, *Manuel républicain* (Paris, 1872), pp. 1–2.
[62] Jules Michelet, *History of the French Revolution*, trans. Charles Cocks (Chicago, 1967), p. 17.

The conflict between the institutional church and an ardently anticlerical state over primary education, which culminated in the separation of Church and state in 1905, dominated French politics from the 1880s to the First World War. Although the Church ultimately fought a losing battle in all but the most Catholic regions of France, during these bitter and strident skirmishes between the Church and the Republic, republican sentiment toward regional languages and culture shifted abruptly. Linguistic unity was soon articulated as a political and national necessity. This shift became clear in 1890, when Armand Fallières, senator of Lot-et-Garonne, proposed legislation that would prevent priests from preaching in local languages. In October 1890 the minister of religious affairs issued a letter to the prefect of Finistère regarding the use of "local dialects and foreign languages" by priests because they might endanger "national unity."[63] He reminded the prefect that the state budget, which paid the salaries of the clergy under the terms of the Concordat, only paid for services performed "in the national language and in the French interest."[64] The minister's circular demonstrates a significant transformation in republican thinking: the French language was now implicitly linked to national unity and identity, and for the republican regime in Paris, regional languages had become an intolerable threat.

The debate that this decree elicited in the Chamber of Deputies demonstrated the degree to which linguistic plurality was deemed a threat to the republican nation itself because of its association with clericalism. Supporters of the measure charged that the ban on the use of regional languages in religious instruction would ultimately disarm the clergy and the enemies of the Republic, depriving them of a vital tool through which to undermine national unity. Although a number of the decree's opponents were republicans, they found it difficult to dispel the association of regional languages with clericalism, superstition, and backwardness.

Thus, the dual challenge of integral nationalists and the Catholic Church reshaped articulations of national identity among republicans. And the politicization of regional culture ultimately resulted in the politicization of language and of regional difference more generally.

By 1900, regionalism and the use of local languages came to be associated with the Church, as a bastion of tradition, and the New Right. When the clergy in Lower Brittany, for example, founded a weekly newspaper, *Feiz Ha Breiz* (Faith and Brittany), whose motto, "Faith and Brittany are brothers and sisters," they clearly wished to use local allegiance as a means of maintaining religious faith. When Barrès attacked the bloodless, reasoned claims to nationality among republicans, he wished less to defend regional culture and local language than to harness them for political ends.

---

[63] A.D. Finistère, 1V56, letter from Dumay to the prefect of Finistère, 30 October 1890.
[64] Ibid.

The newly articulated goal of cultural unity among republicans made the claims of nation and region incompatible and ultimately justified an increasingly aggressive state-sponsored civilizing mission that sought to eradicate cultural difference by creating common cultural referents. This goal was symbolized in a 1903 decree that banned the use of Breton, Basque, Flemish, and Provençal in religious instruction. In a debate over the measure, Emile Combes, the radical leader of the republican/socialist coalition of 1902, told a divided chamber that the use of regional languages was a clear demonstration of a lack of patriotic allegiance.

The political relationship between language, national identity, and republicanism in France indicated the way in which the anticlerical struggles of the 1880s associated cultural pluralism—as manifested in the debate over regional languages—with the interests of the Church. To this extent, shifts in republican articulations of nationality can be directly traced to the political fallout engendered by the Republic's mission civilisatrice, by the anticlerical policies of the French state. Equally important, however, new linguistic policies and articulations of the republican nation must be linked to competing claims to the nation by the Right. It is no accident that republican calls for vigilance and a reconsideration of the language issue became particularly important after the 1885 national elections during which the Right made significant political gains. And as these elections were closely followed by the Boulangist attempt to overthrow the Republic in 1889, republicans in power were particularly concerned about challenges to the new regime.

The broader implications of the New Right's nationalism and its sanctification of provincial languages and traditions were in the end disturbing to the republican consensus. In 1906, Maurice Barrès was elected to the conservative first district of Paris and became concerned with two major problems: How to defend France against the German threat and how to develop the national energy of France. His concern for the individual and the social question, which was worked out in terms of the integration of nationalist and regionalist doctrine, became subordinated to the *revanche*, which translated into the cult of his native province Alsace-Lorraine. In 1904, he wrote that if the French nation was "badly run," then the predominance of southern politicians in the Chamber of Deputies was responsible.

He began to attribute the paralysis and corruption in parliamentary politics to the "preponderance of southerners" in the Chamber of Deputies—to men like the socialists Jean Jaurès and Alexandre Millerand, on whom he blamed the problems in the French national community: "Against this southern preponderance, there are objections, not only those from Lorraine, Normandy, Brittany, Flanders, but French objections."[65] Paradox-

---

[65] Barrès, *Les lézardes sur la maison*, p. 20.

ically, Barrès used regional cultural difference as a basis to attack the republican leadership for undermining French unity. According to Barrès, the crime of southern politicians consisted of either allowing old enmities to reappear or of failing to respect the regional traditions of other parts of France: "Across the Loire river, two angry Frances stare at one another. What is there in common between us? Our [common] interests? You sacrifice them. Our instinctive venerations? You scoff at them. Knowledge of provincial variation should be at the center of a French man of state's science, [just] as the respect for regional characters should be essential to his concerns."[66] The question that Barrès raised—"What is there in common between us?"—was the logical and, for republicans, frightening consequence of a redefinition of the nation in territorial, ethnic, and linguistic terms. Although Barrès continued to argue that regional allegiance formed the primary component of national allegiance, for republicans he confirmed the dangers and apparent contradictions in this view.

The politicization of language and regional culture on the Right ultimately hardened republican opposition in Paris to provincial difference. At the periphery, however, it placed those committed to the Republic in the almost impossible position of reconciling regional and national allegiance. Indeed, these competing allegiances and the Republic's civilizing mission spawned conflicts that would not easily be contained. For it was precisely in a France filled with almost infinite cultural and regional variation that Barrès's question—"What is there in common between us?"—came to haunt the defenders of the Republic.

66 Ibid., pp. 27–28.

2

Regional Economy and Social Change in Lower Brittany

The genius of Brittany is the genius of
untameable resistance and of intrepid,
opinionated, and blind opposition.
(*Jules Michelet*)

THE FEW TRAVELERS who ventured into the province of Brittany in the eighteenth and early nineteenth centuries were invariably struck by the region's isolation, backwardness, poverty, and by the superstition and illiteracy that characterized its population. In 1844, Villermé and Benoiston de Chateauneuf, who journeyed to the five departments comprising the old province on a fact-finding mission for the newly established Academy of Moral and Political Sciences, described a country which, "though united to France for several centuries, still remains, in certain respects, completely separated, and which, when a general revolution has changed everything . . . shows to the surprised traveller its old customs, modes of dress, and language to be intact."[1]

Since the eighteenth century, observers and scholars have viewed Brittany, which remained predominantly rural, as poor, isolated, uncivilized, economically underdeveloped, and sorely lacking in the cultural refinement that characterized France's capital. Following the uprising of the Vendée, western France, including Brittany, has been viewed as a region dominated by an intransigent aristocracy, committed to a retrograde form of conservatism, and populated by a rude and barbarous peasantry completely cowed by *châtelain* and priest.[2] A late nineteenth-century traveler, A. Mahe de la Bourdonnais, for example, noted that he found a striking resemblance between the inhabitants of Lower Brittany and the ostensibly

---

[1] Villermé and Benoiston de Chateauneuf, *Voyage en Bretagne en 1840 et 1841*, ed. F. Elegoet, reprinted in *Tud Ha Bro*, Sociétés Bretonnes, no. 8 (Rennes, 1982), pp. 1–2.

[2] This view was advanced by not only government observers but also novelists, of whom the most celebrated was Balzac in *Les Chouans*. For more recent examples of this view, see Berger, *Peasants Against Politics*, pp. 14–16, 52–53 and Guin, *Histoire de la Bretagne*. For a general discussion of Breton stereotypes, see Catherine Bertho, "L'invention de la Bretagne: Genèse sociale d'un stéréotype," *Actes de la recherche en sciences sociales* (September 1980): 45–62.

primitive "Ladakis, Bouthanis, Tibetains, et Chans" that he encountered in the Orient.[3] Moreover, as most regions of western France were characterized by dispersed settlement patterns, as in the Massif Central, and fields and farms were often separated from one another by dense hedges, western France arguably lacked forms of sociability and communality that were so characteristic of the agglomerated villages and bourgs of southern France.[4] More than perhaps any other region of France, the rural populations of Brittany fitted Karl Marx's description of the French peasantry as having no more relationship to each other than potatoes in a sack.[5]

Less impressionistic assessments of the province suggest, however, that although Brittany can certainly be distinguished from the rest of France by its late agricultural revolution, by demographic patterns peculiar to the region, and by problems associated with its distance from major market centers, in economic and social terms the province had undergone an enormous amount of change between the French Revolution and the early Third Republic and had become well integrated into the national economic system.[6] Indeed, negative appraisals of the region belie the fact that by the beginning of the twentieth century Brittany was a highly diversified region marked by contrasting land tenure systems and political orientations, different tongues and dialects, and diverse social and cultural traditions. The lower Breton department of Finistère, in particular, developed important commercial links with France and abroad and came to be dominated by peasant landowners, as the economic position of the nobility eroded considerably. For these reasons, an understanding of the region's confrontation with the French state at the end of the nineteenth century must be understood less in the context of uniform, unchanging, and relatively static socioeconomic structures than in terms of the deep cultural divide that separated Lower Brittany from the rest of France (maps 1 and 2).

A Country of Bocage

The ancient province of Brittany was defined by a series of geographical, linguistic, agricultural, political, and religious boundaries. Throughout

[3] A. Mahe de la Bourdonnais, *Voyage en Basse-Bretagne chez les 'bigouden' de Pont l'Abbé après vingt ans de voyages dans l'Inde et l'Indo-Chine* (Paris, 1892), p. 13.

[4] Agulhon, *The Republic in the Village*, pp. 124–50.

[5] Berger, *Peasants Against Politics*, p. 18.

[6] Brittany has not generally been the subject of study for economic and social historians of rural France. Notable exceptions to this general rule include T.J.A. Le Goff and D. Sutherland, "The Revolution and the Rural Community in Eighteenth-Century Brittany," *Past and Present* 62 (February 1974): 96–119; Le Goff, *Vannes and its Region*, pp. 151–336; Sutherland, *The Chouans*. The history of the nineteenth and twentieth centuries has, however, been relatively neglected.

N

| 0 | 50 | 100 Miles |
| 0 | 50 | 100 Kms. |

E.McC. '92

Map 1. Departments of France

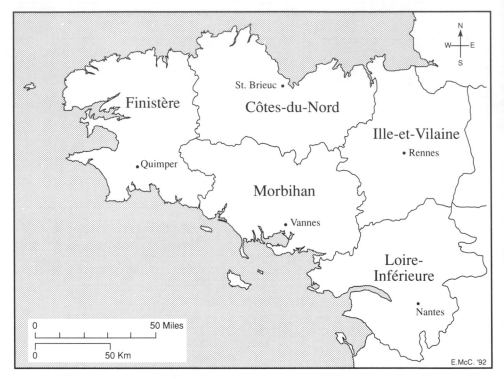

Map 2. Departments of the Breton Peninsula

the nineteenth century "a difficult, almost impenetrable zone" lay between Brittany and the rest of France: "on the border of Normandy, the half-submerged marshes of Dol; all along the Maine and Anjou, a vast, long deserted forested zone."[7] The only real means of communication between Brittany and France came by way of the sea or from the Loire valley to the south until the Third Republic.

A linguistic barrier extending from the bourg of Plouha in the department of Côtes-du-Nord in the north to Muzillac in the department of Morbihan separated Lower or Breton-speaking Brittany from Upper or non-Breton-speaking Brittany. Lower Brittany consisted of portions of the departments of Côtes-du-Nord and Morbihan and all the department of Finistère, France's westernmost department. Within Lower Brittany, three major dialects of the Breton tongue were spoken in the regions of Trégor, Léon, and Vannetais that were absorbed in theory, but not in fact, into

[7] René Musset, *La Bretagne* (Paris, 1942), cited in Chombart de Lauwe, *Bretagne et pays de la Garonne: évolution agricole comparée depuis un siècle* (Paris, 1946), p. 83.

departments during the administrative reorganization of 1790–1791.[8] The inhabitants of the province continued to identify less with the historical province per se than with the commune or region where they were born.

Much of Brittany was a country of bocage, a system in which fields enclosed by dense hedges were cultivated by individual farmers. The origin of the closed field system, which differed from the open fields of the north and the patchwork of fields cultivated in agglomerated villages in the south, is unknown, but Robert Specklin and André Meynier have suggested that the hedges may have protected the fields from the fierce winds that swept the peninsula during the winter months and provided natural barriers in a country that raised livestock.[9] Large aristocratic properties predominated in many parts of the province and corresponded generally with areas of bocage. Property relations and the nature of land tenure in Lower Brittany differed significantly from those in Upper Brittany. Large farms were not the norm in the former, with the exception of some areas of the Morbihan, and throughout the nineteenth century the trend toward land acquisition by the peasantry accelerated; by the end of the century small- and medium-sized farms predominated in Lower Brittany.

As founder of French electoral geography André Siegfried argued in 1913, political temperaments also varied considerably within Brittany, even though it has generally been viewed as a conservative/Catholic bastion. Nonetheless, differences between lower and upper areas of the province were evident in this respect.[10] Much of Lower Brittany was initially favorable to the Revolution and began to resist the revolutionary leadership only after 1791. The memory of the Revolution and the religious turmoil that followed the Civil Constitution of the Clergy remained vivid in the province as a whole. Political factions in the nineteenth century adopted the political discourse of the Revolution, defining political positions in terms of *bleu* (revolutionary) and *blanc* (counterrevolutionary). But the "debate for or against the Revolution did not lead to a dichotomy between fervor and irreligion, but rather to two different formulations, two

---

[8] For the formation of departments in Brittany, see J. Cassard et al., *Histoire de la Bretagne et des pays celtiques de 1789 à 1914* (Morlaix, 1980), pp. 18–19. The linguistic barrier gradually changed over time. See Yann Brekilien, ed., *La Bretagne* (Paris, 1982), pp. 251, 286, for a table of Breton-speaking areas according to the periodic surveys undertaken between 1806 and the 1980s. Also see Charles Berlet, *Les provinces au XVIIIe siècle et leur division en départements* (Paris, 1913); Georges Mage, *La division de la France en départements* (Toulouse, 1924); Marie-Vic Ozouf-Marignier, *La représentation du territoire français à la fin du XVIIIe siècle d'après les travaux sur la formation des départements* (Paris, 1987).

[9] Maurice Agulhon, Gabriel Desert, and Robert Specklin, *Histoire de la France rurale*, vol. 3: *Apogée et crise de la civilisation paysanne* (Paris, 1976), pp. 266–68.

[10] André Siegfried, *Tableau politique de la France de l'Ouest sous la Troisième République* (Paris, 1913).

different modalities even, in relationship with two general visions of things terrestial and divine."[11]

In contrast to most regions of France, Brittany remained staunchly Catholic,[12] but there was no clear correlation between religious practice and political conviction in the countryside stemming from the Revolution, no invisible line dividing the irreconcilable worlds of the devout and the dechristianized.[13] In Ille-et-Vilaine, as in Finistère, devout areas voted for ostensibly anticlerical politicians and Catholic candidates without abandoning their religious devotion. This characteristic has led Lagrée to classify areas of Ille-et-Vilaine in terms of *christianisme bleu* and *christianisme blanc*, as an alternative to the distinction made by electoral sociologists between a perforce areligious, anticlerical Left and a Catholic, retrograde Right.[14]

Although the cultural and political diversity of Brittany as well as its linguistic barrier make it difficult to formulate broad generalizations concerning its political and social characteristics in the nineteenth and twentieth centuries, Upper and Lower Brittany shared several basic traits that distinguished them from the nation as a whole.

Brittany was France's anomaly in demographic terms during the nineteenth and early twentieth centuries. As the birthrate began to fall in rural areas throughout France and as the country became depopulated owing to rural migration to cities and industrial centers by the end of the century, the birthrate remained elevated in Brittany so that by 1900 it was the most populous region of France. Couples in Brittany generally married relatively late and marital fertility was high throughout the nineteenth century. Between 1881 and 1890 Brittany's birthrate was higher than 27 per thousand, whereas the average for France during the same period was 23.9 per thousand.[15] Despite the persistent problem of infant mortality, Breton families were, as a result, generally larger than those in the rest of France. In 1891, for example, 31 percent of Breton families had more than four children in contrast to 21 percent in the rest of France. By the beginning of

[11] Lagrée, *Mentalités, religion, et histoire en Haute Bretagne*, p. 31.

[12] Nonetheless, dechristianized pockets abounded in parts of the department of Ille-et-Vilaine and Côtes-du-Nord. Gabriel Le Bras, *Introduction à l'étude de la pratique religieuse en France*, vol. 1 (Paris, 1942), pp. 101–24, vol. 2 (Paris, 1945), pp. 69–70, and *Etudes de la sociologie religieuse*, vol. 1 (Paris, 1955), pp. 72–84; Lambert, *Catholicisme et société*; Lagrée, *Catholicisme et société*; Isambert and Terrenoire, *Atlas de la pratique cultuelle*.

[13] Lagrée, *Mentalités, religion et histoire en Haute Bretagne*.

[14] Ibid., pp. 73–91.

[15] This figure does not include the department of Loire-Inférieure. Gilbert Le Guen, "D'une révolution manquée à une révolution possible," in *Histoire de la Bretagne*, ed. Delumeau, p. 465.

the twentieth century 41 percent of the Breton population was younger than twenty years of age in contrast to most other rural areas in France where the population aged owing to migration and depopulation.[16]

Within the province, birthrates varied considerably. In general, Lower Brittany's birthrates were higher than those in Upper Brittany.[17] With the gradual lowering of the death rate and without significant out-migration, these elevated birthrates resulted in higher population densities, placing greater demands on the resources of the region. By 1911, the density of the population in the province as a whole was ninety-six per square kilometer in contrast to an average of seventy-five for France.[18] Nonetheless, Brittany had the least number of inhabitants residing in urban areas, communes with a nucleated population greater than two thousand, and this trend continued in the early twentieth century.[19]

Although Brittany clearly did not belong to urban/industrial France, it was not totally lacking in rural and urban industries, but paradoxically, as the population that could fuel such industries increased, the region began to deindustrialize. Between 1780 and 1850, for example, the textile industry witnessed a period of prosperity, which gradually declined in the face of competition from the north and abroad. This decline was evident in the flourishing rural cloth industry. As cheaper cottons came to replace linen in the clothing industry and as the bourgeoisie in the northeast of France began to invest greater amounts of capital in the mechanization of industry, textile production began to disappear in the Breton province.

Brittany was not the only region to experience this process of deindustrialization.[20] The transportation and industrial revolutions, the growth of industrial enterprise in the north, and the spread of urban goods and

[16] Marriage ages could vary considerably in Brittany, however. In the Bigouden region of southern Finistère they were much lower than those observed in the rest of the department and in France as a whole. Segalen, *Quinze générations de Bas-Bretons*, pp. 64–65. Infant mortality figures in Finistère were extremely high before the First World War. See Albert Le Bail, *L'agriculture dans un département français: Le Finistère agricole—étude d'économie rurale* (Angers, 1925), p. 19. Le Guen, "D'une révolution manquée" p. 465. The overall fertility rate in France during the nineteenth century exhibited less regional variation than marital fertility (the number of births per 1,000 married women between the ages of fifteen and forty-four). See E. A. Wrigley, "The Fall of Marital Fertility in Nineteenth-Century France: Exemplar and Exception," *European Journal of Population* 1 (1985): 31–60, 141–177.

[17] Bertillon, *La dépopulation de la France*, p. 105.

[18] Choleau, *L'expansion bretonne*, p. 2; Delumeau, ed., *Histoire de la Bretagne*, p. 464.

[19] Ted W. Margadant, "Proto-Urban Development and Political Mobilization during the Second Republic," in *French Cities in the Nineteenth Century*, ed. John M. Merriman (London, 1982), p. 103.

[20] Michael Burns has argued that the "'modernization' of rural France brought by the 'agencies of change' so expertly outlined by Eugen Weber, led to an ironic consequence . . . the 'ruralization' of modern France." Burns, *Rural Society and French Politics*, p. 23.

values to rural areas accelerated the process of ruralization as well as the rural exodus that so worried observers at the end of the century.

Brittany, too, experienced large-scale emigration during the late nineteenth century, which was spurred by a relatively high birthrate, but the volume of emigration from areas within Brittany cannot be correlated solely with the decline in rural industries or with population increase. The Côtes-du-Nord, which had a more sluggish birthrate than Finistère at the end of the nineteenth century, began to lose an important part of its population early in the Third Republic, while emigration from Finistère did not become significant until after the First World War.

The characteristics that set Brittany apart from the rest of France were accentuated in Lower Brittany's department of Finistère, Pen Ar Bed ("end of the earth"). Finistère was formed in 1790–1791 as an administrative unit, a department, from the region of the Léon in the north, parts of the former dioceses of Tréguier and Vannes, and from most of the region of Cornouaille in the south. The plains of Léon were divided from those of Cornouaille by a long chain of high, barren mountains, the Monts d'Arées, that were hardly amenable to cultivation. Although the northern and southern portions of the armorican peninsula shared a similar geological structure, an impermeable granite base, which, in the absence of fertilizer resulted in very poor soils, the Léon in the north and Cornouaille in the south differed markedly in terms of political temperament, historical development, and, to a certain extent, economic structures. As early as the 1830s, Emile Souvestre commented on differences in temperament between the spirited, gregarious, and festive Cournouaillais and the proud, stolid, taciturn, and profoundly religious Léonard.[21] During the eighteenth and nineteenth centuries the two regions, which were separated by a seemingly impenetrable mountainous barrier, spoke two distinct dialects of the Breton language and exhibited striking contrasting traits with regard to demography, literacy, property relations, land tenure, and religious behavior (map 3).

Demography

Finistère's demographic growth was spectacular in the century following the French Revolution. Indeed, during the course of the nineteenth century it became one of the most densely populated and, at the same time, one of the least urbanized departments of France (Table 2. 1). In the absence of significant immigration, this unusual growth must be attributed to the department's relatively high birth rate. Between 1896 and 1900, the aver-

---

[21] Souvestre, *Les Derniers Bretons*, pp. 1–66.

Boundaries: ——— Canton
—— Arrondissement
—·—·— Department

N
W—+—E
S

0   10 Mi
0   10 Km

Map 3. Department of Finistère, 1911

TABLE 2.1
Urban and Rural Population in Finistère

Year	1821	1872	1886	1901
Urban population	63,052	139,724	169,051	203,600
	(13%)	(21.7%)	(23.9%)	(26.3%)
Rural population	420,395	503,239	538,769	569,414
	(87%)	(78.3%)	(76.1%)	(73.7%)

Source: Collet, "La population rurale du Finistère," p. 85.

age birth rate among Finistère's rural population was 32.78 per thousand and the average death rate stood at a high 20.54 per thousand, which has been attributed to the persistence of contaminated water supplies and infectious disease until the beginning of the twentieth century.[22]

Elevated birth rates did not, however, lead to high levels of urbanization during the course of the nineteenth century. In 1821, Finistère had seven towns, five of which were located in northern Finistère (Brest, Lesneven, Saint-Pol-de-Léon, Morlaix, Landerneau, Quimper, and Quimperlé.) Despite the fact that their number had increased to seventeen and the population of the port of Brest tripled by 1901, Finistère remained predominantly rural until well into the twentieth century. In 1901, 73.7 percent, or six out of eight of the department's inhabitants, lived in rural communes. Of the active population 62 percent were directly engaged in agriculture, but the livelihood of a far higher proportion of the department's inhabitants depended on the agricultural economy. These consisted, for example, of rural craftsmen, who were fast disappearing in the rest of France. Wheelwrights, cartwrights, carpenters, builders, sabot makers, shoesmiths, and saddlers remained an important part of the occupational landscape until the Second World War.

Population densities in rural communities within the department were extremely high (map 4). As early as 1821, these densities were well above the national average, and by the end of the century Finistère was among the most densely populated rural departments in France. Densities were highest in northern Finistère where, for example, the coastal rural cantons of Saint-Pol-de-Léon, Ploudalmézeau, Brest, and Lanmeur accommodated 95 to 120 inhabitants per square kilometer. The number of people residing

---

[22] By the end of the nineteenth century the birthrate was, however, significantly higher in southern Finistère. In Châteaulin, Quimperlé, and Quimper the birthrate was as high as thirty-eight to forty per thousand. The cantons of the Bigouden region in southern Finistère held the record at forty-five per thousand. Collet, "La population rurale du Finistère," pp. 85–99.

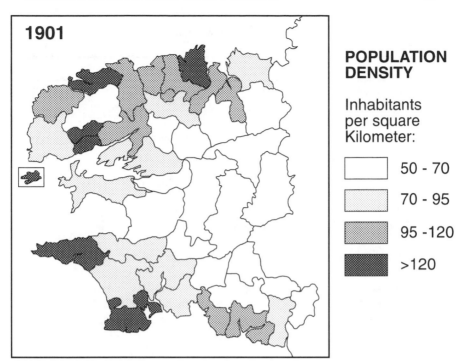

Map 4. Population Density in Finistère, 1901

in rural areas surrounding the port of Brest and the town of Saint-Pol-de-Léon reached 150 per square kilometer at the beginning of the twentieth century.[23] Nonetheless, by 1901 population densities in southern Finistère began to rival those in the north, which resulted in a growing demographic equilibrium between the regions.[24]

The demographic explosion that affected Finistère in the nineteenth century did not contribute to any significant levels of out-migration until well after the First World War. In 1906, for example, Camille Vallaux noted that the population of the Léon, one of the most densely populated areas in France, simply did not "add to any current of emigration out of Lower Brittany" with the exception of temporary migrants from Roscoff who went to England to sell onions grown in the region of Saint-Pol-de-Léon.[25] Although the standard of living tended to be relatively low in Finistére before the Great War, the greater agricultural productivity of northern

[23] Demographic change in northern Finistère varied, however. Ibid., p. 90.
[24] Ibid.
[25] Camille Vallaux, *La Basse Bretagne: Etude de géographie humaine* (1906; reprint, Paris, 1980), p. 276.

TABLE 2.2
Population in Paris Originating from Breton Departments
in 1891, 1896, and 1901

Year	1891	1896	1901
Côtes-du-Nord	25,873	30,044	36,089
Finistère	13,451	14,231	16,549
Ille-et-Vilaine	18,866	20,948	25,809
Loire-Inférieure	16,282	17,683	21,185
Morbihan	13,628	15,750	19,433
Total	88,100	98,656	119,065

Source: Choleau, *L'expansion bretonne*, p. 83.

Finistère may have allowed the region to accommodate its vast population more easily. As late as 1923, government officials claimed that the agricultural labor force was more than adequate to perform necessary tasks in Finistère—in contrast to many other areas of France.[26] Where emigration to cities from rural areas did occur toward the end of the century, migrants generally came from the less wealthy Cornouaille. The reasons for emigration were many: conscription, rural overpopulation in the face of rising prices for land, and low agricultural wages. Choleau suggested that another reason for this trend was the survival in certain parts of Finistère, despite the Napoleonic Code, of inheritance customs that favored primogeniture.[27]

Those who chose to leave the countryside emigrated both to cities within Brittany and to Paris and the department of Seine-Maritime. A relatively insignificant number of those who emigrated to Paris came from Finistère during the first great wave of emigration at the end of the nineteenth century (Table 2.2). The increasing number of migrants from Finistère who arrived in Paris after the First World War never equaled those who came in droves from the Côtes-du-Nord and Ille-et-Vilaine.

Elevated birthrates, comparatively low levels of out-migration, and urbanization in Finistère had several consequences. First, it meant that those who resided in rural communities in the department were far from isolated, except in the more remote, poorer communes of the Monts d'Arées.

---

[26] A.D. Finistère, 7M248, Direction des Services Agricoles, 23 June 1923. Indeed, in 1922–1923 the powerful agricultural syndicat Office Central de Landerneau sponsored the relocation of a number of Breton families in the Dordogne. See A.D. Finistère, 9 November 1923, letter from Hervé de Guébriant to the prefect of Finistère regarding one such voyage; Mévellec, *Le combat du paysan breton*, pp. 211–15.

[27] Choleau, *L'expansion bretonne*, p. 36.

Indeed, the rural inhabitant of Finistère was destined to live in close proximity to neighbors. High birthrates also assured the existence of a plentiful agricultural labor force, but the sheer size of this force drove down wages and fostered increased competition for land and leases. In short, Finistère's demographic takeoff was a double-edged sword that both stimulated agricultural development and aggravated social conflict.

A Failed Agricultural Revolution?

Arthur Young noted in his diary during his travels in Brittany in 1788 that nothing but wasteland could be seen for miles and that he was continually struck by its archaic form of agriculture, by its poverty, and by the savage aspect of its inhabitants: "One third of what I have seen of this province seems uncultivated and nearly all of it in misery."[28] In the absence of detailed studies of lower Breton agriculture in the eighteenth and nineteenth centuries Young's appraisals have generally been accepted by historians. Young, however, tended to emphasize the "dark side,"[29] and his judgments were often based on a superficial knowledge of the region. He failed to visit parts of Brittany where agriculture thrived. He passed through Guingamp, Morlaix, Landivisiau, Châteaulin, and Quimper, thereby missing some of the richest agricultural country in Brittany and France: the *ceinture dorée* (golden belt) surrounding Saint-Pol-de-Léon where crop yields were high, and lucrative market vegetables began to be cultivated early in the nineteenth century. Unlike Jacques Cambry, who published *Voyage dans le Finistère* in 1794 and whose insights are more reliable precisely because of his intimate knowledge of the area, Arthur Young's observations are impressionistic, founded on a cursory contact with the region. Modern economic analyses indicate that during the eighteenth century Breton departments did not differ significantly from other regions of France when one compares agricultural yields. Brittany was not only capable of providing for its own needs, but it also exported large quantities of grain from the ports of Pont l'Abbé, Morlaix, Paimpol, and Vannes at the end of the eighteenth century. As L. Guilhaud de Lavergne argued in 1861, Lower Brittany's reputation for "barbarity and poverty" was only "half deserved."[30]

[28] Arthur Young, *Voyages in France during the Years 1787, 1788, and 1789*, ed. Constantia Maxwell (Cambridge, 1929), pp. 107–15, 109.

[29] Ogès, *L'agriculture dans le Finistère*, p. 11.

[30] Cited in Hugh Clout, "Land-Use Change in Finistère," p. 70. Jean Chombart de Lauwe also takes Young's account to task and presents a more positive view of economic change in Brittany in *Bretagne et pays de la Garonne*. For a discussion of the region's agricultural yields, see Michel Morineau, *Les faux semblants*, pp. 51–3; Jacques Cambry, *Voyage dans le département du Finistère ou état de ce département en 1794 et 1795*.

One of the main reasons for observers' poor assessment of agriculture in Lower Brittany in particular was the widespread prevalence of *landes*, (uncultivated land), which so struck Arthur Young at the end of the eighteenth century. These landes included grazing pasture and land used for occasional cropping and other resources. In fact, it is difficult to substantiate the claim that the landes of Finistère were totally unused in the absence of reliable land-use statistics prior to the *ancien cadastre* of the nineteenth century. The proportion of uncultivated land in the department in the eighteenth century, according to information collected by the *intendant* of Brittany, was extraordinarily high, but differences in the department in this respect were already apparent. In the more prosperous Léon, only 35 percent of land remained uncultivated in the eighteenth century, as compared to 48 percent in Cornouaille.[31] Despite encouragement from the *parlement* and Estates of Brittany and a royal declaration, which gave incentives to those who reclaimed land in the form of exemption from taxation and tithes, land clearance was hardly perceptible until the first half of the nineteenth century.

A number of factors contributed to the preservation of landes in Lower Brittany. First, the complicated rights, usages, and "ambiguities of ownership" governing landes on which peasants grazed their livestock contributed to the difficulty encountered by individuals who wished to reclaim land. Second, a form of tenancy peculiar to Brittany, *domaine congéable* (tenancy at will), which was especially prominent in Cornouaille, militated against land clearance.[32] Domaine congéable provided the tenant farmer little incentive to improve the land he rented. The proprietor owned the land the tenant worked, but the tenant in turn owned the buildings and implements attached to it. Although leases under domaine congéable were generally of longer duration than any other form of lease—sometimes lasting for a generation—and the landlord had to reimburse the farmer for the value of the buildings and any improvements made on the land at termination of the lease, the owner was more often than not reluctant to give his tenants compensation. Indeed, the value of the compensation was frequently a matter of dispute. The tenant, similarly, might be reluctant to make improvements because his tenancy was uncertain, and he could not always be assured of receiving adequate compensation. Third, the peasant saw some utility in moorland for grazing animals in an area where livestock assumed a growing importance. Finally, without fertilizer and an adequate road system, the geography and soil composition of the armorican peninsula discouraged land clearance. The soils of Lower Brittany, which rested on a hard granite base, required calcium, phosphate, or ani-

[31] Clout, "Land-Use Change in Finistère, " p. 74.
[32] Ibid., pp. 77–78.

mal fertilizer to make them suitable for cultivation. In the golden belt surrounding Saint-Pol-de-Léon and Roscoff and in other coastal areas, peasants who had previously discovered the utility of seaweed and sand and broken shells as a natural fertilizer saw the productivity of their land increase dramatically as a result of this discovery. However, without an adequate means of transporting it, such fertilizer could not benefit inland areas. In the first half of the nineteenth century, seaweed was carried inland sixteen to twenty kilometers or more in carts in the arrondissements of Morlaix and Quimper but hardly at all in the southern arrondissement of Quimperlé.[33] The productivity and cultivation of land increased, therefore, at varying rates within the department and were in part dependent on the availability of fertilizer, the disappearance of domaine congéable, and population densities. Increases in population densities encouraged the development of intensive agricultural production, such as annual cropping or multicropping, particularly in northern Finistère.[34] Although change occurred at different rates, by 1850 the agricultural revolution had come to affect all areas of the department. The clearance of landes was an uneven process that began in the eighteenth century and ended in the twentieth.

Lower Brittany was not strictly tied to a system of *polyculture de subsistence*, though a viable commercial market for specialized agricultural production did not develop until the late nineteenth century. Brittany was a major exporter of wheat in prerevolutionary France. As early as the seventeenth century, the northern regions of Trégor and the Léon were part of the capital's breadbasket, and the arrondissement of Morlaix produced some of the best grain from these areas. In the eighteenth and early nineteenth centuries, linen and cloths of various kinds produced from flax grown in northern Finistère were among the area's most important export items. The linen and cloth industry reached its peak between 1756 and 1764 in the region of Morlaix where workers were employed in the production of cloth. In 1763–1764, the royal cloth manufactury was founded in Brest, employing more than 2,515 workers several years later.[35] In the mid-eighteenth century Landivisiau had 1,500 weavers and Saint-Pol-de-Léon 500.[36] By the mid-nineteenth century, this industry, which produced great wealth for farmers and manufacturers in the Léon, was in a decline, as

[33] Ibid., p. 79.

[34] For a discussion of the relationship between population density and varying forms of land-use change, see Boserup, *Population and Technological Change*, chaps. 1–3, esp. pp. 15–28.

[35] Georges M. Thomas, "Contribution à l'histoire de l'industrie et du commerce de la Toile en Basse-Bretagne," *Bulletin de la Société Archéologique du Finistère*, 71 (1944): 28. Louis Elegoet notes that in the bourg of Ploudaniel in the Léon 42 percent of the peasantry contributed to the weaving industry at the beginning of the eighteenth century. By 1790, only 16 percent were involved in weaving. Elegoet, *Saint-Méen*, pp. 86–87.

[36] Ogès, *L'agriculture dans le Finistère*, p. 8.

capital was increasingly invested in the textile factories of the northeast. This decline, which affected other textile areas in France, such as Nîmes in southern France, can be attributed to several causes: the mercantilist policies that resulted in the closing of markets to many French products, the Revolutionary wars, and, above all to government policy. The Breton cloth industry largely depended on outfitting the French Navy, but in 1831 the Ministry of War authorized the use of cotton instead of linen for naval uniforms; the conseil général of Finistère protested this decision and feared its impact on a population of eighty thousand whose livelihood depended in some way on the cloth industry.[37] Indeed, the effect of the government decision was dramatic and marked the demise of the linen industry.[38] In 1832, 4,000 hectares of flax were cultivated in the Léon (Cornouaille never developed a significant cloth industry), but by 1852 no more than 1,000 hectares of flax remained.[39]

In its heyday, the linen industry, enriching the Léon, had a lasting significance in the nineteenth and twentieth centuries in that it helped to foster a "peasant aristocracy," the Julots or Juloded. The Julots became wealthy from growing flax and selling cloth in the sixteenth, seventeenth, and eighteenth centuries, and although they were peasant *cultivateurs*, they lived almost as a closed caste by the nineteenth century, through the acquisition of national lands and the manors of the nobility. With the decline of the cloth industry, they channeled their wealth into land, livestock, stock companies, and banks in the nineteenth and twentieth centuries.[40]

In the eighteenth and early nineteenth centuries, Finistère produced more potatoes, market vegetables, and cereals than it consumed, and surpluses were exported to England, Ireland, and Flanders. In the nineteenth century, the inhabitants of the department tended to consume secondary cereals rather than the more expensive wheat that was shipped to Normandy, the Mediterranean south, and Flanders. Between 1836 and 1842 the department exported most of its wheat.[41] By 1846, Finistère was already a substantial exporter of grain. Of the 239,000 tons of grain exported by France, 121,000 tons were exported from Breton ports, 30,000

[37] Thomas, "Contribution à l'histoire et du commerce," pp. 27–36.

[38] Ibid.

[39] Ibid., p. 32. Elegoet notes that in 1836 there were thirty-two female weavers in the parish of Saint-Méen, but in 1866 only one remained. Elegoet, *Saint-Méen*, p. 152.

[40] Le Gallo, "Une caste paysanne du Haut Léon," pp. 53–82; Ch. Chassi, "Du nouveau et du vieux sur les Julots du Léon," *Le Télégramme*, 8 August 1959; Bernard Verrier, "Le rôle du collège de St. Pol de Léon de 1876 à 1973" (Mémoire de maîtrise, Université de Paris X, 1973), p. 53.

[41] Ogès, *L'agriculture dans le Finistère*, p. 76. Chombart de Lauwe also notes that Brittany as a whole tended to export its wheat, leaving black bread and buckwheat galettes (a kind of thin pancake) for everyday consumption. Wheat export to Britain began in the fourteenth century. De Lauwe, *Bretagne et pays de la Garonne*, p. 51.

of which left the ports of Morlaix, Brest, and Quimper in Finistère.[42] In 1865, Finistère's agricultural exports exceeded its imports and consisted of 1,331,652 kilograms of grain and flour, 7,993,810 kilograms of potatoes, and 773,700 kilograms of green vegetables. These exports only increased as oats, barley, rye, and buckwheat came to be replaced by wheat in the department as a whole, especially in the Léon, and as the livestock farming and the cultivation of market vegetables were intensified.[43]

Whether the gradual increase in crop yields, the accelerated pace of land clearance, and the commercialization of agriculture constituted an agricultural revolution is still a subject of dispute. In the agricultural regions of Lower Brittany the most radical changes in the organization of agriculture were clearing wasteland and developing intensive systems of agricultural production.

One principal factor that delayed the agricultural revolution in Lower Brittany in the eighteenth and nineteenth centuries was the inferior transportation system that characterized the region. Not only were Finistère's land links with Paris weak, but the roads crisscrossing the countryside were often impassable when rain reduced them to muddy troughs. The agricultural population of Finistère therefore relied primarily on the ports of Morlaix, Brest, and Quimper to export their goods. The system of canals whose construction began under the First Empire in Brittany, such as the canal of Blavet (1804–1826) and a canal connecting Brittany's major ports of Brest and Nantes (1806–1842), did not improve communications greatly. Although the Brest-Nantes canal could transport fertilizer to the interior, its total volume of tonnage for all products in 1865 hardly reached 21,767 tons, which included 15,000 tons of coal destined for the Navy in Brest.[44] The new system of railways, whose main lines were installed in the 1860s, vastly improved Lower Brittany's export opportunities, but it did not result in significant changes in the basic modes of production or in the rapid commercialization of agriculture. The railway did, however, contribute to the economic transformation of the most inaccessible portions of the department.

From the 1860s onward railway tariffs were a subject of acrimonious debate,[45] as was the lack of coordination in schedule between the peninsula's southern lines, which were owned by the private Compagnie d'Orléans, and the lines serving the north, which were owned by the state. A few lines connected the north to the south, but schedules were badly timed.

[42] Ogès, *L'agriculture dans le département du Finistère*, p. 88.

[43] France, Ministère de l'Agriculture, du Commerce, et des Travaux Publics, *Enquête agricole*, deuxième série, 3eme circonscription: Morbihan, Finistère, Côtes-du-Nord, Ille-et-Vilaine (Paris, 1867), p. 98.

[44] Meyer, "Une mutation manquée," p. 71.

[45] Ministère de l'Agriculture, *Enquête agricole*, p. 45.

Despite these shortcomings, the introduction of railroads did contribute to
the specialization in lucrative crops other than wheat and forged commercial links with France and abroad that were far from negligible.

One of the most dramatic changes to occur in the development of agriculture in Finistère during the nineteenth century was the introduction and
expansion of new forms of specialized agricultural production for commercial markets. The most important of these were animal husbandry and
market garden farming. The remarkable expansion of animal husbandry
in Finistère was in part fueled by Finistère's demographic growth and the
"vast demand for meat and dairy products in the capital," which stimulated an important commercial market for the sale of Breton butter, milk,
and meat in the twentieth century.[46] Between the 1830s and the eve of the
First World War an increasing number of farmers, particularly in the Léon,
began to channel their energies into the farming of pigs, horses, and cattle.
By 1912, Finistère had one of the highest densities of "livestock units" in
France. Indeed, the geography of livestock farming in France changed
profoundly as the locus of production that had extended across northern
France in the 1830s shifted away from the departments of the northeast to
Brittany, Normandy, Poitou, and to a lesser degree, the Massif Central in
the next three quarters of the nineteenth century. By 1912, "four departments supported more than double the volume of livestock units than
considerations of area alone might suggest," and Finistère was one of the
foremost among them.[47]

Although certain areas of Brittany remained tied to a *polyculture de
subsistence* and hardly engaged in market export, important areas of
Finistère, notably Pont l'Abbé and Plougastel in southern Finistère, and
Saint-Pol-de-Léon and Plouescat in the north, cultivated *cultures maraichères*, early market vegetables such as artichokes, cauliflower, and strawberries that required special climatic conditions.

The export of early market vegetables from the regions of Saint-Pol-de-
Léon and Plougastel began to develop in the early nineteenth century, and
the distribution of these items became organized in the second half of the
century for sale in English, Dutch, and Parisian markets. The farmers of
the Léon early on recognized the value of these lucrative crops. Jacques
Cambry, who visited the golden belt of the Léon in the late eighteenth
century, commented on their abundance, particularly in Saint-Pol-de-Léon
and Roscoff. The region's mild temperate climate, where temperatures
rarely dropped below freezing due to the unusual climatic conditions created by the Gulf Stream, the region's sandy soil, and the early discovery of

---

[46] Clout, *The Land of France*, p. 110; de Lauwe, *Bretagne et pays de la Garonne*, pp. 99–
100.

[47] Livestock units refer to aggregate numbers of horses, pigs, sheep, cattle, donkeys, mules,
and goats. Clout, *The Land of France*, pp. 105, 109–10.

seaweed as fertilizer made the golden belt an excellent environment for cultures maraichères. Moreover, as spring comes two months earlier to Brittany than to Normandy, the Parisian Basin, and other agricultural areas, the region could grow produce unavailable elsewhere for Paris and foreign markets.

In the 1830s and 1840s enterprising farmers began to send their vegetables to Parisian markets or cart them to nearby ports, and trade links between England and Brittany began to be established for these specialized products. In 1830 the first asparagus and artichokes sold in Paris came from Roscoff.[48] During the early nineteenth century Emile Souvestre noted that a number of farmers from Roscoff, who came to be known as "johnnies," began the custom of traveling long distances (particularly across the Channel) to sell produce from the region.[49]

As agricultural statistics from the period prior to the Third Republic are incomplete and sporadic, it is difficult to chart reliably the growth in the number of hectares of early market vegetables. However, the increasing lucrativeness of cultures maraichères can be measured by both the value of land under cultivation and the monetary returns on what was produced per hectare in the region. Ernest Picaud estimated in 1912 that the value of land in the region of Plougastel where strawberries and specialized market produce were intensely cultivated was greater than the national average by several hundred francs per hectare despite the fact that the average value of land per hectare in Brittany as a whole (and more particularly in Lower Brittany) was low in comparison to national averages. In 1912, the value of a hectare of land in Plougastel was 3,000 francs—the French national average was 2,198—whereas the same hectare of land in 1862 was valued at 1,926 francs.[50] The discrepancy in the returns on produce of land in areas where cultures maraichères and other agricultural products were cultivated was evident as early as 1838. Grains were some of the most lucrative agricultural export items; whereas one hectare of cultures maraichères brought a return of 3,000 francs, the same surface of grain yielded a return of 300 francs.[51]

The cultivation of early market vegetables at the turn of the century was primarily concentrated in the arrondissement of Morlaix, more specifically in the cantons of Plouescat, Plouzévedé, Roscoff, and Saint-Pol-de-Léon. The cultivation of these lucrative products accelerated during the first ten years of the twentieth century. Significantly, no special mention was made in the department's annual agricultural statistics of the number of hectares of early market vegetables under cultivation in the arrondissement of Mor-

[48] Ogès, L'agriculture dans le Finistère, p. 15.
[49] Souvestre, Les Derniers Bretons, pp. 176–77.
[50] Picaud, De la culture des primeurs, pp. 43–44.
[51] Ogès, L'agriculture dans le Finistère, p. 15.

laix.[52] These statistics, however, began to be kept in the early years of the twentieth century.[53] In one of the richest cantons in Finistère, Saint-Pol-de-Léon, the number of hectares devoted to early market vegetables almost doubled between the prewar period and 1930, from 1,228 to 2,199.[54] In 1907, early market vegetables occupied 4,075 hectares in the department as whole and increased to 6,420 in 1913. By 1921, the number of hectares of early market vegetables had increased to 8,160, yielding an annual income of 58,668,900 francs, and by 1923, the income produced by 10,542 hectares in the department was 116 million francs annually, more than one-third greater than the income produced by wheat.[55] With the increased cultivation of early market vegetables after the First World War, more produce was of necessity shipped to Paris and abroad. The volume of exports from the region increased significantly.[56] The results of specialization in crops such as early market vegetables and significant increases in exports from the region were twofold: First, the commercialization of these crops by the early twentieth century made the farmer more aware of national price scales, export policies, and transportation systems. This gradual process began early in the nineteenth century. The farmer in Finistère, and more particularly in the Léon, increasingly looked beyond the fence of the family farm for commercial markets.

A second consequence of the commercialization of agriculture and of land clearance was a gradual increase in the value of land in Finistère that initially tended to fall below national averages. Population pressure may also have played a role in augmenting the value of land, however. By the beginning of the twentieth century, there were obvious regional differences within the department in terms of land values. In Cornouaille and Léon, the value of arable land per hectare in 1908–1909 was 1,700 francs and 2,500 for *prairie naturelle*, but in the ceinture dorée a hectare of arable land was worth 2,800 francs and a hectare of prairie naturelle 3,500 francs. A hectare exclusively devoted to early market vegetables could sell for as much as 4,000 or 5,000 francs.[57] Picaud, writing in 1912, put this figure at

[52] A.D. Finistère, 6M1009, "Statistique agricole annuelle, arrondissement de Morlaix, 1895."

[53] A.D. Finistère, 6M1011, "Statistique agricole annuelle, arrondissement de Morlaix, 1904." In Plouescat 86 hectares of "cultures maraichères" were under cultivation; in Plouzévédé 200, and in Saint-Pol-de-Léon 1,228.

[54] A.D. Finistère, 6M1015, "Statistique agricole annuelle, arrondissement de Morlaix," 1930.

[55] Le Bail, *L'agriculture dans un département français*, p. 203.

[56] A.D. Finistère, 7M261, a dossier entitled *cultures diverses* for statistics and correspondence concerning the export of *cultures maraichères*.

[57] France, Ministère de l'Agriculture, Office des renseignements agricoles, *La petite propriété en France, enquête monographique (1908–1909)* (Paris, 1909), p. 82.

TABLE 2.3
Rent per Hectare in the Department of Finistère, 1835–1865 (in francs)

	1835	1845	1855	1865
Terres Labourables	42	50	55	74
Prairie Naturelle	52	62	75	90

Source: Direction des Services Agricoles, Département du Finistère. "Monographie agricole du Finistère, Troisième Partie: L'économie rurale," ms., 1929, p. 8.

6,000 to 8,000 francs minimum in the areas around Saint-Pol-de-Léon and Roscoff.[58]

Increases in rent per hectare reflect a similar rise in the value of land in Finistère, though rent increases show a less linear progress. The greatest increases in the value of rented land in the nineteenth century probably occurred between 1835 and 1865 (Table 2.3). Though the value of land increased, particularly in regions cultivating specialized crops, between 1865 and 1913, it is surprising that rents remained relatively stable. This phenomenon may have been a function of the agricultural downturn of the 1880s and 1890s. Indeed, the war of 1870 and the agricultural crisis of the early Third Republic depressed land prices in general; between 1880 and 1890 these prices actually decreased, although the market began to recover by 1909.

The value of land and the number of sales increased enormously after the First World War. Rents throughout the department, however, remained largely stable until 1922–1923 at which point they experienced a dramatic take-off. By 1929 rents had tripled from their prewar levels in the ceinture dorée, where rents per hectare were often six times the average in the department.[59]

These patterns of land values and rents reflected both national economic cycles affecting French agriculture as a whole and the agricultural revolution in Brittany. Land values began to increase in the first half of the nineteenth century, and particularly between 1830 and 1860 when the initial land improvements were achieved, and then again between 1900 and 1914 when crop specialization was intensified as a result of new forms of market organization and the transportation revolution. In this respect, the Breton pattern of agricultural development may not have been as radically different from the French pattern as has been supposed. It has recently been

[58] Picaud, De la culture des primeurs, p. 102.

[59] Direction des Services Agricoles, Département du Finistère, "Monographie agricole du Finistère, Troisième partie: L'économie rurale" (ms., 1929), pp. 8–9.

argued that the agricultural revolution that ostensibly occurred in all but the most backward areas of France in the eighteenth century was a myth.[60] The most far-reaching changes in French agriculture were the result of a series of revolutions that occurred between the eighteenth and the twentieth centuries, as in Brittany, but more particularly between 1852 and the 1880s. Despite the fact that the agricultural revolution in Finistère resembled in its timing the series of revolutions that occurred elsewhere, it assumed forms peculiar to the armorican peninsula. Agricultural change in Finistère was shaped by climate, soil, and its extraordinary demographic growth. Above all, high population densities in both northern and southern Finistère encouraged an agricultural supply system that tended to combine annual cropping or multicropping with intense animal husbandry, as well as food supply systems increasingly oriented toward a commercial market.[61] Agricultural change in Finistère primarily took the form of land clearance, but this did not transform the basic structure of the rural economy, the individual family farm.

Land Tenure and Social Change

Brittany has been characterized as a region dominated by large landed estates and an intransigent aristocracy whose social and economic supremacy remained virtually unchanged in rural society until the beginning of the twentieth century. However, in the department of Finistère only a handful of communes consisted of large landed farms in the nineteenth century.

The agricultural survey of 1882 provides the first reliable record of the size of farms in Finistère and the relative proportion of those who either owned, rented, or sharecropped these farms during the early Third Republic.[62] The survey indicates that there were very few large farms; most were small (from one to ten hectares) or medium-sized (from ten to forty hectares). A considerable portion of the department's land appears to have been owned by peasant proprietors who farmed their own lands with the aid of family members and hired help.[63] In 1882, 56.08 percent of all

[60] Agulhon et al., *Apogée et crise de la civilisation paysanne*, pp. 8–12.

[61] Finistère's agricultural development lends support to the relationships that Esther Boserup draws between population density and food supply systems in low-technology countries. According to Boserup, low population densities are strongly associated with pastoralism and fallow periods, whereas higher densities are associated with annual cropping and animal husbandry. Boserup, *Population and Technological Change*, pp. 15–33.

[62] None of the agricultural censuses of the nineteenth century provides intradepartmental data on land tenure, and the communal and cantonal questionnaires on which aggregate departmental statistics were based have not survived.

[63] The 1862 census and subsequent censuses provide statistics on the size of farming units

TABLE 2.4
Land Tenure in Finistère, 1882–1929

Year	Working only own lands	Working own plus rented or share-cropped land	Working only rented or share-cropped land	Total
1882	30,822 (39.85%)	12,554 (16.23%)	33,969 (43.92%)	77,345
1892	30,114 (41.49%)	11,687 (16.10%)	30,789 (42.41%)	72,590
1929	34,653 (53.44%)	5,406 (8.33%)	24,790 (38.23%)	64,849

Source: Ministère de l'agriculture, Statistique agricole de la France: résultats généraux de l'enquête décennale de 1882 (Nancy: Berger-Lévrault, 1887), pp. 186–87; Ministère de l'agriculture, Statistique agricole de la France: résultats généraux de l'enquête décennale de 1892 (Paris: Imprimerie Nationale, 1897), pp. 246–47; Ministère de l'agriculture, Les agriculteurs et la propriété foncière, l'évolution des modes de faire valoir en Bretagne, service régionale des statistiques agricoles (Bretagne), no. 53, November 1976, p. 12.

farmers in the department worked their own land, 16.23 percent of whom farmed additional rented or sharecropped land. By 1929 the proportion of farmers in Finistère working their own land had increased to 61.77 percent, but those who worked additional sharecropped or rented land dropped to 8.33 percent. Similarly, the number of those without property who exclusively rented or sharecropped land dropped from 43.92 percent in 1882 of the total number of farmers in the department to 38.23 percent in 1929 (see Tables 2.4 and 2.5).

The pace of land acquisition accelerated following the First World War for several reasons. Many landowners who, before the war, had established long leases at a fixed rent found themselves unable to turn a profit in a changing economic climate and were forced to sell all or part of their land. The farmers who rented the land were often able to benefit from the growing accessibility of land and mortgages as well as farm credits. Indeed, according to the agricultural census of 1929, the interwar period was the apogee of the peasant proprietor who farmed his own land. This phenomenon set a new crisis in motion as the unsettled agricultural market of the l930s and 1940s made it increasingly difficult to pay on these loans. By

---

(exploitations) and on the number of those who owned, rented, and sharecropped land. They do not furnish information on the social status of property owners. These statistics do, however, allow one to make general observations concerning the relative strength of landowning peasant groups and the size and scope of the individual farming unit.

TABLE 2.5
Number of Farms (*Exploitations*) by Hectare in Finistère, 1882–1929

Year	0–5	5–10	10–40	10–50	40+	50+	Total
1882	47,800	14,921	16,974	—	1,694	—	81,389
	(58.73%)	(18.33%)	(20.86%)	—	(2.08%)	—	
1892	41,435	14,914	16,988	—	1,446	—	74,783
	(55.41%)	(19.94%)	(22.72%)	—	(1.93%)	—	
1929	32,840	13,275	—	19,333	—	339	65,787
	(49.92%)	(20.18%)	—	(29.39%)	—	(0.51%)	

Source: Ministère de l'agriculture, *Statistique agricole de la France*, pp. 170–71; Ministère de l'agriculture, *Statistique agricole de la France, 1892*, pp. 218–19, 222–23; Direction des Services Agricoles, Département du Finistère, "Monographie Agricole, 1929," p. 4; Berger, *Peasants Against Politics*, p. 26.

1955 the number of these independent peasant proprietors decreased.[64]

There were nonetheless significant intradepartmental contrasts in the percentage of farmers who owned or leased their farms. The highest proportion of those working their own land could be found in southern Finistère, particularly in the arrondissement of Quimper, while the highest proportions of tenants leasing land were located in northern Finistère (see Table 2.6 and map 5). It must be said, however, that in many northern communes, including Saint-Pol-de-Léon, Morlaix, Brest, and Daoulas, more than half the farms were worked by peasant proprietors.

Although the percentage of peasant proprietors farming their own land increased from the census of 1882 to 1929, this resulted not in increasing the number of small farms, but rather in consolidating five- to twenty-hectares farms at the expense of very small farms and large landed estates. Indeed, Finistère was a close second to the Dordogne in having the greatest number of medium-sized farms in France and was among departments with the smallest number of large estates.[65]

Despite the fact that land acquisition and the size of farms increased between the 1890s and 1920s, changes in land tenure did not eliminate the family farm as the dominant form of agricultural production in the department. It would, however, be erroneous to claim that its survival demonstrated an insensitivity "to changes in market and technology."[66] Changes

[64] Direction des Services Agricoles, Département du Finistère, "Monographie Agricole, 1929," pp. 3–4; France, Ministère de l'agriculture, "Les agriculteurs et la propriété foncière," p. 14.

[65] Le Bail, *L'agriculture dans un département français*, p. 78.

[66] Berger, *Peasants Against Politics*, p. 27.

TABLE 2.6
Land Tenure by Arrondissement and by Canton in Finistère, 1929

Arrondissement and Canton	Farms worked by landowners		Farms worked by leaseholders or sharecroppers		Total
	No.	%	No.	%	
Brest	7,938	48	8,516	52	16,454
Brest	451	58	327	42	778
Daoulas	1,916	58	1,388	42	3,304
Landerneau	887	42	1,225	58	2,112
Lannilis	315	30	736	70	1,051
Lesneven	1,719	46	2,019	54	3,738
Ouessant	—		—		—
Plabennec	1,028	55	841	45	1,869
Ploudalmézeau	541	39	846	61	1,387
Ploudiry	262	41	378	59	640
Saint-Renan	819	52	756	48	1,575
Morlaix	6,514	45	7,899	55	14,413
Morlaix	590	61	378	39	968
Landivisiau	621	46	730	54	1,351
Lanmeur	419	30	978	70	1,397
Plouescat	587	44	747	56	1,334
Plouigneau	856	41	1,232	59	2,088
Plouzévédé	582	38	949	62	1,531
St.-Pol-de-Léon	1,257	58	911	42	2,168
St. Thégonnec	686	46	805	54	1,491
Sizun	587	54	500	46	1,087
Taulé	329	33	669	67	998
Châteaulin	8,132	57	6,139	43	14,271
Châteaulin	1,418	75	473	25	1,891
Carhaix	283	17	1,379	83	1,662
Chateauneuf du Faou	1,799	60	1,200	40	2,999
Crozon	1,421	62	871	38	2,292
Le Faou	478	47	540	53	1,018
Huelgoat	1,351	61	864	39	2,215
Pleyben	1,382	63	812	37	2,194
Quimper	11,723	68	5,400	32	17,123
Quimper	1,333	54	1,135	46	2,468
Briec	1,118	75	372	25	1,490

(continued)

TABLE 2.6
(Continued)

Arrondissement and Canton	Farms worked by landowners		Farms worked by leaseholders or sharecroppers		Total
	No.	%	No.	%	
Concarneau	305	51	293	49	598
Douarnenez	1,172	83	240	17	1,412
Fouesnant	783	48	848	52	1,631
Plogastel-St.-Germain	1,955	73	723	27	2,678
Point-Croix	2,996	83	614	17	3,610
Pont l'Abbé	1,113	51	1,070	49	2,183
Rosporden	948	90	105	10	1,053
Quimperlé	5,461	64	3,068	36	8,529
Quimperlé	466	33	945	67	1,411
Arzano	279	57	210	43	489
Bannalec	1,710	70	733	30	2,443
Pont-Aven	1,760	68	828	32	2,588
Scaër	1,246	78	352	22	1,598

Source: Ministère de l'agriculture, *Les agriculteurs et la propriété foncière, l'évolution des modes de faire valoir en Bretagne,* service régionale de statistique agricole (Bretagne), no. 53, November 1976, pp. 20–21.

Note: There are no existing cantonal data regarding forms of land tenure prior to 1929. As some forms consisted of land that was both owned and rented by farmers (*faire valoir mixte*), some farms may have been counted twice. This might account for the discrepancies in the total number of farms (*exploitations*) contained in this table (70,790) and those reported in the agricultural census of 1929 (65,787).

and variations in both the size of farms, particularly the growing predominance of medium-sized farms, were determined by a number of interdependent variables: soil quality and terrain, access to markets, the growing specialization in the organization of agriculture, and the persistence of varying inheritance customs.

Small farms that ranged from one to ten hectares in size were generally located along the coastal perimeters of the department of Finistére and on the islands of Ouessant and the Batz. These areas, which tended to specialize in cash crops, had most access to markets and benefited from the land improvement through the easy transportation of seaweed and shells that enriched the soils of the armorican peninsula. Farms were perhaps the smallest in size in the ceinture dorée surrounding Saint-Pol-de-Léon and

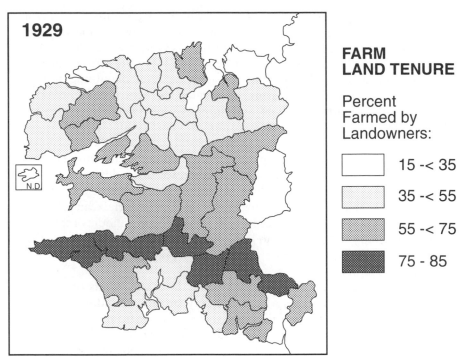

Map 5. Land Tenure in Finistère, 1929

Plouescat, at the forefront in the production of highly lucrative cash crops early in the nineteenth century. Medium-sized farms predominated in the interior of both the Léon and Cornouaille where grazing land coexisted alongside the production of grains that included wheat, oats, buckwheat, and rye, all of which required larger plots of land. The growing importance of livestock farming in the agricultural economy of Finistère, which necessitated wide expanses of grazing pasture, also significantly contributed to the consolidation of medium-sized farms.

The survival of different traditions of inheritance in the prerevolutionary dioceses of Quimper and Léon had a far-reaching impact on the size and types of farming units. In Cornouaille, which was less amenable to cultivation and depended less on cash crops, land was not divided equally among offspring. This practice prevented the excessive division of property that could lead to the impoverishment of proprietors. The size of farms in Cornouaille was therefore somewhat larger than those in the north in the nineteenth century. In the Léon, partible inheritance customs were the norm, which was better suited to cash-crop production and to smaller scale farming. These partible inheritance customs did not, however, lead to serious out-migration because of the labor intensive nature of cash-crop agriculture and because of the way in which the farms were managed, often as family collectives. In the Léon, family members divided the fruits of their labor more equally, whereas in the Cornouaille they were often reduced to little more than wage labor, which led to greater levels of out-migration.[67]

Differences in the size of farms between the northern and southern portions of the department began to disappear in the twentieth century. By 1913, medium-sized properties were important in Cornouaille and in parts of the Monts d'Arées, whereas in the coastal regions of the department smaller plots became the norm and contributed to the cultivation of cash crops and to a family economy whose labor was divided between fishing and farming. Only small pockets of large landed estates owned by the nobility remained intact in the environs of Quimper, Morlaix, and Daoulas by the end of the nineteenth century.[68] Indeed, by the middle of the nineteenth century the nobility had lost whatever economic preeminence they had had; their social influence was based more on cultural precedent than economic power.

Although the peasant gradually became the master of his or her own land in Finistère, both very large and very small landholdings were the exception rather than the rule; rural society was far from homogeneous. Not only did the department have a significant number of those who continued to lease land, but there were subtle distinctions and social gradations among the active population involved in agriculture. In Saint-Méen, a commune in northern Finistère, social stratification within peasant communities was rigid. It was based on wealth and the amount of land peasants farmed. Millers as well as wealthy peasants working their own property and often renting additional land were at the top of the social ladder; they were followed by peasants owning or renting small farms, by rural artisans, including masons, blacksmiths, coopers, weavers, and tailors, by agricultural workers, coal sellers, and beggars.[69] In the Lower Léon, sociologist Fanch Elegoet has preferred to stress the importance of property in defining social order. In terms of social status and power, *propriétaires fonciers* (*moc'heilh* or *moundian*) were followed by peasant smallholders (*en e leve*), farmers renting land (*merour* and *forsal*) and finally by day laborers and servants.[70]

Within this heterogeneous peasant community social hierarchy was translated into political and social privilege. Wealthier peasants often lived

[67] Ogès, *L'agriculture dans le Finistère*, pp. 33–34.

[68] Vallaux, *La Basse-Bretagne*, pp. 107–21.

[69] L. Elegoet, *Saint-Méen*, p. 197.

[70] F. Elegoet, *Paysannes de Léon*, p. 216. Elegoet bases his analysis on interviews with two peasant women, Madeleine, born in 1882 in Guissény, and Thérèse, born in 1892 in Plouguerneau.

in a manner resembling that of their less fortunate neighbors, but subtle social distinctions were evident in dress, education, and social privilege. Not only did wealthier families tend to hold municipal office for generations, but the ritual life of the community, in processions and religious festivals, also adhered to these distinctions. The bearers of banners and religious emblems were chosen according to the standing of the families within communities. Similarly, rites of passage, marriage and burials, were scheduled according to the social standing of the families involved. Pews near the altar were reserved for privileged peasant families in the parish church, whereas the less fortunate were relegated to the rear.[71] Finally, social distinction was reflected in dress, particularly in the shape and height of the *coiffe* (headdress) worn by Breton women, which varied from commune to commune.

A large proportion of land in Finistère was farmed by tenants renting from landowners, who were predominantly peasants. Some land was still subject in the nineteenth century to the disappearing system of domaine congéable that had been widespread in Cornouaille in the eighteenth century, but it had never taken hold in the Léon. This system was gradually replaced by leaseholdings under which the tenant rented land for a period of generally six to nine years. The position of the tenant was always far from secure, but it became particularly insecure in the interwar period. Without sufficient means to acquire property in a vigorous land market— as in 1922 when scores of farmers were evicted from land they had farmed for generations—they could lose their land at short notice. Moreover, they were often subject to political pressure from landlords who could refuse to renew leases without compensation for agricultural improvements if they failed to vote properly.

Although the position of those who leased land was often tenuous and insecure, the lot of the day laborer, servant, and rural artisan was worse and vastly inferior to comparable groups in other areas of France. With the diffusion of urban goods and the decline in rural industries, those who had engaged in the manufacture of goods gradually disappeared and either became part of the vast agricultural labor force or migrated to other areas of Brittany and France.[72]

As Breton families were generally large, there was often little need for salaried labor, but the labor-intensive early market vegetables in the Léon forced peasant proprietors to seek the aid of day laborers and servants. The laborer was generally hired out by the day, particularly during harvests, at a fixed daily rate that varied by region in the department,[73] but payment was

[71] Ibid., pp. 204–5.
[72] Direction des Services Agricoles, "Monographie agricole," p. 16.
[73] Le Bourhis, *Etude de la culture et les salaires agricoles.*

below national averages, owing to the enormous amount of surplus labor during the interwar period.[74] Picard, a professor at the college of Saint-Pol-de-Léon, decried the lot of the *placennen* (day laborer) from the locality at the beginning of the twentieth century; he arose at 2:00 or 3:00 in the morning to meet prospective employers in the market square for whom he would possibly work well into the evening at pitiable wages.[75]

The economic and social position that women occupied in Lower Brittany at the beginning of the twentieth century is still subject to dispute. Jacques Cambry stressed their inferior status during his travels throughout the peninsula at the end of the eighteenth century and suggested that the place occupied by women in rural society diverged markedly from what he observed in other regions of France. According to Cambry, not only did the Breton women that he observed in the Léon eat after their husbands, but they were also servants in their own households, eliciting only disdain.[76] Despite these appearances a number of observers have argued that the woman was the true master of farm: "Behind the facade of patriarchy . . . a reality is hidden which was rather of a matriarchal type. The man strutted, presided at the table, gave the orders, but the important decisions—the purchase of a field, the sale of a cow, a suit against a neighbor, acceptance of a future son-in-law—were made by 'the patronne.'"[77] This appraisal is borne out in the first-hand testimony of Pierre-Jakez Hélias whose mother was far from the submissive, cowed, and malleable servant described in the pages of Cambry. Moreover, in 1929, a small but significant number of women owned and operated their own farms.[78] Recent work by anthropologists Martine Segalen and Agnès Audibert suggests that the women of Lower Brittany, in contrast to their counterparts in Upper Brittany and other regions of France, may have been exceptional in the degree to which they participated in the work of the farm and monetary negotiations at fairs.[79] These differences in the role of women in the agricultural

[74] Ibid., p. 106.

[75] Picard, *L'ouvrier agricole de Saint-Pol-de-Léon* (Brest, 1904).

[76] Cambry, *Voyage dans le Finistère*, pp. 162–63. As a founder of the Napoleonic Académie Celtique, Cambry was not an unsympathetic and insensitive observer.

[77] Brékilien, *La vie quotidienne des paysans en Bretagne*, p. 69.

[78] A total of 2,478 women operated their own farms in contrast to 30,797 men. Direction des Services Agricoles, "Monographie Agricole, Troisième Partie: L'Economie Rurale," p. 6.

[79] See Agnès Audibert, "Paroles de femmes: Jeunes et vieilles agricultrices," in *Mondes paysannes*, Tud Ha Bro, Sociétés Bretonnes, nos. 9–10 (Plouguerneau, n.d.), pp. 59–75; Martine Segalen, *Mari et femme dans la société paysanne* (Paris, 1980). A recent work by a psychiatrist has even argued that this supposed matriarchy may help to explain the prevalence of alcoholism, depression, and suicide among Breton men. See Philippe Carrer, *Le matriarcat psychologique des Bretons: essais d'éthnopsychiatrie* (Paris, 1984). Patrick Le Guirriec suggests, however, that ethnologists may have exaggerated the extent of "Breton matriarchy." He argues, moreover, that in Scrignac, the locus of his study, women were excluded from political discussion and certain labor activities. Le Guirriec, *Paysans, parents, partisans*, pp. 100–106.

economy began to disappear, however, by the end of the First World War, as women gradually retreated from certain agricultural tasks. Moreover, rural historians agree that to the dismay of prospective husbands, the Church, and government officials, young women were more likely to succumb to the lure of the town from the interwar period onward. For those who stayed, technological modernization increasingly encouraged the relegation of women to domestic tasks.

The social gradations and gender difference within the rural community make it difficult to generalize about "the peasantry" as a homogeneous group sharing common attributes and interests. Agricultural downturns, land sales, and the changes in landholding patterns from the early Third Republic to the 1930s aggravated these divisions and often led to serious social tensions within rural society.

Literacy and Poverty

As early as the 1820s, amateur statistician Charles Dupin argued that France was divided by an invisible line that extended from St. Malo in Brittany to Geneva, separating a benighted, illiterate France to the south of the line from a more prosperous and literate north. In 1836, the comte D'Angeville, who was intrigued by this alleged invisible boundary line, undertook a second, far more detailed and culturally sensitive statistical study of each department of France.[80] D'Angeville's study, which focused on the "social" and "moral" aspects of rural France, confirmed Dupin's two-France hypothesis.[81] D'Angeville's study of the three departments comprising Lower Brittany revealed some social and cultural characteristics that epitomized "benighted France." D'Angeville asserted that all three departments of Lower Brittany were afflicted with poverty as manifested in low life expectancies, inferior diet, and short stature of the population. From 1825 to 1832 Finistère had the lowest life expectancy in continental France (29 years), and Morbihan and the Côtes-du-Nord were not far behind with life expectancies of 32 and 33 years, respectively. The national average was 36.7 years.[82] Similarly, of the eighty-five departments comprising France, d'Angeville argued that the departments of Lower Brittany ranked seventy-eight, seventy-nine, and eighty in terms of the quality of

[80] Dupin, *Forces productives et commerciales*; d'Angeville, *Essai sur la statistique de la population française*. Also see Roger Chartier, "The Two Frances: The History of a Geographical Idea," in *Cultural History: Between Practices and Representations*, trans. Lydia Cochrane (Ithaca, 1988), pp. 172–200.

[81] Ibid., p. 16.

[82] Ibid., p. 361. These figures are based on records of births and deaths in 1825, 1826, 1828, 1830, and 1832.

grain consumed by their inhabitants, though modern nutritionists might well take issue with such judgments.[83] These departments did not fare any better when judged in terms of the number of recruits exempted from military service owing to inferior stature per 1,000 recruits between 1825 and 1833. The national average was 260, whereas Finistère had a total of 486, and Côtes-du-Nord 349. Surprisingly, however, Morbihan came close to the national average with only 248 exemptions.[84]

Although Finistère is now among the most literate and educated departments of France, Dupin, d'Angeville, and later Maggiolo each demonstrated that in the Breton departments of France French language literacy levels were abysmally low. Between 1830 and 1833, seventy-seven of every one hundred men recruited into the army from Finistére were deemed wholly "ignorant."[85] Illiteracy levels were only higher in two departments of the Massif Central, Allier and Corrèze, and in the Morbihan.

Louis Maggiolo's monumental educational survey conducted in 1877–1879, which charted the spread of literacy, confirmed and enriched the work of d'Angeville.[86] Not content with looking at a limited sample of conscripts or statistics of school attendance, Maggiolo asked each village schoolmaster to record all those who could sign their name to the marriage register for four periods: 1686–1690, 1786–1790, 1816–1820, and 1872–1876. During the second and third periods under investigation only 20 to 29 percent of men and women in Finistère knew how to read and write, whereas the national average for these periods were 37 percent and 54.3 percent, respectively.[87] By the 1870s the number of those who could read and write increased dramatically in the nation as a whole, but Finistère lagged behind. The national average was 72 percent, whereas in Finistère only 30 to 39 percent of men and women could read and write French in the department.[88]

François Furet and Jacques Ozouf concluded in a study of literacy in France that the coexistence of regional tongues with the French language retarded the spread of literacy. They suggested that in Brittany, as in many non-French-speaking areas of France that are described as "poor" France, "oral" France, "rebellious" France, low literacy levels reflected not a "kind

[83] Ibid., pp. 361–62.

[84] Ibid., pp. 359–61.

[85] D'Angeville, *Essai sur la statistique de la population française*, pp. 362–63.

[86] Born in Nancy in 1811, Maggiolo became an educational official there in 1868. The government gave its blessing to the project but provided him with no financial support. See Furet and Ozouf, *Reading and Writing in France*, pp. 5–6.

[87] Michel Fleury and Pierre Valmy, "Les progrés de l'instruction élémentaire de Louis XIV à Napoléon III d'après l'enquête de Louis Maggiolo (1877–1879)," *Population* 12 (1957): 78, 81.

[88] Ibid., p. 82.

of negative inertia," but rather a "positive rejection, stubborn resistance to that new fangled form of social integration, literacy."[89]

In Finistère, there were, however, differences, as in the case of demographic patterns, in levels of literacy. Marine Bedel-Bernard has observed in a study of primary education between 1863 and 1905 in Finistère that a kind of schism could be perceived between northern and southern Finistère, between Léon and Cornouaille. From 1858 to 1867, in 1878, and in 1899, cantons in the Léon had consistently higher percentages of literate conscripts than those cantons in Cornouaille. In addition, as early as 1863, a higher proportion of boys in the Léon attended primary schools, whether lay or congregational, than in the Cornouaille. In some areas of the Léon literacy levels were equal to national averages by the end of the nineteenth century (Table 2.7 and map 6).

There may be several reasons for this discrepancy. Although both regions were predominantly rural, during the Old Regime a rural textile artisanate was an important element in the local economy where rural industries prospered. Among these craftsmen literacy levels were consistently higher than those of their peasant counterparts. In Cornouaille, the cloth industry was virtually nonexistent. In addition, in terms of agricultural production and output, the Léon was far more prosperous than Cornouaille, and the greater and more precocious prosperity of the Léon led to wider communication with other parts of France and abroad, which required a greater level of literacy.

By the end of the nineteenth century Finistère began to improve its levels of literacy, but its progress was slower than in other regions of France. As François Furet and Jacques Ozouf have demonstrated, the boundaries of the St. Malo/Geneva line began to change by 1900. The new "illiterate" portion of France lay within a triangle whose base was the "Atlantic coast, from Brittany to Landes, and whose apex is the heart of the Massif Central."[90] Brittany still lagged behind northeastern France.

By 1899 conscripts from the arrondissements of Brest and parts of Morlaix, which comprised the Léon, could read and write as well as their counterparts in northeastern France.[91] The Léon, as in earlier periods, was again in the vanguard. In fact, the sons of wealthier peasants in the Léon not only learned to read and write, but they received a secondary education in the Catholic colleges of Lesneven and Saint-Pol-de-Léon, which were avenues through which many entered the priesthood. Although we have few reliable historical statistics on literacy among women in Finistère, from

[89] Furet and Ozouf, *Reading and Writing in France*, p. 299.
[90] Ibid., p. 27.
[91] Bedel-Bernard, "L'enseignement primaire dans le Finistère," p. 67.

TABLE 2.7
Percentage of Illiterate Conscripts in Finistère, 1858–1867, 1878, 1899

Canton	1857–1867	1878	1899	Decrease in illiteracy, 1858–1899 (%)
Northern Finistère				
Brest	24	3.7	0	24.0
Daoulas	57	26	10	47.0
Landerneau	36	19.6	7	29.0
Lannilis	55	41.3	6	49.0
Lesneven	56	21.6	5	51.0
Ouessant	20	0	0	20.0
Plabennec	53	37	10	43.0
Ploudalmézeau	60	42.9	10	50.0
Ploudiry	56.5	34.4	3	53.5
Saint-Renan	50	29.2	4	46.0
Morlaix	48	27.1	7	41.0
Landivisiau	47.5	19.2	8	39.5
Lanmeur	65	32.3	7	58.0
Plouescat	57.5	28.9	10	47.5
Plouigneau	70	51.6	19	51.0
Plouzévédé	61.5	20.5	14	47.5
St.-Pol-de-Léon	51.5	20.2	6	45.5
St.-Thégonnec	63	44.2	20	43.0
Sizun	69	42.9	12	57.0
Taulé	53.5	22.8	5	48.5
Central Finistère				
Châteaulin	56	48.9	18	38.0
Carhaix	70.5	66.9	48	22.5
Chateauneuf-du-Faou	78	61.7	33	45.0
Crozon	66	46.5	9	57.0
Le Faou	63.5	41.2	20	43.5
Huelgoat	66.5	56.8	22	44.5
Pleyben	75	59.3	25	50.0
Southern Finistère				
Quimper	48	24.7	11	37.0
Briec	72.5	34.3	41	31.5
Concameau	63	27.7	15	48.0
Douamenez	66	22.2	12	54.0
Fouesnant	69.5	31.1	30	39.5
Plogastel St. Germain	74	26.2	22	52.0
Point-Croix	40	25.5	10	30.0
Pont l'Abbé	60	28	23	37.0

(*continued*)

TABLE 2.7
(*Continued*)

Canton	1857–1867	1878	1899	Decrease in illiteracy, 1858–1899 (%)
Rosporden	71.5	18.6	21	50.5
Quimperlé	80	31.2	10	70.0
Arzano	93.5	34.7	35	58.5
Bannalec	88	31.8	37	51.0
Pont-Aven	72	30.1	13	59.0
Scaër	88	21.4	33	55.0

Source: A.D. Finistère 1T31 (1858–1867); A.N. F[17] 12318 (1878); A.N. F[17] 14270 (1899); Bedel-Bernard, "L'enseignement primaire dans le département du Finistère," p. 67.

enrollment figures in primary schools in the late nineteenth century, it appears that primary education was more widespread in the Léon, where most girls attended congregational schools.[92]

It must be said that in the work of Maggiolo, Furet, and Ozouf literacy is defined as the ability to read or write the French language. Unfortunately, to date, no studies have been undertaken to measure the ability to read and write regional (as distinguished from patois) languages such as Flemish, Provençal, Basque, and Breton. Such studies might modify the prevailing assessment of levels of literacy in peripheral, linguistically distinct regions during the nineteenth and early twentieth centuries. According to oral testimony collected by scholars associated with the publication *Tud Ha Bro*, many peasants, primarily landowners, knew how to read Breton, and a far from negligible number knew how to write it in the nineteenth century. The texts in circulation encompassed for the most part religious subjects and included *Buhez Ar Zent* (Life of Saints), which in the Léon, according to one source, was read aloud each evening by the head of the household to the assembled family, though this custom declined markedly in the interwar period.[93] In addition, there seem to have been a number of

[92] Corgne, *Histoire du collège de Lesneven*, and Siegfried, *Tableau politique de la France de l'Ouest*, p. 182. For statistics of school attendance among women in the department from the 1860s to the early 1900s, see Bedel-Bernard, "L'enseignement primaire dans le Finistère," pp. 10, 12, 13, 32, 34, 37, 54.

[93] According to sister Marie, a nun of the congregation of the Filles du Saint-Esprit born in 1910 in the Cornouaille where her father was a smallholder, Breton was spoken and read at home, though writing skills were less common. Jean-François Le Duc, "Marie, Fille du Saint-Esprit," in *Les paysans parlent*, Tud Ha Bro, Sociétés Bretonnes, no. 2 (Landerneau, 1979), pp. 33–53. For similar testimony, see Cloitre, "Aspects de la vie politique dans le département du Finistère," p. 735, and L. Elegoet, *Saint-Méen*, p. 228.

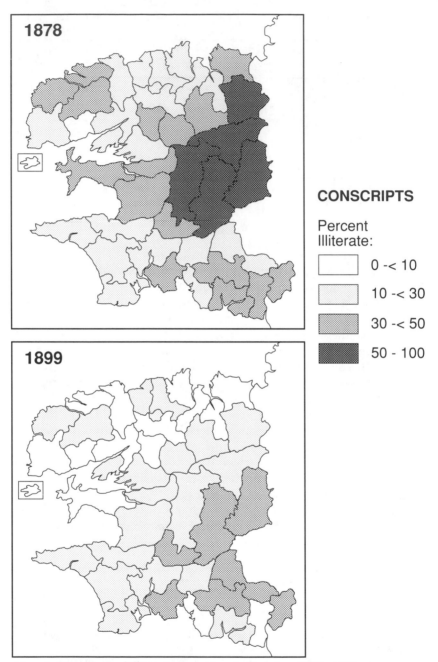

Map 6. Percentage of Illiterate Conscripts in Finistère, 1878–1899

primary schools in the department whose classes were conducted in the Breton language, the *petites écoles bretonnes*, though no systematic study has been undertaken to determine how widespread they were. Marine Bedel-Bernard has shown that the petites écoles bretonnes were prevalent in parts of the Léon. In the 1860s, three-fourths of the primary schools in the department of Finistère were bilingual, if not entirely Breton-speaking.[94] In the commune of Plougastel-Daoulas, the bilingual method was practiced at the school of St. Adrien as early as 1843 and continued despite interdictions by the government in 1902.[95]

Such schools catered to a population that was predominantly Breton-speaking until the First World War. Before the Great War, the majority of Finistère's adult population was unable to understand the rudiments of the French language. Brittany's linguistic difference is borne out by a series of language surveys undertaken between the 1860s and the early twentieth century. In 1863 an inquiry by the Inspection de l'Instruction Primaire found that children and adults alike spoke only Breton, even in the region's cities, with the notable exception of the great port of Brest.[96] Despite attempts to bar Breton from the classroom and the school yard during recreation hours, little progress had been made to spread the French language through primary education. This situation changed, albeit slowly, with the creation of a compulsory, free, primary educational system during the early Third Republic. A survey undertaken by the bishop of the diocese of Quimper and Léon in 1902 found that in the 310 parishes comprising the diocese, out of nineteen thousand children learning the catechism, thirteen thousand learned it in the Breton language. As far as religious instruction in general was concerned, the Sunday mass was spoken exclusively in Breton in 256 of the 310 parishes that made up the diocese. In 49 parishes sermons were delivered in both French and Breton, and in only 5 were they given in French only. In a battle of words, the government took issue with these results, claiming that 80 percent of children learning catechism between the ages of nine and ten could understand the French language and that these children were forced to learn the catechism in Breton.[97] The surveys, which grew out of conflict engendered by government attempts to ban the use of Breton in religious instruction, were clearly shaped by competing aims and agenda. A government report issued by the agency that oversaw the public system in Finistère is probably the most reliable indicator of language usage in the department. It reported in 1902

[94] Bedel-Bernard, "L'enseignement primaire dans le Finistère."

[95] Anne-Marie Bouchy and M. Guilcher, "Plougastel-Daoulas: La vie de famille et d'un village. Le cycle de la vie individuelle dans la société paysanne de 1890 à 1940" (T.E.R., Université de Bretagne Occidentale, 1971), p. 7.

[96] A.D. Finistère, 1T68, report, 3 December 1863.

[97] Jean Louis Le Floc'h, "L'enquête de 1902 sur la langue bretonne dans le diocèse," *Semaine religieuse* (1979): 4–6. The results of the survey were published in the 21 November 1902 issue of the *Semaine religieuse*.

that 80 percent of schools in Finistère were primarily Breton-speaking and
that most children arrived at school not knowing a word of French.[98] The
inspection appeared therefore to corroborate the results of the survey published by the bishop: the survey suggested that if the diffusion of the French
language had made such insignificant inroads among the children of the
department who attended public school, it had almost certainly made even
less headway among the adult population on the eve of the First World War.
By 1929, however, the Direction des Services Agricoles asserted that as a
whole the peasantry's level of education in Finistère was above the average:
"At the present moment there are only a few homes where a weekly newspaper and an annual almanac has not gone. The Breton peasant, above all
peasant women, have a passion for reading."[99]

Finistère and France

Historical evaluations of the response of Lower Brittany to the state's
civilizing mission have hinged on the characterization of the peninsula as
illiterate, poor, lacking in any form of social organization, and in the grips
of a clerico-aristocratic elite who determined the political course of the
region. It must be said, however, that resistance to state policy and the
consequent emergence of the social Catholic movement occurred first in
the Léon, an area that rivaled the wealthiest and most literate areas of rural
France. Moreover, the department as a whole experienced major economic
and demographic changes between the Revolution and the early Third
Republic and was by no means lacking in commercial links with France or
abroad. The Breton farmer, particularly in coastal regions, had access to a
number of ports, and by the end of the nineteenth century Breton agriculture was clearly subject to national economic cycles and downturns as well
as to tariff and trade policies of governments in Paris. Certain traits nonetheless continued to distinguish Finistère from the rest of France: its abun-
dant population; large families; its distance from major market centers in
an area ill-served by roads or railroads; and, above all, its persistent adherence to outward forms of religious devotion. Although it is impossible
therefore to deny that Finistère diverged in important respects from demographic and social trends that could be observed in France as a whole, the
formation of a national and political identity in the region was shaped less
by a supposed static, "traditional" economy, than by religious institutions
and cultural frames of reference. In short, these frames of reference provide
the prism through which to explore the nature and limits of national
integration in the Breton peninsula at the end of the nineteenth century.

[98] Ibid., p. 6.
[99] Direction des Services Agricoles, "Monographie agricole," pp. 10–11.

3

Popular Religiosity and Parish Culture in Lower Brittany

IN 1886 the postimpressionist painter Emile Bernard returned from the village of Pont-Aven to declare, "Brittany has made a Catholic of me again, capable of fighting for the Church. I was intoxicated by the incense, the organs, the prayers, the ancient stained glass windows, the hieratic tapestries."[1] The pronounced religiosity of the Lower Breton peninsula, which so affected Bernard, has been the subject of sustained interest among historians who have observed an invisible "eucharistic frontier" dividing western France from the rest of the nation.[2] To the east of this frontier, Frenchmen honored Catholic rites of passage, but increasingly absented themselves from mass and Easter services. To the west of this frontier, a predominantly rural population faithfully performed their religious duties and encouraged their sons and daughters to enter the Church. The parish clergy, in turn, enjoyed far greater prestige and influence in western France than their counterparts in the south, center, and east, and like the lower clergy in most regions of rural France, the priest was allied politically and ideologically with the landed nobility and had been since the Revolution: In the nineteenth century the parish priest in rural France was a firm supporter of Catholic royalism.

The relationship between the clergy and the nobility in many areas of rural France was, however, strained by the end of the nineteenth century, more often than not as a consequence of personal rivalry and disputes over precedence: The priest bristled at being treated as an inferior dependent or disagreed with the châtelain over parish expenditures.[3] In most cases these quarrels were petty, but in areas like the Mayenne a sort of "class consciousness" began to emerge among the parish clergy.[4] In most areas of the west and the nation as a whole, the ties between the clergy and the nobility nonetheless remained firm as the republican governments of the early

---

[1] Emile Bernard, "Récits d'un passager voyageant au bord de la vie," *Lettres de Paul Gauguin à Emile Bernard, 1888–1891* (Paris, 1954), p. 30. Cited in Anthony D. Smith, *The Ethnic Revival* (Cambridge, 1981), p. xi.

[2] Tackett, "The West in France in 1789," p. 717.

[3] Denis, *Les royalistes de la Mayenne*, chap. 9; Hilaire, *Une chrétienté au XIXe siècle?* 1: 560–66; Weber, "Comment la Politique Vînt Aux Paysans," pp. 368–70.

[4] Denis, *Les royalistes de la Mayenne*, p. 382.

Third Republic increasingly challenged the prerogatives and the political practices of both. Moreover, the parish clergy, reduced to near penury in many parts of France by the end of the century, became more dependent on the financial largesse of the nobility.

In an unprecedented gesture that surprised the public and captured the attention of the national press in the 1890s, the lower clergy of the Breton department of Finistère severed their ties with the nobility by repudiating their royalist convictions and espousing social Catholic republican ideals. This action had far-reaching consequences for a population accustomed to hearing the nobility and clergy speak with one voice. There is no doubt that the clergy was largely responsible for encouraging the peasantry to rally to the Republic and shaping national allegiances in the village.[5] Indeed, religious institutions ultimately structured the ways in which the nation was understood in the towns and rural communities of Finistère. Although in many cases these institutions served as avenues of resistance, the social Catholic movement that emerged from conflicts between Church and state at the end of the nineteenth century acted to reconcile the cultural allegiances of the region with the new political claims of the French nation.

The precise sources of the Church's pervasive influence in Lower Breton society, which has generally been attributed to the credulity and ignorance of the Breton peasant, and the means by which the clergy were able to sever their links with the nobility, in contrast to their counterparts elsewhere, have hardly been explored. The source of the Church's influence on Lower Brittany's parish culture, the relationship between local religious institutions and the parishioner, and more generally the social and spiritual functions of the Church in Lower Brittany's dispersed hamlet communities are the subjects of this chapter.

The Community of the Faithful

The profound religiosity of western France has long intrigued religious sociologists and historians. The origins of this piety have been sought in the history of the conversion of the region from paganism to Christianity by the Jesuits in the seventeenth century, which resulted in successfully grafting Catholic belief and practices onto a rich repository of pagan rituals and rites. Religious sociologists have also emphasized the social origins and

---

[5] Observers and government officials have argued that the electoral success of social Catholic candidates could largely be attributed to the Breton peasantry's blind acceptance of clerical orders. Le Bail, *Une élection législative de 1906*; "Rapport fait au nom de la commission chargée a procéder à une enquête sur l'élection de M. Gayraud dans la 3eme circonscription de Brest," no. 2451, Chambre des Deputés, annexe au procès verbal de la séance du 24 mai 1897.

role of the priest in Lower Brittany, which forged tight bonds between the priest and believer. Finally, government officials and observers such as Villermé and Benoiston de Chateauneuf have suggested that the cultural and linguistic isolation of the Lower Breton peninsula insulated the peasantry from secular cultural currents.

In areas of dispersed habitat such as Lower Brittany, the southern Massif Central, rural Ireland, and areas of northern Spain the parish church structured community life.[6] According to Michel Lagrée, attendance at Sunday mass was a "phenomenon of village sociability."[7] The parish church was not only a place of worship, but Sunday mass also provided an opportunity for parishioners in isolated hamlets to exchange information and news. Alfred de Courcy wrote in 1840 that Sunday in Lower Brittany was not "a day of boredom" as it was in Protestant countries or in nonpracticing areas in the center of France: "They assemble in the cemetery . . . relatives, friends meet, question each other, discuss local news, hopes for the harvest, while outside the young give themselves over to their favorite games of ninepins or boules. The last bell of high mass cuts the games and the conversation short; they enter . . . the church."[8]

Religious devotion was not merely a community affair and an occasion for village sociability, but it permeated the fabric of family life. In Saint-Méen, a parish in northern Finistère, a prayer was said on rising; at seven the *angelus* was rung, and the head of the family abandoned his work and returned to the house in order to recite the prayer with the household. After the midday meal an angelus was again recited, followed by a *de profundis* for each deceased member of the household. According to de Courcy, the de profundis became a sort of regional anthem by the 1840s. Every evening after the evening meal, except in summer, a family member read aloud in Breton from the *Buhez Ar Zent* the life of the saint for that day, after which the family kneeled and recited prayers, including the angelus, litanies, and numerous de profundis. These devotions lasted into the 1950s and took half an hour, including the reading.[9] In addition, signs of the cross were made before undertaking tasks throughout the day, on rising and retiring, before each meal, before beginning work, before changing ones clothes, and when passing a cross or calvaire.[10]

The official religion of Catholicism was grafted onto popular religious

---

[6] See Jones, *Politics and Rural Society*, pp. 128–44; Jones, "Parish, Seigneurie and the Community of Inhabitants in Southern Central France," pp. 74–108; Christian, *Person and God in a Spanish Valley*.

[7] Michel Lagrée, *Catholicisme et société dans l'Ouest*, p. 9.

[8] Alfred de Courcy, *Les bretons et les français peints par eux-mêmes* (Paris, 1842), p. 25; cited in L. Elegoet, *Saint-Méen*, p. 226.

[9] L. Elegoet, *Saint-Méen*, p. 228.

[10] Ibid.

practices and beliefs. The priests and prelates of the old dioceses of Cornouaille and Saint-Pol-de-Léon and, following the French Revolution, of the new diocese of Quimper could boast of overflowing churches in contrast to conditions in most other regions of France, but observers continually noted that the Christian faith was often superimposed on more popular forms of religious practice. During his travels in Finistère following the French Revolution, Jacques Cambry observed that "religion has guided man in this region even more than in the rest of the country. The theocratic government of the Druids, the millions of spirits that inhabit the elements, the power of wise men over nature, all the dreams of the otherworldly, the cult of trees, of fountains, were not destroyed at all by the apostles of Catholicism."[11] As Gabriel Le Bras, a native of Brittany and a pioneer in the field of religious sociology, has observed, "to speak of the traditional faith of the Bretons is to simplify excessively the historical realities" because "there has always been in Brittany a coexistence of primitive beliefs" and "orthodox Catholicism."[12] There were, of course, nonpracticing areas in Finistère in the nineteenth and twentieth centuries, but as a native of one such commune in southern Finistère has argued, whether the inhabitants of the commune went to church or not, they remained Catholics even if nonpracticing, and if one had taken a poll to ask the inhabitants if this commune, Cap Sizun, should be dechristianized, he was convinced that there would be 95 percent nays.[13]

The *culte des ancêtres* (cult of the dead) in Brittany, which has been traced to a pre-Christian, Celtic religion, gave religious practices a special imprint in Lower Brittany that could not be effaced easily. A priest's offices in Finistère consisted in large part of ministering to the dead rather than to the living with the recitation of numerous prayers demanded by relatives of those who had long since passed away.[14] A priest from southern Finistère remarked ruefully in 1982 that the "religion of the dead" that preceded the implantation of Catholicism in Brittany was tenacious.[15]

---

[11] Cambry, *Voyage dans le Finistère* 1: 71.

[12] Le Bras, *Introduction à l'étude de la pratique religieuse en France* 1: 83.

[13] Goardon, "Moeurs et coutumes de Cap Sizun au début du XXe siècle," 102: 270.

[14] In 1908, the abbé Millon, a Breton priest from the diocese of Rennes, had been told that workers who had migrated to Paris could frequently be seen on Sundays, under the pretext of taking the air, wandering between the tombs of the cemeteries of Père Lachaise and Montparnasse in order "to recapture the smell of their distant pays." Croix and Roudaut, *Les bretons, la mort, et Dieu*, p. 239. All Soul's is today one of the most important religious holidays in Lower Brittany, and an anthropologist's recent work on the cult of the dead in the region attests to the fact that it still occupies a very significant place in local cultural life. See Badone, *The Appointed Hour*.

[15] Roudaut and Croix, *Les bretons, la mort, et Dieu*, p. 246.

Pierre-Jakez Helias's sensitive but unsentimental account of his childhood in the Bigouden region of southern Finistère in the early twentieth century provides us with a valuable insight into other popular attitudes toward religious devotion during the early Third Republic. Local saints, canonized or not, abounded throughout Finistère and were invested with magical powers that could affect health, harvests, and human relationships. Helias's mother, who suffered from headaches, went to a chapel far from home to drink water from the chapel's fountain. One of his aunts, who developed scabs on her head and who almost went blind as a result of a home remedy, was ordered by Helias's grandfather to another chapel to partake of the fountain's water. The scabs vanished, and she recovered her sight.[16] Helias suggests that there was enormous faith in these local saints but that reliance on these types of remedies was also necessary in poor areas where doctors were expensive, scarce, and often feared.[17] The power of local saints was not confined merely to the health of persons but also extended to animals and agriculture. Cambry observed that St. Ives, one of the most popular saints in Lower Brittany, was said to make bread rise; if butter formed too slowly, then Saint Herbot was invoked.[18] Similarly, in the Léon, Saint Eloi protected horses. If a horse was thought to be in danger of losing his life, then his owner would pay a certain sum to Church in the name of the saint.[19] As long as parish priests did not interfere with popular practices and beliefs of this kind (and most did not) these beliefs reinforced the religion of the priests. Emile Souvestre in fact argued that the first apostles of the Breton peninsula probably preserved a certain number of popular rituals to make the task of conversion easier, though they gave these practices a new patronage.[20]

A number of religious practices peculiar to Brittany punctuated the seasons. One such devotion was the pardon, originally a penitential religious ceremony that took place annually. The pardon gradually became a festive ceremony as well. The pardon of Sainte Anne La Palud, one of the most important pardons in the Cornouaille around 1850, had both solemn and joyous aspects. On Saturday evening the pardon's procession was a penitential experience in which those attending confessed their sins and were given collective absolution. The next day's procession was festive in character and occurred after high mass. The more important pardons, such

---

[16] Helias, *The Horse of Pride*, p. 80.

[17] "Calling a doctor for anything so unimportant [as minor wounds and temporary ailments] was considered almost a disgrace, a sign of weakness and cowardice . . . not to mention the expense, which, for most of us, wasn't within our means." Ibid., p. 83.

[18] Cambry, *Voyage dans le Finistère* 1: 14–18

[19] F. Elegoet, *Paysannes de Léon*, p. 53.

[20] Souvestre, *Les Derniers Bretons*, p. 91.

as Sainte Anne La Palud in southern Finistère and Le Folgoët in the north, attracted thousands of worshipers from outside these parishes. The popularity of the pardon of Le Folgoët in northern Finistère was such that all agricultural activity ceased in Saint-Méen, a parish dozens of miles away, on the day of the pardon. Until the 1940s the majority of the inhabitants of Saint-Méen went to Le Folgoët on foot, carrying banners, statues, and crosses. In 1888, eighty parishes in the surrounding region were represented in this way, and fifty years later 107.[21] Similarly, a number of saints' days were celebrated throughout the department during the year. In Saint-Pol-de-Léon, not only did the town cease work to celebrate the festival of Saint Pol, but it also spent an entire day preparing for the festival and celebrated other saints' days in the same way.[22] The significance of pardons and saints' days as a collective expression of village sociability has yet to be investigated, but there is little doubt that pardons, in particular, broke down physical boundaries between parishes and contributed to a regional sense of community.

A pastoral inquiry commissioned by the bishop of Quimper in 1909 provides the first quantitative record of religious behavior in Finistère,[23] though this information is limited to a record of the number of parishioners over the age of fourteen who took part in Easter communion. To judge by the diocesan survey, Finistère was one of the most devout departments in France. Although data on outward manifestations of religious devotion such as attendance at mass and Easter services have been used by religious sociologists to chart the religious vitality of the regions of France, some historians argue that such statistics are only of heuristic value:[24] They do not measure the religiosity of an area. If these statistics cannot measure inner faith or orthodoxy, they nonetheless attest to the social importance attached to church attendance in rural communities.

Michel Lagrée has argued that in rural Brittany fewer parishioners took Easter communion in the nineteenth century than attended Sunday mass, so the percentage of parishioners who regularly attended religious service was probably higher.[25] In 1909, 82.5 percent of the population of Finistère

[21] L. Elegoet, *Saint-Méen*, p. 230.

[22] Picard, *L'ouvrier agricole de Saint-Pol-de-Léon*, pp. 19–30.

[23] Archives de l'Evêché de Quimper [A.E.Q.] 3F, "Questionnaire pour la visite canonique (Episcopat de Monseigneur DuParc, 1908–1946)."

[24] Judt, *Socialism in Provence*, pp. 175–76. Judt posits three "levels" of religion: open observance of Catholic ritual, passive observance of Christian practices, and an "almost pagan faith in patron saints, local shrines and the like" (p. 176), and he argues that this pagan faith often flourished in what appear to be "dechristianized" areas. The Lower Breton case indicates that the third level can very successfully be superimposed on the first.

[25] Lagrée, *Catholicisme et société dans l'Ouest*, p. 9.

over the age of fourteen participated in Easter communion. The proportion of those taking Easter communion was slightly higher in the arrondissements of northern Finistère than in the south, if one excludes the the city of Brest. In 1909, then, virtually every member of rural parishes in northern and southern Finistère attended Sunday mass.[26]

In the interwar period there was a decline in the number of parishioners who took part in Easter communion and attended mass in Finistère, but these declines were more significant in the southern portion of the department, as a clear line began to divide the highly devout peasantry of northern Finistère from the more indifferent population in the south after World War I (Table 3.1 and map 7).[27] In cantons comprising the Léon or northern Finistère, where between 97 percent and 99 percent of the population over the age of fourteen attended Easter service in 1909, declines in the number of *pascalisants* (those who attended Easter mass) were relatively insignificant. In the cantons of Landivisiau, Lannilis, Lesneven, Plabennec, Plouescat, Ploudalmézeau, and Saint Renan, the decline was less than 10 percent. In the more urbanized areas of Saint-Pol-de-Léon and Morlaix, the number of pascalisants fell by 18 percent and 32 percent, respectively. By contrast, in southern Finistère these figures were much higher. In the rural cantons of Bannalec, Pont-Aven, and Scaër, pascalisants were more than halved.[28] The decline in the number of churchgoers may be attributed to changes in the social function of the Church with the introduction of television and the communications revolution as well as to the decline in the religious vitality of the region.

By national standards, Finistère remains one of the most Catholic departments in France. In 1958, the number of adults participating in communion (*cenalisants*) at least once a month far exceeded the numbers of cenalisants in neighboring departments in the west. As many as 30 percent to 45 percent of the adult population of the Léon took communion once a month, and in many rural parishes more than 90 percent participated in Easter service.[29] The religious behavior of Finistère indicates, at the very least, that religion and churchgoing were important to the society of the region in the nineteenth and twentieth centuries and that new political currents among the lower clergy would have had ample opportunity for diffusion to the peasantry of the region.

---

[26] A.E.Q., 3F, "Questionnaire pour la visite canonique," and Hilaire, ed., *Matériaux pour l'histoire religieuse*, pp. 206–7.

[27] The bishopric in Quimper did not undertake another survey of religious practice in the diocese until twelve years after the war, in 1957. Lagrée, *Catholicisme et société dans l'Ouest*, p. 65.

[28] Ibid.

[29] Isambert and Terrenoire, *Atlas de la pratique cultuelle*, pp. 36–37.

TABLE 3.1
Pascalisants by Canton, Diocese of Quimper, 1909–1954 (in percentages)

Canton	Pascalisants	
	1909	*1954*
Northern Finistère		
Brest 1	—	—
Brest 2	42.0	—
Brest 3	—	—
Daoulas	90.5	75
Landerneau	86.0	80
Landivisiau	99.6	91
Lanmeur	88.1	44
Lannilis	98.7	92
Lesneven	99.5	92
Morlaix	79.0	46
Ouessant	83.9	84
Plabennec	99.7	97
Ploudalmézeau	98.0	91
Ploudiry	99.4	90
Plouescat	99.3	92
Plouigneau	86.1	38
Plouzévédé	99.4	92
St.-Pol-de-Léon	98.1	80
Saint-Renan	99.1	90
Saint-Thégonnec	95.0	81
Sizun	99.0	82
Taulé	97.3	76
Central Finistère		
Carhaix-Plouguer	83.7	55
Châteaulin	97.2	79
Chateauneuf-du-Faou	97.8	75
Le Faou	93.6	57
Huelgoat	82.7	38
Pleyben	98.6	87
Southern Finistère		
Arzano	90.5	70
Bannalec	97.0	33
Briec	99.5	88
Concarneau	65.0	32
Crozon	—	63
Douarnenez	96.0	73

(*continued*)

TABLE 3.1
(*Continued*)

	Pascalisants	
Canton	1909	1954
Fouesnant	94.2	57
Plogastel-St.-Germain	90.5	70
Pont-Aven	87.0	36
Pont-Croix	96.1	72
Pont l'Abbé	73.8	45
Quimper	80.0	—
Quimperlé	75.0	38
Rosporden	95.2	54
Scaër	92.0	42

Source: Archives de l'Evêché de Quimper, 3F, "Questionnaire pour la visite Canonique" (Episcopat de Monseigneur Duparc), Diocèse de Quimper, 1909; Lambert, *Catholicisme et société dans l'Ouest: Cartes et statistiques*, p. 60.

Missions

The distinctive religious culture that characterizes Lower Brittany has been traced to the missionary work of the Pères Maunoir and Michel Le Nobletz.[30] In the seventeenth century the Breton peninsula was viewed by the Church and particularly by Jesuit missionaries as an area in which the rural population was largely ignorant of the rites and doctrines of the Catholic religion.[31] In 1641 the great missionary of the Breton peninsula, Julien Maunoir, visited the island of Ouessant, which lies off the coast of Finistère, and recorded in his journal that "an ignorance so great has established itself . . . that one can hardly find twelve persons who know the mysteries of the Trinity and of man saved by God, and the precepts of the decalogue."[32] Beginning in the 1640s and 1650s this Jesuit, who was dubbed the "apostle of Brittany,"[33] began to travel on horseback or on foot to the remote hamlets of Lower Brittany. In Finistère he concentrated his efforts in the southern portion of the department, in the former diocese of

[30] Alain Croix et al., "L'Ouest et la Révolution: Traditions et transformation," *Cahiers d'Histoire de Recherches Marxistes*, no. 4 (1981): 8–64.

[31] Daniel, "Religion paysanne et catholicisme romain," esp. p. 704.

[32] Translation of the journal of Père Maunoir by Tanguy Daniel, "Ouessant au XVIIe siècle: les missions du Père Maunoir," *Cahiers de L'Iroise* no. 3 (July–Sept. 1975): 133–34.

[33] Croix and Roudaut, *Les Bretons, la mort, et Dieu*, p. 114.

[34] Ibid., p. 115; Jean Meyer, "La vie religieuse en Bretagne à l'époque moderne," in *Histoire religieuse de la Bretagne*, ed. D. Aupest-Conduche (Chambray, 1980), p. 184.

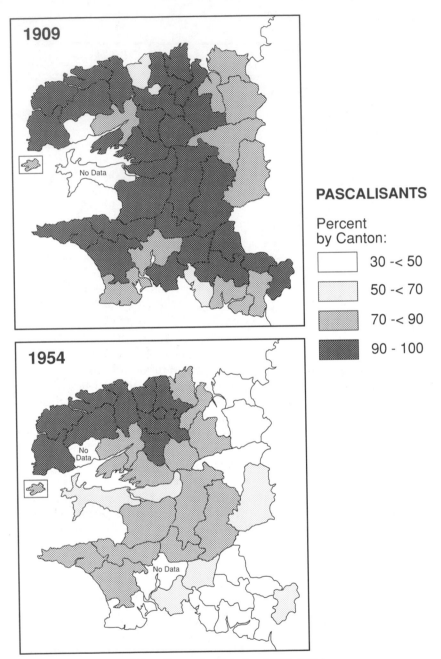

Map 7. Percentage of Pascalisants in Finistère, 1909–1954

Cornouaille. By the end of his life in 1683, he had organized 325 missions in the diocese of Quimper alone.[34]

The missions organized by Julien Maunoir and his Breton compatriot Michel Le Nobletz lasted several days. Parishioners generally abandoned their work to spend five to eighteen hours a day in religious instruction. The missionaries used *taolennou* (pictures representing the stations of the cross, the paths to hell and to heaven, the death of the sinner, and the mortal sins) to inspire hope and, more important, fear in the layman.[35] From the seventeenth century onward missions continued at regular intervals.[36] In June 1950 all the inhabitants of Saint-Méen, with the exception of a dozen workers or so who were employed in Brest, participated in the mission.[37] In the 1970s, several peasant women in Plouguerneau in the Léon recalled the use of taolennou during missions in the parish, and they believed that they had been created by the Pères Maunoir and Le Nobletz.[38]

Although missions played an exceedingly important role in both laying the foundations and reinforcing the unwavering faith that characterized Lower Brittany in the twentieth century, missions in themselves cannot be held accountable for the profound religiosity of the region. Other areas of France also had their missionaries and yet did not manifest a comparable religious history. Perhaps the zeal and talent of the Pères Maunoir and Le Nobletz were unequalled by missionaries elsewhere, but this is doubtful: The map of devout areas in the twentieth century does not necessarily correspond to the missionaries' peregrinations. Maunoir and Le Nobletz concentrated their efforts primarily in southern Finistère, and yet this was the area in which religious devotion declined most rapidly in the twentieth century. Missions undoubtedly led to the christianization of the Breton peninsula, and the regular appearance of missions every eight to ten years anchored the Catholic religion. The parish priest, however, was primarily responsible for inculcating and maintaining the faith and attending to the day-to-day spiritual education and needs of his parishioners. For this reason, many observers have attributed the religiosity of the Breton peasantry to the influence of the parish priest and the importance attached to male and female religious congregations in local communities.

---

[35] The nineteenth- and twentieth-century taolennou differ little in form and content from those of the seventeenth century, but in 1939 a version of hell preserved in the Evêché de Quimper et Léon depicted Marx, Lenin, Hitler, Stalin, and Trotsky.

[36] A mission lasting fifteen days in 1908 and three in 1950 took place in the parish of Saint-Méen in northern Finistère. L. Elegoet, *Saint-Méen*, pp. 228–29.

[37] Ibid.

[38] F. Elegoet, *Paysannes de Léon*, pp. 56–64.

The Parish Priest in Lower Breton Society

The *procureur général* of the *cour d'appel* of Rennes observed in the 1880s
that all the Breton clergy's efforts were directed at keeping their parishioners in a state of *obscurantisme*: "Their piecemeal culture, their lack of
intelligence, the narrowness of their views and vulgarity of their manners
help a great deal in developing this vain complacency to which these par-
venus deprived of primary education are ordinarily accustomed."[39] Whatever views observers held regarding the parish priest in Lower Brittany, no
one denied that he wielded enormous temporal and spiritual power. What
was the source of the real or alleged power of the parish priest in Breton
society? What position did the priest actually occupy?

Accounts written by travelers to the region in the nineteenth century and
reports by government officials indicate that Finistère, particularly the
Léon, was a clerical society where priests reigned supreme. In the 1840s
Emile Souvestre wrote that the priest's influence in rural society was enormous but that this influence was not simply the result of "fervent beliefs, it
is also the fruit of the good accomplished in the countryside by the Catholic
priests. The Breton priest is not only a minister of heaven, but a friend and
counselor, a precious protector of the things of this world."[40] The priest
fulfilled more than the spiritual needs of his parishioners. He served as a
mediator with the outside world, a source of information and charity, and
an authority to represent the interests of the parish to the outside world
because he was one of the few members of the community who could speak
French. According to Emile Souvestre, the priest was an integral and important part of the parish: "Only lately having left the plow, his hands
hardened by the elements, his cassock faded by the rain, the Breton priest
could be observed on muddy roads, crossing inaccessible heathland to
bring the viaticum to the ill and prayers for the redemption of the dead."[41]
His authority was grounded in a long tradition that the new and less
legitimate authority of the state had difficulty challenging. Louis Hémon, a
moderate republican deputy in the department of Finistère during the
Third Republic wrote that "when administrative pressure manifests itself,
when a prefect . . . speaks, he speaks in the name of a transitory authority
subject to discussion. . . . But when the priest speaks, when he addresses
himself to populations who believe like ours that his words will echo in the
depths of their souls then . . . things change face."[42]

"Rural clericalism" had long distinguished the West from other regions

---

[39] A.N. F19 5610, 15 July 1888.
[40] Souvestre, *Les Derniers Bretons*, p. 24.
[41] Ibid., p. 25.
[42] A.D. Finistère, 18J Fonds Louis Hémon, handwritten notes 1897.

of France.[43] This clericalism and the distinctive brand of rural Catholicism were integral components of village society in Finistère, but more particularly in the Léon, in the nineteenth century. This rural clericalism may be explained in terms of clerical structures in the West, which differed from those in the rest of France before the French Revolution, most especially in terms of the status and position of the parish priest in rural society. Three aspects of these clerical structures in western France differed markedly from those found in the center, south, and in the Parisian Basin: the density of the parish clergy in rural society, its wealth, and clerical recruitment. Timothy Tackett has found, based on studies of the ecclesiastical revenues in the four dioceses comprising the old province of Brittany that the parish clergy—not bishops, priors, canons, or monastic houses—controlled a major portion of the wealth given to the Church in rural parishes, though these revenues appeared to be considerably less in Lower Brittany than in northern France. Moreover, the much despised *portion congrue*, a fixed revenue given to resident priests by an often nonresident tithe-holder, was quite rare in Lower Brittany.[44] Significantly, the practice was only widespread in the Lower Breton diocese of Tréguier where anticlericalism became rife and where Church attendance declined rapidly in the twentieth century.[45] The commune of Plozévet, the *enfant terrible* of the diocese of Cornouaille, was one of the least practicing communes in the entire diocese following the Revolution, and it paid two-thirds of revenues owed to the Church to an absent canon who resided in Quimper.[46] The portion congrue did not foster resentment in Finistère, as in the north or center of France, except in isolated pockets within the department. Complaints against the clergy as such were infrequent because their wealth was not siphoned out of the community. Much of this revenue was, in fact, distributed to the poor. In contrast to most areas of France, complaints regarding the tithe and the way in which it was collected, as reflected in the *cahiers de doléances* that were drawn up in preparation for the Estates General in 1789, were insignificant. The wealth of the parish priest (curé or recteur), which varied from diocese to diocese in Lower Brittany, made him a member of the community who commanded respect and authority.

In contrast to the center, southwest, and much of the Parisian Basin, the rural clergy was far more conspicuous—judging by figures of regional clerical density—and the social bonds between priest and parishioner were

[43] Tackett, *Religion, Revolution and Regional Culture*, pp. 226–50.

[44] Tackett, "The West in France in 1789," pp. 720–21.

[45] Ibid., p. 721. The department of Côtes-du-Nord, which circumscribes the old diocese of Tréguier, had one of the highest levels of portion congrue in France.

[46] M. Cl. Gasnault-Beis, "Enquête pluridisciplinaire sur Plozévet. Partie historique—L'évolution socio-culturelle: Foi et laïcisme, la paroisse de Plozévet à l'époque contemporaine," A.D. Finistère (ms. 1965), pp. 5–6.

extraordinarily close. Before the Revolution of 1789 more than 50 percent of the clergy in several dioceses in western France came from rural areas where they later served as priests.[47] In the rest of France the gradual "ruralization" of the parish clergy did not occur until the nineteenth century.[48] In some cases it did not occur at all. Toward the mid-nineteenth century many parish clergy in the diocese of Orléans were recruited from among townsmen, many of whom were not native to the area.[49] The cultural gulf between the peasant and priest was often a source of bitter conflict.[50]

During the French Revolution there was little evidence of hostility directed toward the parish clergy in rural areas of Finistère.[51] In Guiclan in northern Finistère, a parish that belonged to the former diocese of Saint-Pol-de Léon, the priest was designated president of the municipal assembly, and the second *vicaire* drew up the cahiers de doléances on behalf of the parish on 29 March 1789.[52] At the beginning of the Revolution the curé was favorable to the revolution and the reforms it promised to enact, as was the majority of the local population in the department.[53] As in most other parishes in Lower Brittany, the attitude of the clergy and the people changed in Guiclan as the revolutionary tide turned against the Church in 1791. The curé of Guiclan refused to take the oath to the constitution vowing obedience to the revolutionary state, and refractory priests in the area continued to perform their functions illegally. The religious history and behavior of the parish of Guiclan mirrored the events that occurred in countless parishes in Finistère where the intrusion of the state in local affairs in the form of military conscription and what was perceived to be religious persecution aroused hostility among the peasantry. During the periods when the central government embarked on a campaign to dechristianize France and substitute the Catholic faith with the worship of the Supreme Being, local opposition to the state became particularly apparent. On 19 April 1793, for example, peasants who intended to take part in the procession of the Chapelle Sainte Brigitte, which was closed as were other chapels under the orders of the revolutionary armies, gathered in Guimiliau and were fired on by local troops. On 13 December 1793, saint's day of the patron saint of the cathedral of Quimper, an official charged with reviewing the accounts of the municipality ordered the closing of all

[47] Tackett, "The West in France," p. 724.

[48] Tackett, *Priest and Parish in Eighteenth-Century France*, p. 306.

[49] Christiane Marcilhacy, *Le diocèse d'Orléans au milieu du XIXe siècle: Les hommes et leurs mentalités* (Paris, 1964), pp. 222–23.

[50] Ibid.; Agulhon, *The Republic in the Village*, pp. 103–4.

[51] Only in urban areas was radical anticlerical sentiment expressed. Tackett, "The West in France in 1789," pp. 738–39.

[52] Yves Miossec, *Une vieille paroisse bretonne: Guiclan* (Brest, 1975), pp. 131–32.

[53] René Kerviler, *La Bretagne pendant la Révolution* (Rennes, 1912), pp. 11–17.

churches. He moreover proceeded to destroy the statues and ornamentation both inside and outside the cathedral, and he ended his exploit by urinating in the ciborium before a crowd of peasants who had come from the countryside to take part in the festivities of Saint Corentin. These incidents only stiffened the resistance of the local population against the Revolution after 1792. Indeed, the clergy and their parishioners began to oppose the Revolution after the imposition of the revolutionary government's religious policies, though it must be said that they did not engage in extensive chouannerie or guerrilla warfare against the revolutionary armies, a phenomenon that affected much of French-speaking Brittany and the Vendée.[54] The revolutionary experience nonetheless left important traces in the collective memory of the region and created a profound popular mistrust of the French state.

If in most regions of France the revolutionary decade appeared to separate "a world of almost unquestioned obeisance to catholic teaching from one in which significant sectors of the populace slipped away into indifference,"[55] the religious history of the lower Breton department of Finistère was quite different. In Lower Brittany the Revolution introduced, as it did elsewhere, national political issues and a new political vocabulary to a peasant population. The sale of national lands wrought profound changes in the social relations of the countryside as the town dweller or wealthy peasant, such as the Julots in the Léon, profited from the opportunity of buying former Church and noble lands. The old administrative ecclesiastical structures were dismantled as well. In an attempt to foster new allegiances, to impose a new administrative apparatus bearing no resemblance to the old order, provinces, pays, and dioceses were obliterated by a new administrative unit, the department, whose borders circumscribed the new dioceses. Thus, the new diocese of Quimper and Léon, whose episcopal seat was in Quimper, comprised most of the old dioceses of Saint-Pol-de-Léon and Cornouaille. In one simple gesture the revolutionary state abolished the province of Brittany as well as the particular privileges granted to it by the royal government. Administratively, the old province was effectively absorbed into the French nation. Despite these administrative and legal changes inaugurated by the French Revolution and the presence of the revolutionary armies in Lower Brittany, the revolutionary decade did not in fact result in large sectors of the population slipping into religious indifference. Nor did it affect the authority of the parish priest in the new department of Finistère.

[54] Miossec, *Une vieille paroisse bretonne: Guiclan*, p. 161; Roger Dupuy, "La période révolutionnaire et la réconstruction concordataire," in *Histoire religieuse de la Bretagne*, ed. D. Aupest-Conduche, p. 243. Moreover, Saint-Pol-de-Léon experienced anticonscription riots in 1793.
[55] Olwen Hufton, "The Reconstruction of a Church," p. 21.

Religious Vocations and the Postrevolutionary Settlement

Following the Revolution, parish priests in Finistère continued to be re-cruited largely from among the peasantry, and ties between a largely Breton-speaking peasantry and the lower clergy remained tight.[56] A boy destined for the seminary was generally recommended by a priest and sent to Pont Croix, Lesneven, or Saint-Pol-de-Léon. His studies were paid for by the Church, and members of the clergy in the diocese with salaries ade-quate to add to a diocesan fund would see this money distributed among those on scholarship.[57] Ordination records prior to 1905 do not contain precise information about the social origins of the parish clergy, but after the separation of Church and state in that year, the superior asked for information on the social situation of candidates, which provides more specific data on the social origins of the clergy in the interwar period. An overwhelming majority of the priests ordained came from relatively well-to-do peasant households. A small number of the priests ordained during this period came from wealthy urban households or were the sons of parents from the liberal professions. The priests whose families did not come from the social group broadly defined as the peasantry came from households in which the father was employed as an artisan, a shopkeeper, a worker from the arsenal of Brest, a fisherman, or a domestic servant.[58] Great prestige was attached to the priesthood in rural areas. In the 1840s, Villermé saw parents bow before their son who had become a priest and wait on him at table.[59]

As in most other regions of France, between 1789 and the restoration of the Bourbon monarchy, there were few ordinations in Finistère. Following the Concordat concluded between Napoleon and the Pope in 1801, an agreement that allowed the state to exert greater control over ecclesiastical affairs, the Church was faced in all dioceses with the problem of recruiting and training new personnel after nearly a decade of revolution that had left many parishes without priests. This problem was solved with varying degrees of success, and this success depended in part on the appeal of the profession of the priesthood. Only after 1815 did the number of ordina-tions in the department begin to increase perceptibly.[60] During the early years of the Restoration the image of the priest as a white-haired old man began to change with the influx of younger men. However, with the fall of the Bourbon monarchy in 1830 and the disappearance of some material advantages accorded the Church during this period, the number of ordina-

[56] This situation contrasts sharply with that observed by Maurice Agulhon in southern France. See Agulhon, *The Republic in the Village*, pp. 98–104.

[57] Girard, "L'évolution quantitative du clergé diocésain de Quimper," p. 155.

[58] Ibid., pp. 157–59.

[59] Villermé and Benoiston de Chateauneuf, *Voyage en Bretagne en 1840 et 1841*, p. 18.

[60] Girard, "L'évolution quantitative du clergé diocésain de Quimper," p. 89.

tions again declined in France as a whole. This decline has been attributed in part to the limitation of the number of pupils attending seminaries under the Martignac ministry and to the decline in the number of births in the country as a whole during the Napoleonic Wars.[61]

The peaks and troughs in national ordination statistics can be correlated with both state policies and the material rewards afforded those entering the clerical profession. During the Bourbon Restoration, for example, ambitious young men, such as Stendhal's Julien Sorel, flocked to the Church, which offered opportunities for social advancement and prestige. The ordination figures available for the nineteenth century for the new diocese of Quimper and Léon, however, demonstrate no clear correlation between the number of priests ordained and the state's material incentives to attract young men to the priesthood. In other regions of France such a correlation is plain, and the number of men choosing the priesthood declined steadily from the 1850s onward as the material advantages associated with the priesthood disappeared. In the Breton department of Finistère, by contrast, the number of ordinations steadily increased, reaching a peak at the height of the Third Republic's anticlerical campaign between 1899 and 1902,[62] a fact that has led one historian to remark that "it is curious to see that it was in this period, when the state attacked the Church with the greatest virulence, that vocations were the most numerous."[63] The surplus of population in Finistère as well as the shrinking of economic opportunities owing to the economic depression of the 1880s and early 1890s may account in part for these patterns. However, 1899 marked the beginning of the economic recovery, particularly in agriculture. The Church seemed to exert another sort of appeal.

The Lower Breton department of Finistère was then extraordinarily rich in clerical vocations, but between 1803 and the First World War the Léon provided the department with the majority of its priests. In Cornouaille only two cantons, Plouaré and Quimper, furnished between 51 and 100 priests during this period, whereas fourteen cantons in the Léon—including Plouguerneau, Plabennec, Kernouès, Guipavas, Landerneau, Ploudaniel, Landivisiau, Plounévez-Lochrist, Plouvorn, Saint Thégonnec, Morlaix, Cléder, and Plouénan—could be counted among those cantons furnishing between 51 and 100 priests between 1803 and 1907. Saint-Pol-de-Léon, the old episcopal seat of the prerevolutionary diocese, provided 185 priests, outstripping all other cantons in the department.[64] Pierre Jakez Hélias recalls that in the Bigouden region of southern Finistère (Cornouaille), priests generally came from the Léon, from the seminaries of

[61] Ibid.
[62] Ibid., pp. 89–90.
[63] Ibid., p. 90.
[64] Ibid., map 1.

Saint-Pol-de-Léon and Lesneven, and the books of catechism that they used were written in the dialect of the Léon rather than that of Cornouaille.

Although existing records of clerical recruitment suggest that the religious vitality of southern Finistère began to wane toward the end of the nineteenth century, the Revolution did little to alter the authority and influence of the parish priest in rural society in northern Finistère.

Clerical Income and the Independent Parish Clergy

Levels of clerical recruitment in the new diocese of Quimper in the nineteenth century do not correlate with either state policy or the relative material advantage accorded the priesthood, for, unlike the lower clergy in most other regions of France following the French Revolution, parish priests in Finistère were largely independent of the salary provided by the state under the terms of the Concordat and were far wealthier than their counterparts in central or southern France. A substantial portion of their income was derived from surplice fees (*casuel*) and parish collections (*quêtes*), and this relative wealth made them financially secure and added to their prestige in rural society.

The tithe was abolished in all dioceses of France during the French Revolution, and the Civil Constitution of the Clergy of 1791 established state salaries for the lower clergy. Although these salaries were temporarily discontinued in 1794, the Concordat, which was ratified in September 1801, reestablished state salaries for all the upper and lower clergy until the Separation of Church and State in 1905. These salaries, however, were relatively meager, in comparison with the income of priests in other European countries. The average annual income of a curé in France before 1830 was 750 francs, whereas in Austria a priest's average income was 1,263 francs, in Prussia 1,460, in Spain 1,430, and in Portugal 2,926.[65] Moreover, the salaries of the parish clergy in France in the nineteenth century were not increased to keep pace with the salaries of other functionaries. By the second half of the nineteenth century a number of pamphlets and books appeared on the miserable plight of the parish clergy with titles such as *Les prolétaires dans le clergé français* and *Le clergé fin-de-siècle*, which popularized the economic condition of the parish clergy.[66] In *L'épiscopat sous la joug*, Guy de Pierrefeu argued that whereas the salaries of state functionaries and those of the liberal professions had doubled and tripled over the course of the nineteenth century, clerical salaries remained the same even though the priest sometimes had to use his salary to pay for his books, journals, charitable works in the parish, and his basic material needs as well as to support his parents.[67] From the 1840s onward, curés and *desser-*

---

[65] Brugerette, *Le prêtre français* 1: 34.
[66] Dupont, *Tribulations du desservant*; Pottier, *Les prolétaires dans le clergé français*.
[67] Guy de Pierrefeu, *L'épiscopat sous la joug*, 20 ed. (Paris, n.d.), p. 13.

vants began to write anonymously to the Ministry of Religious Affairs regarding their financial difficulties.[68] In 1866, a curé wrote to the emperor to call his attention to the plight of clergymen like himself in rural areas where the surplice fees were not sufficient to compensate for the low salary received by the curé.[69] Desservants, in addition, who did not have tenured (*inamovible*) positions like the curés, were often dismissed on the whim of the government or the ecclesiastical hierarchy in the diocese. These desservants often, therefore, found themselves in a precarious position and received little sympathy from the local population or the government. When it was suggested in the Senate in 1862 that clerical salaries for all priests be increased, the suggestion was opposed because there was ostensibly no evidence that the lower clergy were unhappy with their position. In the early 1870s, an open letter was addressed to the archbishop of Rennes by abbé X regarding the minister Jules Simon's proposal to increase the number of tenured curés, which the archbishop opposed.[70] According to one critic the postrevolutionary Concordat made the parish priest in rural areas dependent on the local nobility, who supported him financially and put him entirely at the mercy of his bishop.[71] The position of the parish clergy as depicted in various publications by the end of the nineteenth century was indeed sorry. The *Revue des Deux Mondes* described the parish priest in 1892 as a man "banished from the school, excluded from the committee directing public charities, regarded with malicious distrust and jealous hatred by the mayor and the schoolmaster, kept at arm's length as a compromising neighbor by the minor officials employed by the commune or the state, spied on by the innkeeper, exposed by anonymous denunciations by the local newspaper. . . . He spends his mornings reciting prayers to empty pews and his afternoons planting cabbages and pruning roses."[72]

The status and particularly the financial position of the parish priest could not have been more different in Finistère. At the end of the nineteenth century the parish priest received an annual salary allotted by the government of 900 francs for desservants, 1,200 francs for curés of second class, and 1,500 for curés of first class. However, the income of the parish priest in the department was actually much higher. In 1904, the subprefect of Châteaulin noted that the wealth of the parish clergy was substantial even in the poorest areas in the department. In Lannédern, one of the smallest communes in Finistère, the annual income of the parish priest—2,330

---

[68] A number of these letters are contained in A.N. F^{19} 6117. Under the terms of the Concordat, priests assigned to cantonal seats were curés. Priests serving in other communes were desservants who earned less in the way of salary.

[69] A.N. F^{19} 6117, 4 March 1866.

[70] A.N. F^{19} 2653. In 1873, Jules Simon suggested making all desservants over the age of fifty *inamovible*, but this proposal was rejected by the Church. Brugerette, *Le prêtre français* 2: 71.

[71] De Pierrefeu, *L'épiscopat sous le joug*, pp. 1, 89.

[72] Cited in McManners, *Church and State in France*, p. 168.

francs—was derived from surplice fees, quêtes, collections organized by the priest in money and in kind, and gifts. This revenue consisted in part of fees from five marriages at 8 francs, twenty baptisms at 4 francs, fifteen burials at 20 francs, three weekly services for the deceased at 150 francs, and other special services at 30 francs, one mass per day at 2 francs, collections in kind, and 400 francs from parish properties. In Brennilis, a commune created in 1884, which housed only one priest, the priest had an annual income of 3,000 francs. Two priests in the parish of Loqueffret shared an annual income of 3,500 francs, and two priests in Cloitre Pleyben shared 4,500 francs a year. In Brasparts, three priests shared an annual income of 12,000 francs, and in Plonevez-du-Faou, the desservant earned 10,000 to 15,000 francs per year.[73] The arrondissement of Châteaulin was not the wealthiest area in Finistère, so we may assume that these figures were even higher in the Léon and the richer communes of Cornouaille. In 1904, a government official reported that in Plogoff, a commune in southern Finistère, the clergy earned 9,200 francs annually, in Plouhinec 11,000, and in Briec and Cléden-Cap-Sizun, they had an income as high as 35,000 and 37,500 annually.[74] Following the legislative elections of 1906 in the second district of Quimper, the revenues of the clergy in Cléden-Cap-Sizun, in particular, were publicized by the anticlerical republican deputy of Finistère, Georges Le Bail. According to Le Bail, the parish clergy exerted undue influence over the electorate in an attempt to defeat the republican candidate who supported the Combes ministry. Le Bail argued that using conservative estimates the three priests serving the parish of Cléden-Cap-Sizun, which had a population of 2,146, shared an annual income of 24,000 francs. This revenue included 7,522 derived from baptisms, burials, and marriages, 3,840 francs collected during pardons, 2,620 francs given to the clergy in the form of gifts, and 1,980 francs collected on behalf of saints and other services.[75]

It is difficult to estimate with any certainty the revenues of the parish collected by the lower clergy in kind during traditional quêtes, as this revenue was not declared. Nonetheless, there is no doubt, based on governmental and ecclesiastical reports, that this revenue was considerable. In many parishes, quêtes were organized twice a year by the resident clergy, who traveled from farm to farm in horse-drawn carts collecting butter and wheat. The revenues derived from the surplice fees were also very high.

The substantial income of the lower clergy in Finistère afforded them a degree of independence from the ecclesiastical hierarchy in the diocese and from the local châtelain that was unknown in most other regions of France.

[73] A.D. Finistère, 1V58, 26 September 1904.
[74] A.D. Finistère, 1V58, reports of a *commissaire spécial des chemins de fer* of 14 and 30 September 1904.
[75] *Le Citoyen*, 21 April 1906.

At times it seemed to the government that even the bishop of the diocese was unable to exert control over his clergy, particularly in the Léon. During the early Third Republic prefects continually complained of the insubordination of the lower clergy, and the government attempted to combat the problem by establishing a practice in 1887 of only accepting the appointments of non-Breton bishops to the department: A Breton bishop might only reinforce the clergy's tendency to resist the administrative measures. Louis Hémon voiced this argument in an open letter to the government in 1887 and suggested that the new bishop appointed to assume the place of Monseigneur Nouvel de la Flèche, the deceased bishop of the diocese of Quimper, should be chosen from outside the diocese and, if possible, outside Brittany.[76] Despite the government's attempts to choose bishops who were not native to the region, the clergy nonetheless remained intransigent. In 1895, the prefect informed the minister of religious affairs that the bishop, Monseigneur Valleau, had no control over the parish clergy in the diocese and suggested that he be replaced.[77]

The lower clergy appeared to the government to have every intention of maintaining their independence from the administration in Paris, as well as from the ecclesiastical hierarchy, despite measures taken by the government to combat the problem. After 1887, the lower clergy was frequently at odds with the ecclesiastical hierarchy, and the bishops of Quimper were more often than not simply unable to exert their authority. Monseigneur Dubillard, who was appointed bishop of Quimper in 1899, even intimated that the lower clergy had led his predecessors to an early grave.[78] By the end of the nineteenth century some argued that relations between the bishop and the lower clergy were so strained that the diocese was in a state of anarchy.[79]

According to the government, the lower clergy had long been "bellig-

[76] Prior to that time, however, it was impossible for the prefects to agree on whether the lower clergy led Monseigneur Nouvel de la Flèche or whether the bishop led them. A.N. F^{19} 2564, handwritten note on Monseigneur Nouvel de la Flèche. Letter, Louis Hémon, 9 June 1887.

[77] A.N. F^{19}2564, memorandum from the prefect of Finistère to the minister of religious affairs, 27 December 1895.

[78] Letter from Monseigneur Dubillard to Abbé Ollivier, 29 March 1902, cited in Jacques Roué, "Etudes sur la vie paroissiale et religieuse de Lannilis, commune de Léon du Concordat à 1914" (mémoire de maîtrise, Université de Bretagne Occidentale, 1970). Lamarche, Dubillard's immediate predecessor, died only five years after being appointed bishop of Quimper, and Valleau, Lamarche's predecessor, after only seven years in the position.

[79] A.D. Finistère, 18 J 21, Fonds Louis Hémon, notes. According to Hémon, the diocese was "in a state of anarchy. Parish priests were directors of newspapers, directors and organizers of unions, electoral agents, conference organizers, and electoral speech-givers. . . . One might have asked oneself if there were a bishop in the diocese of Quimper. . . . There was one, but a bishop who seemed quite ill informed" about the political and organizational initiatives undertaken by the lower clergy.

erent,"[80] bypassing or simply ignoring authorities, whether they assumed the form of the ecclesiastical hierarchy or the government. At times the government withdrew their salaries, and the nobility refused to contribute generously to the Church coffer, but the clergy was not significantly affected. Moreover, the government's apparent decision to appoint bishops foreign to the region only appears to have exacerbated the division between the ecclesiastical hierarchy and the lower clergy, many of whom had scarcely ventured beyond the geographical perimeters of the department. Monseigneur Dubillard, for example, made it known when he arrived in the diocese of Quimper in 1899 that he did not approve of the use of Breton in religious instruction and that he intended to "break the resistance of his priests and to subjugate them."[81]

One of the clergy's traditional sources of local power resided in their knowledge of both Breton and French. In a region that remained predominantly Breton-speaking until after the First World War this provided the clergy with an immense amount of influence. They became the mediators and conduits through which official information passed. According to the prefect, Dubillard's initial hostility to the Breton language cost him his authority among the parish clergy.[82] In short, Dubillard was no more successful than his predecessors in coming to terms with the parish clergy, and the prefect claimed that the real leaders of the diocese were abbé Roull (curé of Saint Louis in Brest), abbé Ollivier (curé of Lannilis and former head of the Grand Séminaire de Quimper), abbé Grall (curé of Ploudalmézeau), and abbé Rossi.[83]

Clericalism and Anticlericalism in Finistère

The adjective *clerical* began to be used with frequency from 1848 onward, appearing in Littré's dictionary in 1863.[84] The term *anticlerical* first ap-

---

[80] A.N. F¹⁹2564, memorandum from the prefect of Finistère to the minister of religious affairs, 17 June 1888.

[81] A.N. F¹⁹2564, memorandum from the prefect to the minister of religious affairs, 8 January 1903.

[82] Ibid.

[83] Ibid. Rossi was born in Quimper in 1844 of a German mother and an Italian father, and according to the prefect, was the "veritable leader of the diocese . . . the upper clergy acts on his orders." A.N. F¹⁹2564, memorandum from the prefect to the minister of religious affairs, 5 November 1892. Abbé Roull was born in Landerneau in 1843 and attended the college of Saint-Pol-de-Léon before entering the seminary of Quimper in 1862. See Marie-Thérèse Cloître, "Les années 1898–1914 vues par 'L'Echo Paroissal de Brest,'" in *Etudes sur la presse en Bretagne aux XIXe et XXe siècles*, ed. Jean-Yves Veillard et al. (Landerneau, 1981), pp. 72–73.

[84] Maurain, *La politique ecclésiastique*, p. 960.

peared during the Second Empire in administrative correspondence from two of the most religiously devout departments in France, Finistère and the Nord. The prefect of the Nord described in a report of 21 May 1852 the "anticlerical reaction" in his department, and in 1859 the prefect of Finistère reported that the bourgeoisie in the department were anticlerical in sentiment.[85]

Anticlericalism in France in the nineteenth century embraced different forms of opposition to the Church and the clergy. This opposition and the struggle against the Church more generally constituted, according to one historian, "possibly the major conflict of the nineteenth century,"[86] and they were by no means confined to republican politicians such as Leon Gambetta who declared war on the Church with the battle cry, "Clericalisme, voilà l'ennemi!"

The term anticlerical first surfaced in Finistère, and it is clear from official reports that anticlerical sentiment ran high in the port of Brest. In 1903, the Fête Patronale of the rural commune of Lambézellec close to the city of Brest resulted in a brawl between Brest's working class and the peasantry, which left sixteen people injured. A police official in Lambézellec estimated that there were three thousand anticlerical demonstrators.[87] Urban anticlericalism that was expressed in this form was often an expression of the deep-seated and profound hostility between town and country, a hostility that was culturally as well as economically based.

There was little direct evidence of resentment toward the clergy in rural areas of Finistère. As it surfaced sporadically in both highly devout and indifferent communes, rural anticlericalism is more difficult to analyze. Complaints of clerical abuses and evidence of anticlerical sentiment appeared most frequently in areas where religious practice was declining or where mayors and municipal councils vied with the priest for political ascendency. Anticlerical sentiment was frequently expressed in terms of

---

[85] Ibid.

[86] Zeldin, "Introduction: Were there Two Frances?" in *Conflicts in French Society*, p. 10. Unfortunately, the origins and nature of anticlericalism among these varied social and professional groups still remain obscure, despite some recent, but somewhat isolated, studies of this phenomenon. See the essays contained in ibid., esp. Zeldin's "The Conflict of Moralities: Confession, Sin and Pleasure in the Nineteenth Century," which explores the way in which the priest's scrutiny of the sexual and private lives of his parishioners generated fierce anticlerical sentiment, and Roger Magraw, "The Conflict in the Villages: Popular Anticlericalism in the Isère (1852–1870)." Also see Agulhon, *The Republic in the Village*, pp. 99–111; Goldstein, "The Hysteria Diagnosis," pp. 209–39; Magraw, *France 1815–1914*, pp. 332–38; and for Finistère, Le Gallo, "Aux sources de l'anticlericalisme en Basse-Bretagne," pp. 803–48.

[87] A.D. Finistère, 1V49, report by the commissaire de police of Lambézellec to the subprefect of Brest, 25 June 1903.

resentment of the wealth of the parish priest and the way in which it was used to assert his authority over parish society. The concern over the tactics used by priests to amass personal wealth represents a recurrent theme in the history of anticlericalism both before and after the French Revolution in France as a whole. Although these complaints existed in Finistère in the eighteenth and nineteenth centuries, they were relatively rare precisely because the priest's revenue stayed within the confines of the parish and even after the Revolution was used in part for charitable purposes.

Nonetheless, in the early 1900s one battle fought at the local level between municipal authorities and the parish clergy centered on the Breton custom of taking a collection in kind two to three times a year, especially during the harvest season. The prefect of Finistère noted in a report to Minister of the Interior Emile Combes that this practice was a "continuation of the tithe," which had been abolished during the French Revolution.[88] He claimed that the lack of open protest against such practices in the department was owing to the "fear of being the object of public humiliation by the clergy," and, "kept in this fear, the peasants continue to give."[89] According to the prefect, some even deprived themselves and their children of food in order to satisfy the demands of the priest.

Several municipal councils, primarily, though not exclusively, in the arrondissement of Morlaix, where religious practice declined rapidly in the twentieth century, requested that either the government ban these quêtes altogether or that the municipality regulate them in such a way as to prevent abuses. To this end, a number of municipal councils proposed that the council would provide a fixed sum to the parish priest to supplement his income. Quêtes, which were frequently justified as public collections for charitable purposes, were in fact legal. For opponents of the quêtes, however, the clergy was usurping the functions of the *bureaux de bienfaisance* established in the wake of the French Revolution to replace the Church as institutions of public assistance.[90] In rural Finistère the Church never relinquished its hold on the organization of charitable activities in the parish. The bureaux de bienfaisance existed side by side with older traditions of charity that continued to be accepted by the local population.[91]

One government official investigating electoral fraud in the department argued that the peasantry often submitted to the priest's political directives unwillingly and out of material necessity. According to a local expression,

[88] A.D. Finistère IV50, 9 July 1903.
[89] Ibid.
[90] Jones, *Charity and Bienfaisance*, pp. 159–257.
[91] Historians of rural France are only beginning to discover the degree to which rural areas resisted directives from Paris and maintained time-honored institutions. In the Massif Central, for example, the peasantry found ways of ignoring the inheritance laws of the Napoleonic Code. See Jones, *Politics and Rural Society*, p. 103.

the clergy was very *aumonieux* (inclined to almsgiving), and gave a major part of its revenues to the parish in the form of indispensable charitable services.[92] Many peasants in rural parishes of Finistère were indebted to the priest in a way that would have surprised the parishioner in southern France where priests had no extra income at their disposal. In Finistère the parish treasury, which often possessed more substantial funds than the municipal treasury, was frequently controlled by the priest.

In 1879 the subprefect of Morlaix was asked to adjudicate a conflict between the priest and municipal council regarding the annual quête in the commune of St. Jean du Droigt. He ruled that the right of collection outside the physical confines of the Church "belongs in principle to the bureaux de bienfaisance" because they were often made for charitable purposes, but the law also seemed to acknowledge that collection "made on behalf of desservants in the arrondissement where they exercise their functions does not constitute unlawful begging."[93] As a result, in the arrondissement of Morlaix two municipal decrees that forbade quêtes were declared illegal. Moreover, in 1881, the prefect informed the subprefect of Quimperlé that, according to the minister of the interior, a municipal council could not substitute revenue derived from quêtes with a municipal grant.[94] A year later the subprefect of Brest was roundly reprimanded by the prefect for having forbidden quêtes in the arrondissement of Brest: "You will be obliged to kindly refer [these matters] to me in the future before making decisions of this kind. In fact, the right of collection, outside the Church, does not exclusively, as you seem to believe, belong to the bureaux de bienfaisance, and the freedom to take up collections or organize subscriptions has not been taken away from citizens by any law."[95]

Government officials viewed these attempts to regulate the clergy's collections as "a protest movement" against the clerical abuses in the departments of Brittany.[96] Nonetheless the government appeared to resist efforts by local authorities to assume new financial powers, and, in the heat of its struggle with the Church over the control of primary education, the government ironically upheld the rights of the clergy to continue collecting

[92] A.N. F¹⁹5620, "Rapport fait au nom de la commission chargée à proceder à une enquête sur l'élection de M. Gayraud dans la troisième circonscription de Brest," no. 3451, Chambre des Deputés, annexe du procès verbal de la séance du 24 mai 1897, p. 7.

[93] A.D. Finistère, letter from the subprefect of Morlaix to the prefect of the department, 6 August 1879. In 1888 Victor Jeanvrot published a legal handbook that would address such matters. See Victor Jeanvrot, *Manuel de la police des cultes à l'usage des maires et fonctionnaires de l'ordre administratif et judiciaire* (Angers, 1888).

[94] A.D. Finistère, IV50, letter from the prefect to the subprefect of Quimperlé, 20 June 1881.

[95] A.D. Finistère, 1V50, letter from the prefect to the subprefect of Brest, 23 November 1882.

[96] A.D. Finistère, 1V50, letter from the prefect to the minister of the interior, 18 July 1888.

what some considered to be a "continuation of the tithe." In 1888, several mayors, *conseillers généraux*, *conseillers d'arrondissement*, and other local elected officials in the arrondissement of Morlaix, drew up a petition for regulating ecclesiastical collections.[97] In most cases municipal councils in Finistère did not go so far as to suggest that the clergy was not entitled to any additional income. Throughout the nineteenth century the Conseil Général of Finistère proposed that the government increase the salaries of desservants in order to prevent abuses.[98]

The conflict between the clergy and municipal councils over collections was a manifestation of both a political battle between local notables over the control of local institutions and popular anticlericalism that was perhaps fueled by the priest's reprisals in the form of ostracism and public humiliation of members of the community who would not contribute to the collections. In 1902, Madame Le Poher, a native of Bolazec in Finistère, wrote to the president of the Conseil d'Etat and complained of the behavior of the parish priest of Plougras in the lower Breton department neighboring Finistère, Côtes-du-Nord, where she had been living for twelve years. When the priest organized a quête for the collection of butter in the parish on 31 May and she refused to contribute, she claimed that the priest began to slander her in public. She was, moreover, refused communion and accused of immorality.[99]

Reprisals against individuals for not following the clergy's directives could take other forms. In the commune of Plonéour-Trez, a collectively signed formal letter, drawn up in 1897, complained that the desservant refused the mayor, who was known for his republican sympathies, absolution and was generally disrespectful toward the members of the republican municipal council.[100] In certain cases priests punished all members of a family if one member of the household was found to have erred. Pierre-Jakez Helias's mother was allegedly "certainly one of the best Catholics in the parish flock" but when he was sent to a state school, his mother was "deprived of taking the sacraments at Easter" and humiliated from the pulpit.[101]

In some parishes of Finistère, particularly in the Léon, a parish priest might find himself confronted with the curious situation of a people who were "clerical in their social structures and anticlerical in their instinctive reactions."[102] Louis Keraudren, who was born in southern Finistère, was

---

[97] Ibid.

[98] Ibid. The prefect noted that the Conseil Général had repeatedly called for an increase in clerical salaries as a means of controlling quêtes as in 1824, 1831, 1832, and 1833.

[99] A.N. F[19] 5971, letter from Madame Le Poher to the president of the Conseil d'Etat, 10 July 1902.

[100] A.N. F[19] 5620, letter from the prefect to the minister of the interior, 12 July 1897.

[101] Helias, *The Horse of Pride*, p. 139.

[102] Le Gallo, "Aux sources de l'anticlericalisme en Basse-Bretagne," p. 821.

appointed to the parish of Guimiliau in the heart of the Léon in 1897. The parish was inhabited by a rich peasant aristocracy, the Julots or Juloded, many of whose sons entered the priesthood and attended the Catholic colleges of Lesneven and Saint-Pol-de-Léon. This parish, along with those bordering it, was among the most devout in France. Yet the priest claimed that the Julots consistently opposed his request for funds for the parish budget and showed him little respect. It appeared that the political and personal rivalry between the temporal and spiritual leaders of the parish led to hostility and reprisal, a form of anticlericalism based on struggles over the exercise of political power and the authority of the priest vis-à-vis his benefactors, the Julots. These conflicts were by no means confined to Guimiliau.

Anticlerical sentiment did not, however, surface frequently in rural Finistère where the priest, particularly in the Léon, was a powerful and influential member of the parish. His position may have allowed him to stifle open criticism or his reputed arrogance may have been outweighed by the services he performed in rural parishes.

Religious Congregations and "le catholicisme au féminin"

Although the social role of the priest in large measure helps to explain loyalty or opposition to the Catholic Church in Finistère, religious congregations were equally important to the fabric of local life. Between the seventeenth and nineteenth centuries France witnessed a dramatic increase in the number of active religious congregations—so much so that by the end of the eighteenth century members of communities devoted to active service outnumbered the contemplative orders. In contrast to men and women belonging to contemplative orders, these *congréganistes* did not take formal vows and lived in the communities in which they worked. Moreover, they tended to have a greater degree of independence because they were only under the nominal control of the episcopacy and the superior of the *maison mère*.

Although there was a slight decrease in the proportion of men entering congregations in France on the eve of the Revolution, the number of women who joined communities tended to increase throughout the eighteenth century.[103] One estimate based on an 1817 list of religious pensioners, which probably underestimates the number of women in congregational

[103] For a discussion of the beginnings of the feminization of the Catholic Church in seventeenth-century France, see Rapley, *The Dévotes*. Olwen Hufton and Frank Tallett evaluate the significance of the movement away from contemplative orders toward the more practically oriented congregations among women in eighteenth-century France in "Communities of Women," pp. 75–85. Even in the devout Lower Breton diocese of Vannes the number of men entering religious congregations and orders dropped by 1789. Le Goff, *Vannes and Its Region*, pp. 266–71.

establishments and tertiary roles, nonetheless indicates that "more women than men sought a religious life in the eighteenth century" (70 percent versus 30 percent).[104] Moreover, whereas female congréganistes constituted only 11 percent of women with religious vocations at the beginning of the century, by 1789 that proportion had increased to 21 percent.[105]

During the nineteenth century there was a spectacular growth in the number of women entering congregations, such as the Filles de la Charité, established before the Revolution. The expansion of well-established houses, however, was complemented by the foundation of a virtual plethora of new female congregations. According to one estimate, there were more women religious in 1880 than there were in 1789.[106]

These statistics confirm the now overwhelming evidence that suggests that the practice of the Catholic religion became increasingly feminized in France during the nineteenth century.[107] Claude Langlois's path-breaking history of this phenomenon, whose origins and consequences still require further systematic investigation, charts the foundation of four hundred new female religious communities in France during the first eighty years of the nineteenth century. Although men in the Catholic west deserted church pews for the tavern and open air less frequently and there was little difference in religious practice among men and women in Finistère, Brittany was no exception to the increasing tendency among women to join religious communities devoted to active service. In Brittany, as in France as a whole, the number of women who entered religious congregations grew substantially during the course of the nineteenth century, and much of the growth in Brittany occurred from 1850 to the early twentieth century.[108]

In contrast to male congregations, female communities provided a multiplicity of social services. Whereas male congregations focused their attention almost exclusively on educational activities, female communities performed more diversified roles as providers of medical care, public charity, refuge, pharmaceutical remedies, childcare, and education.

The sharp increase in the number of women entering religious congregations can in part be attributed to the growing demand for education and welfare in a century during which the state refused to provide them. After the revolutionary decade, the successive governments of the nineteenth

104 Hufton and Tallett, "Communities of Women," pp. 77, 83–84. In addition to women in orders and congregations were examples of pious spinsters who devoted themselves exclusively to the community service. The *béate* of the Velay in Haute-Loire, who performed good works in the local community, is a case in point.

105 Gibson, *A Social History of French Catholicism*, p. 106.

106 Langlois, *Le catholicisme au féminin*.

107 See Olwen Hufton's important article on the role of the Revolution in this process, "The Reconstitution of the Church, 1796–1801." This phenomenon was not confined to France but also became apparent in America and Europe during this period. See, for example, Caitriona Clear, *Nuns in Nineteenth-Century Ireland* (Dublin, 1987).

108 Gibson, *A Social History of French Catholicism*, pp. 114–15.

century left the business of charity, education, and medicine in the hands of the Church. The establishment of the Third Republic marked the end of Catholic dominance in primary education, but the new Republic still proved reluctant to assume the financial burden that a state-funded system of public assistance would entail. Congregations provided women who did not marry for reasons of choice, for lack of a dowry, or through family pressure with an active vocation that afforded them, in addition, some security in old age. Moreover, in areas that were poor, like the Massif Central, or that witnessed a demographic upsurge, families often depended on religious orders for survival.[109]

Few detailed diocesan studies chart the recruitment and growth of male and female congregations during the nineteenth century.[110] It has been estimated that in Brittany there were 119 masculine religious establishments and 94 female communities in 1789.[111] The religious policies of the French Revolution sent many members of such communities into hiding or exile. However, during the first decade of the nineteenth century, the Napoleonic regime, which pursued a policy of religious appeasement and sought the social services that congregations—particularly female communities—were willing to provide, authorized the reestablishment of a great number of teaching and nursing congregations throughout France. Between 1803 and the early years of the Restoration, a number of male and female religious orders reconstituted themselves, and additional new congregations came into being in Brittany. Among the most important of the male orders in Brittany were the Frères des Ecoles Chrétiennes, and the significant female congregations included the Filles de Saint-Thomas, Soeurs de la Charité, Ursulines, and Filles du Saint-Esprit.

Until the late nineteenth century, whatever inroads were made in raising literacy levels among children in Finistère were largely achieved through the efforts of female religious congregations. In 1863, 40 percent of all children who attended primary schools attended congregational establish-

[109] Jones, *Politics and Rural Society*, p. 287.

[110] These studies cover the devout area of Nantes, the more dechristianized region of Montpellier, and the Creuse. See, for example, M. Faugeras, "Vocations religieuses d'hommes dans le diocèse de Nantes au XIXe siècle (1803–1914)," *Bulletin de la Société Archéologique et Historique de Nantes* 118 (1982): 39–59, and "Les vocations religieuses de femmes dans le diocèse de Nantes au XIXe siècle (1802–1914)," in *Enquêtes et documents (Université de Nantes)* 1 (1971): 239–81; G. Cholvy, "Le recrutement des religieux dans le diocèse de Montpellier (1830–1856)," *Revue d'histoire de l'eglise de France* 141 (1958): 57–73; L. Pérouas, "Les religieuses dans le pays creusoise du XVII au XXe siècles," *Cahiers d'Histoire* 24, no. 2 (1979): 17–43. Michel Tanguy's "L'implantation des congrégations masculines et féminines dans le Finistère, 1790–1902" (maîtrise, Université de Bretagne Occidentale, 1988) is a welcome addition to this literature.

[111] Jean Meyer, "La vie religieuse en Bretagne à l'époque moderne," pp. 204–6. These figures may be somewhat misleading, however, as Meyer does not include the congregation of the Filles du Saint-Esprit, founded in 1706 in Ploermel, which became one of the most important female religious congregations in Finistère.

ments, but this proportion was much higher for girls (54 percent) than for boys (30 percent).[112] At the beginning of the Third Republic a governmental list that ranked the female religious communities in Finistère in order of educational importance put the Filles du Saint-Esprit in first place. This congregation maintained ninety-eight schools that served 11,023 children. The sisters of the Immaculate Conception, the second-ranked congregation, fell far short of this number; they operated only sixteen schools that were attended by 1,486. The remaining eighteen female congregations played a relatively negligible teaching role. Collectively they taught 7,969 children.[113] Indeed, an 1880 report noted that three-quarters of the congregational schoolteachers belonged to the Filles du Saint-Esprit.[114] The quality of congregational instruction varied widely, according to governmental reports.

Like many congregations, the Filles du Saint-Esprit provided medical care and instruction. Generally living in groups of two or three, they were scattered throughout the countryside. Like their male counterparts, the Frères de l'Instruction Chrétienne, the Filles du Saint-Esprit, who tended to be based in rural areas to a greater extent than the Ursulines, for example, formed an integral part of parish culture and the village economy. As greater and greater numbers of women entered these congregations, their visibility and social importance only increased toward the end of the nineteenth century.

Both male and female congregations were, then, part of the economy and cultural fabric of village life in Lower Brittany. If female congregations were more important in the acculturation of women as opposed to men, by providing care to the sick and help to the needy, they were nonetheless a highly significant and necessary part of a village society that experienced increasing demographic strain.

The dramatic shift in the political orientation of the peasantry of Finistère from royalism to republicanism was, as government officials argued, largely the result of the influence of the Church. The priest certainly capitalized on his authority in the highly clerical parish culture of northern Finistère, but this authority cannot simply be attributed to the ignorance and credulity of the Breton peasant, as government reports implied. This authority was predicated on the close social ties between the laity and the clergy, on the charitable and social services performed by male and female religious congregations alike, and more generally on the social and cultural role of the Church in dispersed hamlet communities.

[112] Bedel-Bernard, "L'enseignement primaire dans le Finistère, 1863–1905," p. 239.

[113] A.N. F¹⁷9261. "Liste des congrégations (femmes) établies dans le département dans l'ordre de leur importance," [1880].

[114] A.N. F¹⁷9261, Report from the Inspection de l'Académie at Rennes to the minister of education, 24 June 1880.

4

Religion and Popular Politics

THE POLITICAL identity of Brittany in the nineteenth century was one that government officials repeatedly defined in terms of antirepublicanism, conservative reaction, and isolationism. This identity was largely shaped by the memory of the counterrevolution of 1793 and 1794 and by the long-standing postrevolutionary political alliance between the parish clergy and a royalist landed aristocracy. By the early 1890s, however, the lower clergy throughout western France began to repudiate royalism and to reexamine their historic alliance with the nobility. In Finistère, the parish clergy went so far as to embrace the Republic, supporting social Catholic political candidates in opposition to royalist incumbents. The election of Albert de Mun in 1893, and, more important, the success of Christian Democratic priest abbé Gayraud in 1897 marked the dissolution of political ties between an increasingly embattled royalist nobility and the parish clergy.

The profound rift that developed between these former political allies and the gradual democratization in local styles of politics in the 1890s clearly surprised government administrators and the Parisian press. It marked a fundamental turning point in the political evolution of the region: Abbé Trochu, founder of the first social Catholic regional daily, *L'Ouest Eclair*, observed that the election of abbé Gayraud to the third electoral district of Brest in 1897 made a "considerable stir" in France as a whole because it inaugurated a new attitude among Catholics and consecrated the division that would soon occur in conservative (Catholic) circles between republicans and monarchists.[1]

According to government officials and republican politicians in the region, however, the conversion of the clergy to the Republic merely signified an attempt to maintain their increasingly precarious position in rural society by staving off true republicanism and socialism. Georges Le Bail, the most vociferous anticlerical republican deputy in Brittany during this period, summarized this appraisal in no uncertain terms: "Paul Bert had well foreseen the danger when he denounced the peril that would result from the clergy's adherence to the Republic. The clergy calls itself republican today. I am surprised that they did not think of this tactic sooner."[2] Accord-

[1] Delourme, *Trente-cinq années de la politique religieuse*, p. 23.
[2] Le Bail, *Une élection législative de 1906*, p. 71.

ing to Le Bail, a clerical republic could better assure the clergy's dominant position in rural society than a monarchical form of government.

Observers and historians have since explained the origins of the break between the priest and the châtelain, which did not occur in most other areas of France, and the Breton lower clergy's unreserved acceptance of Pope Leo XIII's call for Catholics to rally to the Republic in terms of the social origins of the clergy and the influence of ultramontanism: The parish clergy of Finistère was largely recruited from among the lower Breton peasantry; the clerics therefore had little social loyalty to the aristocracy, who often treated them with disdain. Once the tide turned against royalism and the clergy was encouraged to accept the Republic, it was all too willing to do so. If the clergy's allegiance lay anywhere, it was with neither the nobility nor the ecclesiastical hierarchy, with which the lower Breton parish clergy was in continual conflict, but with Rome, which often adjudicated these conflicts. According to the anticlerical republican politician, Théodore Le Febvre, who garnered only a few votes in his bids for election in the 1890s, Brittany had never "known a Gallican spirit."[3] By implication, the clergy's new commitment to democracy was no more than an indication of obedience to the Pope.

Although these arguments are at first persuasive and may in part explain the conversion of the parish clergy to social Catholicism in Finistère, they are nonetheless problematic: The parish priest came from the popular classes throughout France where the tradition of ultramontanism was strong, but the spirit of the Ralliement was only tacitly accepted in most areas of France, if at all. After 1898 a large number of priests in rural areas found their spiritual home in the newly formed royalist organization of the Comité de l'Action Française and openly opposed Christian democracy.[4] In some regions, moreover, the lower clergy welcomed the Ralliement but nonetheless felt restrained from showing sympathy for fear of losing livelihood. Monseigneur Turinaz, the bishop of Nancy, was reported to have said that if he "showed his loyalty to the Republic, he would not have a farthing to bless himself with the next day."[5] Another bishop allegedly told a Catholic reporter why he found it difficult to come out in favor of the Republic: "Do you think my diocese is made up of so many parishes? If so,

---

[3] A.N. F¹⁹5620, "Rapport fait au nom de la commission chargée a procéder à une enquête sur l'élection de l'abbé Gayraud dans la troisième circonscription de Brest," p. 111.

[4] The battle between Catholic royalists and republican social Catholics was fought out until the papal condemnation of the Action Française in 1926 in both Paris and the provinces. Paul Delourme, alias abbé Trochu, a prominent Christian Democratic priest, who was largely responsible for creating the regional social Catholic daily, L'Ouest Eclair, testified to the difficulties faced by Catholics committed to republicanism in the diocese of Rennes where the bishop openly supported the Action Française. See Delourme, Trente-cinq années de la politique religieuse, pp. 229–55.

[5] Dansette, Religious History of Modern France 2: 94.

you are mistaken. It is made up of 150 manors that provide money for my various Catholic enterprises. The rest of the diocese is nothing more than a financial burden. When I visit twenty-five of these manors, I find a portrait of Prince Victor, which I salute. In twenty-five others, I find photographs of the Prince Imperial and the comte de Paris, set in a single frame. I bow to them twice over. In a hundred of others, the family of Orléans holds undisputed allegiance and I bow three times. In all these houses, I find help for my schools and for the poor that I find nowhere else."[6] To a certain extent, the financial independence and relative wealth of the lower clergy in Finistère might explain how the priest opposed the châtelain so easily, but it does not explain why the clergy embraced republican social Catholicism so wholeheartedly.

Historians and political scientists have nonetheless since adopted, though often in modified forms, contemporary republican views of Breton social Catholicism or "clerical republicanism." They argue that it served as an ideology of cooptation propagated by rural elites, the clergy and the nobility, to maintain their dominant position in traditional rural society. Moreover, the resounding electoral success of social Catholic candidates in this period has been attributed to no more than the clergy's powerful influence in local society. To government observers, the conversion of the peasantry to the Republic was therefore more apparent than real. Before the development of commercial and social links with worlds beyond the parish, electioneering and political contests were directed and decided by the châtelain and the priest. While voters remained ignorant of the French language and national political issues, it was still possible to lead obedient flocks to the polls, especially in areas such as Brittany where the priest was a feared and revered member of the community. The Breton clergy, in this view, eventually understood that the defense of the Church and priestly prerogative in the face of the state's growing intervention in local affairs during the early Third Republic necessitated a new political program. It became increasingly difficult, however, to espouse such a program and defend the social interests of a landed nobility.

The gradual penetration of the state into local affairs and the growing rift between the clergy and the nobility thus threatened the very foundations on which traditional society rested in the department and created a political crisis for the nobility. In Finistère, elites, drawing on the social Catholic doctrines that had orginally threatened their political preeminence, organized the peasantry into corporatist agricultural organizations aimed at preserving traditional social relationships in the countryside, the hegemony of the nobility. These unions, it is suggested, ultimately formed a state within a state, and politics in the region turned solely on religious issues.[7]

[6] Cited in ibid., p. 94.
[7] Berger, *Peasants Against Politics*, pp. 51–54.

These assessments of social Catholicism are predicated on an instrumental view of religion that strangely ignores the development of the movement outside agricultural syndicalism. Social Catholicism ultimately assumed various forms in the department in the twentieth century, and although it served as a locus of resistance to the cultural mission of the French state in its political, not syndicalist, form, it helped to bring the nation to the village by representing local interests and allegiances in the larger national community.

In building the social Catholic movement, traditional methods of political persuasion—songs, almanacs, ostracism, and the refusal to grant absolution—were employed along with methods of modern electoral politics, which included open meetings, the press, and public debate. This contributed to the democraticization of the political process, which inaugurated a decisive change in local styles of politics and political practices. The movement thus helped to politicize a largely quiescent electorate and to foster a new national consciousness at the periphery. As government officials, priests, anticlerical neophytes, and landed elites fought to gain the sympathies of the local electorate, Breton men and women became aware of their own political stake and importance in the larger national community.

Social Catholicism among the Parish Clergy in Finistère

Although social Catholicism as a social and political ideology had been an integral part of the French political and social landscape since the 1840s,[8] it did not gain widespread popular support as a political movement until the end of the nineteenth century. Social Catholicism as a political and social movement centered on Catholic initiatives to come to terms with the social and economic problems afflicting modern society, and prior to the revolution of 1848 the movement included royalists such as Villeneuve-Bargement, who was inspired by an idealized notion of a hierarchical Christian social order associated with the Middle Ages that emphasized the social duties of the rich toward the poor, as well as social Catholics such as Lamennais and Lacordaire, who advocated social justice and a democratic republic based on universal manhood suffrage in the 1830s and 1840s. Social Catholicism encompassed a myriad of political and social groups that appeared in France in the nineteenth century. Although these groups shared a common rejection of a social and economic order predi-

---

[8] Dansette, *Religious History of Modern France* 2: 112–13; Duroselle, *Les débuts du catholicisme social*; Cholvy and Hilaire, *Histoire religieuse de la France contemporaine* 1: 66–72.

cated on liberal principles that advocated Christian, corporatist solutions to the ills afflicting industrial society, they can be divided into two distinct camps: First, the aristocratic and paternalist emphasized Christian charity, social reconciliation, and the duties of the rich to the poor. Second, the democratic accepted the political fact of the Revolution of 1789 and stressed principles of social justice rather than charity.

An aristocratic tradition of social Catholicism flourished from the Restoration to the Third Republic in the form of charitable organizations such as the Society of St. Vincent de Paul. In 1833, Frédéric Ozanam founded the conferences of St. Vincent de Paul in Paris to serve the material and spiritual needs of the poor. As a charitable organization, St. Vincent de Paul recruited from a social elite who were moved by the plight of the working classes in a number of cities in France. Seven years later, St. Vincent de Paul had a membership of two thousand in fifteen towns in France.[9] Along with Armand de Melun, Ozanam also initiated the *patronage*, a religious and social apostolate for the young that established a system of hostels throughout France and workshops to train its members for the workplace. This institution has had a long legacy and provided a haven for the young and unemployed particularly during the severe economic depression of the 1840s.

The origin of the democratic variety of social Catholicism of the 1890s also dates from the early attempts to reconcile the Church with modern French society during the Restoration and July Monarchy. In France, the Breton patriarch abbé Felicité de Lamennais, together with Père Lacordaire and comte Charles Forbes de Montalembert founded the journal *L'Avenir* in 1830, whose motto, "God and Liberty," embodied its essential message. It encouraged French Catholics to reexamine the historic ties that had been forged between throne and altar during the French Revolution and advocated universal manhood suffrage, freedom of the press, separation of church and state—because it would afford the church greater autonomy— and freedom of association. *L'Avenir* developed a critique of modern liberal society by arguing that the social relations between classes were as much governed by moral laws as the relations between individuals.

L'Avenir was denounced by an intransigent legitimist ecclesiastical hierarchy that was unwilling to accept any political and liberal principles associated with the French Revolution. Pope Gregory XVI sided with the French ecclesiastical hierarchy and forced Lamennais and his disciples to make a declaration of doctrinal submission in 1833. Lamennais lived out the last years of a now embittered life writing in defense of democracy and refusing to bow to papal authority.

Lamennais's disciple Lacordaire, who distanced himself from the master

---

[9] Dansette, *Religious History of Modern France* 1: 254.

soon after 1833, became a spokesman for the social dimension of Catholicism in the 1840s and during the Second Republic and founded a new journal, *L'Ere Nouvelle*, two months after the February revolution in 1848. *L'Ere Nouvelle* in part represented an attempt to rechristianize an increasingly indifferent working class. The prospectus of *L'Ere Nouvelle* declared: "There are only two forces that count—Jesus Christ and the People. An alliance between them will be the salvation of France and it is therefore the duty of Catholics to accept the Republic."[10] *L'Ere Nouvelle* inaugurated the first popular movement in France that could be characterized as Christian Democratic. It criticized an unregulated economic system that tended to concentrate wealth in the hands of a few to impoverish the many and argued that the Church had to do more than dispense charity to alleviate the plight of the oppressed. Its priests had to become interpreters of the spiritual and material needs of their parishioners and promote social justice. *L'Ere Nouvelle* called for profit-sharing partnerships between management and labor as well as far-reaching social legislation. The publication soon boasted a circulation of twenty thousand, but Catholic liberals who had been associated with Lamennais's *L'Avenir* attacked the new enterprise and the doctrine it represented. Montalembert was, in contrast to Lacordaire, prepared to accept liberal society and the economic system in France in the nineteenth century. He advocated political reforms but not fundamental social reforms. As Adrien Dansette has put it, "While the diehard Catholics mourned the Old Regime or the Middle Ages and Catholic liberals were satisified with the bourgeois society of the nineteenth century, the Catholic democrats wanted a new society from which the worker would not be excluded."[11] This populist, reformist strand of social Catholicism fed into the ideology of the Left during the revolution of 1848,[12] but the Vatican and the vast majority of the ecclesiastical hierarchy remained hostile to these initiatives for another forty years; they preferred the social solutions advocated by liberal and intransigent Catholics in the form of charitable enterprises. Indeed, the hostility of the institutional church to this form of populist Catholicism drove a wedge between the republican Left and the Church, which profoundly shaped the politics of the early Third Republic.

L'Ere Nouvelle, failing with the collapse of the democratic republic in June 1848, was discredited because it became associated with social upheaval that was feared by intransigent and liberal Catholics alike. The

[10] Quoted in ibid. 1: 256–57. See Berenson, *Populist Religion*, and Bowman, *Le Christ des barricades*, for a discussion of the ways in which popular religious sentiment was channeled into the democratic movement that overthrew the July Monarchy during the Revolution of 1848.

[11] Dansette, *Religious History of Modern France* 1: 257.

[12] See Berenson, *Populist Religion*.

violence and unrest associated with the democratic revolution of 1848 discredited democratic aspirations among social Catholics, who faced bitter opposition from an uncompromising and politically conservative Vatican until the 1890s.[13]

The largely paternalistic social initiatives therefore became the focus for social Catholics during the Second Empire and early Third Republic. Albert De Mun, a noble army officer who became a leading social Catholic politician of the early Third Republic, founded the *Oeuvres des Cercles*, workers' clubs, in 1881. Through such organizations De Mun wished to effect an alliance between the people and an aristocracy that had ostensibly long forgotten its social obligations. These clubs were directed and funded entirely by wealthy employers and aristocrats. Both de Mun and his comrade in arms, the comte de La Tour du Pin, were aristocratic royalists who sought social reconciliation through such enterprises but who also called on the state to intervene to limit working hours, improve working conditions for women and children, and institute the five-and-a-half-day week, insurance against industrial accidents, and pension plans. In the 1880s, Albert de Mun and La Tour du Pin were revolutionary on social issues but counterrevolutionary as far as political issues were concerned. Indeed, La Tour du Pin, in particular, hoped to revive corporate institutions of the Old Regime. As military attaché in Vienna from 1877 to 1880, La Tour du Pin came under the influence of Baron von Vogelsang and the Prince of Lichtenstein who called for more than charity to resolve the social question and encouraged maintaining a strong professional guild system to counter the ill effects of a liberal, individualistic economic order. In France in the absence of guilds, which had been abolished during the French Revolution, La Tour du Pin and Albert de Mun hoped that new professional groupings would be created that included management.

The initiatives of de Mun and La Tour Du Pin were given a new force in 1891 as a result of Pope Leo XIII's promulgation of *Rerum Novarum*, which reminded Catholics of the pressing need to come to terms with the social question, and *Au Milieu des Sollicitudes*, which encouraged French Catholics to rally to the republican regime. The Ralliement—the rallying of Catholics to the Republic in the 1890s[14]—and Rerum Novarum gave rise to a new incarnation of social Catholicism that ultimately assumed democratic political form. And unlike the social Catholic, Christian Democratic movement of the 1830s and 1840s, this new movement proved a lasting force in French politics.

These new "democrats of Christian inspiration" advocated a social and political system based on republican principles and universal suffrage,

[13] Dansette, *Religious History of Modern France* 2: 114.
[14] Sedgewick, *The Ralliement in French Politics*.

which included the vote for women. To the extent that they repudiated the changes wrought by economic modernization, they hardly differed from intransigents and paternalists, but to the extent that they embraced the republican ideals of the French Revolution, they represented a phenomenon in French politics that cannot easily be understood in terms of the political categories of Left and Right.

This movement was by no means universally welcomed by the Catholic hierarchy, but the lower Breton department of Finistère rapidly became one of its most important strongholds. The parish clergy greeted Rerum Novarum and Au Milieu des Sollicitudes with overwhelming enthusiasm and set out to proselytize the cause. How and why did the Ralliement and social Catholicism come to be so widely accepted among the lower clergy of Finistère when in many parts of France and in areas of the west (for example, the Mayenne) such initiatives met with hostility? Why was the clergy, and especially the younger clergy of Finistère, willing to embrace the new political and social orientation of the Vatican so wholeheartedly? The answers to these questions are twofold: First, a successful campaign of promotion and propagandizing was organized through the seminary of Quimper. Influential clerics in the department recognized the importance of coming to terms with the social problems afflicting their parishioners if they wished to stay the tide of secularization that they observed elsewhere. Second, a receptivity among the lower clergy was fostered by their social roots among the peasantry of Finistère, their financial independence from the French state, and a consequent tradition of autonomy in the face of the ecclesiastical hierarchy and aristocracy.

The social Catholic movement and the Ralliement had support from influential clerics in Finistère in a way that the movement lacked in most dioceses in France. It was officially endorsed and sponsored by the superior of the seminary of Quimper, which became the ideological center of social Catholicism in the diocese of Quimper. One of the chief architects of the Ralliement in Finistère was abbé Ollivier, curé of the commune of Lannilis, who allegedly had more influence and authority than the bishop himself. Ollivier was superior of the seminary of Quimper from 1879 to 1893 and later became one of the *grands électeurs* of Léon when he was appointed curé of Lannilis. Abbé Ollivier played an instrumental role in fostering the dissemination of social Catholicism in three ways: First, he instituted a course of study within the seminary of Quimper that diffused the precepts of social Catholicism; second, he created an electoral organization and press loyal to the Ralliement; and third, he sponsored the candidacy of social Catholic political hopefuls.

Abbé Ollivier instituted a new course of study in the curriculum of the seminary in 1885. The first session of this *cours d'oeuvres*, whose aim, according to Ollivier, was to "oppose the incessant and always progressive encroachments of freemasonry" by defending the "material and spiritual interests of the faithful,"[15] began in June of that year. The cours d'oeuvres met once or twice a week and consisted of a presentation and general discussion of an assigned topic. The cours fostered an intellectual climate in which the new ideals of social Catholicism were discussed among seminarists. It provided future priests, in addition, with precise information on the economic and social problems facing different social groups in Finistère, including the agricultural crisis of the 1880s and 1890s.[16]

The early meetings of the cours d'oeuvres focused on the discussion of both established charitable institutions sponsored by the Church, such as the Society of St. Vincent de Paul and *patronages* (charitable organizations founded in honor of a patron saint), and the role of temperance societies and organizations to help military conscripts. From the early 1890s onward, however, the emphasis of the cours d'oeuvres changed as discussions focused less on charity than on social obligation, the ill effects of economic liberalism, the agricultural crisis, and the role of professional organizations, including unions and cooperatives, in alleviating these problems. The debates that followed these conferences reflected broad differences of opinion among participants and the rejection by some of the traditional solutions advocated by the Catholic Church to social problems.

After 1891 most seminarists who participated in the cours d'oeuvres seemed to share the view that economic liberalism, capitalism, and individualism were largely responsible for the social problems facing modern society. According to one seminarist, economic liberalism was merely a "despotism of high finance, the tyranny of money."[17] Although liberal economists "still say that free competition will make monopolies disappear," it would in fact result in the "destruction of the poor, in the disappearance of the middle classes themselves, and capital would concentrate itself in a small number of hands."[18] Seminarists repeatedly cited liberalism, an offshoot of individualism, as the main cause of the crisis afflicting agriculture and industry with deleterious social consequences. To this extent the seminarists' analysis of the social crisis allegedly afflicting France was identical with positions traditionally held by intransigent conservative Catholics who identified individualism and economic liberalism, resulting from the French Revolution, as the root causes of the crisis. Where intransigent Catholics advocated a return to the hierarchically ordered corporatist society of the ancien régime, the seminarists rejected the political prin-

[15] A.E.Q., 2H310, minutes of the session of 11 June 1885.

[16] The minutes of the sessions of the cours d'oeuvres from 1885 to 1908, when they were abolished, have been preserved in the diocesan archives of Quimper, Fonds du Grand Séminaire de Quimper, 2H310–313.

[17] A.E.Q. 2H312, De Kervenoael, minutes of the session of 13 December 1894.

[18] Ibid.

ciples on which such a society was based even as they supported corporatist solutions to the social ills afflicting modern society.

The solutions and strategies discussed by the seminarists participating in the cours d'oeuvres reflected the language and strategies advocated by republican social Catholics at the ecclesiastical congresses held at Bourges and Reims between 1896 and 1900 where the principles of Christian Democracy or republican social Catholicism were popularized.[19] These congresses were attended by the new leaders of the nascent Christian Democratic movement in France, such as abbé Lemire, who had been elected to the Chamber of Deputies from French Flanders; the abbés Garnier and Naudet of *Le Peuple Français* and *La Justice Sociale*, respectively—two newspapers guided by the new ideals of Christian democracy; and Georges Fonsegrive, the pen name of Yves Le Querdec, who in 1895 published *Lettres d'un curé de campagne*, a book popularizing the ideal of a new breed of parish priest dedicated to social reform. Léon Harmel, the eccentric industrialist from Val de Bois in the Ardennes, who promoted the idea of a partnership between management and labor in industry and helped to form worker associations excluding management, also attended.

Four features distinguished Christian Democracy from the paternalistic tradition of social Catholicism: (1) the role it granted to the state in intervening in social and economic affairs; (2) its explicit commitment to republican political institutions in the spirit of the Ralliement (*avant la lettre*); (3) the greater emphasis it placed on social justice and Christian duty as opposed to charity; and (4) its emphasis on regionalism.[20]

Many of the most prominent organizers of the third ecclesiastical congress, which was given the title of "congrès [de la] démocratie chrétienne,"[21] rejected some of the more paternalistic solutions to social problems that had been promoted with all good intentions by Albert de Mun, for example, in the 1880s. De Mun had established the Oeuvres des Cercles Catholiques d'Ouvriers, worker's associations consisting of management and labor, though they were wholly directed and funded by the former. After a law legalizing trade unions was passed in 1884, de Mun encouraged the formation of *syndicats mixtes*, trade unions consisting of management and labor.

Representatives of the new Christian Democratic movement, such as the abbés Lemire and Gayraud, who helped to organize the congresses of Bourges and Reims, adhered to the associational solution, but they saw the necessity of more direct action on the part of the state in alleviating the

[19] Rémond, *Les deux congrés ecclésiastiques.*
[20] Poulat, *Eglise contre la bourgeoisie*, pp. 135–72.
[21] McManners, *Church and State in France*, p. 94.

plight of the poor. Some, like Harmel, favored the formation of autonomous worker trade unions instead of syndicats mixtes.

The influence of the reformist doctrines of the Christian Democratic movement were clearly reflected in the way in which issues were articulated in the cours d'oeuvres at the seminary of Quimper after 1896. The chairman of the cours d'oeuvres in 1898, Auffret, actually visited Harmel's factory at Val de Bois along with several other seminarists. Auffret praised the "generosity" and enthusiasm of "des hommes du Nord." The secretary of the proceedings noted that Auffret's "patriotism" led him to want Brittany to guard against falling behind the Nord.[22] François-Marie Madec, who became one of the most active members in the social Catholic movement in Finistère in the twentieth century, was librarian of the cours d'oeuvres from 1900 to 1901 and cited a report of the ecclesiastical congress of Reims in a discussion regarding associations.[23]

By 1898 the goal of the cours d'oeuvres was still primarily evangelical, concerned with protecting the material and spiritual interests of the people with greater emphasis placed on ministering to the former. The newly elected president of the cours d'oeuvres announced at the opening session of 1898–1899, which was attended by more participants than ever before, that it was necessary to go directly to the people and to concern oneself with their material interests and improve their situation not with *oeuvres de charité* but with *oeuvres économiques*. According to Auffret, works of charity were necessary, but they were only a palliative. The problems of society had to be attacked at their root, "that is to say to cry justice to society and improve the organization of work."[24] In establishing an agenda for the year, therefore, discussion of charitable organization was all but omitted. The cours d'oeuvres focused on (1) professional organizations, (2) a series of theoretical discussions on liberalism and individualism, (3) organizing workers politically, and (4) regional issues. A seminarist by the name of Gouchen argued that it was imperative to study social questions so that the priest would not become a "victim" in the "democratic movement that is emerging today in France."[25] The underlying evangelical motives were never absent from these formulations. Auffret warned that it was important to remember that the votes of the people are not conquered overnight but "through the modest labor of social works."[26]

The principal solutions proposed by the seminarists in the cours d'oeuvres to the problems of modern French society were to be found in professional associations—unions and cooperatives—and in the limited

[22] A.E.Q., 2H312, minutes of the session of 10 November 1898.
[23] A.E.Q., 2H312, minutes of the sessions of 8–15 February 1900.
[24] A.E.Q., 2H312, minutes of the session of 10 November 1898.
[25] Ibid.
[26] A.E.Q., 2H312, minutes of the session of 24 November 1898.

intervention of the state in social and economic affairs. François Madec argued in a 1901 session that professional organization was an alternative to the only existing alternatives, liberalism and socialism. Madec rejected the liberal solution that held that happiness would result from the free exercise of "social forces," regulated only by charity, because this view ignored the facts that *liberté du travail* was a contradiction in terms and that charity by itself was incapable of solving the problems from which society suffered.[27] Similarly, Madec rejected the socialist solution on the grounds that the state becomes both the source and the end of all social action. Madec argued that the state should play a limited but clearly circumscribed role in regulating social and economic affairs.[28]

There was by no means an absolute consensus among seminarists participating in the cours d'oeuvres and indeed among social Catholics regarding the social function of the state.[29] One seminarist argued that state interventionism was both necessary and legitimate to protect the home, the life of the family, to ameliorate the lot of the worker, and to protect the nation's wealth.[30] Seminarist Goanac'h saw a certain danger in the centralizing tendencies of the modern state, which opened the way for socialism, and he called for decentralization.[31] According to seminarist Guéguen that decentralization might be achieved by restoring the prerevolutionary provinces. A certain M. Gouchen countered that this solution could present a "danger to national unity," and he proposed instead the creation of charitable, professional, and trade organizations that would represent the interests of various trades and professions in the social polity.[32] The seminarists' evident commitment to the nation and national unity appears to have been shared by other participants in the cours d'oeuvres. Even as they called for decentralization, corporatist solutions, and the maintenance of the Breton language, they recognized the French state as a given and never questioned its legitimacy. Goanac'h's sensitivity to the implications of regionalism suggests the clear line drawn between supporting regionalism and threats to the unity of the Republic. Indeed, these early discussions reflect nascent attempts in social Catholic circles at the periphery to reconcile the interests of the nation with the region.

Madec and countless other speakers in the cours d'oeuvres advocated a "Catholic" solution to the social question primarily in the political arena through democratic action and the creation of trade unions, cooperatives, and professional chambers. Most other seminarists, unlike their more radi-

[27] A.E.Q., 2H312, minutes of the session of 7 February 1901.
[28] A.E.Q., 2H312, minutes of the sessions of 29–30 January 1900.
[29] Ibid.
[30] Ibid.
[31] Ibid.
[32] Ibid. Also see 2H312, minutes of the sessions of 31 January and 7 February 1901.

cal Christian Democratic counterparts in the congresses of Bourges and Reims, supported the syndicat mixte. Madec, however, insisted that unions, which would include management and labor, be organized in a democratic fashion, and he was confident that such organizations would ultimately lead to regenerating society.[33]

Participants in the cours d'oeuvres not only advocated unions to represent the economic interests of professional groups in society, but in addressing themselves to the agricultural crisis of the 1890s, they emphasized the benefits of cooperatives, and *caisses rurales*, which would provide peasants with insurance in case of fire, poor harvests, and the death of livestock. Cooperatives were thought to be particularly atttractive to the peasant landowner because they eliminated the middleman and the profits they allegedly made at the farmer's expense. Seminarists, most of whom came from and served in rural parishes in Finistère, hardly seemed concerned with the plight of the shopkeeper, the small rural businessman. Auffret argued that from a social point of view small tradesmen or shopkeepers were parasites deriving more than their share in profits from their customers so that their gradual disappearance in the face of competition from cooperatives was not to be lamented.[34] According to Auffret, the gradual growth of cooperatives would simply allow the tradesman or shopkeeper to seek other means of existence.[35]

The seminarists discussed the benefits of unions, caisses rurales, and cooperatives at length, and these discussions bore fruit. By 1909, twenty-eight rural organizations had been formed in Finistère. Those with the largest membership were located in the Léon and included the Syndicat Agricole du Canton de Daoulas with 586 members and the Syndicat Agricole de Ploudaniel with 783 members.[36] By 1914, there were fifty-six caisses rurales sponsored by the clergy to insure several thousand members in case of fire.[37]

The syndicalist and cooperative movements were regarded favorably by the Church hierarchy, even as a succession of bishops in the diocese of Quimper from the 1890s onward regarded the lower clergy's Christian Democratic sympathies with disapproval and distrust for fear that such sympathies might lead to class warfare.[38]

[33] Ibid.

[34] A.E.Q., 2H312, minutes of the session of 9 May 1899.

[35] Ibid.

[36] A.D. Finistère, 7M78, "Etat de syndicats agricoles, 1909."

[37] *Bulletin mensuel des oeuvres. Diocèse de Quimper et Léon*, no. 10, 14 April 1914, pp. 166–68.

[38] A.D. Finistère, Fonds Trémintin, 104J3, memo on an interview between Monseigneur Duparc, bishop of Quimper, and Pierre Trémintin on 4 July 1913 at Chatel-Guyon, 24 November 1964.

The cours d'oeuvres, a unique course of study founded by abbé Ollivier in 1885, established an avenue through which to disseminate social Catholic ideas as well as to heighten the social consciousness of future priests of the diocese of Finistère. There is no doubt that it helped to train a new leadership and, through attending such gatherings as those at Bourges and Reims, that this leadership served as a conduit between the nation and the region. Moreover, it is no accident that some of the most ardent supporters of the social Catholic movement in the diocese of Quimper were recruited from among the younger clergy and seminarists, who took their message to rural Finistère after they were ordained. Seminaries proved the primary recruiting ground for Christian Democratic militants in France as a whole, but discussions were more often than not held clandestinely and did not have the official blessing of the superior. The ecclesiastical hierarchy in most dioceses was suspicious of independent initiatives taken by the lower clergy. Finistère was no exception, but it was clear to government observers that the bishop, who after 1889 was deliberately selected from among non-Breton candidates, had no authority and power in the diocese. Effective power rested in the hands of the abbés Olliver and Grall, who formed the real clerical leadership in the department. Indeed, the lower clergy's support of social Catholic candidates, according to Louis Hémon, a moderate republican deputy of southern Finistère, revealed their open revolt against the upper clergy and the bishop, which became particularly marked during the legislative elections of 1902.[39]

Without the sponsorship of abbé Ollivier and abbé Grall, it is doubtful that social Catholicism would have spread as rapidly and as successfully among the lower clergy. The government recognized Ollivier's influence over the parish clergy, and local officials attributed this influence to the fact that Ollivier was superior of the seminary of Quimper for fourteen years.[40] His power and authority were regarded with some suspicion, and it appeared that the republican regime was largely responsible for removing him from his position as superior of the seminary in 1893 because they viewed him as a reactionary and recognized the extent of his influence. The prefect of Finistère initiated Ollivier's ouster from the seminary: "My predecessors and myself, we have pointed out to you the hostile attitude of this priest. I believe that the direction he gives to the education of seminarists contributes to a very great extent to the maintenance of the hostile spirit which the government confronts among the clergy of the department. The position of the superior of the seminary gives him a very great influence. These are the considerations that I have already discussed, which led you to make M. Valleau [bishop of the diocese] take the formal step to replace M.

[39] A.D. Finistère, 18J19, Fonds Louis Hémon.
[40] A.N. F¹⁹5620, "Rapport . . . sur l'élection de l'abbé Gayraud," p. 15.

Ollivier as superior of the seminary when he [Valleau] was nominated to the seat of Quimper."[41] The bishop kept his promise to the prefect and suggested the appointment of Ollivier as curé to the parish of Lannilis in the Léon. The prefect was satisfied with this appointment because Lannilis was located in a region where the local population was, in his view, entirely dominated by the parish clergy. Therefore, his presence would be less harmful than if he had been appointed to a "republican" parish.[42]

Although government officials tended to regard Ollivier as an intransigent Catholic conservative who ruled by the sheer force of his personality, Ollivier was among the first zealous supporters of the Ralliement and Rerum Novarum, and his influence over the parish clergy can be attributed more to his successful propagandizing, especially as superior of the seminary of Quimper, than to the forceful imposition of his will.

The appeal of social Catholicism among the younger members of the lower clergy can perhaps be measured in terms of clerical ordinations, which reached a record high between 1898 and 1902—years that coincided with the implantation of a clerically inspired social Catholic movement. In 1899, fifty-six priests were ordained, a greater number than in any single year since the beginning of the Third Republic.[43] The appeal of social Catholicism among the lower clergy of Finistère was complex. The lower clergy undoubtedly believed that the Church's interests would be best served and that they had a greater chance of combatting anticlerical republicanism and socialism if they responded to the social problems that socialists sought to address and moderate republicans often neglected. Many were probably moved by the social plight of the peasantry during the agricultural depression of the 1880s and 1890s. Their commitment to social Catholicism was therefore as much strategic as ideological. But ultimately, the democratic priests in Finistère began to use the electoral arena to promote their cause by employing traditional and new methods of political persuasion, which included the almanac, popular press, and public meeting.

Organizing the Masses

In the dispersed hamlet communities of lower Brittany printed songs and popular almanacs hawked by itinerant *colporteurs* (peddlers) or by the songwriters themselves had long played a crucial role in disseminating

[41] A.N. F¹⁹5006, Letter from the prefect of Finistère to the minister of religious affairs, 27 June 1893.

[42] Ibid.

[43] Girard, "L'évolution quantitative du clergé diocésain de Quimper," pp. 90, 93; Delumeau, ed., *Histoire de la Bretagne*, p. 438.

local and national news. During the nineteenth century these songs told rural communities about the assassination of the duc de Berry, of the *trois glorieuses* of 1830, of the 1839 volcanic eruption in Guadaloupe/ Martinique, of the revolution of 1848, and of the 1859 war in Italy. They also reported the first train accident to occur in France in 1842 and the opening of the road between Quimper and Morlaix, which linked northern and southern Finistère. Charles Chassé has concluded that "it does not appear that a single important [political] event was silenced by our poets . . . whether it was the Revolution of 1789 or the separation of Church and State."[44]

Two Frenchmen and one Englishman emphasized the social and cultural importance of the popular song to the Breton peasantry. Emile Souvestre claimed in 1836 that the song was in essence both a form of literature and journalism: "Active, garrulous, changing like the penny press [presse timbrée], the song runs, flickers . . . and makes the round of the diocese in 3 days."[45] Alfred de Courcy, who visited Lower Brittany in the Restoration, described the way in which the song could be used to raise money for families ruined by fire and that such families, going from farm to farm, would sing of their misfortunes.[46]

Much of this oral tradition was preserved through the good graces of local antiquarians, the most renowned of whom remains a Breton noblemen, Théodore Hersart de la Villarmarqué, whose famous anthology, *Barzaz Breiz*, popularized Lower Brittany's rich oral literature. This tradition was both revitalized and altered significantly by the establishment of a number of important regional printing houses. Brest and Morlaix became the department's publishing centers by the early nineteenth century, though Carhaix, Châteaulin, Landerneau, and Quimper could also boast of flourishing printing businesses. Perhaps the largest of these businesses for the department as a whole, however, were Lefournier and Anmer of Brest and Lédan of Morlaix. All these houses were established toward the end of the eighteenth century, but they did not specialize in the publication of Breton works on a large scale until the nineteenth.

The Lefournier house, situated in the port city of Brest, was one of the most important regional publishers of literary, popular, and religious works after the French Revolution. Lefournier, for example, was responsible for publishing the influential and popular *Istor Breiz ou histoire populaire de la Bretagne par une Fille du Saint-Esprit*. The book, published in 1868, went through four editions by 1893. The bilingual text by Anne de Jésus, a member of one of the largest female congregations in Finistère, the

[44] Preface to Ollivier, *Catalogue bibliographique de la chanson populaire bretonne*, p. xl.
[45] Cited in ibid., p. xxxvii.
[46] Cited in ibid.

Filles du Saint-Esprit, represented a relatively early attempt to record and disseminate local customs and culture by the local clergy. Destined for a rural readership, this 868-page tract brought together the history of the peninsula from its alleged Druidic past to the Napoleonic Empire in the form of thirty-six *veillées* (stories).[47] *Istor Breiz* was not without polemical purpose, however; ten of the veillées concern the religious persecution of the French Revolution, thereby demonstrating the ways in which a popular text could be used with political intent.

Alexandre-Louis-Marie Lédan, born the son of a shoemaker in Morlaix in 1777, became the most enthusiastic publisher of Breton works by launching an enterprise to publish popular songs on loose sheets that could be sold by songwriters or colporteurs for a sou in the surrounding countryside. Indeed, owing largely to his ardent interest in Breton titles, the nineteenth century became the golden age of the *chanson populaire bretonne sur feuilles volantes*.[48]

In 1854, Thomas Price wrote that in his travels through Brittany he witnessed "numerous peasants, speaking Breton" coming to the local printer and bookseller, a certain Monsieur Lédan, in Morlaix to buy a number of these small tracts: "M. Lédan assured me that Breton peasants were more disposed to develop their taste for reading than the same category of persons in France [as a whole]."[49] The Breton poet Angela Duval has confirmed that this practice continued into the twentieth century. On Sunday afternoons, members of her parish went visiting and memorized the songs that had been bought from traveling peddlers who sold them as loose sheets at markets.[50]

Most of these tracts consisted of songs printed by the local presses, composed by itinerant singers, and sold by the singers themselves or colporteurs in the region. During the first third of the nineteenth century Finistère witnessed a veritable proliferation in the number of songs printed on loose sheets by local publishers, most of which were concentrated in northern Finistère.[51] Although many of these songs were purchased in market centers throughout the department, they were also sung by the composers themselves who made rounds of the department, visiting pardons, fairs, and markets. These singers and peddlers came from a variety of social milieus. Records maintained by the prefecture of Finistère indicate that the majority of colporteurs in Finistère during the nineteenth century

---

[47] The French text is complemented on facing pages by a Breton version. De Jésus, *Istor Breiz*.

[48] Cited in Girauden, "Chanteurs populaires," p. 415.

[49] Cited in ibid., p. 416.

[50] Anjela Duval, "Ma vie," ed. Christian Brunel, in *Changer de monde*, Tud Ha Bro, no. 7 (1981): 10

[51] Ollivier, *Catalogue bibliographique de la chanson populaire bretonne*.

submitted requests to sell songs.[52] Only toward the end of the nineteenth century did newspapers assume an equally important place in their business. These colporteurs included protestant preachers, schoolteachers, farmers, tailors, carpenters, weavers, soldiers, and a considerable number of blind men and women who told their tales, performed their songs, and sold their sheets. Perhaps the most notorious peddler and traveling singer at the end of the nineteenth century was Marie Kastellin, immortalized in photographs while seated in her makeshift dogcart.

The rich store of popular printed songs has largely disappeared, but those that have survived[53]—most of which were printed by the Lédan house of Morlaix—suggest that they covered a wide range of subjects: farewell odes of conscript soldiers; sensational crimes; stories of infanticide; supernatural apparitions; duels; betrayals; and tragic love affairs. Many provided practical, scientific information concerning disease and hygiene. For example, "Cholera morbus and the means to protect oneself as much as possible," a song consisting of forty-eight couplets, was published in 1832 in Morlaix.[54] Songs told of miraculous events from as far away as Lourdes, Auray, and La Salette. They documented the healing of Jeanne Bescon of paralysis at Auray and the resurrection of the child of a merchant who was allegedly eaten by a pig while in the care of a wet nurse. An increasing number of songs, however, particularly those printed by local printing houses from the 1820s onward, concerned national events, local politics, and news in brief.

Before the advent of the printing press, then, popular songs peddled at fairs, markets, and pardons spread local scandals, national news, and political messages in the countryside.[55] No doubt songs helped to shape local awareness of national events. Lédan and other houses popularized the military exploits of Napoleon as early as 1806 and provided news of events in Paris in 1835.[56] In 1849, Desmoulins of Landerneau printed a song that

[52] A.D. Finistère, 2T78.

[53] Although a considerable portion of the Bibliothèque Nationale's collection of *chansons sur feuilles volantes* has disappeared, a number remain in two cartons that are numbered Yn1–512. Moreover, the BN's manuscript section contains handwritten songs (with French translations) from various regions of France in *nouvelles acquisitions françaises*, ms. 3342. The municipal libraries of Quimper, Brest, and Morlaix also house collections.

[54] This practical advice, which made its rounds in Finistère, contrasts sharply with Souvestre's portrayal of the ignorant, fearful peasantry in the grips of the cholera epidemic, who attribute earthly disaster to divine intervention and who only sought divine solutions. Cited in Berger, *Peasants Against Politics*, p. 34.

[55] Charles Chassé, preface to Ollivier, *Catalogue bibliographique*, p. xc.

[56] "Detaill ha circonstanzço remer . . . an impar campagn . . . Napoleon" (Morlaix, 1806); "Detaill demeus an torfet euzus coumettet e Paris an 28 eus a vis gouere 1835" (Morlaix, 1835). In 1840, Lédan, who was an ardent admirer of Napoleon, printed a eulogy on the death of his hero.

essentially served as advice to electors, and a printer in Brest sold a song that warned against the evils of communism and socialism.[57] Indeed, in the 1840s during his travels through Brittany Anthony Trollope talked with a colporteur who told him that images and "objects of fine art are life's most noble attraction, and those who distribute them are the most powerful agents of civilization."[58]

By the Third Republic the popular Breton song assumed more distinct political forms. As early as 1874, the prefect of Finistère, recognizing the political significance of the popular song and almanac, sought ways to require publishers to submit translations of their tracts. Laws governing colportage and the press did not, however, explicitly address the issue and the printed song so that Breton language publications continued to proliferate.[59] Popular composers of all political shades used the song as a vehicle of political expression both to lambaste individuals and to proselytize their cause. At the height of local struggles over the secularization of educational institutions in the department, songs became broadsides against the national assembly itself:

Je vois bien de gens dans l'embarras,
surtout dans mon pays;
ils sont à se tourmenter l'esprit
pour essayer de comprendre les décrets;
mais jamais cela n'arrivera;
ni dans ce pays ni dans aucun autre,
si on ne sait comment est composée
l'Assemblée Nationale.
On a d'abord choisi
dans tout le Royaume
en ville aussi bien que dans les campagnes
les hommes les plus insolents, les plus affrontés
hommes sans raison, sans religion, sans éducation
s'ils savaient parler.[60]

---

[57] "Instruction var an electionou" (Landerneau, 1849); "Canaouen var zujed ar communiset ac ar zocialistet" (Morlaix, 1850).

[58] Quoted in Michael Burns, *Rural Society and Politics*, p. 80.

[59] The government attempted to get around this situation with the following arguments: "il n'est pas possible que l'administration accorde l'estampille à des écrits dont elle ne connaitront pas le contenu." A.D. Finistère, 2T73, letter from the Service de la Presse et du colportage to the prefect of Finistère, 18 November 1874.

[60] The manuscript collection of the Bibliothèque Nationale contains a rich store of songs from various regions of France, including Brittany and the Basque region, that were collected and translated by an anonymous translator. Fr. nouv. Acq. 3342, chanson 418, "L'Assemblée Nationale," dictated in Plouaret.

Songs, which became an important vehicle of right- and left-wing political expression, also found their way into almanacs that were published in Breton and French throughout the nineteenth century. The almanac comprised a medley of different elements that included songs, train timetables, schedules of fairs and market days, meteorological predictions, practical agricultural advice, stories, and events of local and national history. The almanac was particularly popular in rural areas in the eighteenth and nineteenth centuries, and as Lise Andries has recently suggested, it was also used for ideological purposes by the Jacobin Left during the French Revolution.[61]

At the end of the nineteenth century political groupings in both Paris and the provinces increasingly came to capitalize on the pervasiveness of these popular tracts in the countryside. In 1889 the bilingual *Almanach breton-français: An den honest* announced that the "sole aim of this publication is to show to all the necessity of appointing Christian deputies, *conseillers généraux*, mayors, and municipal councillors."[62] It appealed to "Breton mothers" and "Christian wives" to use their influence in favor of "traditions of faith and honor" by opposing the nefarious influence of the republican state. The almanac accused the new society and *nouvelles couches sociales*, extolled by republicans like Gambetta, of having the utmost contempt for the peasantry and promised to show the ways in which the political changes in Paris affected property, faith, and the family.[63]

These political charges were not lost on republican groups who answered in kind. The Morlaix publishing house issued a republican bilingual almanac that sold 5,000 copies in fifteen days.[64] *The Almanach de Léon et de Cornouaille: Gallek ha Brezonek* of 1884 featured an essay on the death of the legitimist Comte de Chambord; it claimed that monarchists were now "bodies without heads": "The Republic can sleep peacefully. . . . Let us learn to keep the Republic, which is our own sovereignty, well, and let us mock the monarchists with their kings and pretenders."[65] The almanac, which is only incompletely preserved in the department of Finistère's *dépôt légal*, was published from the 1870s to the 1890s, but its format and scope changed significantly in these years. It continued to provide advice on elections to the Senate and the Chamber of Deputies as well as brief summaries of "what the republic has done for Finistère."[66] Initially the almanac featured a calvaire and parish church on its cover, but by the early 1890s this religious imagery disappeared, even though

---

[61] Andries, "Almanacs," pp. 203–22.

[62] *Almanach breton-français: An den honest* (1889), p. 16.

[63] "Les prétendus démocrates manifestent un grand dédain pour le paysan." Ibid., p. 53.

[64] Ollivier, *Catalogue de la chanson populaire breton*, p. 424.

[65] *Almanach de Léon et de Cornouaille: Gallek ha Brezonek* (Morlaix, 1884), p. 42.

[66] Ibid., pp. 66–72.

the publication continued to draw on the conventions of the popular song, including the *disput*, which figures prominently in the loose-sheet songs printed by Lédan:

> YAN—Ce qui est le pis, c'est que les prêtres, du moins, beaucoup d'entre eux sont toujours aussi acharnés contre la République. Ils disent partout qu'elle est l'ennemie de la religion.
> ALAIN—Ce sont ces prêtres-là qui sont les plus grands ennemis de la religion.[67]

The ideological war between almanacs was played out with fierce intensity in the 1880s in right-wing publications that included *Almanach royaliste des départements de l'Ouest par un ami du peuple, Mon Almanach* (printed by La Croix's Maison de bonne presse) as well as in republican almanacs that included the Parisian *Almanach républicain électoral illustré* destined for a readership in the provinces. As a subsequent chapter suggests, by the early 1900s, the social Catholic movement itself began to appropriate both song and almanac for their own political uses in an increasingly strident war of words.

The Catholic press, like the almanac and popular song, had long played a significant role in local politics, but until the 1890s it was synonymous with the royalist press. This press had to a large extent been directed by the *Comité Royaliste du Finistère* and in the late 1880s included *Feiz Ha Breiz*, a weekly newspaper written entirely in Breton that was founded in 1865, *L'Union Monarchique du Finistère, La Résistance-Croix de Morlaix, L'Océan*, perhaps the longest living Catholic royalist newspaper, first established in June 1848, *L'Etoile de la Mer*, and *Courrier du Finistère*, both of which began to appear in 1880. However, the Catholic press of Finistère gradually came to endorse the clergy's repudiation of royalism, and, in the late 1890s, the *Courrier du Finistère* ousted partisans of the royalist cause from its ranks after bitter struggle.

The history of the *Courrier du Finistère* illustrates the complicated struggle that led to an independent and highly successful Catholic press in the department and to the creation of a cohesive social Catholic political organization. In fact, the *Courrier du Finistère*, which was essentially directed to a rural readership, became one of the most widely distributed newspapers in the department in the late 1890s.[68]

In January 1880, the first edition of the weekly newspaper, *Courrier du Finistère*, appeared under the editorship of Hippolyte Chavanon, an ardent royalist who also edited *L'Océan*. A close association existed between the newspapers, and in 1885 the latter was purchased by the former. When Chavanon stepped down for reasons of health in 1890, it seemed only

---

[67] *Almanach de Léon et de Cornouaille: Gallek ha Brezonek* (Morlaix, 1885), p. 40.
[68] Veillard, "Un hebdomadaire à la fin du XIX siècle," p. 65.

natural that the editor of *L'Océan*, Ambroise Dumont, should succeed him. A year later, the *Société anonyme de l'Océan* decided to discontinue publication of the rapidly declining *L'Océan* and to create instead a sister publication for the primarily northern *Courrier du Finistère*. Thus, for the southern portion of the department the *Courrier de la Cornouaille* was born. Both publications were now headed by Dumont, a fervent Catholic and an even more ardent royalist.[69]

In the early 1890s dissension began to surface within the Société anonyme de l'Océan regarding the political orientation of the newspapers. In particular, abbé Ollivier and abbé Grall could hardly conceal their growing disenchantment with legitimism, which led to a number of clashes between Dumont and the influential abbés and finally to the dismissal of Dumont in 1895, a date that marked the newspaper's abandonment of legitimism.

In 1892, Dumont published a defamatory article about schoolteachers in the department, which led to assessing considerable damages against the newspaper. This antagonized shareholders of royalist persuasion as well as *ralliés*, including the abbés Ollivier and Grall. Two years later Dumont sent a telegram of condolence on behalf of the *Courrier du Finistère* to the family of the comte de Paris, which further irritated his associates.[70]

On 3 April 1895, the rallié contingent of the board organized a secret meeting, from which Dumont was excluded, and at which abbé Grall was elected president of the Société Anonyme de la Presse Catholique du Finistère. Despite the secrecy of the meeting, the prefect came to hear of it, objected to a cleric assuming such a role, and presented a formal protest to the bishop in which he requested that Grall be asked to step down. Grall did resign, but only in name: The new president, a M. Caroff, was a notable from Grall's parish of Ploudalmézeau.[71] Dumont was then asked to submit his resignation; when he refused, he was expelled from the newspaper's offices.[72]

Henri de Trémauden became the new editor of the *Courrier*. De Trémauden had been a journalist with *L'Indépendence Bretonne*, but he left the newspaper when the editorial board would not declare its support for the Ralliement. Following de Trémauden's appointment to the *Courrier*, all references to the reestablishment of the Bourbon monarchy and to royalism disappeared. The *Courrier du Finistère* began to focus on defense of the Church, but it did not attack the Republic per se.[73]

---

[69] Raoul, *Un siècle du journalisme breton*, p. 219.
[70] Ibid., p. 220.
[71] Ibid.
[72] Veillard, "Un hebdomadaire à la fin du XIX siècle," p. 64.
[73] Raoul, *Un siècle du journalisme breton*, p. 221.

The new orientation in the Catholic press was reflected in the proliferation of parish bulletins throughout the department in the late 1880s and early 1890s. Although they did not explicitly deal with political issues, the social question was a major focus, as they encouraged the formation of caisses d'assurances, unions, and cooperatives. One of the most successful bulletins of this kind in terms of its circulation and longevity was the *Kannad ar Galoun Zakr a Jezuz*, a Breton language version of the *Messager du Sacre Coeur de Jesus*, under the editorship of abbé Grall, curé of Ploudalmézeau. The bulletin was founded in 1888 and ceased publication in 1951. By 1913, the circulation of the bulletin exceeded seven thousand.[74]

By 1897 the nascent social Catholic movement had an effective organizational network in place in the form of the parish and press organization, the Société Anonyme de la Presse Catholique du Finistère, which published the *Courrier du Finistère*. The abbés Ollivier and Grall, spokesmen for the lower clergy of the Léon, were instrumental in using the Catholic press and political organization to proselytize the social Catholic cause in defiance of the bishop. Ollivier and Grall, however, were not simply generals directing soldiers to march. They acted as political leaders, recognizing the importance of propaganda and political persuasion.

In addition to the popular press and more traditional channels of social communication, including song and almanac, the social Catholic leadership used the new medium of the open meeting, as opposed to private gatherings, as a forum in which to garner support. When Paul Rosec, the curé of Pleyben, held a Catholic republican meeting in preparation for the 1894 elections, he invited the participants to subscribe to the *Courrier de la Cornouaille*, which the prefect characterized as a "clerical newspaper" that attacked the government, administration, and republicans.[75] The press, and more particularly the Société Anonyme de la Presse Catholique du Finistère, stood at the center of the organization of public meetings. The Société Anonyme de la Presse Catholique du Finistère, which represented a newly coordinated popular press, was formed in 1895, becoming the principal organization that selected, endorsed, and actively campaigned for social Catholic candidates. The Sociète Anonyme de la Presse Catholique du Finistère, abbé Ollivier, and abbé Grall organized a Catholic congress resembling those held at Bourges and Reims in Finistère in 1896 and popularized the movement beyond the confines of the seminary. Local officials initially claimed that the congress of Landerneau had little effect on the public and passed virtually unnoticed. A police official in Landerneau, who attended the congress, informed the prefect that far from having the

---

[74] Ibid., pp. 282–83.
[75] A.N. F¹⁹5627, report from the prefect of Finistère to the minister of religious affairs, 20 July 1893.

"optimism" of "certain men and certain newspapers who loudly proclaim that all these institutions signify nothing" and that the clergy's initiatives were "worthy of scorn, the impression made on me by what I saw, heard, and perfectly understood, was that at the present hour the so-called Christian democrats are in the process of overhauling the country and that they have already won to their cause more than 100,000 individuals."[76] The police official characterized the leaders of the movement as practical men, who "know the aspirations of the masses."[77] Those who participated in debates at the congress came from various parts of Brittany and as far away as Paris and the Nord. The program of the congress, almost identical to the yearly agenda of the cours d'oeuvres, included discussions of patronages, caisses rurales, and the agricultural crisis. The political motives behind such a conference were clearly reflected in a speech by chanoine Dulong du Rosnay of Morlaix: "If we want the numerous class to adopt our ideas and to do something for us, it is first necessary to do something for it. Let us speak to them of their needs, let us render them services, let us organize conferences . . . and we are certain to succeed."[78]

Popular Politics at the Periphery

In 1894 and again in 1897 the political calm that had characterized local politics and the deep cultural and political isolation of the region were breached by the election of two social Catholic candidates sponsored by the lower clergy. Prior to 1894 the clergy and the nobility in Finistère carefully managed elections that were conducted in an atmosphere of political consensus. Prefects and local officials assigned to the department frequently commented on the political apathy of the local populace who unquestioningly followed the directives of a royalist nobility and clergy. The subprefect of Morlaix described this indifference in a way that echoed the appraisals of subprefects of the other arrondissements in the department: "The population, in general, would concern itself little with politics, and thanks to its somewhat fatalistic temperament, would willingly accommodate itself to any form of government if the aristocracy and the clergy did not use all legal and extralegal means to pit them against the republican regime, which they [the aristocracy and the clergy] can neither dominate nor exploit."[79]

---

[76] A.D. Finistère, 1V40, police report from Landerneau to the prefect of Finistère, 13 September 1896.

[77] Ibid.

[78] Ibid.

[79] A.D. Finistère, 1M136, memorandum from the subprefect of Morlaix to the prefect of Finistère, 30 April 1889.

Prior to 1894, the transitions from one regime to another in the nineteenth century were hardly felt, in contrast to central and southern France. Nonetheless Finistère exhibited some original political characteristics in the nineteenth century that pointed to a greater degree of political awareness and heterogeneity than was generally supposed.

Finistère was one of the few rural regions in France that did not vote for Bonaparte in December 1848; it preferred the republican General Cavaignac.[80] Moreover, certain political developments that occurred during the Second Republic revealed strains in the alleged untroubled fabric of rural politics. In March 1849, the subprefect of Brest forwarded a petition from the Committee of Rural Populations from the Arrondissements of Brest and Morlaix; it demanded the independence of the Church, freedom of religion and education, the lowering of taxes, administrative decentralization, and the development of agriculture. The committee consisted largely of peasant landowners from Julot communes in the Léon, and the subprefect claimed that many viewed this committee as a direct challenge to royalist groupings in northern Finistère and as an attempt on the part of the countryside to free itself from the exclusive leadership of the "comités des villes et des Messieurs."[81] Although royalism was strong in the department in the nineteenth century, the formation of such a committee during the Second Republic revealed the subterranean tension between the local nobility and a prosperous landowning peasantry.

In the 1870s, southern Finistère, "the cradle of republican Brittany,"[82] began to support moderate anticlerical republicans and continued to elect moderates on the Left through the 1880s, 1890s, and early 1900s. Similarly, the Monts d'Arées, the rugged mountainous region separating southern Finistère (Cornouaille) from the north (Léon), elected moderate and radical republicans during the early Third Republic. However, rural areas of northern Finistère, with the exception of the first electoral district of Morlaix, remained firmly in the hands of royalist deputies until the 1890s.

Northern Finistère was a bastion of royalism during the early Third Republic. The royalist party, the party of the nobility, which, after the death of the Comte de Chambord, was reorganized in the department under the aegis of de Kermenguy (president), Boucher (conseiller général of Landerneau), and de Chamaillard (a lawyer from Quimper), by all accounts owed its strength to the influence of the parish clergy. After the legislative elections of 1885, which returned many conservative candidates in France as a whole, the prefect of Finistère wrote to the minister of the interior that

---

[80] Cloître, "Aspects de la vie politique," pp. 746, 754.
[81] Ibid., p. 761.
[82] Siegfried, *Tableau politique de la France de l'Ouest*, p. 164.

reactionary committees were being formed in each arrondissement in the department, though it was almost "superfluous to create such an organization in Finistère" because "the true royalist association, that exercises its action in the smallest hamlet, is the clergy."[83]

In an area where the nobility lacked significant economic influence to promote royalism among the peasantry of the region by themselves, they had to rely on the influence of the clergy to advance their cause. Popular support for royalism was in fact rather tepid during the early Third Republic. In 1887, the prefect of Quimper reported that the passage of the Comte de Paris, heir to the French throne, through Brittany to Jersey "elicited no emotion in Finistère."[84] If his intention was to stir up the ardor of his supporters, then he "obtained no result." Those who turned out for the occasion were nobles of royalist conviction. According to the prefect, the absence of the Breton peasantry showed they were hardly "disposed to encourage the pretender's visits,"[85] and local reaction to the death of the Comte de Paris in 1894 seemed to confirm the prefect's impressions. The subprefect of Morlaix reported that only a few people, primarily nobles in the countryside surrounding Morlaix and Saint-Pol-de-Léon, mourned the death of the royalist incumbent.[86]

In 1893, the second electoral district of Morlaix in northern Finistère was represented by Emile de Kermenguy, an eighty-three-year-old royalist nobleman who had been deputy since the advent of the Third Republic in 1871 and, according to government officials, was "supported by the clergy and the great landowners."[87] The second electoral district of Brest was represented by Emile Villiers, a large landowner, who was viewed as a "reactionary with liberal tendencies."[88] Monseigneur d'Hulst, a cleric, represented the third electoral district of Brest and was supported by the clergy and the landed nobility in an area that the government viewed as "fanatically religious."[89] Although d'Hulst was a royalist, André Siegfried has characterized this district as a "clerical democracy": The parish clergy had chosen candidates for election in the district since 1881 when they supported d'Hulst's predecessor, Monseigneur Freppel, bishop of Angers, who was also an ardent legitimist.[90]

---

[83] A.D. Finistère, 1M229, memorandum from the prefect of Finistère to the minister of the interior, 4 April 1886.

[84] A.D. Finistére, 1M229, memorandum from the prefect of Finistère to the minister of the interior, 5 July 1887.

[85] Ibid.

[86] A.D. Finistère, 1M136, memorandum from the subprefect of Morlaix to the prefect, 1 October 1894.

[87] A.D. Finistère, 3M287, electoral notes, 20 August–3 September legislative election, 1893.

[88] Ibid.

[89] Ibid.

[90] Siegfried, *Tableau politique de la France de L'Ouest*, p. 194.

In 1893, the comte de Kermenguy, president of the royalist party of Finistère and deputy of the second arrondissement of Morlaix, died suddenly. For the first time, however, the lower clergy of northern Finistère chose not to sponsor a royalist candidate but rather to support Albert de Mun, who declared his allegiance to the Republic and was well-known for his social Catholic sympathies. Three years later, the lower clergy again backed a social Catholic republican candidate, abbé Hippolyte Gayraud, in the third electoral district of Brest, breaking an alliance with the nobility that had effectively been forged in 1793. These elections attracted the attention of the national press because in most areas of France the alliance between the clergy and the nobility remained firm, despite Pope Leo XIII's promulgation of Au Milieu des Sollicitudes, which encouraged French Catholics to rally to the Republic.

The election of Albert de Mun marked a turning point in the political evolution of Finistère and indicated the ways in which the clergy grafted new political practices and ideologies onto older political traditions—the effect of which was to democratize the electoral arena and to construct a bridge between national politics and a *politique du clocher*.

In the early 1880s, the newly established republican government had sought to promote policies of national integration and to reduce the clergy—their time-honored enemies—to political impotence. The principal strategy used by the government was the policy of laicization in education because, absent such a policy, it was in Catholic-dominated educational institutions that future citizens of the Republic would be educated.

The Breton clergy and members of religious congregations, who occupied a large number of teaching posts and who controlled most educational institutions in Lower Brittany in the 1880s, fought bitterly against the *écoles sans Dieu* and made the church-state conflict the key political issue on which elections turned in the department before the advent of the social Catholic movement in the 1890s.

In the early 1890s the clergy began to broaden the basis of their criticism of the republican government, however, and pointed to the latter's inability to deal with the agricultural crisis. In the 1880s and 1890s France suffered from a severe economic depression that afflicted agriculture as well as industry. Foreign competition from Latin America, Australia, the United States, and Russia threatened the livelihood of wheat producers. Dairy produce from Denmark and the Netherlands affected the demand for French production, and the winegrowers of the south were not only facing disaster as a result of the phylloxera epidemic that destroyed half the vineyards in southern France, but Spanish and Italian viticulture began to compete more successfully with the French industry. The government seemed unable to deal with the crisis in the 1880s, at least until the National Assembly passed the Méline tariff in 1892, a protectionist measure that ultimately raised agricultural prices that had fallen as a result of the crisis. Nonetheless, French agriculture did not fully recover from the economic downturn until the early twentieth century.[91]

Existing agricultural institutions attempted to deal with the crisis, and conferences were held throughout France, including Finistère.[92] These efforts yielded little, and the problem as a whole became a volatile political issue in most affected areas of France. According to government officials in Finistère, the clerical party began to capitalize on this issue and delivered a two-pronged attack on the anticlerical policies of the republican regime as well as on its apparent inability to deal with the problems of French agriculture. On 4 June 1893, for example, the priest of Pleyben organized a meeting whose goal was to defend "agricultural and religious interests" in the 1894 elections.

When the seat of the comte de Kermenguy, royalist deputy of Finistère, became vacant in 1893, the lower clergy of northern Finistère proposed the candidacy of Albert de Mun at a meeting comprising local notables and priests on 5 January 1894. About one hundred priests from the district attended the meeting. The comte de Mun's candidacy was suggested by one of the most distinguished clergymen in the Léon, the curé of Saint-Pol-de-Léon. The curé argued that de Mun would make an excellent choice because he was a talented orator and would "through his votes . . . and words defend our religious faith and our mother church."[93] For the subprefect of Morlaix, who had received reports of the meeting, this declaration was a clear indication that de Mun was the "official candidate of the clergy."[94]

Albert de Mun's nomination was bitterly opposed by the local nobility. Though once a royalist deputy who represented Pontivy in the lower Breton department of Morbihan, he later renounced his legitimism, and his social Catholic views were deemed revolutionary. De Mun was no radical, but in 1888 had attempted to form a Catholic party free from all attachments to royalism and modeled on the German Center party. The local nobility of Finistère distrusted and even scorned him, despite his aristocratic lineage. The comte de Nanteuil claimed in the royalist *Gazette de France* that de Mun had come to Brittany to "preach *jacquerie* under the pretext of bringing us solutions to the social question."[95]

[91] Agulhon et al., *Apogée et crise de la civilisation paysanne*, pp. 387–413. It may be argued that the depression had more disastrous effects in Brittany than in northeastern France because falling agricultural prices did not result in a decrease in land values and rents. They in fact increased by 18 percent in Finistère between 1879 and 1912, which created additional difficulties for the peasant farmer; see p. 403.

[92] Le Roux, *Conférences sur la crise agricole*.

[93] A.D. Finistère, 1V69, memorandum from the subprefect of Morlaix to the prefect, 21 January 1894.

[94] Ibid.

[95] *Gazette de France*, 20 December 1893.

De Mun arrived in Saint-Pol-de-Léon to begin his electoral campaign on 7 January 1894. He traveled to all thirty one communes comprising the second electoral district of Morlaix and received zealous assistance from the parish clergy. In Santec, Roscoff, and Carantec, the desservant rented the hall where de Mun introduced himself to voters. In Locquénolé, the *vicaire* signed the invitations to the electoral meeting. The responsibility for putting up posters and distributing electoral brochures and photographs of the candidate was assumed in most of the communes by the parish clergy. The presbyteries received packets of newspapers from the editorial offices of the *Courrier du Finistère*, which endorsed de Mun, for distribution after Sunday mass.[96] Many of de Mun's supporters allegedly resorted to giving money to electors. The mayor of the republican commune of Sibiril claimed that more than ten people were bribed in the commune.[97]

The nobility of the region feared that de Mun was quite simply a socialist. The republican newspaper, *L'Union agricole et maritime*, perhaps wishing to discredit de Mun in the eyes of both the Right and the Left, argued that the conservatives of Finistère had "chosen a *socialist* as a candidate . . . that de Mun embellishes his socialism with the title *Christian*. . . . It is still socialism . . . like the deputy Jaurés, M. De Mun is a partisan of agrarian socialism."[98] The nobility of Finistére accused de Mun of bringing only firebrand speeches as solutions to the social question, even though noble proprietors in the region let their land at low rents and used a considerable portion of their income to transform the notorious Breton hovel into a comfortable home.[99]

De Mun and the clergy who supported him did not openly attack or challenge the nobility. On the contrary, they actively tried to solicit their support and goodwill. To this extent, de Mun's electoral tactics did not break with tradition. Messager, the curé of Saint-Pol-de-Léon who promoted de Mun's candidacy, worked hard to reconcile the Catholic party with the party of the nobility, and, according to a police official from Morlaix, used all the influence he had to persuade the father of the mayor of Saint-Pol-de-Léon, the comte de Guébriant, whom the nobility preferred as a successor to de Kermenguy, to accept de Mun's candidacy.[100] After a *visite de politesse* at de Guebriant's home, the château de Kerneven in Saint-Pol-de-Léon, de Mun told Messager that he had not been satisfied

[96] A.D. Finistère, 1V69, memorandum from the subprefect of Brest to the prefect, 21 January 1894.

[97] Ibid.

[98] *L'Union Agricole et Maritime*, 19 January 1894.

[99] *Gazette de France*, 20 December 1893.

[100] A.D. Finistère, 1V69, report from the commissaire de police of Morlaix to the subprefect of Morlaix, 27 January 1894.

with the meeting and that de Guébriant had refused to give him his support.[101] Messager allegedly promised that these difficulties would be resolved, and within two days de Guébriant promised to endorse de Mun.[102]
The royalist party did not in fact propose an alternative candidate, and de
Mun ran against a republican adversary.

The *Résistance de Morlaix*, the "royalist/Catholic" newspaper founded
in 1885, supported de Mun from the beginning of the campaign, despite
his repudiation of royalism. Following the election it intended to publish a
speech that de Mun had given several months earlier and in which he
accused the nobility and large landowners of being hostile to Christian
Socialism, but before the article appeared, the printer considered it best to
send the proofs to Messager, curé of Saint-Pol-de-Léon, to strike out the
passages of de Mun's speech that he thought might be offensive to the local
nobility.[103]

The results of the election of 21 January 1894 demonstrated a relatively
high rate of abstention, and a not insignificant number of votes were given
to de Mun's republican adversary, Caill, a landowner and mayor of the
commune of Plouzévédé (Table 4.1). Despite the clergy's efforts, de Mun
did not win as resounding a victory as his royalist predecessor who won the
previous legislative election by 8,849 votes. Nonetheless, a higher proportion of the electorate voted in the 1894 by-election than in the general
election of 1893. This discrepancy may in part be explained by either
parish rivalries or the fact that de Mun was not native to a region where
local ties, as government observers and politicians readily pointed out,
were of such importance, particularly during the early Third Republic. In
1898, however, de Mun had enough support to win a clear victory, obtaining 12,080 votes, whereas his opponent won only 1,555.[104]

The electoral campaign of 1894 in the second district of Morlaix did not
signify a radical change in electoral strategies and tactics, even though it
represented an important change in the clergy's political sympathies.
Meetings held by de Mun in the communes comprising the electoral district were carefully organized private affairs, by invitation only, and were
attended primarily by the local notables. The election, however, revealed a
profound, though concealed, rift within the Right. The subprefect of Morlaix claimed that the legislative election of January 1894 in the arrondissement "has accentuated the already acknowledged division . . . between the
clerical party and the conservative party. Despite appearances, the latter
retains a considerable influence in the second district. The clericals only

---

[101] Ibid.
[102] Ibid.
[103] Ibid.
[104] A.D. Finistère, 3M294.

TABLE 4.1
Results of 21 January 1894 Election in the Second Electoral District
of Morlaix

Canton	Registered Voters	No. of Voters	Caill	de Mun
Landivisiau	3,673	2,940	928	1,994
Plouescat	2,989	2,443	961	1,462
Plouzévédé	3,272	2,620	1,388	1,226
St-Pol-de-Léon	5,321	4,237	1,989	2,228
Taulé	2,698	1,875	619	1,244
Total	17,953	14,115	5,885 (42%)	8,154 (58%)

Source: A.D. Finistère, 3M290.

triumphed in a modest way: the republicans are satisfied with the result."[105]

The victory of de Mun in 1894 heralded the initial decline of royalism as a significant political force in the department and the beginning of the conversion of the region to Christian democracy. However, the populist nature of the movement did not become evident until the election of abbé Gayraud in 1897 in the neighboring arrondissement of Brest. Within three years a more efficient social Catholic electoral organization was in place making new tactical choices.

The Election of Abbé Gayraud and "Class War"

Monseigneur d'Hulst, who had been elected deputy of the third electoral district of Brest as a royalist, did not share the local clergy's new enthusiasm for republican values or institutions. He complained to a friend that the clergy was completely caught up in Catholic republicanism: "Without paying [any] attention to my Orleanist attachments, they have only wanted to see the priest in me and have hoisted me like a flag against the pretensions of royalist nobles."[106]

[105] A.D. Finistère, 1M136, report from the subprefect of Morlaix to the prefect, 30 January 1894.

[106] Quoted in Queré, "L'élection de l'abbé Gayraud," Diplôme d'Etudes Supérieures, Université de Paris IV, 1965, p. 48.

When Monseigneur d'Hulst died in 1896, the clergy made sure to endorse a candidate with Catholic republican views to assume d'Hulst's place. On 10 December 1896 de Trémauden, editor of the *Courrier du Finistère*, sent abbé Gayraud in Paris a telegram asking him if he would be willing to stand as candidate in the third district of Brest. Abbé Gayraud was a Dominican priest from southern France who had taken an active part in the Catholic congress of Reims and who was known for his Christian democratic sympathies. A few days later he received a letter from abbé Ollivier reaffirming the proposal.[107]

According to Gayraud, before he was actually endorsed as candidate by an important group of electors in the Léon, there were acrimonious debates (*tiraillements*) among the clergy, peasants from the district, and rich landowners regarding his nomination.[108] Monseigneur Cabrières, the bishop of Montpellier, had initially been asked to stand as candidate in the district, but when he would not renounce his royalist convictions, an influential segment of the clergy would not accept him as candidate.[109] During the early months of 1897 abbé Ollivier went to Montpellier to try to persuade Monseigneur Cabrières to run as a Catholic republican candidate because there was some opposition to Gayraud.[110] E. de Poulpiquet, a conseiller général, testified that abbé Grall made it known to Cabrières that he would not be accepted as a candidate by the clergy of the Léon unless he demonstrated his sympathy for the Republic. De Cabrières flatly refused. On 9 January a "congress" of Catholic priests was held in abbé Ollivier's parish of Lannilis where abbé Gayraud was chosen to stand as candidate by a majority of only two votes, and on 11 January a second assembly was held to confirm this choice. Approximately eight hundred people, forty of whom were priests, attended the meeting, and the rest consisted of local delegates. According to Gayraud, a considerable number of those who attended did not wish to accept a stranger.[111]

The lower clergy of a predominantly rural electoral district sponsored abbé Gayraud, as they did Albert de Mun, but the electoral tactics they used differed significantly from those used by de Mun's supporters in the second district of Morlaix in 1894. Gayraud, like de Mun, toured the countryside to introduce himself to the electorate, but he tended, unlike de Mun, to hold public rather than private meetings, thus democratizing the rules of the traditional electoral game, which previously was decided among rural elites. On 14 January 1897, Gayraud invited his opponent,

---

[107] A.N. F¹⁹5620, "Rapport fait au nom de la commission chargée à procéder à une enquête sur l'election de l'abbé Gayraud," pp. 90–93.
[108] Ibid.
[109] Ibid.
[110] Ibid., p. 167.
[111] Ibid.

the comte de Blois, a royalist, to participate in debates in Saint-Renan on 16 January, in Ploudalmézeau on 17, and in Lesneven on 18. Blois replied that he saw no reason to "overexcite" the voters and that it was more desirable to state one's position dispassionately in a printed "profession de foi."[112]

The comte de Blois had announced his profession de foi on 10 January 1897, declaring himself to be a "man of the region" and a defender of the faith who, like those who had held the seat of deputy from the third district, was in favor of a constitutional monarchy. The comte de Blois was far from being a man of the people, however. In 1869, he obtained the legion of honor for his role in a labor dispute that resulted in the death of several miners. In 1870, he participated in the siege of Paris, and after having become a *procureur de la république* in 1874, returned to his home, the château de Kerascoet in Coat Méal in northern Finistère, where he was elected mayor and finally conseiller général of the canton of Plabennec. He was, moreover, an ardent Catholic.[113]

In his *profession de foi*, Gayraud declared himself to be an admirer of tradition, but one who did not advocate revolution to restore a defunct monarchy. Clearly putting himself on the side of the Republic, he professed to be a Catholic candidate opposing state laws governing the exclusion of religious congregations from teaching positions. He strongly advocated unions and associations to protect the interests of the peasantry and working classes, protectionist policies for agriculture, and administrative decentralization. In addition, he emphasized his own humble origins by presenting himself as a "child of the people," who had been born in an agricultural region in the department of the Tarn in southern France and therefore understood the problems and misery of those engaged in agriculture. *L'Etoile de la Mer*, a Catholic newspaper supported by the Société anonyme de la presse catholique du Finistère, argued that Gayraud should be admired for his "tireless energy," his "oratory power," and his gift of "stirring the masses," which would allow him to become a sort of "Gambetta of Catholicism."[114]

Gayraud's candidacy received support from the national Catholic press, faithful to the spirit of the Ralliement. He was firmly supported by Veuillot's *L'Univers* through articles written by Emmanuel Desgrées du Lou, a young lawyer from Brest.[115] The unusual electoral alliances formed during this election were of particular interest to the national press. *L'Univers* claimed, for example, that the comte de Blois invited republican

[112] Ibid.
[113] Queré, "L'élection de l'abbé Gayraud," pp. 106–7.
[114] *L'Etoile de la Mer*, 16 January 1897.
[115] Delourme, *Trente-cinq années de la politique religieuse*, p. 23.

schoolteachers to a private electoral meeting in Ploudalmézeau on 22 January and that he was supported by anticlerical republicans.[116]

The by-election of 1897 confirmed the final break between the nobility and the clergy, and the success of abbé Gayraud bore witness to the power of the lower clergy to effect political change in the region. Gayraud, like de Mun, did not win an overwhelming victory; he captured only 7,326 votes, whereas his opponent won 5,976 votes.[117] A second election was held on 29 August 1897, after the January election was invalidated following an electoral investigation initiated by the nobility who had supported Blois and who claimed that the clergy had used undue influence over voters. On 29 August Gayraud won a greater victory, in part because there were fewer abstentions and in part because Gayraud won votes from former supporters of Blois.

Gayraud, like Blois, considered himself a Catholic candidate, but in his speeches he put overriding emphasis on the problems facing agriculture in an area hard hit by the economic depression of the 1880s and 1890s. Indeed, he used the defense of religion and agriculture as principal mobilizing issues. The third arrondissement of Brest circumscribed a subregion within the Léon, the lower Léon, which was much poorer than the upper Léon and which had a higher proportion of tenant farmers who rented their land from peasant proprietors. The nobility was hardly a significant economic force in the region. According to the census of 1896, there were few noble families in the area. To be precise, there were only twenty-six[118]—five in the canton of St. Renan, four in Ploudalmézeau, ten in Lannilis, and seven in Lesneven. It appears, however, that either these families exerted some influence or the influence of the clergy was not as absolute as has been supposed because Gayraud did not win majorities in Ploudalmézeau and Lannilis, despite the presence of Grall and Ollivier as curés of these parishes. Gayraud, nonetheless, won significant victories on the island of Ouessant that was formerly not very favorable to d'Hulst or Freppel and not traditionally under the tutelege of the clergy. The island now transferred its support to Gayraud. It is thus difficult to maintain the thesis that Gayraud's election represented political continuity and that the peasantry simply transferred their allegiance from one candidate to another under the direct orders of the clergy.

The tone of the conflict was highly charged and steeped in the discourse of class conflict, which resulted in bitter recriminations between former allies. At the height of the parliamentary electoral investigation, abbé Gayraud argued in the Chamber of Deputies that the nobility had instigated the

---

[116] L'Univers, 22 January 1897.
[117] A.D. Finistère, 3M291, "Elections législatives, 24 janvier 1897."
[118] Quéré, "L'élection de l'abbé Gayraud," p. 15.

proceeding because he was a commoner, a fact that, along with his political convictions, they resented highly.[119]

In 1902, the legislative campaign in the third electoral district of Brest was just as bitter. This time the lower clergy supporting Gayraud had to contend with the bishop of Quimper as well as with the nobility. Monseigneur Dubillard, who was appointed to the diocese in 1898, argued that abbé Gayraud encouraged clerical insubordination and class conflict in the region and suggested that he not run for reelection in the department in 1902. He endorsed the candidacy of abbé Stephan, who was a curé of Saint-Renan and a native of Finistère.[120] Stephan referred to the campaign as an "open war" between the bishop and his clergy.

Monseigneur Dubillard was the principal proponent of abbé Stephan's candidacy in 1902, though we do not know how the curé of Saint Renan came to the attention of the bishop. Stephan's candidacy was bitterly opposed by the *grands électeurs* of the Léon, the abbés Ollivier and Grall. At a diocesan synod in 1902 the bishop made it known that he did not favor the reelection of abbé Gayraud. Rumors circulated in the press that Jacques Piou, leader of the Catholic political party formed in 1901, Action Libérale Populaire,[121] would stand as candidate in order to resolve the deadlock.[122] Abbé Ollivier argued, however, that the candidacy of "Piou himself would, at the present moment, have no chance of succeeding."[123] It appears that Monseigneur Dubillard attempted to have the Pope intervene to force abbé Gayraud to step down, an act that prompted Ollivier to write a formal

[119] *Journal Officiel*, Chambre des Deputés, session of 4 March 1897, pp. 601–17.

[120] The government also appeared to regard Stephan favorably. In 1901, he was recommended and appointed to Saint-Renan, an important post in the Léon. The prefect then wrote that Stephan was "très intelligent . . . d'une instruction bien supérieure à celle de la moyenne du clergé du Finistère." More important perhaps for the government, while desservant of Plounéour-Trez, his political conduct was *très correcte*. The prefect contended that he was so esteemed by the local population that on the death of Monseigneur d'Hulst, deputy of the third electoral district of Brest, in 1897, a certain number of voters wished for him to stand as candidate. The prefect did not know whether Stephan had the ambition of becoming deputy, but the prefect was sure that he harbored a certain bitterness toward abbé Gayraud, who became d'Hulst's successor. A.N. F^{19}5006, prefect of Finistère to the minister of religious affairs, 23 January 1901.

[121] Action Libérale Populaire (ALP) was formed in 1901 by Albert de Mun and Jacques Piou to challenge the political preeminence of the Radicals and socialists following the Dreyfus Affair. The ALP was, through de Mun, heir to the Ralliement and Social Catholicism, but in 1902 it was primarily a movement of religious defense. See Martin, "The Creation of the Action Libérale Populaire," pp. 660–89.

[122] *La Patrie* reported that the abbés Gayraud and Stephan withdrew owing to pressure from Rome to let Piou stand as candidate in what was described as a *coup de théatre*. A.N. F^{7}12541, Notes on *La Patrie* dispatch, 16 April 1902. This did not in fact occur, though Piou was proposed as candidate.

[123] Letter from abbé Ollivier to Monseigneur Dubillard, 16 April 1902, cited in Roué, "Etude sur la vie paroissiale et religieuse de Lannilis," p. 275.

letter of protest that was signed by forty-three other priests in the Léon.[124] Abbé Ollivier requested that the bishop put nothing in the way of abbé Gayraud's candidacy and claimed that his request represented the opinion of the lower clergy in the area.[125] In his letter, abbé Ollivier argued that Gayraud was the only "foreign candidacy" that Catholics in the third district of Brest wanted,[126] and he claimed that his letter reflected the opinion of the clergy.[127]

The legislative elections of 1902 in the third electoral district of Brest attracted as much attention from the national press as the election of abbé Gayraud in 1897 because the lower clergy were again prepared to defy not only the nobility in their choice of candidate—they preferred a deputy with republican convictions—but also their bishop. *La Patrie* characterized the situation as being "unique" in the "annals of universal suffrage." According to *L'Ouest Eclair*, the Christian democratic newspaper based in Rennes that strongly suppported Gayraud, the bishop appeared to ally himself to the Ministry of Religious Affairs in order to assert his authority and rid the department of abbé Gayraud.[128] The standoff between abbé Ollivier, curé of Lannilis, his compatriots among the lower clergy, and Monseigneur Dubillard was only resolved by the results of the election. Abbé Stephan won a considerable number of votes, though Gayraud clearly had the majority behind him. The votes, however, were not divided in the same way they were in 1897 when Gayraud contended with the comte de Blois, a Catholic royalist supported by the local nobility. No common geographical pattern of opposition was visible. The voters of Lannilis, abbé Ollivier's cure, did give a sizeable number of votes to abbé Stephan, just as they had to the comte de Blois—suggesting perhaps that the nobility preferred to vote for a nonroyalist as long as he was not the democratic demagogue Gayraud—but the canton of Ploudalmézeau backed Gayraud solidly, in contrast to 1897. The bishop was forced to admit defeat in his attempt to displace Gayraud, who in fact remained deputy of the third arrondissement of Brest until his death in 1910. Dubillard, like bishops in

---

[124] Ibid. The letter was signed by the grands électeurs of Léon, the abbés Ollivier and Grall and by abbé Roull, of Saint Louis in Brest, who was responsible for the creation of the cercles d'études attached to the patronage de Saint Louis as well as by a priest in Monseigneur Dubillard's own home ground, Coat, archiprêtre of St. Corentin de Quimper.

[125] "L'intervention de Rome a été très malencontreusement sollicitée. D'ailleurs si Rome savait que les catholiques, dévoués avant tout à l'Eglise de Saint Père, sont contrariés dans leurs préférences, très justifiées, la candidature de M. abbé Gayraud continuerait à avoir son approbation." Ibid.

[126] Ibid.

[127] "Ce voeu est celui du clergé dont nous sommes certains d'être les interprètes." Ibid.

[128] F712541, copy of an article by Diraison, former editor of *L'Etoile de la Mer*, now editor of *L'Ouest Eclair*. According to notes on the article, the Breton population was beginning to wonder if "Monseigneur Dubillard is the representative of Jesus Christ" or the "valet of the free mason M. Dumay" [republican minister of religious affairs].

other parts of France who were unsympathetic to the Christian democratic movement, tried to call on Rome to adjudicate the conflict, but they achieved only incomplete success.[129] Monseigneur Dubillard was vanquished, as his predecessors had been, by the lower clergy.

Abbé Gayraud was scorned by both the Left and the Right, though the most bitter attacks on his program and person came from the Right. Gayraud answered his conservative critics who accused him of sowing revolutionary ideas by affirming his republican principles: "I accept as a historical evolution of the dogma of Christian fraternity the maxim of political and civil equality which is one of the conquests of the [French] Revolution. That is why I am a democrat."[130] By contrasting his ostensibly pluralistic conception of the Republic with that of traditional Left and the royalist Right, he recognized the hostility that his espousal of republican claims would elicit: "this moderate, liberal Republic has enemies to the left and to the right. The enemies to the left are free masons and jacobin sectarians, the enemies to the right have done as much harm to religion as enemies to the left. In fact, by their intransigence, they have made believe that the throne and altar were intimately linked, so much so that moderate republicans believed that to preserve the Republic it was necessary to destroy religion."[131]

A correspondent of the *Figaro* was told by a resident of Brest that what one took to be a "conflict of electoral ambitions" in Paris was quite simply a "class war"[132]: "There is on one side the bishop and the châteaux and on the other the people and the republican lower clergy."[133] A resident from Lannilis told the reporter that "we will re-elect him [Gayraud]. Priests and laymen, we are in agreement. A class war, exactly! We have had enough of leaders by right of birth . . . and we are not Jacobins here," and he pointed to a large crucifix on the wall above his head.[134]

Religious Identity and National Politics

Social Catholicism, which was first introduced to the department of Finistère by the parish clergy who opposed the nobility and ecclesiastical

---

[129] The bishop of the diocese of Cambrai in the department of the Nord asked Pius X to forbid abbé Lemire from running for reelection in Hazebrouck in 1906. Although the pope declared that priests could not run for office without permission, he stipulated that it would be imprudent to oppose the candidacy of priests who were already in office. Mayeur, *L'abbé Lemire*, pp. 328–30.

[130] A.N. F^{19}2564, 14 May 1902, letter printed in *Verité française* on 9 June 1902.

[131] A.N. F^{19}2564, speech delivered at Lannilis, reported in the *Dépêche de Brest*, 24 April 1902.

[132] A.N. F^{19}5621, *Le Figaro*, 26 April 1902.

[133] Ibid.

[134] Ibid.

hierarchy, emerged in the context of the state's attempts to impose the secular nation at the periphery. Indeed, the principal poles around which the clergy organized their political campaigns centered on the defense of religion, Breton agriculture, and the peasant farmer. The Republican state's mission civilisatrice explicitly called the the religious claims of the Church into question and implicitly made those claims incompatible with those of the republican nation. Until the 1890s, local populations had to choose between an increasingly anticlerical republican Left, which attacked the pretensions of the clergy and nobility, and a royalist Right, which defended the religious identity of the region. In the 1880s many cantons of southern Finistère voted for anticlerical republicans to represent them in parliament. The highly devout north consistently voted for royalists who defended the interests of the Catholic church. The introduction of the social Catholic movement in the department, which rejected the hierarchical, antirepublican politics by birthright while simultaneously voicing the legitimacy of the religious identity of the region, provided the electorate with a means to reconcile the democratic claims of a larger republican nation with religious and regional loyalties. The nascent movement, predicated on both social reform and religious defense, challenged elite control of local politics. It therefore came to occupy an ambiguous position between Left and Right, both advocating resistance to the state's religious policies and accepting the nation's claims on the region. The appearance of this hybrid political movement ultimately succeeded in destroying the calm that had characterized local politics during the nineteenth century. The public could no longer remain indifferent as they watched the bitter vituperations exchanged between châtelain and priest, both of whom were forced into competing for allegiance rather than commanding it. The intense struggle between these former allies heightened the political awareness of the voter, who now had to choose between conflicting loyalties, and the rules of the local political game would no longer be the same.

5

The Resistance of 1902

DURING THE 1890s the nascent social Catholic movement was largely confined to former royalist enclaves in northern Finistère. It had little support in the south where moderate anticlerical republicans controlled the majority of arrondissements. By 1902, however, the social Catholic movement began to make political headway in southern Finistère even in the most anticlerical communes. This political change of heart was the result not of clerical action but of government policy, which reflected a shift in republican attitudes toward cultural pluralism and brought into bold relief the growing conflict between regional cultural attachments and the republican articulations of national identity. This shift was perhaps best symbolized in the 1 July 1901 Law on Associations and in the banning of the use of regional languages in religious instruction.

The Law on Associations and the Ministry of Père Combes

The Law on Associations, passed in July 1901, was a part of the Republic's larger effort to "civilize," integrate, and republicanize the far reaches of the French hexagon. It grew, moreover, out of a specific political context. It was an immediate consequence of the Dreyfus Affair, which divided the country into two opposing camps and helped to bring a rabidly anticlerical majority to the Chamber of Deputies in 1899. In the wake of the Affair, the appeasing cabinets of the Méline era came to an end. René Waldeck-Rousseau, a lawyer from Nantes, formed a new ministry of republican defense in 1899. One of Waldeck-Rousseau's primary concerns was to force the army and the Church, which had appeared to threaten the existence of the Republic during the Affair and had violently opposed Dreyfus, to submit to republican discipline. Waldeck-Rousseau appointed General de Gallifet, who had won fame for his suppression of the Commune in 1871, as minister of war to accomplish the first task. To exert greater control over the clergy, particularly some of the regular orders such as the Assumptionists,[1] who had launched a blistering attack on the Republic

[1] The Assumptionists had not supported the Ralliement. Zeldin, *France 1848–1945*, p. 313.

during the Dreyfus Affair, Waldeck-Rousseau devised the Law on Associations,[2] or more specifically a new "concordat of congregations."[3]

Religious congregations were not explicitly included in or governed by the Concordat of 1801, but they multiplied in number during the nineteenth century under the benevolent eyes of the Restoration, July Monarchy, and Second Empire. By the 1880s, the regular clergy formed the backbone of the primary and secondary educational system in the country.

The bill that Waldeck-Rousseau proposed would require congregations to both be authorized by the Conseil d'Etat and accept the jurisdictional authority of the bishop. By forcing congregations to recognize the authority of the bishop, who, under the terms of the concordat, was appointed with the consent of the state and paid from the public treasury, Waldeck hoped to have greater control over the affairs of religious orders. The bill was changed significantly by parliament, and the altered version eventually became law on 1 July 1901. The new bill stated that within three months congregations were to seek authorization from parliament, not a legal court, or face dissolution. The bill also stipulated that no member of an unauthorized religious congregation would be permitted to teach. In the hands of a hotly anticlerical parliament, as opposed to the courts, the law could be used not simply to regulate congregations, as Waldeck-Rousseau had intended, but to eradicate them entirely. Waldeck-Rousseau, who remained in power until 7 June 1902, promised the Vatican that the law would be applied with *un libéralisme le plus bienveillant*.[4]

A great deal of confusion surrounded the interpretation of the law. Many congregations did not seek authorization because they believed themselves to be in conformity with the law, while others defiantly chose not to apply for authorization because they wished to maintain their independence and refused to place themselves under the jurisdiction of a bishop.[5]

The Law on Associations was one stone in an edifice dedicated to a secular republic that was slowly built by republican politicians between the 1880s and 1914. It did not, however, provoke serious opposition until Emile Combes came to power in June 1902.[6] The legislative election of May 1902 was a resounding victory for the Dreyfusards, hence the Re-

---

[2] This law governed all associations other than professional associations, which were governed by the law of 1884.

[3] Mayeur, *La vie politique sous la Troisième République*, p. 184.

[4] Dansette, *Histoire religieuse de la France contemporaine*, p. 571.

[5] Ibid., p. 572.

[6] Mayeur contends that the 1902 elections centered on the *question religieuse* and more specifically on the law on associations. However, in Finistère there was little mention of the law in electoral tracts and public speeches, and it did not appear to become an issue as such until after Combes began to attempt to enforce the law. Mayeur, *La vie politique sous la Troisième République*, p. 185.

public. Republicans won 370 seats against 220 held by the opposition. The Radical faction within the republican bloc viewed the returns as their own victory. Waldeck-Rousseau may have been convinced of this himself for he resigned on 4 June 1902. Emile Combes was called upon to form a government.

The *petit père* Combes (1835–1921) had attended Catholic schools, had written a doctoral thesis on Thomas Aquinas,[7] and had wanted to enter the Church but was advised against doing so because he allegedly did not have the vocation. He eventually traveled to Paris, where he received a degree in medicine; he returned to Pons in the Charente-Inférieure to become a successful republican politician.[8] He was elected senator in 1885. As rapporteur of the Law on Associations, he seemed a worthy successor to Waldeck-Rousseau.

As soon as he was in power, Emile Combes began to implement his plan to republicanize the army and administration. In June 1902 he issued a circular instructing prefects to "reserve favours which the Republic disposes of" for friends of the government.[9] His Minister of War General André, who as a result of General Gallifet's reforms had sole power over all appointments and promotions in the army, was determined to promote only those who could clearly show their republican and anticlerical sympathies. To verify these credentials, General André established files on the religious and political affiliations of officers by using informers from lower commissioned and noncommissioned ranks, particularly Freemasons.[10]

While in power, Combes abandoned all moderation and ruthlessly applied the Law on Associations. Only a few orders that were useful to the government because of their missionary activities were given authorization.[11] In most areas of France these measures met with indifference.[12] In the department of the Var in southern France the Law on Associations elicited no opposition at all.[13] In more devout areas such as the Nord, republican and conservative municipal councils condemned the legislation but did not actively resist the closure of congregational schools.[14] By contrast, the application of the 1901 Law on Associations encountered armed resistance and public demonstrations in many parts of Lower Brittany. It

---

[7] Ibid.

[8] Zeldin, *France 1848–1945*, pp. 319–24.

[9] Alfred Cobban, *A History of Modern France*, 3 vols. (Harmondsworth, 1965) 3: 61.

[10] This system, revealed to the public as the *affaire des fiches*, eventually led to the political ouster of first General André and then of Combes himself. See Douglas Porch, *The March to the Marne: The French Army, 1871–1914* (Cambridge, 1981), pp. 92–104.

[11] See Partin, *Waldeck-Rousseau, Combes, and the Church*, pp. 135–87.

[12] Mayeur and Rebérioux, *The Third Republic*, pp. 241–42.

[13] Judt, *Socialism in Provence*, pp. 181–82.

[14] Hilaire, *Une chrétienté au XIXeme siecle* 2: 743–45.

resulted in nothing less than an armed insurrection against the state in both northern and southern Finistère, in "republican" as well as in "clerical" communes.[15] This insurrection inspired the imposition of additional anti-clerical legislation in these regions by the government, which included banning the use of regional languages in religious instruction in 1903.

In the department of Finistère, government officials were cudgeled, taunted, and drenched with buckets of "dirty water and fecal matter" dumped from windows and from behind overturned carts that served as barricades.[16] Newspaper reporters who flocked to the little-known communes of Saint-Méen, Folgoët, and Ploudaniel to report on these events recognized the chouan in the faces of men throwing stones. Photographs of peasants shod in sabots and armed with sticks appeared in the pages of the illustrated press where specific references were made to chouannerie and the Vendée.[17] The republican newspaper, La Dépêche, characterized the population of Saint-Méen as "ignorant and fanatical,"[18] while Bretagne Nouvelle, in an article entitled "Congregationists and Chouans," went so far as to describe the peasants of Saint-Méen as "savages."[19]

Government officials largely shared this opinion. In reporting on the events that occurred in Finistère, where the resistance came to be seen in terms of a "revolt,"[20] officials attributed the actions of the local populace to religious fanaticism, to pressure exerted by the clergy on superstitious parishioners, and to the nobility's manipulation of their tenants. Government officials attributed this resistance to the actions of a half-crazed and submissive rural population who, plied with drink, pressured by the local châtelain, and threatened with damnation by the curé, marched to the orders of local elites. In short, the rejection of the state's civilizing mission in Finistère was explained in terms of atavistic allegiances, superstition, and venality.

Historians have adopted, albeit in modified forms, these interpretations

[15] All the communes, for example, in the arrondissement of Quimper that took part in the revolt returned anticlerical republican candidates during the 1902 elections. Morlaix strongly supported Emile Cloarec, an anticlerical republican. Roscoff, Saint-Pol-de-Léon, Carantec, and Cléder were in cantons that voted for the Comte de Mun, and Saint-Méen was in abbé Gayraud's electoral territory. Only Landerneau, another site of unrest, voted for a candidate that was clearly antirepublican. A.D. Finistère, 3M297, élections législatives, 27 April 1902. Moreover, in 1905 all these communes, with the exception of Quimper, were dominated by medium-sized property holders, not the nobility who leased their property. Camille Vallaux, La Basse-Bretagne: étude de géographie humaine (Paris, 1980), pp. 107–21.

[16] A. D. Finistère, 1V1157, report by the commissaire spécial des chemins de fer, 13 August 1902.

[17] L. Elegoet, Saint-Méen, p. 296. Postcards were also printed by local publishing houses.

[18] Cited in ibid., p. 295.

[19] Cited in ibid., p. 299.

[20] Combes, Mon ministère, pp. 55–56.

of the resistance and, more generally, the language and assumptions of French officialdom. Robert Gildea, for example, has recently argued that in Upper Brittany resistance to the Law on Associations was explosive where clericalism combined with royalism and that notables played an important role in communes where resistance occurred.[21] Yannick Guin suggests that the resistance of 1902 in Lower Brittany demonstrated that local notables (the landed aristocracy and the clergy) were still "capable of manipulating the peasantry to resist urban enterprises" and that these elites "held Breton peasants in firm economic dependency and in a propitious isolation through the mediation of the curé."[22]

The fact that the resistance occurred in a number of left-wing communes and urban centers and that only one particular religious congregation was at issue poses problems for these lines of interpretation. The form that the resistance assumed suggests that the rejection of the state's policy was selective. The defense of the Filles du Saint-Esprit and a network of schools only recently created in the department raises particular questions regarding the nature of the "tradition" being defended and the rationale for what appears to be a gender-specific response to state policy. Moreover, although the majority of communes protesting the closure of congregational schools run by the Filles du Saint-Esprit were rural, a significant number of regional market centers including Landerneau, Morlaix, Saint-Pol-de-Léon, and Quimper as well as the seaport of Concarneau violently opposed the Law on Associations. In characterizing the resisters as atavistic "chouans," government officials and the press wittingly or unwittingly ignored the fact that the resistance centered on the schools run by only one particular female religious congregation, and the populations of communes in Finistère were prepared to accept substantial losses to keep them open. The peasantry abandoned their crops in the midst of the harvest season, and republican communes were willing to defy the government despite the consequences such an action might have in terms of future government favors. For these reasons it is difficult to understand this incident of resistance in terms of the rhetoric of French officialdom, as a product of elite manipulation.

What then accounts for the violent resistance to the closing of girls' schools run by the Filles du Saint-Esprit, and what was the long-term significance of this incident? Why were the Filles du Saint-Esprit and the system of female education they established particularly valued by local communities in Lower Brittany? An explanation must be sought in the experiences and cultural perceptions of provincial communities adapting to social and economic change. The keys to unlocking the meaning of the

[21] Gildea, *Education in Provincial France*, p. 169.
[22] Guin, *Histoire de la Bretagne*, pp. 159–60.

resistance of 1902 in Finistère will be sought in the actions of the protestors, in the articulation of local concerns that led to these actions, and in the social and cultural functions performed by the Filles du Saint-Esprit during the early Third Republic.

"Breton Insurrection"

A free, secular, compulsory system of primary education, introduced in the still largely illiterate department of Finistère in the 1880s, was bitterly opposed by the parish clergy in Finistère, who railed against the *écoles sans Dieu*. Opposition to the dissemination of primary education by the state was tame in comparison to the events of 1902, however. In the 1880s the Church responded to the first challenge by founding a number of new congregational schools, particularly for girls. The expansion of female education in the department may in part have been a clerical strategy to maintain women within the fold in order to assure the future vitality of the Church in the region. It was also one solution to the demands placed on localities that were called upon to build or secularize schools for boys and felt they could not afford to provide similar schools for girls as well. The educational initiatives of the Church and the state appeared to bear fruit by the turn of the century. Whereas in 1878 the percentage of illiterate conscripts from Finistère was as high as 59.3 in some cantons,[23] the number of illiterate conscripts fell dramatically by 1899, particularly in northern Finistère, where conscripts could read and write as well as their counterparts in northeastern France.[24]

In July 1902, several weeks after Emile Combes had formed his cabinet, the prefect of Finistère issued an order: all congregational schools that did not conform to the law of 1 July 1901 be closed by order of the government on 21 July. By 22 July all the unauthorized schools run by male orders were closed without incident, and little or no controversy surrounded the closing of schools run by most female orders.[25] There was, however, fierce

[23] Notably in Pleyben; see Bedel-Bernard, "L'enseignement primaire dans le Finistère," p. 67.

[24] Literacy levels were generally higher in northern Finistère, which was more prosperous than the south and where a peasant aristocracy, the Juloded, often obtained a secondary education. Corgne, *Histoire du collège de Lesneven*, and André Siegfried, *Tableau politique de la France de l'Ouest sous la Troisième République* (Paris, 1913), p. 182. Also see Le Gallo, "Une caste paysanne du Haut Léon," pp. 53–82, and C. Chassi, "Du nouveau et du vieux sur les Julots du Léon," *Le Télégramme*, 8 August 1959.

[25] No incidents of resistance occurred in the arrondissement of Quimperlé where schools run by the Filles de Jésus de Kermaria closed. The subprefect noted, "no agitation occurred when the nuns departed. . . . Up to this day, the laicizations in the arrondissement of Quimperlé have taken place not only without incident but even with some success, which in certain

opposition to the closure of thirty seven schools operated by the Filles du Saint-Esprit, a Breton order whose maison mère was in the neighboring department of Côtes-du-Nord.[26] The prefect, who tried to enlist the help of the bishop of Quimper to close the thirty seven schools, was informed by the vicaire général that he had no jurisdiction over them because these orders were based in another diocese.[27]

On 23 July, the mayor of the republican commune of Plogonnec, which had voted for the Radical deputy Georges Le Bail, a supporter of the Combes government, addressed a letter to the prefect that reflected the sentiment of republican communes that had heard of the imminent closure of schools run by unauthorized religious congregations:

> The undersigned municipal councillors of Plogonnec have the honor of extending to you the expression of their sincere devotion to the republican cause of which they have been ardent defenders at every moment and in every circumstance. . . . They have, however, as representatives of the commune, the duty to take into consideration the almost unanimous sympathy of the inhabitants of the commune for the sisters of the congregation of the Filles du Saint-Esprit whose establishment is to be closed imminently. They [the municipal councillors] do not believe they are overstepping their rights in making it known to you their intention of giving a favorable judgment to their [the nuns'] request to become authorized if, as they [the councillors] hope, they [the nuns] make a request.[28]

Most communes in Finistère became aware through the press by mid-July of the order that schools run by unauthorized orders were to be closed.[29] On 22 July, a group of residents of the seaport of Concarneau in southern Finistère went to Quimper to speak with the prefect. While the prefect was away, a delegation of ten was admitted to the prefecture and had an audience with the secrétaire général. He informed them that the government would maintain its position and that it would be ready to use armed force if it encountered resistance.[30] The group therefore returned to

---

cases has gone beyond all [our] hopes." A.D. Finistère, 1V1158, report from subprefect of the arrondissement of Quimperlé to the prefect of Finistère, 26 August 1902.

[26] The prefect wrote to the minister of the interior at the end of July and noted that of the thirty eight establishments remaining to be closed, thirty seven belonged to the Filles du Saint-Esprit and one to the Filles de Jésus whose "maison mère" was in Plumelin in the Morbihan. A.D. Finistère IV1152, prefect of Finistère to the minister of the interior, 29 July 1902.

[27] Ibid.

[28] A.D. Finistère, 1V1157, Mairie de Plogonnec to the prefect of Finistère, 23 July 1902. The Filles du Saint-Esprit did not consider making a formal request for authorization until quite late because they believed their order was in conformity with existing laws.

[29] In Concarneau, residents heard of the imminent closing on 10 July, but they did not learn that it would occur on 21 July until 16 July, and in Saint-Méen inhabitants learned of the closings on 14 July. See Les soeurs blanches de Concarneau: expulsion du 13 août 1902 (Vannes, n.d.), pp. 4, 7, and L. Elegoet, Saint-Méen, p. 287.

[30] Anonymous, Les soeurs blanches de Concarneau p. 9.

Concarneau empty-handed and circulated petitions that obtained 1,524 signatures from eligible male voters in the commune, and 1,240 female signatures.[31] In other communes, such as Saint-Méen in northern Finistère, events took a more violent turn. On 21 July six hundred armed peasants confronted two gendarmes who came to notify the nuns who ran the Ecole Sainte-Anne of their imminent eviction if they did not voluntarily comply with the government's order. When the schoolteacher of the public primary school in the commune tried to show the gendarmes where the sisters could be found he was seized by the collar and then fled from the angry shouts of the crowd. The gendarmes were forced to leave the village without having accomplished their mission.[32] The schoolteacher, who feared reprisals, returned to his family in Saint-Renan.

The prefect noted on 29 July that the communes in which the "stir caused by the measures taken with regard to congregational establishments" was the "most spirited" were Quimper, Kerfeunteun, Ergué-Gabéric, Pluguffan, Concarneau, Douarnenez, Pont-Croix, Plogonnec, Treffiagat, and Audierne in the arrondissement of Quimper; Morlaix, Roscoff, Saint-Pol-de-Léon, Carantec, and Cléder in the arrondissement of Morlaix; and Landerneau and Saint-Méen in the arrondissement of Brest.[33] Although some government officials consistently argued that the clergy and the antirepublican nobility were behind the unrest,[34] most of these communes were situated in cantons that had obtained republican majorities during the 1902 legislative elections, particularly in southern Finistère.[35]

Violent incidents occurred in both northern and southern Finistère in late July, causing local authorities concern. In Quimper, two schools belonging to the Filles du Saint-Esprit remained open, and a peaceful demonstration that began in front of the prefecture ended in violence: The crowd marched from the prefecture to the house of Georges Le Bail, archanticlerical deputy of Quimper, attempted to enter his home by force, and broke several panes of glass. Blows were exchanged, and the gendarme as well as a schoolteacher were severely bruised.[36] In Douarnenez the primary

[31] Ibid., p. 10. This was a considerable number as the total population of the commune in 1901 was 7,635, and 3,534 voted in the legislative elections of 1902. Charpy, "Dénombrements de la population des communes du Finistère," p. 858, and A.D. Finistère 3M297, élections législatives, 27 April 1902.

[32] L. Elegoet, Saint-Méen, pp. 288–89.

[33] A.D. Finistère, IV1152, report by the prefect, 29 July 1902.

[34] A.D. Finistère, 1V1164, report by the commissaire spécial de Morlaix, n.d. [1902].

[35] A.D. Finistère, 3M297, élections législatives, 27 April 1902.

[36] A.D. Finistère, 1V1152, report from the prefect of Finistère to the minister of the interior, 29 July 1902. Two arrests were made during this incident, and one offender was sentenced to fifteen days in jail. The crowd also demonstrated in front of the residence of Louis Hémon, moderate republican deputy of the first electoral district of Quimper, but the demonstration remained peaceful.

congregational school remained open, and the population was visibly angry. In Saint-Pol-de-Léon a peaceful demonstration of about one thousand peasants took place on 28 and 29 July.[37]

From mid-July onward watches were established in a number of communes. In Ploudaniel and Saint-Méen, barricades consisting of overturned carts chained together were placed at the entrances of the congregational schools. Waldeck-Rousseau, author of the new law governing religious associations, questioned the legality of Combes's application of the law in a letter to Delcassé;[38] he was disturbed by Combes's calm in the face of the staunch opposition to the law in Brittany: "What is happening in Brittany disturbs me a great deal. My compatriots are slow to stir, but once stirred, they are capable of going all the way."[39] Waldeck-Rousseau's uneasiness merely surprised Combes. Indeed, Combes as well as some of his supporters in Finistère were taken aback by the violent response of the local populace to the closing of institutions run by the Filles du Saint-Esprit. Georges Le Bail, for example, wrote to the prefect of Côtes-du-Nord in October 1902 in this regard: "Finally, would it be indiscreet to ask you, in your opinion, the motivation behind sisters of this congregation submitting in your department while they adopt an absolutely different attitude in the department of Finistère."[40]

The situation took a turn for the worse in August, when the government, with the help of the army, began to close the congregational schools . The evictions did not begin in earnest until the second week in August, and only then in areas that did not appear heavily guarded by the local population. On 1 August, the commune of Douarnenez resisted the police who tried to evict the nuns from the congregational schools.[41] On 8 August, pieces of coal and large quantities of mud were thrown at the police from the walls and door inside the congregational school run by the Filles du Saint-Esprit in Treffiagat.[42] On 11 August, a gendarme was hit in the chest with a cudgel, and a police official had a bucket of water thrown on his head in Fouesnant.[43] Resistance took similar forms in Quimper, Audierne, Concarneau, Kerfeunteun, Pont-Croix, and Beuzec, all of which were located in the arrondissement of Quimper.[44] The number of men who gathered to resist the police in communes in southern Finistère was large, and the

[37] Ibid.

[38] A.N. F¹⁹6268, 6 August 1902, cited in L. Elegoet, *Saint-Méen*, p. 307.

[39] Ibid.

[40] A.D. Côtes-du-Nord, V3969, letter.

[41] A.D. Finistère, 1V1157, report, commissaire de police of Douarnenez, n.d.

[42] A.D. Finistère, 1V1157, report, commissaire de police of Pont l'Abbé, 24 August 1902.

[43] Ibid.

[44] Ibid. For Beuzec, see report by the commissaire spécial de la police des chemins de fer, 13 August 1902, A.D. Finistère, 1V1157 who claimed that authorities were drenched with "dirty water and fecal matter" when they tried to enter the school run by the Filles du Saint-Esprit in the commune.

number of women was even larger.[45] In the republican commune of
Plogonnec, whose municipal council had written to the prefect on behalf of
the Filles du Saint-Esprit, 200 people demonstrated,[46] and in Le Guilvinec,
1500 persons—80 percent of whom were women—out of a population of
3,884 demonstrated.[47] Virtually the entire population of the commune of
Treffiagat, in addition to persons from the surrounding area, must have
taken part in the demonstration against police, if official estimates were
correct.[48] To deal with these widespread disturbances, the prefect had to
call out between three and twelve brigades of gendarmerie, depending on
the locality.[49] In Concarneau twelve brigades of gendarmerie and three
hundred infantrymen were on hand to evict five nuns from the congregation of the Filles du Saint-Esprit.[50] Similar forces were employed in Beuzec-
Bourg and Douarnenez.[51]

By 17 August most evictions had been accomplished in southern
Finistère, and all the nuns evicted belonged to the order of the Filles du
Saint-Esprit. On 18 August, a demonstration held in Quimper to protest
the evictions was led by Albert de Mun, de Chamaillard, a member of the
Action Libérale Populaire, Emile Villiers, deputy of the second electoral
district of Brest, and Gabriel Miossec, republican deputy of the first electoral district of Châteaulin.[52] The protesters arrived from areas surrounding Quimper and from the Léon and marched through the city carrying the
tricolor.[53] "Defenders" from what came to be called "three citadels" of the

[45] The commissaire spécial de la police des chemins de fer of Quimper claimed that most of
those who resisted the law were women following the order of the clergy and that if men took
part, this was owing to the influence that women had over their husbands. In addition, he
claimed that in Quimper, many demonstrators were paid to cry, "Vivent les soeurs!" A.D.
Finistère, 1V1157, commissaire spécial des chemins de fer to the minister of the interior,
31 July 1902.

[46] A.D. Finistère, 1V1157, "Tableau indiquant les établissements congrégationistes de
l'arrondissement de Quimper dont la fermature a été poursuivie . . . la nature et le caractère
de l'opposition . . . ainsi que les mésures que leur résistance a rendu nécessaire." Préfecture du
Finistère.

[47] Ibid. Charpy, "Dénombrements de la population des communes du Finistère," p. 858.

[48] Ibid., p. 882. According to officials, 1,800 to 2,000 took part in the resistance against
the police, in a commune whose population was 1,819 in 1901.

[49] A.D. Finistère, 1V1157, "Tableau indiquant les établissements congrégationistes de
l'arrondissement de Quimper dont la fermature a été pousuivie" Préfecture de Quimper.

[50] Ibid.

[51] Ibid.

[52] Villiers was a conservative with monarchist leanings, and Miossec was a moderate
republican who opposed the radical ministry of Combes. He was described by the prefecture
in the 1902 elections as a "républicain antiministériel." A.D. Finistère, 3M297, élections
législatives de 1902. Abbé Gayraud was in Saint-Méen, which was in a state of insurrection as
the army and police attempted to close the Ecole St. Anne.

[53] The communes represented were Saint-Pol-de-Léon, Roscoff, and Commana in northern Finistère, Brasparts in the central part of the department, and Concarneau, Douarnenez,

Léon, Saint-Méen, Folgoët, and Ploudaniel were missing, as the local population in these communes were battling with the police and the army who were attempting to evict the sisters of the Filles du Saint-Esprit from educational establishments run by the nuns in these communes.[54] According to one observer, 30,000 demonstrated in Quimper, but a police official of Quimper estimated that only 2,000 were present.[55] On 18 August, the conseil général of Finistère condemned the measures in a near unanimous vote, as would a number of municipal councils in the department.[56]

On the same day, the government began its assault on Saint-Méen, Ploudaniel, and Folgoet. The prefect, who had attended a meeting in the nearby commune of Lesneven on 11 August, had the opportunity to see at first hand the unrest in the area and anticipated that 200 infantrymen as well as 50 gendarmes would be necessary to enforce the Law on Associations in the communes of Ploudaniel and Folgoët, but that 300 infantrymen and 80 gendarmes would be required in Saint-Méen.[57] The state of excitement was so great in Saint-Méen that abbé Gayraud, who represented the district in parliament, decided to stay in the commune, which had been anxiously awaiting government troops for over three weeks. A copy of the Declaration of the Rights of Man and Citizen was posted on one of the doors of the Ecole Sainte-Anne which was blocked by makeshift barricades.[58]

On Monday, 18 August, at 11:00 A.M. a battalion of 400 men from the colonial infantry, 75 gendarmes, several members of the police from Brest and Lambézellec, a locksmith, and the subprefect of the arrondissement of Brest arrived in the commune. The subprefect and abbé Gayraud exchanged words, but as no compromise was reached, the subprefect ordered the troops to dismantle the barricades erected at the head of the path leading to the Ecole Sainte-Anne.[59] One policemen was wounded in the head by stones thrown, along with sand and mud, at the soldiers. The crowd gave way to the second barricade erected in front of the presbytery where they chanted, "Vivent les soeurs! A bas Combes! Vive la Républi-

---

Pont-Croix, Audierne, Pluguffan, Penhars, and Kerfeunteun from the southern part of the department. Goyen, *Expulsées*, p. 149.

[54] Ibid.

[55] Ibid. A.D. Finistère, IV1157, report by commissaire de police, 19 August 1902. This discrepancy may be attributed to the fact that Goyen, an alias for abbé Cornou, may not have been the most objective of observers. Goyen became editor of a newspaper in the interwar period that many considered to be the mouthpiece of the Evêché de Quimper. A.D. Finistère, 1M133, "Presse du Département de Finistère," [1924].

[56] Goyen, *Expulsées*, p. 149. A.D. Finistère, 1V1160.

[57] L. Elegoet, *Saint-Méen*, p. 294.

[58] Ibid.

[59] Ibid., pp. 296–97.

que!" The soldiers ultimately reached the school, where the locksmith was required to open the doors. Scuffles between the crowd and the soldiers continued. The parish priest and several young women guarding the court-yard of the school were thrown to the ground, as mud, stones, and sand were thrown at the troops. The soldiers forced the four nuns out of the school, after the superior had presented a letter of protest to the subprefect, and the nuns took refuge in the home of a certain Madame Aballéa in the village. Twelve peasants and ten young women received wounds of varying degrees of seriousness; on the government side, seven, including a police official and gendarme were wounded. Eight arrests were made.[60] In Folgoët and Ploudaniel, events did not take as violent a turn,[61] but the local popu-lation resisted the troops nonetheless. The press attributed this moderation to the senators Cuverville and Pichon, who were in the communes to restrain the crowd, and to the prefect, who ordered that no bullets be fired by the army or the gendarmerie.[62] By 20 August, all thirty seven schools run by the Filles du Saint-Esprit, which had been denied authorization, were closed by force in the department of Finistère, and those arrested during the revolt were tried in September and October 1902.

The geography of the resistance indicates that local protest was not solely confined to isolated semiliterate rural communes as government officials implied in their reports. Market towns and seaports played an active role in the resistance in July and August, but their protests were more rapidly suppressed than the revolt of the three "citadels" of the Léon. This may in part be attributed to the fact that the rural communes of Saint-Méen, Ploudaniel, and Folgoët were less accessible to government troops than urban centers. It became evident, however, that when the secularizing policy of the French state was concerned, many urban populations of Lower Brittany had more in common with their provincial rural counter-parts than with the administrators and institutions of the capital.

Interpretations

A report written by a police official on 31 July 1902 regarding unrest in the area is typical of many reports explaining the nature of the resistance to the Law on Associations in Finistère in the summer of 1902. According to the official, the agitation was superficial, and most resisters in the city of Quimper were paid to cry "Vivent les soeurs!"[63] In the countryside, the

---

[60] Ibid., p. 298.

[61] There were no injuries. Ibid., p. 299.

[62] *Le Temps* also praised abbé Gayraud by implying that the situation could have been worse in Saint-Méen. Ibid.

[63] A.D. Finistère 1V1157, report from the commissaire spécial of Quimper to the minister of the interior, 31 July 1902. In succeeding years Emile Combes attributed the resistance in

clergy, allegedly behind the campaign in favor of the nuns, promised this "people still faithful to mysticism every indulgence possible," as the peasantry by nature would not become involved until they were given some material interest in the matter.[64] The subprefect of Brest argued that in Landerneau monarchists, who had always viewed the city as their "center of action," had continued to stir up the local population over whom they held some sway because they were tenants or because they were the nobility's suppliers.[65] Local officals also charged that the widespread and indiscriminate use of alcohol among the peasantry was in part responsible for the summer violence. The resistance of 1902 cannot, however, easily be explained in terms of clerical manipulation, bribes, or alcohol consumption because considerable evidence contradicts such explanations.

The clergy did actively participate in many of the thirty seven communes where the expulsion of the nuns took place. In Saint-Méen, where the government encountered the fiercest resistance, the parish priest abbé Manac'h was in the middle of the fray, as were the curé and vicaire of Ploudaniel.[66] In southern Finistère several priests were even arrested for the part they played in the resistance.[67] This participation was by no means universal, however. A policeman who had witnessed the expulsion of the Filles du Saint-Esprit from Ploumoguer reported that the vicaire of the parish was "favorable rather than hostile to the accomplishment of our mission . . . he preached calm" and that it would be "inexact" to say that "priests organized the resistance";[68] rather the mayor of the commune, who resisted the authorities, was reported to have prevented the soldiers from obtaining food from local shops.[69] In some communes the peasantry appeared to have resisted the government whether or not the clergy took an active role. It would be difficult to argue that the priest had an unshakable hold on the behavior of his parishioners, for only four years later, when the

---

Finistère to the prefecture of Finistère: "I had sent to the prefects of the departments concerned confidential instructions, pressing them to implement the decrees from one day to the next. The prefect of Finistère was absent from Quimper, called, he told me, to the bedside of his very ill mother. He could not return to his post in time and was very badly served by his secretary." Combes, *Mon ministère*, pp. 55–56. This view of events reflects Combes's blithe refusal to consider the local causes of the resistance and his confident belief that all opposition could ultimately be repressed.

[64] Ibid. "The Breton peasant only takes sides in a question if he believes there is something in it for him and he feels himself to be the stronger."

[65] A.D. Finistère, 1V1157, report from the subprefect of the arrondissement of Brest to the prefect of Finistère, 24 July 1902.

[66] L. Elegoet, *Saint-Méen*, p. 299. A.D. Finistère, 1V1157, report from the subprefect of the arrondissement of Brest to the prefect of Finistère, 24 July 1902.

[67] They were arrested for violating the *loi sur attroupements* in Pont l'Abbé and Concarneau. A.D. Finistère, 1V1157, report by the commissaire de police of Douarnenez, n.d.

[68] A.D. Finistère, 1V1154, report by the commissaire de police of Brest, 14 August 1902.

[69] Ibid.

clergy in many communes, such as Guimiliau,[70] tried to organize a protest against the government's taking an inventory of church property following the separation of church and state in 1905, the local populace refused to support them.[71] There appears, moreover, little relationship between statistics on levels of religious practice and opposition for the centers of resistance in southern Finistère—Concarneau, Crozon, and Pont l'Abbé— had among some of the lowest levels of participants in Easter mass in the department (see Table 3.1).

Similarly, the charge that the nobility, through bullying and buying off their tenants, were behind the resistance could only be justified in a few communes that took part in the revolt. The commissaire spécial of Morlaix reported that "enormous pressure" had been exerted by the nobility on their tenants and employees.[72] Only in parts of the arrondissement of Morlaix, where the nobility still owned substantial tracts of land, and in pockets within the arrondissement of Quimper and Châteaulin, where similar reports were made, would such harassment have been possible. In a report regarding the extent to which landowners and industrialists had played a role in instigating the resistance, the subprefect of Châteaulin noted that resistance was particularly serious in three communes: Crozon, Brasparts, and Gouézec.[73] In Brasparts and Gouézec, farmers were allegedly given indemnities to abandon their harvest, and crops apparently suffered as a result.[74] The same could not be said of Crozon where violent demonstrations occurred. As property in this commune was particularly subdivided, no landowner was capable of having any sway over tenants, and the subprefect had had no reports that workers from the canneries in the area had been *embrigadé* by their employers.[75]

In fact, the majority of communes that revolted against the application of the Law on Associations were dominated by peasant landowners, particularly in communes that experienced the most serious outbreaks of violence. In Saint-Méen, the peasantry abandoned crops at the height of the harvest season so that there would be enough men to stand watch. There is no explicit mention in either the press or government reports, with the exception of the subprefect of Châteaulin's October memorandum, of the effect

[70] L. Elegoet, *Saint-Méen*, p. 310.

[71] Finistère remained relatively quiet during the taking of the inventory in 1906. See Mayeur, "Géographie de la résistance aux inventaires," pp. 1259–72.

[72] A.D. Finistère, 1V1164, report by the commissaire spécial of Morlaix, n.d.

[73] A.D. Finistère, 1V1164, report by the subprefect of the arrondissement of Châteaulin to the prefect of Finistère, 11 October 1902.

[74] A.D. Finistère, 1V1164, report by the prefect of Finistère to the minister of the interior, 18 October 1902.

[75] A.D. Finistère, 1V1164, report by the subprefect of the arrondissement of Châteaulin to the prefect of Finistère, 11 October 1902.

that the resistance might have had on crops, but in communes such as Saint-Méen, Ploudaniel, and Folgoët, composed primarily of peasant smallholders,[76] watches had been organized for several weeks, and the peasant stood to lose from his participation in the resistance.

To judge from the record of arrests, most agitators who went to trial were employed, established members of the community over the age of twenty three, indicating that the principal participants were neither tenants nor the young vagrant poor who could be bought off by wealthy landholders.[77] Two of the principal organizers of the resistance in Concarneau were Pierre Henri Le Marié, a fish salesman, and Auguste Toulgoat, a twenty-three-year-old cannery worker. Jean Gwenolé Droalan, a forty-two-year-old ship carpenter with seven children, was arrested for erecting barricades.[78] In Saint-Méen, Jean-Marie Roudaut, a thirty-nine-year-old widower with one child, was arrested for having shouted "A bas l 'Armée."[79]

At the trials of those arrested, charges were made that the peasantry in Ploudaniel, Folgoët, and Saint-Méen had consumed 45,000 more *petits verres* between 17 July and 18 August 1902 than they had during the same period during the previous year, a charge that prompted the prefect to investigate the amounts of alcohol consumed in 1901 and 1902 in the communes that took part in the revolt of 1902.[80] The prefect found that, while consumption increased in some communes, in others, many of which experienced the most violent incidents, consumption of alcohol was slightly or substantially less than in 1901. In Saint-Méen, Folgoët, and Ploudaniel, where the resistance was fiercest, the local population drank 0.02 hectolitres less in 1902 than in the same period in the previous year; in Beuzec, 4.90 hectolitres less; whereas in Brasparts, 1.26 more hectolitres of alcohol were consumed.[81] The prefect did find that for thirty three out of the thirty seven communes about which such information could be gathered, a total of 23.58 more hectolitres of alcohol were consumed in 1902 than in the same period in the previous year,[82] but this number was far

[76] Vallaux, *La Basse-Bretagne*, pp. 99–121.

[77] A.D. Finistère, 1V1167, Cahiers des mesures disciplinaires par ordre alphabétique des communes, 1902.

[78] Among the other individuals noted for their involvement in incidents in Concarneau and Beuzec were three priests, a twenty-eight-year-old unmarried négociant De Malherbe, a medical student, a lawyer, Conseiller Général de Servigny, a seminary student, a shoemaker, and the mayor of Concarneau, an industriel. A.D. Finistère, 1V1157, report by the commissaire de police of Concarneau, 21 August 1902.

[79] A.D. Finistère, 1V1154, report, brigade of Plouescat, 18 August 1902.

[80] L. Elegoet, *Saint-Méen*, p. 308; A.D. Finistère, 1V1162, report by the director of the Direction des Contributions Indirectes du Département du Finistère, 14 September 1902.

[81] A.D. Finistère 1V1162, report by the directeur des contributions indirectes du département du Finistère, 19 September 1902.

[82] Ibid.

from the 45,000 petits verres allegedly consumed in the "three citadels" of the Léon, Saint-Méen, Ploudaniel, and Folgoët, where the local inhabitants actually consumed less alcohol in 1902 than in the previous year.

Brittany was renowned for relatively high levels of alcohol consumption in the nineteenth and twentieth centuries, but the association of drink with social disorder among the "dangerous" or popular classes figures more generally in official reports and the social literature of nineteenth-century France. In 1840, Eugene Buret compared the condition of the besotted Paris worker with that of the unruly savage in *De la misère et des classes laborieuses en Angleterre et France.* By the early Third Republic local officials used similar comparisons to describe the peasantry throughout France, and, like Buret, they viewed the peasant's alleged unrestrained alcohol use as a manifestation of his savage condition and a cause of social unrest. After the Commune radicalism came to be linked with alcoholism, but in the Breton case it was linked with reactionary violence.[83]

Some newspaper accounts, evoking the chouannerie, suggested that the peasantry's response to the expulsions was merely part of a political tradition of reactionary politics. Finistère had never, however, taken part in chouannerie,[84] and many communes that took part in the resistance of 1902 had backed, in the Combes ministry's understanding of the term, republican candidates in the legislative elections of 1902.[85]

Provincial response to the closing of congregational schools, moreover, was selective. Armed resistance occurred only in communes where the law applied to a specific female congregation, the Filles du Saint-Esprit. In their case, the government's closures were widely considered illegal. Many congregational establishments founded by the Filles du Saint-Esprit were created before the Revolution and during the First Empire and as such were authorized, as was the maison-mère in Saint-Brieuc, by the decrees of 1810 and 1813. Others, established between 1825 and 1880, were regulated by a *Décret de souveraineté* and a *Décret de tutelle.* Those founded after

---

[83] Susanna Barrows has argued that the problem of alcoholism became a politically charged issue after the Paris Commune of 1870–1871 as politicians, men of property, and government officials tried to understand the Paris uprising and the military defeat of France during the Franco-Prussian War. Barrows, "After the Commune," pp. 205–18.

[84] Only one minor incident occurred in the commune of Pont de Buis in Finistère, and Lower Brittany, as a rule, with the exception of incidents of chouannerie in what became the department of Morbihan, remained relatively quiet. Skol Vreiz, *Histoire de la Bretagne et des pays celtiques* Vol. 4: *La Bretagne au XIXe siècle* (Rennes, 1980), p. 43.

[85] The second district of Quimper, the site of significant resistance, was the electoral fiefdom of the passionately anticlerical radical deputy Georges Le Bail. Moreover, there was no significant clerical party to party to speak of in the area. In 1902, Le Bail's opponent, Delaporte, was classified as a *républicain modéré antiministeriel.* In Pont Croix and Dounarnenez, which was an important locus of resistance, Le Bail garnered 3,396 votes against Delaporte's 2,704. A.D. Finistère 3M297.

1880, however, following changes in the law, could not strictly be regarded as authorized. Precisely this category of schools was affected by the Combes decree of July 1902.[86] The legality of this decree was questionable, however, as article 14 of the new Law on Associations stated that members of authorized congregations had the right, without seeking authorization under the law, to teach in private schools. For this reason, most congregational schools founded after 1880 in Brittany did not seek authorization before the summer of 1902. The decree of the Combes ministry seemed to be clearly in violation of the original text and principle of the 1901 law. Many superiors of congregational schools were undoubtedly aware of these legal considerations, which were made known to the village notables.

Municipal councils of the thirty seven communes affected, including those that had voted for the Radical deputy Georges Le Bail, sent letters of protest to the government; they argued that state educational institutions simply could not accommodate the displaced pupils. Many communes, in the process of building state facilities for boys, contended that they did not have the revenues to provide facilities for girls as well.

The peasantry did not actively oppose the closing of schools run by male orders. Statistics on the number of state and congregational schools in the department from 1880 to 1905 indicate that secular education among boys became widely accepted in the department. The number of state schools for boys more than doubled from 1880 to 1905, from 399 to 824,[87] whereas the number of "public" congregational schools—schools officially patronized by communal authorities—declined from 151 in 1880 to 33 in 1905.[88] By the early 1900s, no matter how loudly the parish priest might rail against the écoles sans Dieu and against the families who patronized them, the number of male pupils in state schools continued to grow.

In Finistère it appears that almost without exception money that was voted by municipalities for the construction of secular primary schools to be staffed by state-trained schoolteachers went to the construction of boys' schools first. Such actions made it appear that resistance to state policy was gender-specific and that communities in Finistère more readily handed their sons over to the state and were miserly when it came to female education. Obvious distinctions seem to have been made between male and female education, and a greater value was attached to preserving a strong religious direction in the instruction of young girls. These values were undoubtedly encouraged by the Church whose strength and survival largely depended on its female parishioners at the end of the nineteenth century.

[86] L. Elegoet, *Saint-Méen*, p. 306.
[87] Bedel-Bernard, "L'enseignement primaire dans le Finistère," p. 5.
[88] Ibid.

Attitudes toward male and female education may have played a part in shaping the response of the peasantry to the secularization of primary education, but it does not explain why only girls' schools run by the Filles du Saint-Esprit were vigorously defended. The peasantry of Finistère did not resist the closing of all primary schools for girls in the department. The closings of schools staffed by the Filles de Jésus de Kermaria, the Soeurs de la Providence, and the Soeurs de l'Immaculée Conception, all of which were subject to the Law on Associations, were not contested. This suggests that more was at stake in the resistance of 1902 than considerations of gender and religion. What made the Filles du Saint-Esprit unique and particularly valued by the peasantry?

The Filles du Saint-Esprit was a Breton congregation initially founded in the diocese of Saint-Brieuc, neighboring Finistère, in 1706. The community began as a charitable and nursing congregation that gradually established a system of primary schools throughout the Breton peninsula.[89] After the Revolution, the congregation received official recognition from the French government for eight establishments as well as authorization to found additional institutions "in accordance to the need for hospitals and of the poor and at the demand of communes."[90] Although the congregation grew by leaps and bounds during the course the nineteenth century, it remained regionally based. The eight religious houses formally recognized by the government in 1810 had grown by 1888 to 290 "maisons d'instruction et de charité" that served 38,000 children.[91] By the end of the nineteenth century, the Filles du Saint-Esprit had more members working in Finistère than in any other department in Brittany, and in Finistère itself the order had more members than any other religious teaching order. By 1878, the Filles du Saint-Esprit was ranked among the largest orders in France.[92]

The Filles du Saint-Esprit recruited primarily from among the daughters of the Breton peasantry who generally served in the areas from which they came. At midcentury, the diocese of Saint-Brieuc recruited the largest number of young women into the congregation.[93] By 1880, however, the Filles du Saint-Esprit drew more novices from Finistère than from any other

---

[89] Langlois, Le catholicisme au féminin, pp. 316, 416.

[90] "Décrets imperiaux," 13 November 1810, Bulletin des lois de l'empire français 13, no. 338 (Paris, 1811), p. 680.

[91] Abbé Lemercier, Notice sur la congrégation des Filles du Saint-Esprit, 1706–1850 (Saint Brieuc, 1888), pp. 160–63.

[92] Langlois, Le Catholicisme au féminin, p. 335.

[93] Between 1850 and 1860, 140 women from the diocese of Saint Brieuc entered the congregation, and 80 came from the diocese of Quimper. Michel Tanquy, "L'implantation des congrégations masculines et féminines dans le Finistère, 1790–1902," vol. 1 (Maitrise, Université de Bretagne Occidentale, 1988), pp. 361–62.

region in France, including the diocese of Saint-Brieuc.[94] Similarly, the number of religious houses dispensing charity, medical services, and providing primary instruction in Finistère increased dramatically during the course of the nineteenth century. Between 1819 and 1902, 110 new communities of the Filles du Saint-Esprit were founded in the department.[95] Collectively, they ran seventy-seven operations that combined medical and charitable services with primary instruction, twenty four that devoted themselves exclusively to primary instruction, and a number of maisons de charité, dispensaries, and hospices. The majority of the one hundred ten houses assumed, then, multiple roles, and half of these houses were formed during the early Third Republic. By 1890, the Filles du Saint-Esprit was the largest female religious congregation in Finistère.

The rise in the number of young women who entered the Filles du Saint-Esprit during the early Third Republic can in part be attributed to the availability of a vast pool of young women in a region due to the "demographic explosion" that affected the department.[96] Alternatives to rural exodus were sought, and agricultural prosperity in certain areas of the department may have alleviated the pressure of population. Entry into religious congregations such as the Filles du Saint-Esprit provided an honorable and preferable alternative to emigration for the daughters of the Breton peasantry, and perhaps the growing visibility of the Filles du Saint-Esprit among a highly devout population stimulated interest in the congregation.[97]

The closing of congregational schools run by an order that had close ties to local communities throughout the department meant that the fate and livelihood of these nuns, the daughters and sisters of the lower Breton peasantry, were in question. When all unauthorized schools run by female congregations were finally closed in 1903, 363 nuns and 10,762 of their pupils were affected by the Law on Associations in Finistère.[98] Of these nuns, 236 belonged to the Filles du Saint-Esprit; because they could not be readily absorbed into the congregation's main establishment in Saint-Brieuc, they faced an uncertain future. The violent response to the closing of schools run by the Filles du Saint-Esprit may then in large part be viewed as a reaction to what would become an important social, economic, and moral problem for the rural communities in which the nuns served.

---

[94] In the decade between 1870 and 1880, 192 nuns from Finistère entered the congregation, whereas the diocese of Saint Brieuc followed with 152. Ibid.

[95] Ibid., pp. 260–63.

[96] Segalen, *Quinze générations de Bas-Bretons*, p. 139.

[97] Although the Filles du Saint-Esprit recruited among young women throughout the department, larger numbers came from regions that experienced economic difficulties from between 1870 and 1880. Tanguy, "L'implantation des congrégations masculines et féminines," pp. 362–64.

[98] *La Semaine religieuse du diocèse de Quimper et Léon*, 29 August 1903, p. 565.

The close social bonds between the Filles du Saint-Esprit and the local communities in which they served are important in understanding the geography of the resistance of 1902, but the congregation was unique given its multiple social roles in the region. By 1902, no other female religious congregation was as evenly distributed in the department, had as many religious houses, and combined the multiple social functions performed in local communities by the Filles du Saint-Esprit.

In an area ill-served by physicians at the turn-of-the-century,[99] and where in many cases the local population could not afford their services,[100] the nuns provided free health care and dispensed highly valued remedies to the local population. In 1881, there was only one physician for every 5,000 inhabitants in the department of Finistère, whereas the national average was one physician for every 2,500.[101] The subprefect of Morlaix, for example, noted that the departure of the superior of a school in the commune of Carantec would be "sincerely regretted" because of the medical care she gave to the sick (the other nuns would be missed less).[102] The municipality of Penhars claimed that if the Filles du Saint-Esprit were forced to leave the commune, indigents in the region would be deprived of free medical care.[103] A local organization formed to protest the expulsion of the Filles du Saint-Esprit in Locmaria Plouzané argued that in a commune "lacking in resources the departure of the sisters will leave a number [of people] without indispensable care if they become ill."[104]

Just as, if not more, important, the Filles du Saint-Esprit had established a system of nursery schools (écoles maternelles), particularly in coastal regions of southern Finistère and provided charity during a period in which the chaotic French system of public assistance was badly strained. On 15 July 1902, the wife of a fisherman addressed an impassioned, barely literate plea requesting that the government allow the Filles du Saint-Esprit to continue their activities in the port town of Douarnenez:

> "For the love of us let our good sisters stay. They do no harm the reverse they only do good above all for the poor. For myself I am a mother, the mother of 15 children and a lot of others like me who have to leave them from morning to night

[99] Jacques Léonard, Les médecins de l'Ouest au XIXeme siècle (Lille, 1978).

[100] Helias, The Horse of Pride, p. 85.

[101] Skol Vreiz, Histoire de la Bretagne et des pays celtiques 4: 112.

[102] A.D. Finistère, Iv1156, 26 August 1902. Also see Christiane Nasquer, "Exercice illégale de la médecine et de la pharmacie par les soeurs, en 1903, à Carhaix et Henvic" (Mémoire des Idées Politiques, Faculté de Droit, Brest, 1976–1977), and Marie-Noelle Cordon, "La loi du 1 juillet 1901: Expulsion des Filles du Saint-Esprit à Morlaix" (Mémoire des Idées Politiques, Faculté de Droit, Brest, 1976–1977).

[103] A.N. F¹⁹6079. Petition, 8 August 1902.

[104] A.N. F¹⁹6079. "Protestation des pères et méres de Locmaria Plouzané," 12 August 1902.

to help get them some bread for you know the life of poor fishermen is very hard. Our children are kept with the good sisters and are given food they are very good to the poor and to all of us. Mr. President, have the goodness to grant us this grace you can do it we are more than 2,000 mothers all republicans. . . . Vive la République! Let us keep our sisters."[105]

The subprefect of Brest, the commissaire spécial of Quimper, and many other local officials noted that women formed an important element in the resistance.[106] In the port towns of Douarnenez and Concarneau, for example, women dominated the crowd protesting the closure of schools run by the Filles du Saint-Esprit. Their closure unleashed a fury among women who went so far as to rip the clothes of a government official to shreds. Ironically, one of the most ardent supporters of the state's anticlerical policies, the Radical deputy Georges Le Bail, requested that the government keep open the écoles maternelles staffed by the Filles du Saint-Esprit. Perhaps fearing the electoral consequences, Georges Le Bail concluded that it would be impossible to close schools because they performed an irreplaceable "mission de bienfaisance et d'assistance."[107] In Douarnenez, more than four hundred preschool children were enrolled in these institutions, and according to the prefect, the wives and daughters of the fishermen employed in factories were unable to stay at home to tend to the children affected by the closures without losing a substantial source of family income.[108] In effect, the prefect requested that the government find a loophole to allow the écoles maternelles to remain open,[109] for in the towns of Tréboul, Douarnenez, Audierne, Le Guilvinec, and Pont l'Abbé the loss of what in essence constituted day-care for children provided by the Filles du Saint-Esprit created serious problems for already fragile family economies. Nonetheless, Georges Le Bail was mystified with the tenacity and violence of the resistance and wrote to the prefect of Finistère to obtain his thoughts on the reasons for the marked attachment to the congregation in Finistère.[110]

In 1902 the women of Finistère appeared to reenact the collective protests that occurred in many parts of France between 1794 and 1799,[111] but

[105] A.N. F¹⁹6079.

[106] A.D. Finistère, 1V1157, report from the subprefect of Brest to the prefect, 24 July 1902. The subprefect described them as "unbelievably overexcited" and claimed some went so far as "to utter death threats."

[107] A.N. F¹⁹6079, letter from Georges Le Bail to the minister of the interior, 16 July 1902.

[108] A.N. F¹⁹ 6079. Letter from the prefect to the minister of the interior, 16 July 1902.

[109] "Je vous prie, en conséquence, d'examiner si, par une mésure exceptionelle, il n'y aurait pas lieu de surseoir à la fermature des écoles maternelles privées." A.N. F¹⁹6079.

[110] A. D. Côtes-du-Nord, V3975. There appears to have been little resistance to the closure of congregational establishments in the neighboring department of Côtes-du-Nord.

[111] See Hufton, "Women in Revolution," pp. 90–108, and "The Reconstruction of a Church," pp. 21–52; Tackett, "Women and Men in Counterrevolution," pp. 680–704;

women do not appear to have led the resistance, as they had during the revolutionary period, perhaps because their relative impunity before the law no longer existed. Legal codes had changed by the twentieth century, and, indeed, many women were tried and sentenced in 1902. However, in 1902, as in the 1790s, women acted as defenders of the "moral economy" of the community.[112]

The highly visible participation of women in all demonstrations protesting the closure of schools run by the Filles du Saint-Esprit can in part be explained by the fact that they stood to lose most from the cultural policies of the Combes regime. However, as the plea from the mother in Douarnenez indicates, protests and petitions were not couched in anti-republican terms. In Saint-Méen, the Declaration of the Rights of Man and Citizen was posted in the commune, and the most common slogans were denunciations of Combes rather than of the Republic. In the thirty eight petitions submitted to the government from Finistère, Bretons used the language of the Republic itself to attack its mission.

In the partisan discourse of the period, the dominant role assumed by women in the resistance was a manifestation of their ignorance and of the hold that the parish clergy had on their female subjects. Indeed the behavior of women in the incident seemed to confirm the fears raised by the increasing feminization in the practice of religion in nineteenth-century France: as men increasingly absented themselves from Church, women entered and defended the religious institutions in greater and greater numbers. This was illustrated most dramatically in the startling growth in the size and number of female religious congregations, in statistics of attendance at Sunday and Easter mass, and in the numbers of educational institutions for girls established by women religious. In its baldest terms this phenomenon could be reduced to biology: Frequent confrontations with the specter of death and childbirth forced women to think more often of their souls. In a modified version of this view, it has been argued that the increasing confinement of women in a separate and domestic sphere following the Revolution made them less likely to experience the diversions that called their piety into question.[113] Harriet Martineau, commenting on the propensity of American women to immerse themselves in religious activities of all kinds, observed in 1837 that women pursued religion as an

---

Dupuy, "Les femmes dans la contre-révolution dans l'ouest," pp. 61–70; Desan, *Reclaiming the Sacred*, pp. 165–216.

[112] See, for example, E. P. Thompson, "The Moral Economy of the English Crowd in the Eighteenth Century," *Past and Present* 50 (1971): 76–136; Davis, "The Rites of Violence," and recent critiques of these approaches, including Desan, "Crowds, Community and Ritual," and Geertz, "Blurred Genres: The Refiguration of Social Thought," in *Local Knowledge*, pp. 19–35.

[113] See Bonnie Smith's argument in this regard in *Ladies of the Leisure Class*, esp. pp. 93–122.

occupation because they were prevented from assuming the wide range of social and intellectual roles open to men. The origins, impact, and long-term ramifications of the feminization of religion in France and in the West as a whole are far from clear. Nonetheless historians and anthropologists have noted the sexual division of labor in matters of religion in Brittany as well as other regions of France. In the Basque community of Sainte-Ignace female heads of households served as the link between the living and the dead as the guardian of the funeral cloth, and until the 1960s the elder female head of the household went to mass every evening as well as to a special Friday mass.[114] Martine Segalen has argued in Lower Brittany women were largely responsible for "religious relationships with the Catholic community which she embodied in the domestic sphere."[115] This division of spiritual space was not confined to Brittany, however. In many areas of France women took primary charge of the religious life of the family.[116]

This phenomenon assumed important political dimensions. Jules Michelet, denied access from the deathbed of his mistress by a Jesuit priest, attributed the religiosity of French women to the influence of the father confessor and early on in 1845 in *Le prêtre, la femme et la famille* railed against their subjugation. According to Michelet, the pernicious influence of the priest on women was making the French home uninhabitable, as the priest through the auricular confession obtained information about the habits and political behavior of her husband. The priest, Michelet explains in a telling passage, "always has the stick of authority in his dealings with the wife, he beats her, submissive and docile, with spiritual rods. There is no seduction comparable to this."[117] Republican politicians worried that these devout and therefore of necessity politically conservative mothers would undermine the Republic through their children, and indeed this was one justification for imposing a secular compulsory system of primary education during the early Third Republic in the first place.

Anticlerical republicans regarded the growing bifurcation in the practice of religion as a manifestation of a clerical plot. Indeed, when one of the prefect's assistants remarked to a priest on the extraordinary number of schools for girls run by the Filles du Saint-Esprit in the department, the priest replied, "C'est par la femme que nous tenons l'homme."[118]

---

[114] Nancy F. Cott, *The Bonds of Womanhood: "Woman's Sphere" in New England, 1780–1835* (New Haven, 1977) pp. 137–38. Sandra Ott, *The Circle of Mountains: A Basque Shepherding Community* (Oxford, 1981), pp. 45, 82. For similar practices in a rural community in Spain, see Christian, *Person and God in a Spanish Valley*, pp. 121–68.

[115] Segalen, *Love and Power in the Peasant Family*, p. 149.

[116] Ibid.

[117] Cited in Zeldin, "Conflict of Moralities," p. 15.

[118] F¹⁹2564, confidential memorandum from the prefect of Finistère to the minister of religious affairs, 12 May 1899.

For many communes, the expulsion of the sisters represented an infringement on local liberties and a source of serious financial hardship, as the government had not provided funds for communes that would be losing schools. Each commune affected by the measures was expected to provide the necessary funds either to rent or construct a new school building. For the populace who did not share Combes's dream of ridding France of all clerical influence, the expulsion of the members of the Filles du Saint-Esprit from three dozen communes in Finistère appeared not only illegal but also financially irresponsible.

The prefect of Finistère was perhaps the only government official to recognize the deleterious political and social consequences that the execution of the Law on Associations in Finistère might have. On 22 August 1902, the inspecteur de l'académie reported that in thirty one of the communes affected by the measures, which applied to schools that had been run by the Filles du Saint-Esprit and by male teaching orders, existing buildings were sufficient to house the students who would be displaced by closing the congregational schools, but that it was necessary to ask the mayors to furnish supplies, such as tables and benches. In fifteen of these communes additional facilities were needed, and in six it would be necessary to ask the municipalities either to make available facilities that were at their disposal or in some cases to furnish these facilities. Three communes in Finistère, according to the inspector, did not have facilities for a girl's school. These included Kerfeunteun and Mahalon in southern Finistère and Saint-Méen in northern Finistère.[119] Although it appeared to the prefect that the existing institutions would ultimately be sufficent to serve the needs of the students displaced by the expulsion of the teaching orders in Finistère, he noted that municipalities would be required to supply resources "which will be insufficient almost everywhere" and that the government was sure to encounter the "ill will" and "open hostility" of republican and reactionary municipalities alike.[120] The prefect wrote to Paris that although he was in agreement with the inspector concerning the steps needed to assure that scholastic resources were maintained in the department, he could not hide the fact that there would be no definitive solution to the problem unless the government made generous subsidies available to provide for the scholastic needs of the department. He noted that this would be the only means to avoid the delays that could result due to the "ill will of municipalities, even republican [municipalities]."[121]

As the prefect tried to assure that facilities would be sufficient to provide for students displaced by the closing of congregational schools, he con-

---

[119] A.D. Finistère, 1T79, report by the inspecteur de l'académie, 22 August 1902.
[120] Ibid.
[121] A.D. Finistère, 1T79, report by the prefect of Finistère, 24 August 1902.

tinued to encounter difficulties. In communes where it was possible to acquire or rent buildings to house students, the municipal council could legally refuse to make the necessary funds available,[122] and in some cases those funds were in fact unavailable. In other localities the government encountered even more formidable obstacles: There were no buildings available to rent.[123] This remained a problem. At the end of the 1902–1903 school year and during the succeeding years, these problems were not resolved. In May 1903 the prefect wrote a letter reiterating his request for funds and resources to the minister of public instruction.

The gender-specific response of the lower Breton populace in defending the closure of schools run by the Filles du Saint-Esprit must in part be understood in terms of the value placed on the social and spiritual services provided by the congregation. In closing educational establishments run by the Filles du Saint-Esprit the government wished to take the ideological instrument of the primary school out of the hands of the Church in order to inculcate republican values, but the government failed to realize that the desired impact of these reforms would be lost when communities were forced to provide financial resources for new state institutions and, at the same time, to give up what had become a vital network of public assistance.

Reprisals

Tempers had barely had an opportunity to cool after the resistance of August 1902 when Emile Combes aroused more discontent by effectively barring priests from preaching to their parishioners in Breton. As functionaries of the state, parish priests were required to submit proof every three months that they had performed their duties. This took the form of a certificate of residence, verified by municipal authorities, without which the priest would not receive his salary. On 29 September 1902 Combes introduced a new element into the certificate of residence. The mayor of the town in which the priest resided was required to attest that the priest was of French nationality and during the course of the previous trimester had given his religious instruction in the French language. Thus, the salary of each priest was inextricably tied to whether or not he used the Breton language in religious instruction.

As this circular followed close on the heels of the incidents of the summer of 1902, many speculated that it amounted to a reprisal directed against the clergy of Finistère whom Combes held responsible for the resistance. The salaries of twenty priests had been suspended for the third trimester

---

[122] A.D. Finistère, 1T79, report by the prefect of Finistère, n.d. [August].
[123] Ibid.

owing to their roles in the revolt. Several had been tried in court. The incidents of the summer of 1902 may also have demonstrated to the government the degree to which the peasantry of Finistère, twenty years after the introduction of a universal, free educational system in the 1880s, remained ignorant of the French language, as interpreters were needed in the trials of those arrested during the resistance of 1902.

In November 1902, the prefect reported that he thought the measure requiring priests to teach the catechism in French would "encourage families to send their children to school," but that the number of schools available was not sufficient to accommodate them.[124] He also noted that in a great number of communes in the Léon, republican or not, ignorance of the French language was universal; most men older than forty could only understand the Breton language.[125]

Combes viewed Breton, and indeed any regional language, as a language of reaction that was used by the clerico-aristocratic elite to shield the peasantry from the world beyond the parish,[126] and more specifically from republican ideas, arguing in defense of his measure that the catechism in Breton contained electoral as well as religious instructions.[127] Combes had some justification for this claim. In 1891, the inspecteur de l'académie reported that in the canton of Arzano, the Breton catechism contained a special section regarding the duties of voters:

Is it a duty to vote on election day?
Yes, it is an important duty and those who fail in it sin.

Is it a sin to vote badly on election day?
Yes it is a sin to vote badly on election day.

Why is it a sin?
Because in voting badly on election day, we choose the enemies of God, and by the same, the enemies of the country, to govern.[128]

The prefect as well as a number of republican politicians in Finistère questioned both the justification and the political wisdom of Combes's language policy. The prefect pointed out in the fall of 1902 that there was

[124] A.N. F¹⁹ 5503, report by the prefect of Finistère to the Direction Générale des Cultes, 5 November 1902.

[125] Ibid.

[126] Combes's position is not lacking in foundation. Fanch Elegoët cites the example of the periodical *Feiz ha Breiz* (Faith and Brittany) that was established in 1899 as a means of preserving and diffusing the Breton language in Finistère. See Elegoët, "Prêtres, nobles, et paysans," pp. 40–90. Gérard Cholvy, however, argues that the clerics were often used as agents of centralization as well. See his "Régionalisme et le clergé catholique au XIXe siècle," pp. 187–201.

[127] Le Floc'h, "L'enquête de 1902 sur l'usage de la langue bretonne dans le diocèse de Quimper et Léon," p. 6.

[128] A.D. Finistère, 1V56, report by the inspecteur primaire, 6 December 1891.

no correlation between the use of Breton and the political commitments of the population of Lower Brittany. Breton was used universally in the republican enclave of the Bay of Audierne in southern Finistère, whereas French was spoken almost exclusively in Concarneau, where the local population was clearly reactionary and where they actually appeared to "disdain the Breton language."[129] The prefect warned that the Breton was strongly attached to his native language and that it would offend the local population to implement such measures.[130] He argued before Combes had inaugurated his campaign against the Breton language in earnest that the measure would be the object of universal opposition, which "will necessitate the suspension of the salaries of the great majority of the department's priests" and deeply offend the local population.[131] He predicted, moreover, that the local population would see the measure as a first step toward the closing of churches—a fear the clergy had helped to foster to serve their interests. According to the prefect, religion played a very powerful role in the ordinary life of the Breton, and by ignoring this fact, one would only produce a movement as profound as that which emerged among Protestants in France when they were forbidden to preach in the sixteenth century. Most important, the prefect warned that the measure would result in a major setback for republican groups in the department and would therefore work against the government's political interests: "electors [will] hold the department's republican representatives responsible and [will] support the most clerical candidates presented to them."[132] Moreover, the situation in his view would be rendered even more difficult because "*it is not* certain that the best republicans support the administration."[133]

The prefect's appraisal of the situation in Finistère, shared by a number of republican mayors and deputies in the department, evoked the wrath of the Parisian newspaper, *Lanterne*, which accused the prefect of being "reactionary" and of taking part in an "anti-French and clerical campaign which the hobereaux lead in Brittany, under the pretext of regionalism."[134] The

[129] A.N. F[19] 5503, report by the prefect of Finistère to the Direction Générale des Cultes, 5 November 1902.

[130] Ibid. Collignon, the prefect of Finistère, seemed to be surprisingly sympathetic to those who wished to maintain regional languages, especially as such a position would provoke considerable consternation in the Combes era: "It is not to be doubted that any kind of measure restraining the use [of Breton] will severely offend his [the Breton's] affection for the language that he learned growing up, which is in some sense an integral part of this spiritual sustenance that he finds in his churches and would not know how to do without for a long time hence."

[131] A.N. F[19]5503, prefect of Finistère to président du conseil, ministre de l'intérieur et des cultes, n.d. [Sept. 1902].

[132] Ibid.

[133] Ibid.

[134] *Lanterne*, 20 September 1902. According to the newspaper, Collignon also declared his support for the equal maintenance of the Breton language at school in a session of the Conseil Général to the applause of the reactionaries.

Lanterne argued, echoing the position taken by the Combes regime, that the so-called regionalist initiative in Finistère was a matter of shielding Bretons from French culture and in consequence from ideas of progress and democracy.[135] Nonetheless, mayors, conseillers généraux, and deputies from the department protested against these measures as did literary societies and organizations devoted to the study of the Breton language. Many of these formal protests addressed to Emile Combes were written in Breton, such as those emanating from the cantons of Landivisiau and Châteaulin.[136] In many cases, as the prefect had predicted, mayors ignored and refused to have anything to do with the measure.[137] When the salary of the vicaire of the republican commune of Plogoff in southern Finistère was suspended, one municipal councillor of the commune resigned. In his letter to the prefect he pointed out that only Breton was used in sessions of the municipal council because most councillors did not understand French and that all secular marriages performed at the mairie were also conducted in Breton.[138]

All republican deputies were fearful, as was the prefect, that Combes's language policy would undermine support for republican groups in the department: "Do you think that we can watch with an indifferent eye two or three decrees sweep from this Breton soil republicans' thirty years of work?"[139] The republican regime's attacks on the language spoken by the majority of the adult population in Lower Brittany was as much an affront to local customs and values as was its insistence on the closure of congregational schools run by the Filles du Saint-Esprit. In the government's zealous pursuit of its civilizing mission, it risked losing whatever cultural and ideological legitimacy it had had in the region since the early Third Republic.

Consequences

In a practical sense the government failed utterly in ridding the department of the Filles du Saint-Esprit, many of whom continued to reside and teach in the communities where they had taught before 1902. The peasantry

[135] Ibid.

[136] Le Floc'h, "L'enquête de 1902 sur l'usage de la langue bretonne dans le diocèse," p. 7.

[137] A.N. F¹⁹5503, Report from the prefect to the minister of the interior, 24 November 1902. "I have reason to think that some will omit mention of religious instructions and the catechism, that others will not concern themselves with what happens in church anymore than at school."

[138] Le Floc'h, "L'enquête de 1902 sur l'usage de la langue bretonne dans le diocèse," p. 11.

[139] Louis Hémon's personal notes from this period are full of bitter comments on political consequences of Combes's regime. In 1903, Hémon wrote, "Radical Jacobin politics, with its incoherence and its brutality, its hollow declarations, its pretentions . . . is everything that is most repugnant to the independent temperament of this region. . . . It is only by violently attacking their nature that one can wrest Radical votes from Bretons." A.D. Finistère, 18J21, Fonds Louis Hémon. Charles Tréboul argues, however, that Hémon was somewhat contradictory in his behavior, for he was interested in defending the Breton language but happy to suppress the clerical threat in any form. See Tréboul, "Louis Hémon," p. 263.

supported and protected their activities in defiance of Paris. In December 1902, four months after the expulsion of the Filles du Saint-Esprit from schools throughout the department, the subprefect of Brest reported to the prefect that nuns who were expelled from the school they ran in Roscoff continued to run a school, give music lessons, and campaign for the re-opening of the school from which they were evicted.[140] Similarly the Filles du Saint-Esprit continued to teach on the island of Batz where monthly public collections assured their livelihood.[141] Their school, which had been taken over by the state was, according to the subprefect, boycotted by the local inhabitants.[142] This problem was not merely one of transition. In 1921, the government received complaints of teachers in a number of private schools in Finistère donning religious habits. Mlle. Tersiquel, head of the private school in Saint-Méen, declared in a sworn statement that when she began wearing a religious habit in September 1919 she did not believe that she was violating the law because she thought that with the end of the war "religious questions would no longer be a matter of discussion."[143] She added that she could also not afford to replace her worn-out clothes, one main reason for wearing her habit.[144] It appears that Mlle. Tersiquel's case was not unique. The prefecture advised against prosecution because there were a number of similar cases in the department, and all the nuns concerned belonged to the Filles du Saint-Esprit.[145] Moreover, the statistics on the ratio of public to private schools between 1901 and 1905 clearly demonstrate that the number of private schools in the department did not decline precipitously as the government had hoped; they had actually increased.[146] Most of these schools had clerical backing and were probably manned by the displaced Filles du Saint-Esprit. Combes, therefore, failed in ridding educational institutions of women from teaching orders in the department.

[140] A.D. Finistère, 1M151, report from the subprefect of Brest to the prefect, 7 December 1902. The nuns even began to give catechism lessons in Breton to all pupils in the commune. Report from the subprefect of Brest to the prefect, 26 October 1903.

[141] A.D. Finistère, 1M151, report from the subprefect of Brest to the prefect, 25 January 1903.

[142] A.D. Finistère, 1M151, report from the subprefect of Brest to the prefect, 15 February 1903. Only twenty eight pupils attended the school, the other eighty continued to be taught by the Filles du Saint-Esprit.

[143] A.D. Finistère, 1T78, letter, 21 April 1921.

[144] Ibid.

[145] A.D. Finistère, 1T78, report from the commissaire spécial of Brest to the subprefect of Brest, 1 July 1921. The commissaire spécial cited nine cases in which teachers in private schools began wearing their habits in 1919.

[146] Bedel-Bernard, "L'enseignement primaire dans le Finistère," p. 55. The number of private schools for women dropped from 151 to 148 between 1902 and 1903 but then increased to 150 in 1904 and to 154 in 1905. The number of public schools for girls outnumbered private schools both before and after the application of the law on associations, but these numbers hardly seemed affected by the government's measures.

The government believed the resistance of 1902 was orchestrated by the local nobility and the parish clergy, but this appraisal of the situation in Finistère demonstrated a profound ignorance, despite local reports, of the change in political alliances that had occurred in the countryside. The resistance occurred spontaneously and had broad-based bipartisan support. The anticlerical measures of the Combes regime merely strengthened popular support for the Christian democratic movement and associated the issue of regionalism and the defense of local culture with this new group of clerical republicans. These measures had a direct effect on the 1906 legislative elections in the department where republican deputies associated with the regime faced stiff challenges from the opposition after a number of years of undisputed success. The electorate did not go so far as to elect reactionary or monarchist deputies, but clearly showed their displeasure through the ballot. Most important for the Christian democratic movement, which was beginning to face problems from the Vatican and the ecclesiastical hierarchy, these events merely broadened the social base for the movement, particularly in southern Finistère. The issue of cultural and regional defense replaced the agricultural crisis as one main issue to mobilize the rural electorate. The cultural politics of the Combes regime therefore played directly into the hands of the Christian democratic movement, providing it with a volatile and popular issue to mobilize support. Combes chose perhaps the worst moment to implement his anticlerical campaign, for had he been more conciliatory, he could have undercut one appeal of the movement in a department where the electorate rejected reactionary politics but was unyielding on questions of local liberties and culture.

By suspending the salaries of the clergy who did not obey ministerial directives regarding the use of French in religious instruction, the government hoped to hurt them financially. Although the parish clergy lost a considerable amount of revenue, they were able to defy the government because of the amount of income they customarily had at their disposal from quêtes.[147] The government further hoped to disarm the Church through the Separation of Church and State which was enacted in December 1905. By 1906, however, it was clear to observers in the department and evident in election results that the government had utterly failed in its objectives and had, in fact, achieved the opposite result. In 1902, virtually all electoral districts in southern Finistère returned ministerial republicans who did not face serious challenges from the opposition, but by 1905,

[147] See chap. 3, "Clerical Income and the Independent Parish Clergy." The subprefect of Brest suggested that the suspension of the the clergy's salary may have made the transition between the régime concordataire and the Separation of Church and State less difficult as the parishoners were accustomed to providing the salary of their priest by 1906. A.D. Finistère, 1M134, report by the subprefect of Brest to the prefect, 29 September 1906.

voters were disenchanted with the anticlerical republicanism that lacked, in addition, an effective organizational base. Moreover, these measures had a lasting effect on politics in the region; the memory of these events determined political choices for some time to come. This is not to say that politics in the region turned on the religious issue. More was at stake in the mass resistance to the expulsion of the Filles du Saint-Esprit and to the language policy of Emile Combes. Republican deputies such as Louis Hémon realized that these measures, profoundly offensive to local sensibilities, were viewed as an attack on local liberties. The prefect reported on the eve of the 1906 legislative elections that the eviction of the Filles du Saint-Esprit and the question of separation of Church and state had inspired deep opposition to the government. The decree banning the use of Breton in religious instruction was exasperating because most voters over the age of forty did not understand enough French to comprehend a sermon in the national language, and the government had long failed to provide the department with a sufficient number of schools where the French language could be taught.[148] The prefect argued, moreover, that if the clergy had actually obeyed the decree banning the use of Breton in religious instruction, the peasantry would have resorted to force as they had in August 1902.[149] The prefect would not venture to predict the outcome of the elections because the peasantry seemed totally mute and inscrutable, which was not a good sign.[150] In 1907, the peasantry in the arrondissement of Brest seemed to have lost confidence in the government and began withdrawing money held in banks and caisses d'épargne.[151]

The legislative elections of 1906 demonstrated the depth of voter dissatisfaction, particularly in former Radical enclaves in southern Finistère. Georges Le Bail, radical deputy of the second electoral district of Quimper, faced a serious challenge from a reactionary, Henri de Servigny, member of the Action Libérale Populaire (ALP). Le Bail narrowly won by 143 votes,[152] largely owing to support from the urban commune of Douarnenez, for de Servigny won majorities in the other four cantons, two of which had actively participated in the revolt of 1902 (Pont-Croix and Pont l'Abbé) (Table 5.1). Similarly, in the second district of Châteaulin and the

[148] A.D. Finistère, 3M301, élection législative of 6 February 1906. Report by the prefect to the minister of the interior, 10 October 1905.

[149] Ibid. According to the prefect, the clergy made a "fortunate blunder" when it "refused to preach in French," as this would have resulted in a "revolt in the entire countryside."

[150] Ibid.

[151] A.D. Finistère, 1M134, report from the subprefect of Brest to the prefect, 2 January 1907. "This state of mind is disturbing and merits the government's attention."

[152] Le Bail blamed his political difficulties on clerical meddling and devoted a book to the subject, but priests had evidently tried to influence the vote in previous elections and had not achieved such a degree of success, so other elements must have been at work. See Le Bail, *Une élection législative de 1906*.

TABLE 5.1
1906 Legislative Election in the Second Electoral District of Quimper

Canton	No. of voters	Georges Le Bail (Radical)	Henri de Servigny (ALP)
Douarnanez	7,120	3,889	3,218
Plogastel-St. Germain	4,435	2,033	2,395
Pont Croix	6,300	3,107	3,179
Pont l'Abbé	6,305	3,086	3,180
Total	24,160	12,115 (50.14%)	11,972 (49.55%)

Source: A.D. Finistère, 3M300, élections législatives de 1906.

first district of Morlaix the republican and radical candidates Louis Dubuisson and Emile Cloarec faced formidable challenges from ALP candidates. The results in the first round were so close that a runoff was held. Although the republican Louis Dubuisson and the radical candidate Cloarec ultimately won against their ALP contenders, their victories were narrow.[153]

The results of the 1906 legislative elections in the first electoral district of Morlaix and the second district of Châteaulin illustrate another consequence of implementing Combes's regime's anticlerical policies. Not only did they alienate a number of steadfast republican voters, but they also created divisions in republican ranks. The prefect reported in 1905 that these issues had initiated a "dangerous division" between moderate republicans and radicals, who had previously cooperated with one another during elections to defeat "clerical" and reactionary candidates.[154]

In the second electoral district of Châteaulin a Radical candidate ran against the incumbent republican deputy who had not supported Combes's language policy; this challenge resulted in the division of the republican vote and left the door open for the ALP candidate. In the first electoral district of Morlaix, an anticlerical socialist candidate ran against Cloarec, the incumbent radical who had voted against implementing the measure to ban Breton in religious instruction; he thereby divided the vote, which necessitated a runoff. In both cases the ALP candidate lost, albeit narrowly

153 A.D. Finistère 3M300, élections législatives de 1906.
154 A.D. Finistère, 3M301, Elections législatives de 1906, report by the prefect to the minister of the interior, 10 October 1905.

in Châteaulin, as traditional republican groups were able to rally their supporters. This lasting division between moderate and Radical republicans resulted in disunity in republican organizations. In 1906, local officials reported that republican electoral groups in southern Finistère were moribund and totally lacking in organization. In the first district of Quimper, republican committees and unions were allegedly "inactive" and republican politicians did not seem to try to give a "new drive" to republican ideas.[155] In 1907, the suprefect of Brest wrote that republicans were "scattered," lacking in organization: it was difficult for the government to count on them, for they at times allied themselves with"conservatives."[156] In 1909, the subprefect of Brest reported that only one party made any organizational effort in the arrondissement, the social Catholic sillonistes, and in the second district they were a political group with considerable support.[157]

The Combes regime was directly responsible for the electorate's disaffection with traditional republican groups and inadvertently for the splintering of the republican party in the department. Some politicians reconsidered their allegiance to the délégation des gauches. Republican, Christian democrat, and reactionary alike objected to the way in which the government implemented the 1901 law on associations, and some questioned the legality of the measure. Although the enforcement of the law resulted in a mass resistance in 1902, Combes's language policy provided the real issue of contention. Breton deputies of all political colorations heard Combes question their national loyalty in a full session of the Chamber of Deputies. Despite protests launched by republican deputies in Finistère against the Combes regime and unanimous rejection of the language measure, the regional issue came to be associated with the opposition and an integral part of the program and platform of the Christian democrats in particular. The social Catholic movement profited most from the Combes's regime political blunder, for these clerical republicans provided an alternative to traditional parties of the Right, whose social and political views were unacceptable to the electoral majority in Finistère and to traditional parties of the Left, who were intimately associated with Emile Combes.

The political furor caused by Combes's anticlerical campaign marked a turning point for the Christian democratic movement because it helped to create a mass-based following and a bridge between town and country

[155] A.D. Finistère, 1M175, report by the commissaire spécial of Quimper to the prefect, 29 December 1906.

[156] A.D. Finistère, 1M134, report by the subprefect of Brest to the newly appointed prefect on the political situation in the region, 31 October 1907.

[157] A.D. Finistère, 1M136, report by the subprefect of Brest to the prefect, 1 November 1909.

throughout the department by increasing its ranks in southern Finistère. It also created a new set of issues that became an integral part of the movement's platform. Whereas republicans at the center increasingly articulated national loyalty in terms of secular culture that denied the legitimacy of local or regional claims, Christian democrats at the periphery sought to reconcile regional identity with that of the larger French nation. By 1910, the movement that had been launched to defend religion and reform society had also become a movement to defend the region's cultural identity.

The events surrounding the secularization of education in Finistère and the resistance of 1902 indicate that during the early Third Republic provincial appropriation of Parisian values and institutions through the agency of the state was selective. Instead of adopting the cultural practices generated at the center, local populations often created indigenous institutions in response to initiatives in Paris. Shifting economic trends and demographic patterns shaped the way in which the institutions and values of the capital were adapted or transformed at the periphery. Far from defending tradition in 1902, Bretons rallied behind newly created institutions that addressed the needs of a society adapting to social and economic change. For example, the écoles maternelles created by the Filles du Saint-Esprit responded to the challenges posed by the formation of new industries in port towns such as Douarnenez. In founding such institutions and in expanding its social and educational functions, the congregation provided at the same time new opportunities for women in a region experiencing a demographic explosion.

A number of historians have recently suggested that forging a national identity through a gradual process of acculturation involved the replacement of rural cultural traditions by urban values and institutions.[158] The geography of the resistance of 1902, which included both urban and rural communes, makes it difficult to equate the urban culture of Paris with that of towns in Lower Brittany. Townspeople in the seaport of Concarneau and in the rural village of Ploudaniel shared common values and defended local cultural practices and forms of public assistance in opposition to the center. Indeed, this case study suggests that at the periphery the cultural boundaries that divided Paris and provincial towns may have been more sharply drawn than the cultural frontiers dividing towns and rural hamlets.

In a broad sense, the implementation of the 1901 Law on Associations in the department of Finistère illuminates the gulf of misunderstanding between the administrative halls of Paris and the byways of provincial France during the early Third Republic. In face of the mass resistance to its policies, the government continued to attribute the resistance in the region to

[158] See, for example, Weber's "Cultures and Civilizations," in *Peasants into Frenchmen*.

a tradition of religious extremism and antirepublicanism. But Bretons framed their petitions and protests in the language of the Republic and in the terms of the revolutionary Declaration of the Rights of Man and Citizen, a framework indicating the degree to which these admittedly devout communities had assimilated and transformed the discourse of the Republic into a public defense of local institutions.[159] The government, and to a large extent historians who have adopted its language, took the incidents of 1902 in Finistère to be a revolt of a superstitious and barbarous population completely cowed by châtelain and priest. This merely reinforced the government's belief in the legitimacy of the state's mission civilisatrice. The peasants and fishing families of Finistère, however, could only view the government legislation as a policy whose result would be the financial ruin of communes and families and the collapse of local institutions and networks of public assistance. When Breton women and men placed barricades in village roads and threatened military troops in the summer of 1902, they were not defending a world they had lost but a world they were in the process of creating.

[159] Similarly, during the religious revival of the revolutionary period, communities, using the rhetoric of revolutionary ideology to defend their right of worship, infused that ideology with new meanings. See Desan, "Redefining Revolutionary Liberty," pp. 1–27.

6

Religion and the Politics of Dissent, 1903–1911

DURING THE first decade of the twentieth century the state's anticlerical campaign strengthened the social Catholic movement considerably as it steadily made headway in Finistère's towns and cities. Although the movement's urban following was not as large as that of the countryside, its eclectic ideology, which initially appealed to the country dweller, came to be embraced by urban dock workers, postal employees, shopkeepers, and students. The expansion of the movement's social base, however, ironically coincided with the withdrawal of women from any form of public expression. The resistance of 1902 marked only the fleeting involvement of women in local politics.

As the social Catholic movement spread among urban and rural groups alike, elements within it grew more independent of the ecclesiastical hierarchy, and its leadership became less clerical. The gradual declericalization of the movement ultimately contributed to its democratization and coincided with the emergence of the Sillon, a social Catholic youth group initially founded in Paris in 1894. Finistère became one of the most important silloniste strongholds in France and helped to transform the social Catholic movement in the department.

In the first decade of the twentieth century the Sillon recruited from among democratic priests, those who had backed abbé Gayraud and Albert de Mun, and the working classes of Brest and Quimper. Initially, it identified itself as a Catholic movement dedicated to social reform and left political action to the Action Libérale Populaire. When sillonistes began in 1906 to question the political and social aims of the ALP and the Association Catholique de la Jeunesse Française, a youth group closely associated with it, the movement split into two distinct factions that each embodied different social and political goals. The ALP devoted its political efforts primarily to the defense of religious interests. Sillonistes, who had previously abstained from politics, increasingly argued that political action should be used to redress social and economic problems afflicting modern society. The ALP articulated their social goals primarily in terms of charity and benevolence, while sillonistes stressed the principles of social justice and Christian duty.

Pope Leo XIII initially encouraged the social Catholic movement in France and Italy, but he became increasingly fearful that elements within the movement had become too independent of ecclesiastical authority and aggravated the social tensions latent in the Catholic community. On 18 January 1901, he issued the papal encyclical *Graves de Communi*, which warned Christian democrats against adopting socialism and provoking class warfare. He decreed that Christian democracy should mean no more than "a benevolent Christian action toward the people."[1]

His successor, Pius X, who became pope in 1903, merely hardened this new position toward social Catholicism. Pius X was intensely conservative and lacked Leo XIII's urbanity and interest in the "intellectual ferment stirring within Catholicism."[2] Although he was the only pope in the two hundred years before 1958 to have been born in true poverty, he did not share Leo XIII's concern for the social question. Moreover, Pius X chose Cardinal Merry del Val, a Spanish aristocrat who had little sympathy for the spirit of the Ralliement, as his papal secretary. On 18 December 1903, Pius X issued *Motu proprio*, which stipulated that Christian democrats were to obey ecclesiastical authorities and obtain permission for publications, and on 8 September 1907, *Pascendi*, which condemned Modernism.

Armed with these documents, Monseigneur Dubillard, who was appointed bishop of Quimper in 1899, succeeded in achieving what he and his predecessors had failed to achieve prior to 1903. He forced the lower clergy of Finistère to abandon positions of leadership and to withdraw open support for the independent, democratic, and socially progressive groups within the social Catholic movement.[3] The clergy's loss of its financial independence after the Separation of Church and State in 1905 facilitated Monseigneur Dubillard's task. The separation resulted in the fiscal reorganization of the French Catholic Church and the disappearance of the lower clergy's practice of taking independent public collections.

The vicissitudes of Vatican policy and internal divisions in the social Catholic movement resulted in the gradual fragmentation of the movement in Finistère. By 1908 the Sillon, a socially progressive Catholic group, was pitted against the conservative ALP, and the Pope finally condemned the Sillon's social and political positions in 1910. Papal condemnation and the consequent declericalization of the social Catholic movement in Finistère led to the emergence of a lay leadership from among its ranks, which ultimately revitalized and strengthened the movement's political base.

The Changing of the Guard

The Sillon, a social Catholic youth group founded in Paris by students at the Catholic Collège Stanislaus in 1894, rapidly spread to Finistère. Marc

---

[1] Quoted in McManners, *Church and State in France*, p. 99.
[2] Ibid., p. 134.
[3] He was later well rewarded and became a cardinal in 1911.

Sangnier and Paul Renaudin, its principal leaders, were strongly influenced by the democratic priests associated with the Christian democratic movement and the Ralliement, by the Catholic philosopher Maurice Blondel and by the social Catholic industrialist Léon Harmel. Under Sangnier's auspices and with his financial help, in 1894 the group began to publish *Le Sillon*, which was intended to propagate the silloniste ideas. The Sillon was dedicated to creating a democratic and socially just Christian society and to combatting dilettantism, pessimism, and art for art's sake, all of which were ostensible manifestations of the spiritual emptiness of modern industrial society.[4] In its early days the Sillon met as a study group in the crypt of the Collège Stanislaus and discussed the problems facing Catholics in modern society. Its members were largely confined to an intellectual elite of students and professors. By 1899, however, the Sillon began organizing *cercles d'études* (study groups) to bring students and the working classes together to discuss matters of faith as well as the social question. Soon thereafter periodic congresses of the study groups were held. These study groups differed in important respects from those organized by the Association Catholique de la Jeunesse Française (ACJF), a youth group established by Albert de Mun in 1886 and whose motto was "piety, study, action." The ACJF clearly obeyed the ecclesiastical directives, whereas the Sillon gradually became independent of the ecclesiastical hierarchy in social and political matters. This stance in fact led to its condemnation by the Vatican in 1910, even though the Sillon exercised strict obedience in religious matters.

Like the Christian democrats of the 1890s, the sillonistes were above all interested in rechristianizing modern society. They were, however, regarded with some suspicion in certain Catholic circles because of their social progressivism and the methods they used to disseminate their message. Marc Sangnier willingly participated in large public meetings where he debated outspoken anticlericals and socialists, including Jules Guesde. In 1901, the Young Guard, established "to ensure liberty of speech and discussion," stood in readiness at such meetings to suppress hecklers and those who tried to disrupt the proceedings.[5] The Young Guard was trained in boxing, fencing, and served as a paramilitary force at the often tumultous debates held in Paris. The Sillon, moreover, encouraged the formation of an elite from among the study groups and staged theatrical and musical productions as well as public lectures through Instituts Populaires in order to reach a wider audience.

The Sillon was initially a movement of young students and professors from the Parisian bourgeoisie, but after 1901 it rapidly spread to other

---

[4] McManners, *Church and State in France*, p. 100ff.
[5] Ibid., p. 100.

segments of society and other parts of France. The Sillon was particularly successful in the Northeast and Brittany. The lower clergy of Finistère who had sponsored the candidacies of abbé Gayraud and Albert de Mun avidly embraced the social initiatives of the Sillon. Finistère became one of the movement's most loyal strongholds, which may in part be explained in terms of the prior implantation of social Catholicism in the area.

On 10 June 1904, the first issue of *L'Ajonc*, a monthly publication established by the Sillon of Brittany, began to be published in Rennes,[6] and students and seminarists who joined the Sillon began to edit their own publications, such as *Nos Vacances* and *La Semence* in Finistère. A number of study groups were established throughout the department, recruiting initially from the ranks of the lower clergy, students, and the bourgeoisie. Early issues of *L'Ajonc* reflected silloniste activity in northern Finistère, but in 1906 references began to be made to silloniste groupings in Quimper.

According to the 15 July 1906 issue of *L'Ajonc*, the Sillon was not a "confraternity to obtain indulgences, it is not a school of catechism. What it wants is to improve the destiny of people and the government of the country."[7] The means through which the Sillon hoped to obtain its goal centered on creating an elite that "thinks, acts, teaches, goes among and wins over the masses."[8] The principal leaders in the Sillon hoped to achieve this through the creation of study groups as well as unions, which would form responsible, Catholic, democratic "apostles."[9] The sillonistes in Finistère increasingly referred to themselves in meetings as "républicains démocrates" as well as "catholiques convaincus."[10]

The Sillon was grafted onto the Christian democratic movement in Finistère and drew on preexisting study groups in the department to recruit new members, particularly among the young. Until 1907, there was close cooperation between the Sillon and the Christian democratic priests who had organized such groups prior to 1900. One of the most successful study groups founded by the lower clergy in the diocese was situated in the parish of St. Louis in Brest. The curé of the the parish, abbé Roull, had firmly backed abbé Gayraud in 1898 and 1902, and, along with abbé Ollivier and abbé Grall, he was one of the most influential priests in the diocese, as a "grand électeur du Léon."[11] In 1896, he helped to found a study group

---

[6] Similar regional publications began to appear in the center, north, and east of France. Caron, *Le Sillon et la démocratie chrétienne.*

[7] *L'Ajonc*, 15 July 1906, "Au Sillon" (text in Breton and French), p. 159.

[8] Even claimed that the Sillon did not pretend to attract everyone, but to create an elite. *L'Ajonc*, April–May 1907, Speech by Michel Even, president of the Sillon de Bretagne, congress in Fougères, Ille-et Vilaine, p. 16.

[9] *L'Ajonc*, 15 January 1906.

[10] *L'Ajonc*, 15 June 1905, evening meeting in Pleyben, 15 May 1905.

[11] Abbé Roull was one of the priests who opposed Monseigneur Dubillard's choice of abbé

that was attached to the Patronage de Saint Louis on 15 May. The purpose of the group was to formulate and implement practical solutions to social problems. An adult group met regularly on Friday, a youth group on Thursday. During its first two years of existence, the groups were responsible for creating a consumer cooperative, a family fund, and a union. The patronage, moreover, formed a library that made Catholic publications— *Le Sillon*, *l'Univers*, and *La Vie Catholique*—available to participants.[12] The Patronage of Saint Louis and its study groups also organized a series of special lectures and conferences sponsoring, for example, a regional congress on 22 March 1903 attended by the charismatic leader of the Sillon, Marc Sangnier.[13]

Study groups and silloniste meetings drew from all social classes and particularly recruited from among adolescents between the ages of fifteen and twenty. Many of the latter became involved in such activities through the influence of Eugène Le Berre, the young *vicaire* of the parish of St. Louis, and abbé Calvez.[14] Lawyers such as Jacques Fonlupt, Pierre Trémintin, Paul Simon of Landerneau, and Emile Kellersohn, professor of German at the Lycée of Quimper, represented the social Catholic movement's new urban and secular constituency and increasingly participated in silloniste activities.[15]

A significant number of the early leaders of silloniste groups in the department were also recruited from the working classes of Brest and Quimper, such as Jean Barré, a woodworker and vice president of the group formed in Quimper, Jean Le Gac, a tailor, Phillipe, an arsenal

Stéphan as candidate for the third arrondissement of Brest during the 1902 legislative elections. He was born in 1843 in Landerneau and had been appointed principal of the collége of Lesneven in 1872. As such, he wielded an enormous amount of power. The prefect of Finistère referred to him as the "bishop" of the Léon. In 1892, his candidacy was considered when the bishop of Quimper died but was rejected because of his purported political "meddling" and native birth in the region. He was appointed curé of the parish of St. Louis in 1892. See Cloître, "Les années 1898–1914 vues par *L'Echo Paroissial de Brest*," pp. 72–76.

12 *L'Echo Paroissial de Brest*, 23 December 1900, pp. 2–3.

13 Ibid., 13 April 1903, p. 3. From 1,200 to 1,500 persons attended these conferences according to *L'Echo Paroissial de Brest* and official government reports. In October 1905 a meeting of the cercles d'études in the region of Brest took place at the Patronage St. Louis, which was attended by at least 1,500, 500 of whom were men, 60 priests, 250 young people, and the remaining number women. A.D. Finistère, 1M200, report by the commissaire spécial of Brest to the subprefect of Brest, 30 October 1905.

14 Personal interview in Brest, 4 October 1984, with Albert Berthou, who began to attend silloniste meetings in 1906. Berthou became a postmaster and continued to be an ardent silloniste and member of the Jeune République during the interwar period.

15 A police official reported to the prefect that Pierre Trémintin and Le Goasquen, vicaire of the cathedral, were in the process of forming a silloniste youth group in Quimper and pledged to attend twice a week. A.D. Finistère, 1M228, report by the commissaire de police of Quimper to the prefect, 13 July 1906.

worker in Brest, and Herry, an employee in Morlaix's tobacco factory. By 1907, silloniste meetings and social initatives were not exclusively dominated by the clergy, as were Christian democratic social initiatives of the 1890s. A new lay leadership had emerged, and the Sillon was successful in introducing its variety of social Catholicism into an urban setting.

The Sillon and Rural Organization

After 1906, the Sillon in Finistère made the greatest progress in rural areas through the formation of agricultural unions and cercles d'études.[16] These initiatives were by no means new; a number of rural unions created by the lower clergy in the 1890s had been strongly influenced by Christian democratic ideas. However, the aims of rural organizations that were formed under silloniste auspices posed a new threat to rural elites whom they challenged publicly.

The democratic priests of the 1890s had been responsible for founding cooperatives, insurance funds, and unions; by serving the material needs of their parishioners, they hoped to stay the tide of secularization. In general, these unions included large and small landowners, tenants, and rural workers. This form of syndicat mixte, according to many social Catholics, would assure social reconciliation and unity and therefore avoid the element of class conflict associated with socialist unions. Some of the earliest rural unions in Brittany were formed under the auspices of the Confraternity of Notre Dame des Champs, but these organizations were generally dominated by large noble landowners, who in turn belonged to the conservative Union Centrale des Syndicats.[17] Of the 224 participants at the 1906 congress of the Union des Syndicats Agricoles et Horticoles de Bretagne, 77 were nobles, 22 were priests, and the rest were bourgeois or individuals who could not be considered peasant; only 2 could claim that title.[18] For this reason, the Union des Syndicats Agricoles et Horticoles de Bretagne that was formed in 1894 was not to the liking of all peasants, some of whom claimed that the organization was run by hobereaux and priests, not farmers.

[16] A strategy often used to recruit the peasantry was to stage theatrical productions, to organize "silloniste days" three times a year that would be followed by a conference. L'Ajonc, 15 January 1906. When the congress of study groups was held on 28 January 1906, more than 600 participants from over fifty predominantly rural communes attended. L'Echo Paroissial de Brest, 4 February 1906.

[17] The confraternity Notre Dame des Champs in the region of Saint-Pol-de-Léon was led by a noble landowner, Henri de Goesbriand. Bulletin des syndicats agricoles de Basse Bretagne, 23 June 1899. For a discussion of the division of the national syndical movement between a republican left and conservative right before the First World War, see Cleary, Peasants, Politicians, and Producers, pp. 33–47.

[18] Raoul, Un siècle de journalisme breton, pp. 605–6.

Sillonistes increasingly raised the question of whether this form of organization best served the interests of the small farmer or rural wage earner. At the 1908 regional silloniste congress held in Quimper, Saik Ar Gall, a peasant farmer from Plabennec who had formed a union and study groups in his parish, suggested that the Sillon might organize separate unions for agricultural wage earners.[19] Although it was generally agreed that separate organizations might be unnecessary because wage workers were often the sons of farmers in Brittany and became farmers themselves, Saik Ar Gall argued that more attention should be devoted to the farmer leasing land from large landowners, many of whom charged exorbitant rents for their land. He also complained of the rapacious middleman, who was responsible for setting prices and robbing the peasant of the true value of what he produced.

In answer to many of these concerns, on 31 May 1909 Hirrien and Eugène Berest of Saint Malo formed the Syndicat de Saint-Pol-de-Léon, which initially consisted of 1,500 farmers.[20] They invited all tenant farmers, landowners working their own land, and sharecroppers regardless of sex or age to join, but excluded all landowners who lived off the rent received from their land. This bold departure illustrated the tensions that began to be expressed between farmers, middlemen, and large landowners in the Léon during a period of growing agricultural prosperity. Farmers in the region objected to the practices of middlemen who dominated the market in Saint-Pol-de-Léon. The farmers, for example, claimed that the middleman often forced the producer to sell below a fair price. The statutes of the union were no less than a declaration of war against the large landowner and middleman. Article 4 stated that the goal of the union was to hasten the moment when the farmer himself owned the land he tilled individually or collectively. According to Louis Le Dissès, its president, the union should assume this form because the peasant who tilled the land and rented from large landowners was "weighted down by the competition with the rich, the masters of commerce, factories and land."[21] The peasant was a victim of the large landowner who leased his land and the merchant, both of whom exploited the peasant mercilessly in their passion to get rich.

[19] "Congrès régional du Sillon en Bretagne. Quimper, 7 & 8 juin 1908," L'Ajonc, July–August 1908.

[20] F. Elegoet, Révoltes paysannes en Bretagne, pp. 89–94. In 1909, the subprefect of Morlaix reported that the syndicat of Saint-Pol-de-Léon had been formed by a group of landowners and led by well-known sillonistes. A.D. Finistère, 1M136, report by the subprefect of Morlaix to the prefect, 29 May 1909.

[21] "Petra eo eur Syndicat.—Perak eo bet savet hini Kastell" (What is a Syndicat.—Why was one formed in St. Pol) by Louis le Dissès, Ann Hader, October 1909, p. 4. The stipulation, according to Louis Le Dissès, that only those who actually worked on the land should be members of the union won the Syndicat de Saint-Pol-de-Léon the enmity of the nobility and bourgeoisie.

One means of combatting this problem was to form an agricultural union along new lines. Existing unions, according to Louis Le Dissès, were no more than cooperatives established to buy seed, fertilizer, phosphates, and farm machinery at prices cheaper than those on the open market. They were, moreover, dominated by individuals with considerable wealth. What was needed was a new kind of union to unite those exercising the same profession, to improve the material conditions in which they lived and worked, and to "put pressure on deputies to change [existing] laws" and establish new ones.[22] The union's larger purpose was to eradicate customs and practices that oppressed the peasantry and harked back to a period of virtual slavery; the union sought to combat excessive rents and improve the housing conditions of laborers employed by farmers in order to change the relationship between farmer and master.[23] According to Le Dissès, the rich landowner, who had formerly dominated agricultural unions, would no doubt view such an organization as an "entente of fire and war," but he argued that he and his compatriots were fervent Catholics with no desire to establish a collectivist system that would convert the peasant into a new form of slave.[24]

The leaders of the Syndicat de Saint-Pol-de-Léon were silloniste militants whose leadership included president Louis Le Dissès, François Cabioch of Roscoff, and Hirrien of Tréflouénan. The bilingual Catholic newspapers *Feiz Ha Breiz* (Faith and Brittany) and *Courrier du Finistère* strongly supported the union and cooperative.[25] Several months after its foundation, its members and other prominent sillonistes from the Léon launched a bilingual publication, *Ann Hader* (The Sower), that was strictly devoted to agricultural syndicalism and rural issues. The editorial board consisted of three leaders of the Syndicat of Saint-Pol-de Léon, Louis Le Dissès, Louis Emily of Cléder, and Hirrien, as well as Saik Ar Gall and abbé Grindorge, the author of a column concerning agricultural issues in *L'Ouest Eclair*, the social Catholic newspaper based in Rennes.[26] Jacques Fonlupt and Paul Simon, both of whom were lawyers in Brest, as well as Francis Bellec, a notary from Landivisiau, were also members of the editorial board.

[22] Ibid.

[23] Ibid.

[24] Ibid.

[25] These Catholic affiliations may have been one reason why the subprefect of Morlaix characterized the members of the group as "reactionnaires" and argued that there may have been political implications to the formation of such a group as the middlemen were "republicans." A.D. Finistère, 1M136, report from the subprefect of Morlaix to the prefect, 29 mai 1909.

[26] *L'Ouest Eclair*, was founded in 1899 through the efforts of abbé Trochu and Desgrées du Loû, a lawyer from Brest, who had been a strong supporter of abbé Gayraud in 1897 and who wrote several articles in favor of Gayraud's candidacy in *L'Univers* at the time of the

Ann Hader was modeled on the immensely popular almanac and loose sheet songs hawked by colporteurs. The monthly publication pictured a youthful farmer sowing seeds in a field beside a church or chapel placed off in the distance. The resemblance of the cover of *Ann Hader* to popular almanacs published in the region is unmistakable, though the young farmer is less identifiable as a Breton. The first issue of *Ann Hader*, which appeared in October 1909, was subtitled "Kazeten al Labourien-Douar e Breiz-Izel" (Journal of the Peasantry of Lower Brittany). The first issue contained a long article by Louis Le Dissès on why it came to be formed; the journal itself was dedicated to the creation of unions and cooperatives on a broader scale in order to enable the peasant who worked his land to protect his interests.[27] The introductory articles by Fonlupt and Francis Bellec constituted an open declaration of war against merchants—that is, the middlemen—and *grands propriétaires*. *Ann Hader* was clearly committed to preventing large landowners from infiltrating agricultural syndicalism: "The large landowners would like to be the masters of unions at any price just as they are masters of the land. The dominant classes will try at whatever cost to turn the peasantry away from their efforts. With vigilance, we will fight against this attempt."[28]

Louis Le Dissès, Francis Bellec, and Jacques Fonlupt declared in the first issue of *Ann Hader* that the syndicalism they espoused was not "political" and that the journal would not treat political issues. The professed goal of their form of agricultural syndicalism was professional. It was dedicated to emancipating the peasant and improving the material conditions under which he worked and lived.[29] The journal also vowed not to discuss matters of religion, another divisive issue. They hoped to organize the peasantry regardless of their political conviction. Despite this declaration of political neutrality, *Ann Hader*, however, did not advocate forming a state within a state in order to discourage the peasantry from using the electoral arena for resolving social and economic issues. Jacques Fonlupt clearly stated in the publication's first issue that its founders were "republicans

---

contested election. The founders of *L'Ouest Eclair* were strong supporters of Christian democracy and later of the Sillon, which incurred the wrath of the archbishop of Rennes. The newspaper, despite the hostility of local notables, became a very successful enterprise—ultimately the largest regional daily in France. See Delourme [alias abbé Trochu], *Trente-cinq années de politique religieuse*, and Arnal, "The Nature and Success of Breton Christian Democracy," pp. 226–48.

[27] Jacques Fonlupt, "Aux ruraux," *Ann Hader*, October 1909, p. 3.

[28] Ibid., p. 4

[29] Francis Bellec, "D'Al Labourien-Douar" (To the Peasantry), *Ann Hader*, October 1909, p. 1. "There will never be a question of politics among us. . . . Politics is something which sows discord here; we, we strive to unite the peasantry, and to help them to improve their situation in all respects."

resolutely attached to republican ideas."[30] Louis Le Dissès asserted that a primary goal of the new form of agricultural organization that they hoped to create was to have its voice heard in the Chamber of Deputies and to establish more equitable laws.[31]

The creation of the Syndicat de Saint-Pol-de-Léon and the publication of *Ann Hader* caused consternation in some Catholic circles. Abbé Roull, curé of Saint Louis in Brest, who had been an ardent supporter of the Sillon and the Christian Democratic movement, began to lambaste the enterprise in *L'Echo Paroissial de Brest.* In an article dedicated to *Ann Hader*, it became clear that abbé Roull's principal objection to the publication was that it propagated "class warfare." He argued that certainly some farmers suffered from the demands and injustices of landowners but that all landowners were not "without heart and a sense of justice."[32] Abbé Roull considered the poem that concluded the first issue of *Ann Hader* to be nothing less than a communist "International." "The Song of the Sower" contained verses that abbé Roull argued were so socially divisive they only created friction among Catholics:

Le temps des droits anciens qui pliaient la tête du Peuple
Sous la main du bourgeois, ou sous la semelle du noble,
Le temps de Yann Gouer [du paysan] d'être maître à son tour
Et de jeter son licol au nez du maître.

Et la semence que nous répandons à travers la terre de Basse-Bretagne
C'est la semence que l'on verra se lever
Le peuple nouveau doit briser le lien
Et, droit sur la terre, culbuter le Peuple ancien.

Culbuter le Peuple ancien, briser les lois
Qui pèsent sur chaque esprit comme de lourdes chaînes
Et les remplacer par le lien d'amour
Qui devra toujours être la loi du Peuple nouveau.[33]

Ann Hader was increasingly criticized by the landowning elite in the region surrounding Saint-Pol-de-Léon, by abbé Roull, and by the clerical

[30] "Aux ruraux," p. 4.

[31] Louis Le Dissès, "Petra eo eur Syndicat.—Perak eo bet savet hini Kastell," *Ann Hader*, October 1909. Le Dissès, Francis Bellec, and Jacques Fonlupt declared that they were republican in political conviction and Catholic. Ibid. "Most of those who will write in this journal are republicans, that is to say people who think that it is fitting to each to have the right to have his say concerning the country's affairs. . . . We declare . . . we are and want to be *Christians above all else* [emphasis in original]. It is in the teachings of religion and in our faith that we find the courage to accomplish our task."

[32] *Echo Paroissial de Brest*, 14 November 1909, p. 2.

[33] Verses 11–13, "Guerz An Hader" (Le Chant du Semeur), *Ann Hader*, October 1909, p. 8, trans. Christian Brunel.

hierarchy in Quimper for espousing firebrand politics while pretending political neutrality. In September 1910, Francis Bellec published a public statement in answer to these claims. According to Bellec, *Ann Hader*'s activities were directed toward the professional and social concerns of the laboring peasantry, and he and his colleagues had never indicated that *Ann Hader* had silloniste sympathies.[34] Despite this declaration, it became increasingly difficult for *Ann Hader* to claim its independence from the Sillon: most members of the editorial board were also sillonistes, and the ideas the publication espoused were identical to those expressed by the Sillon. For this reason, as the Sillon in the department of Finistère came into conflict with the ecclesiastical hierarchy, so did *Ann Hader* and the form of agricultural syndicalism it represented.

Papal Condemnation

Prior to 1906 the Sillon's attitude toward politics was ambiguous at best. Marc Sangnier and silloniste publications insisted that the Sillon's mission was social and intellectual, not political: To ensure a tolerant democratic society, it was necessary to change the outlook of individuals rather than to involve oneself in the electoral arena.[35] A principal leader of the Sillon in the department of Côtes-du-Nord argued that it was best not to raise political questions as no consensus would be possible.[36]

It became increasingly clear that Marc Sangnier himself and a certain segment within the Sillon were not altogether convinced that the Sillon should shy away from politics indefinitely and that they did not support either the ALP's brand of politics or the *jaunes*,[37] a form of Catholic trade unionism that many sillonistes believed served the interest of capital rather than labor. Marc Sangnier emphasized at the third regional congress of the "Sillon en Bretagne" that it would be "ridiculous" for the Sillon to involve itself in politics when its democratic ideas had not achieved sufficient influence in the country: "Politics is not, in fact, a goal, a result, but a means. We would like politics to be the fulfillment of popular aspirations and, in consequence, we must develop those aspirations."[38] Sangnier's insinua-

[34] Francis Bellec, "A nos lecteurs," *Ann Hader*, September 1910.

[35] According to a 1906 article in *L'Ajonc*, the Sillon did not involve itself in politics: "We do not practice politics. We do not step into the arena where parties slaughter each other for a future France. We do not think that the future of democracy depends on the fate of an election. Changing the inner man, that is what we work for, our work is purely moral and social from this point of view." *L'Ajonc*, "La vie du Sillon en Bretagne," 5 January 1906.

[36] Paul Rivière, "Trouvons mieux," *L'Ajonc*, 15 August 1906.

[37] A.D. Finistère, 1M228, report by the commissaire spécial des chemins de fer to the prefect, 6 August 1906, and 1M228, report by the commissaire spécial de Brest, 29 July 1906.

[38] "Compte rendu du 3eme congrès régional du Sillon en Bretagne—23, 24, 25 Avril 1905, Saint-Brieuc," p. 86.

tions that the Sillon would enter the political arena were hardly veiled, however. He declared that the Sillon was not currently involved in politics, but perhaps "in fifty years" or sooner.[39]

In 1905, Sangnier was clearly more concerned with defending the interests of the Catholic church and believed that one should vote with these interests in mind.[40] Between 1908 and 1911 this priority changed, and some members of the Sillon hoped to see it become an active political movement. Saik Ar Gall, a principal organizer of rural unions under silloniste auspices in northern Finistère, declared at the Sillon's regional congress in Quimper in 1908 that he hoped to see "Bretons assume the honor of taking our movement to the Palais Bourbon."[41]

By 1906, members of the Sillon in Quimper as well as Marc Sangnier began to make political statements that disturbed the bishop and the ALP. Monseigneur Dubillard therefore encouraged young Catholics in Finistère to join the Association Catholique de la Jeunesse Française, and in August 1906 he forbade all priests and seminarists from attending a silloniste congress.[42] All priests in the department, with the exception of abbé Clec'h of the collège of Saint-Pol-de-Léon, obeyed. Six priests from other dioceses attended.[43] Marc Sangnier described this move as a mistake because it would be severely judged by the Catholic laity and priests in the diocese of Quimper. He declared that sillonistes, inasmuch as they were Christians, had the obligation to obey religious authority, but inasmuch as they were citizens "do not depend on the bishop."[44] On 7 August 1906, the Sillon of Morlaix under the leadership of Jean Marzin declared itself independent of diocesan organizations.[45]

At the congress held in Brest on 5 August 1906, Marc Sangnier set out to define the political position of the Sillon vis-à-vis the Left and Right.

[39] Ibid.

[40] "Sillonistes must vote. It is a duty of conscience and they must let the interests of the Church come before political interests, whatever they are." Ibid., p. 87.

[41] "Congrès régional du Sillon en Bretagne," Quimper, 7, 8 juin 1901.

[42] This order was published in the *Semaine Religieuse de Quimper* on 3 August 1906. A.D. Finistère, 1M228, reports from the commissaire de police of Quimper to the prefect, 13 July 1906, 3 August 1906.

[43] A total of 300 people attended the congress, 30 of whom were women. For official comments, see A.D. Finistère, 1M228, report by the commissaire spécial to the prefect, 6 August 1906.

[44] Ibid.

[45] Quéméneur, "Le Sillon à Morlaix, Landivisiau, Saint-Pol-de-Léon 1903–1912," pp. 11–12. Many members of the parish clergy disapproved of these declarations of independence and openly attacked sillonistes during religious services. When a silloniste congress was held in Landivisiau, a town in northern Finistère, on 27 January 1907, the curé of Landivisiau declared from the pulpit that the sillonistes had a right to attend mass and receive communion, but "I must protest against their behavior, in my name and in the name of the bishop. . . . They wanted to organize their congress outside of the hierarchy. . . . Politico-socio-religious groups like the Sillon do not have the right to absolute independence." Ibid., pp. 24–25.

Sangnier declared that the current government in France was not a democratic republic but a "monarchy without a king, a bastard government."[46] Adversaries on the Right resented the Sillon because they claimed that it wanted to transform society. Without denying this goal, Sangnier launched a blistering attack on the egoism of the Right, which wished simply to maintain a blatantly unjust economic system. Adversaries on the Left, according to Sangnier, also wished to enslave the people. Socialists who wanted to abolish management merely wished to replace it with the tyranny of the state, which was even more dangerous. Instead, Sangnier called for the support of worker legislation in accordance with proposals presented by socialists and social Catholics such as Albert de Mun.[47] Sangnier nonetheless argued that, when the education of the proletariat was completed, "management will disappear, and worker groups will replace it."[48] He declared that the Sillon would "refuse to follow political directions from curés and bishops."[49]

This message was reiterated by the members of the Sillon in Quimper several days later on 9 August 1906. At a meeting attended by 500 people and presided over by carpenter Jean Barré and tailor Jean Le Gac, Barré declared that workers need not simply be wage earners but should have a role in management.[50] Sangnier, who spoke at the meeting, claimed that in order for citizens to be aware of the interests of the French nation, it was necessary to have effective legislation, social initiatives, and a truly democratic spirit. He concluded that "land should be possessed by those who cultivate it, mines by miners. . . . Capitalism is an obstacle. The Church does not protect capitalism. One can replace it, or rather replace management by groups of workers."[51]

Soon after the meeting rumors circulated in the seminary of Quimper, which had become a breeding ground for the Sillon, that the future of the cours d'oeuvres was in jeopardy. The superior of the seminary of Quimper had warned the seminarists to submit to [episcopal] authority at the first session of the cours d'oeuvres in 1901 but assured them that the bishop looked on their activities favorably. According to the secretary, this was said to "stifle certain sinister noises regarding the cours d'oeuvres' state of health" and to dampen the hostility toward the cours d'oeuvres that was evident in certain quarters.[52] The superior repeated his warning in 1906. He instructed the seminarists to devote themselves to the study of the social

---

[46] A.D. Finistère, 1M228, report by the commissaire spécial to the prefect, 6 August 1906.
[47] Ibid.
[48] Ibid.
[49] "In as much as we are devout, we submit to them, but we do not admit anyone the right to impose political opinions on us ." Ibid.
[50] A.D. Finistère, 1M228, report by the commissaire of police of Quimper to the prefect, 9 August 1906.
[51] Ibid.
[52] A.E.Q., 2H312, Minutes of the cours d'oeuvres, session 19 November 1901.

question but in a spirit of submission to ecclesiastical authority to avoid being branded "independents."[53] The superior announced his intention to attend sessions of the cours d'oeuvres assiduously to ensure that studies "always remain on the correct path."[54] Following 29 November 1906, however, no further meetings were held for nearly a full year; only in November 1907 were sessions resumed. The president of the cours d'oeuvres, in stark contrast to his predecessors, emphasized that the "social question is a question of charity," rather than a question of justice, and that the cours d'oeuvres would now resume after having been interrupted "by the events you know about."[55] The resumption was short-lived. The last entry in the cours d'oeuvres book of minutes mused, "When will the meetings of the oeuvres be resurrected? Soon, one must hope. Meetings discontinued on 21 May 1908."[56]

The Catholic press in Finistère, such as *L'Echo Paroissial de Brest*, supported the Sillon and its initiatives wholeheartedly prior to 1907, in spite of open attacks by other Breton publications such as the *Nouvelliste de Bretagne*, based in Rennes, and by ecclesiastical authorities in other dioceses. In 1904, *L'Echo Paroissial de Brest* published an eloquent defense of the Sillon after it had been allegedly attacked by the *Nouvelliste de Bretagne*: It argued that simply because the *Nouvelliste* strongly supported the more conservative youth organization, Association Catholique de la Jeunesse Française, it had no right to portray sillonistes as insubordinate—"always ready to rise up against ecclesiastical authority"—citizens who "think and act like socialists."[57]

In early 1907 the tone and content of *L'Echo Paroissial de Brest* and other Catholic newspapers changed markedly.[58] On 29 September 1907, *L'Echo Paroissial* published remarks allegedly made by the Pope to the bishop of Bayonne regarding the Sillon: "I have fears regarding the Sillon. I have read the speeches of Marc Sangnier. I have also read a few of his articles. All of this disturbs me. These young people are following an unfortunate path. Priests should not become involved."[59]

---

[53] A.E.Q., 2H313, Minutes of the opening session of the cours d'oeuvres, 18 November 1906.

[54] Ibid.

[55] A.E.Q., 2H313, Minutes of the cours d'oeuvres, session of 14 November 1907.

[56] Ibid., session of 21 May 1908.

[57] *L'Echo Paroissial de Brest*, 21 August 1904.

[58] *La Quinzaine Ouvrière*, founded in Brest by abbé Madec, who had as a seminarist participated actively in the cours d'oeuvres, was an exception. In 1908, Madec declared that the *Quinzaine Ouvrière* was not, strictly speaking, a silloniste publication, but that it adhered to silloniste "economic methods" and "social ideas." *La Quinzaine Ouvrière*, 11 April 1908, p. 1. Madec, however, was careful to declare that his publication, which was authorized by the bishop, was an "enemy of politics" and that its only aim was to serve the "religious and material interests of the region." *La Quinzaine Ouvrière*, 12 October 1907, p. 1.

[59] *L'Echo Paroissiale de Brest*, 29 September 1907, p. 3.

After 1907 the Action Libérale de Quimper, through its new publication, *L'Indépendent du Sud-Finistère*,[60] launched fierce assaults on the Sillon in the department. On 25 September 1907, *L'Indépendent du Sud-Finistère* reported that the Sillon's current motto appeared to be "Cléricalisme, voilà l'ennemi!" because of remarks made by Henri Teitgen, a well-known silloniste from Brest at a congress of the Sillon in Douarnenez.[61] Teitgen responded to the attack by declaring that he did indeed express his horror of "clericals," whom he defined as those who used religion rather than served it.[62] *L'Indépendent du Sud-Finistère* went so far as to accuse sillonistes of being Christian anarchists and of giving Radicals, Socialists, and all anti-Catholics "the weapons to combat the religion of Christ."[63]

The sudden rejection of the Sillon by the *Indépendent du Sud-Finistère*, the official newspaper of the ALP in Finistère, reflected a gradual repudiation of republican varieties of social Catholicism owing to the change of tide in Rome in 1907, particularly after the publication of the encyclical *Pascendi*, condemning Modernism. The repudiation also showed that the bishop of Quimper's efforts to force the clergy to submit to ecclesiastical authority were finally successful, after his abortive attempts during the reelection of abbé Gayraud in 1902.

Once freed from the Concordat after the Separation of Church and State in 1905, the bishop, who had never been sympathetic to the Christian democratic movement or the Sillon, controlled the purses of the lower clergy and was therefore better able to exert his will. Clerical salaries supplied by the state were abolished as a result of this legislation, which would have been no great loss to the lower clergy of Finistère had new fiscal policies not been implemented by the Church. The clergy were required to report collections taken in their parishes, and the ecclesiastical hierarchy in the diocese determined how these funds would be redistributed and used. The bishop, therefore, had more effective instruments at his disposal to control the activities of the lower clergy. The subprefect of Brest reported in 1906 that the lower clergy were disappointed that *associations cultuelles communales*, which would be independent of diocesan authority, were not established. Without associations cultuelles, revenues collected in the parish would be "centralized in the hands of the bishop who will redistribute them."[64]

On 25 August 1910, Pope Pius X officially condemned the Sillon for

[60] *Action Libérale de Quimper*, which was founded soon after the ALP committee in Quimper, ceased publication in 1906.

[61] *L'Indépendent du Sud-Finistère*, 25 September 1907, p. 3.

[62] Ibid., 28 September 1907, p. 2.

[63] Ibid.

[64] A.D. Finistère, 1M134, report from the subprefect of Brest to the prefect of Finistère, 27 October 1906.

acting independently of ecclesiastical authority, collaborating with Protestants and free-thinkers, and encouraging social divisiveness. This condemnation was not surprising, for in 1907 *le plus grand Sillon* agreed to accept Protestants and free-thinkers into its ranks. Marc Sangnier stood for election twice during this period, albeit without success, campaigning on the issues of an income tax, minimum wage, retirement pensions for workers, and the right of civil servants to form trade unions.[65] Pius X did not condemn the social initiatives of the Sillon entirely, however, but he argued that the movement had strayed from the Catholic path when it began to reject ecclesiastical authority and create divisions among Catholics.[66] The Pope indicated that silloniste Catholics should be free in their political preferences, but only insofar as those preferences were purged of all that was not "entirely in conformity with Church doctrine."[67]

Pius X's letter of condemnation marked the beginning of a bitter struggle for ascendency among Catholic groups in France, which included the socially conservative Association Catholique de la Jeunesse Française, the right-wing Action Française, and the center/left-leaning Sillon. The Action Française, a nationalist political action group formed by Charles Maurras in 1898, and the ACJF began to fight a vituperative war with the Sillon.

As a devout Catholic, Marc Sangnier submitted to the Pope's letter of condemnation and disbanded the Sillon as an organization, which helped initially to temper clerical criticism. On 18 September 1910, the new bishop of Quimper, Monseigneur Duparc, praised the members of the Sillon in his diocese for following suit.[68] Monseigneur Duparc advised his parishioners to observe the lesson provided by the Sillon, to follow the path of obedience, and to unite in order to defend Catholic interests.[69]

Not only did members of the Sillon in the department of Finistère submit to papal authority, but ultimately *Ann Hader*, which had tried to disassociate itself from any political or ideological grouping, ceased publication. The editorial board explained that as members of the Sillon they had submitted to ecclesiastical authority and that *Ann Hader* would be discontinued because its continuation might imply that their submission was insincere.[70]

---

[65] McManners, *Church and State in France*, p. 172.

[66] Letter of condemnation reprinted in *La Semaine Religieuse de Quimper et Léon*, September 1910, 599–605, 618–25, 670–75.

[67] Ibid., p. 674.

[68] "Lettre pastorale de Mgr l'Evêque de Quimper et de Léon, promulgant la Lettre du Souverain Pontife, relative au Sillon." The bishop of Quimper announced that the members of the Sillon should be applauded for their actions. *La Semaine Religieuse de Quimper et Léon* September 1910, 694.

[69] Ibid., p. 698.

[70] *Ann Hader*, September 1910, no. 12.

The papal condemnation of the Sillon and the disappearance of publications like *Ann Hader* did not eradicate these initiatives, but they did result in both the declericalization of social Catholicism in Finistère and the definitive splintering of the original social Catholic movement into three groups: L'Union des Catholiques sponsored by the bishop, the Office Central de Landerneau created by the landowning nobility, and the Fédération des républicains démocrates du Finistère established by sillonistes. Each of these organizations was formed in 1911, one year after the condemnation of the Sillon.

New Departures

In his pastoral letter condemning the Sillon, Monseigneur Duparc, who was appointed bishop in 1908, called for Catholic unity and the creation of a "tight alliance" of "religious defense" among Catholics.[71] A year later he announced the formation of L'Union des Catholiques, an association of Catholic defense intended to "(1) foster works useful to the diocese and parish and (2) organize Catholic defense."[72] The Union des Catholiques focused on the education of its members specifically with regard to the rights of the Church, the laws that violate those rights, and the implications of the Separation of the Church and State.[73] The Union, moreover, formulated its demands with the approval of the bishop and voiced them through petitions, conferences, and demonstrations, and in the press. L'Union des Catholiques ostensibly shied away from politics. It accepted Catholics of all political parties and did not advocate a "purely political program," but it did instruct its members: "You know the program of the liberties of the Church. All of you vote for men who are prepared to defend them."[74] The bishop was determined to maintain firm control over defining the rights of the Church and religious issues. A diocesan committee chosen by the bishop oversaw all parochial and cantonal unions composing the diocesan L'Union des Catholiques.[75]

In essence, Monseigneur Duparc created a political pressure group that drew on the new tactics inaugurated by the lower clergy in the region. However, it drew on only one set of issues used by the democratic priests in the 1890s to mobilize the electorate. L'Union des Catholiques subordi-

---

[71] "Lettre Pastorale de Monseigneur l'Evêque de Quimper et de Léon, promulgant la Lettre du Souverain Pontife relative au Sillon," *La Semaine Religieuse*, 18 September 1910, p. 698.

[72] *La Semaine Religieuse de Quimper et Léon*, 24 November 1911, p. 846.

[73] Ibid., p. 847.

[74] Ibid., p. 848.

[75] Ibid., pp. 861–62.

nated all other concerns and issues—political, social, and economic—to religious defense.

L'Office Central de Landerneau, an agricultural union founded on 16 September 1911,[76] also represented a continuation of social and economic initiatives of the democratic priests of the 1890s and of the Sillon. But l'Office Central opposed the brand of agricultural syndicalism espoused by the silloniste Syndicat de Saint-Pol-de-Léon formed in 1909. L'Office Central was founded by the landowning nobility in the Léon, many of whom had been staunch supporters of Action Libérale Populaire and opponents of the Sillon. The leaders of the new union included the mayor of Saint-Pol-de-Léon, the comte de Guébriant, A. de Boisanger, A. de Nanteuil, and A. de Vincelles, all of whom possessed considerable property, as well as non-nobles who owned medium-sized farms: François Tynévez, Yves Ellegoët, and Mathurin Thomas.

The Office Central de Landerneau included—in contrast to the Syndicat de Saint-Pol-de-Léon—all social groups involved in agriculture. Its professed goal was to defend the corporate interests of the profession. Office Central was designed to foster social reconciliation and claimed that only an organization that included tenants, landowners, and laborers could best represent the interests of the profession. To this extent the Office Central was predicated on the long-standing cultural division between town and country in Lower Brittany, and its founders argued that social tensions and divisions in the countryside could be adjudicated within the union.

The founders of the movement wished, like the Union des Catholiques, to steer clear of political parties and programs. The Office Central explicitly banned all political discussions within the union and refused either to sponsor or endorse political candidates: Political involvement would only disturb the professional unity advocated by the association.

The underlying purpose of the Office Central was to establish what amounted to a state within a state to shield the peasantry from politics in order to preserve existing hierarchical relationships in the countryside. The formation of the Office Central de Landerneau was a direct response to the mobilization of the peasantry by the democratic priests in the 1890s and organizations like the Syndicat de Saint-Pol-de-Léon that had threatened those relationships.[77]

If the Office Central de Landerneau shunned political patronage, however, it actively sought and received the patronage of the Catholic Church. At the first congress of the Office Central de Landerneau held in 1912, de Boisanger, a principal founder of the Office Central, announced that the

---

[76] F. Mévellec, *Le combat du paysan breton*, pp. 113–59, and Berger, *Peasants Against Politics*.

[77] Berger, *Peasants Against Politics*.

members of the association belonged to a "common profession" but because they were "Catholics before being farmers" they would follow the dictates of the Church.[78] The bishop of Quimper, Monseigneur Duparc, in turn welcomed such an initiative because the new organization could act as a Christian order in the agricultural sphere.[79] Indeed, he declared that the Office Central was an "extension of L'Union des Catholiques."[80] More important for the bishop, the union was based on the "harmony which should exist between the diverse social classes,"[81] which could heal the wounds caused by the "spirit of the Sillon."[82] Whereas the Syndicat de Saint-Pol-de-Léon was nonconfessional, de Boisanger declared at the first congress of the Office Central that members would not conceive of the exercise of their profession outside the "paths traced by the Church."[83]

The creation of an alliance between Union des Catholiques and Office Central did not result in the suppression of the political aspirations of republican Catholics with democratic aspirations. In 1911, sillonistes in Finistère founded a political organization, the Fédération des républicains démocrates du Finistère (FRDF), that became an important political contender in the department's legislative and local elections in the interwar period.

The president of the newly formed FRDF was the well-known silloniste Pierre Trémintin, a lawyer and conseiller général of Plouescat, a commune in northern Finistère. The vice president was Paul Simon, the son of a shopkeeper in Landerneau, the secretary Francis Bellec, a notary and municipal councillor of Landivisiau was the treasurer and a founding member of the silloniste Syndicat of Saint-Pol-de-Léon. The program of the organization placed it squarely between the Right and the Left, between the parties of reaction and revolution. Indeed, the formation of the Fédération des républicains démocrates du Finistère reflected the political aspirations of former sillonistes. It was, moreover, the clearest expression of the new political identity that was brought into being in the Breton peninsula in the 1890s. It represented a novel attempt to reconcile the Republic with religion and the nation with the region.

[78] Report of the congress in *La Semaine Religieuse de Quimper et Léon* , 1 November 1912, pp. 749–50.

[79] Ibid., p. 750.

[80] *La Semaine Religieuse de Quimper et Léon*, 1 November 1912, p. 751.

[81] Quoted in Mévellec, *Le combat du paysan breton*, p. 135.

[82] Two years later the bishop wrote that he hoped that the "divisions, class hatreds, the spirit of the Sillon" would be avoided through Catholic union. *La Semaine religieuse de Quimper et Léon*, 20 February 1914, "Lettre pastorale de Mgr. L'Evêque de Quimper et de Léon portant publication du décret sur l'heroïté des vertus du venerable Michel Le Nobletz," p. 118.

[83] Quoted in *La Semaine religieuse de Quimper et Léon*, 1 November 1912, p. 749.

In general terms, the FRDF program advocated "liberty of conscience" and "religious peace" as well as the recognition of the spiritual rights of the Church and the continuation of diplomatic relations with Rome. It also called for freedom in education, that is, the development of Catholic schools. The FRDF did not, however, characterize itself as a Catholic party and devoted the majority of its platform to political, social, economic, and regional issues.[84]

The FRDF advocated social security legislation, land leases of longer duration to give tenants greater protection, lending institutions in the form of agricultural credit banks, and low-income housing. Although the FRDF was not a regionalist party per se, in 1911 and throughout the interwar period it promoted administrative decentralization, electoral reform, proportional representation, and the depoliticization of the administrative bureaucracy.

During a period in which a number of important regionalist and autonomist organizations were founded in the Breton peninsula, the FRDF articulated its program in terms of both the unity and the plurality of the French nation. Like the Christian democratic priests of the 1890s the new lay leadership of the FRDF never questioned the legitimacy of the French nation or claimed the sovereign autonomy of Brittany. In its 1911 manifesto, the group clearly identified the Republic with the nation but defined its interests in local terms. The FRDF's understanding of the constituent elements of national community had much in common with that of Maurice Barrès. It shared with the Right a common rejection of the omnipotent state and the consequences of raw-toothed individualism, arguing in favor of the creation of intermediate professional and corporate bodies.[85] Its regionalism was therefore an expression of a corporatist vision, but that vision explicitly rejected the paternalism and hierarchical conception of society that the Right embraced. The regionalism of the FRDF was translated into a consistent defense of regional culture and the Breton language. But regional defense was not predicated on a romantic attachment to a preindustrial or prerevolutionary past, like the Union Régionaliste Bretonne. Rather, its regionalism was predicated on a pragmatic defense of the region's future. For this reason the regionalism of this group was expressed in demands for developing the economy and com-

[84] "Programme de la Fédération des républicains démocrates du Finistère, 1911," A.D. Finistère, 104J, Fonds Trémintin.

[85] For a discussion of the social Catholic regionalism, see Mayeur, "Démocratie chrétienne et régionalisme," pp. 445–60. In a path-breaking article on the ideological origins of Christian Democracy, Mayeur argues that intransigent Catholicism and Christian Democracy share a common intellectual heritage. Mayeur, "Catholicisme intransigeant, catholicisme social, démocratie chrétienne," pp. 483–99. Also see Poulat, Eglise contre la bourgeoisie, pp. 135–72.

merce of the region and placing Brittany on an equal economic footing with the other regions of France. It insisted, moreover, on integrating Breton language into the state's primary and secondary school curriculum. Far from undermining efforts to propagate the French language, they argued, Breton could be used to teach French more effectively. The recognition and fostering of palpable, grassroots attachments, they suggested, would only strengthen the larger nation.

The républicains démocrates, whose leadership consisted of laymen, gave the social Catholic movement a new political and organizational basis, particularly after the death of abbé Gayraud in 1910. The FRDF was soon put to its first test—a major electoral battle fought in the second arrondissement of Brest in 1913.

On 20 January 1913, Emile Villiers, the conservative deputy of the second electoral district of Brest, stepped down to become senator of Finistère. The nominations of candidates to replace him unleashed a bitter struggle between the newly formed Fédération des républicains démocrates du Finistère and conservative Catholic groups. The choice of conservative Catholics was Gaston de l'Hopital, a wealthy aristocratic landowner and the mayor of Landerneau, endorsed by Villiers himself, the bishop of Quimper, "the aristocracy and the older members of the parish clergy." De L'Hopital identified himself as a "liberal Catholic republican."[86]

Paul Simon, a twenty-seven-year-old lawyer and vice president of the Fédération des républicains démocrates du Finistère, presented himself as a democratic republican and was supported by the "younger members of the clergy in the district" despite the bishop's opposition.[87] The other principal candidates represented the Radical and Socialist parties respectively.

Simon espoused the FRDF program of 1911 but emphasized his support for a national income tax, long-term agricultural credit, and compensatory awards for peasants who improved the land they farmed. De l'Hopital focused primarily on the issue of religious defense.

According to the prefect, the electoral battle would be confined between the two Catholic candidates, Simon and de l'Hopital, and reflected the "profound divisions" that had occurred among Catholics in France as a whole: Some remained obedient to the orders of the upper clergy, and others, the "more and more numerous, Christian democrats or sillonistes have evolved toward modern ideas."[88] This division, according to the prefect, could ultimately help republican parties in the district because the struggle between the two Catholic candidates had already assumed a

---

[86] A.D. Finistère, 3M311, miscellaneous electoral notes.
[87] Ibid.
[88] A.D. Finistère, 3M311, letter from the prefect to the minister of the interior, 26 March 1913.

"violent character" that would render any reconciliation "difficult and uncertain."[89]

The electoral contest between Paul Simon and Gaston de l'Hopital resembled the battle between abbé Gayraud and the comte de Blois, but Simon, in contrast to abbé Gayraud, did not have the support and endorsement of the Catholic press as a whole in Finistère. The *Progrès du Finistère*, edited by F. Goyen, who was suspected to be none other than canon Cornou of the Evêché of Quimper, attacked Simon for sowing discord among Catholics.[90] He claimed that the Sillon, which had been condemned by the Pope, survived in the form of the Fédération des Républicains Démocrates du Finistère and continued to disturb the "authorized directors of Catholic conscience in the diocese."[91] Goyen, moreover, accused Simon of destroying the political civility that had characterized elections in the district: "We now have come to know political meetings as people like them in the Midi . . . where one makes [a lot of] noise, where one yells, [where] interruptions, denunciations roll like a tempest."[92]

The prefect of Finistère predicted that anticlerical republican voters might vote for Simon because of his program, which, leaving aside the religious issue, was "very progressive."[93] The prefect attached particular importance to the outcome of the election because it could "orient politics in a new direction."[94] He feared, however, that sillonisme corresponded exactly to the Breton state of mind, which was religious but attached to republican institutions: Simon's success could give the Fédération des Républicains Démocrates du Finistère "considerable scope," which "could become menacing not only for traditionally conservative Catholics, but also for republican deputies."[95]

Paul Simon followed in the footsteps of the democratic priests of the 1890s and held a number of large public meetings throughout the district, in contrast to his opponent. The results of the 30 March election were inconclusive. De l'Hopital won 5,524 and Simon 5,008 of the 12,512 votes cast. The remainder were divided between Sauveur Salahun, a Radical, and F. Le Gall, a socialist. A runoff was scheduled for 13 April 1913.

The April election was a success for Paul Simon, who garnered 6,103 of the 12,729 votes cast, and he had clear majorities in the cantons of Daoulas and Plabennec where peasant landowners were in a majority. De l'Hopital

---

[89] Ibid.

[90] *Le Progrès du Finistère*, 13 March 1913.

[91] Ibid., 8 March 1913.

[92] Ibid., 29 March 1913.

[93] A.D. Finistère, 3M311, letter from the prefect to the minister of the interior, 26 March 1913.

[94] Ibid.

[95] Ibid.

received 5,825 votes. The *Progrès du Finistère* attributed this success not to Simon's platform, but to the "remarkable organization" of Simon's party and to support among anticlericals.[96] The *Courrier du Finistère* had a more philosophical interpretation of Simon's success: "The people increasingly evolve toward the pursuit of happiness . . . and the election of Monsieur Simon appears to simply mark a new phase in this evolution like, before it . . . the elections of the comte de Mun and abbé Gayraud."[97]

Le Citoyen, the Radical newspaper owned by the anticlerical deputy of Finistère, Georges Le Bail, interpreted Simon's success more cynically: the election represented the success of the younger clergy over the older clergy, "the bishop of Quimper vanquished by the pseudo-democratic Sillon," and "clerical demagoguery over conservative clericalism."[98] For Radicals, the peasantry's republican sentiments in the district were more apparent than real: "They believe themselves to be republican, but they are not. . . . It could not be otherwise in a country where the Church stifles all public spirit and all efforts at reflection."[99] The only positive outcome of the election for true republicans, in this view, was that the discord in clerical ranks would undermine the authority of the Church.

Government observers worried that Paul Simon's success in the second electoral district of Brest would probably lead to "very great political changes in all of northern Finistère" and would certainly strengthen the newly formed party: "Should we desire the success of this new party? I don't think so. Whatever they say, the sillonistes of Finistère are pure clericals, partisans of equal funding for state and private schools and great enemies of secular education. I would prefer, for my part, the success of the liberal candidacy of M. de l'Hopital who has only frequented Church since he became a candidate. We would have in him a less hardened adversary of lay education."[100]

Paul Simon and the Fédération des républicains démocrates were distrusted and shunned by the Catholic Right as well as the anticlerical Left. F. Goyen argued in the *Progrès du Finistère* that neither true Catholics nor the Radicals were interested in such "hybrid products": "M. Simon, rebuffed

[96] *Le Progrès du Finistère*, 26 April 1913, 19 April 1913.

[97] *Le Courrier du Finistère*, 10 April 1913. The *Courrier du Finistère* was one of the most widely read newspapers among the peasantry in the Finistère. Monseigneur Duparc believed that the positions it and the regional daily, *L'Ouest Eclair*, took were open to criticism. A.D. Finistère, 104J, Fonds Trémintin, "Entretien avec Monseigneur Duparc, 4 July 1913, Chatel-Guyon" by Pierre Trémintin, president of the FRDF. There were perceptible differences of view in the Catholic press in Finistère.

[98] Camille Vallaux, "Après l'élection de Landerneau," *Le Citoyen*, 19 April 1913.

[99] Ibid.

[100] A.D. Finistère, 3M311, report from the subprefect of Brest to the prefect of Finistère, 24 March 1913.

to his right and to his left, will be left with the ridicule of having sought the cooperation from all and of not having inspired confidence in anyone."[101]

The severest critics of the newly formed Fédération des républicains democrates du Finistère were on the Right, however, and the FRDF faced the formidable opposition of the bishop of Quimper. In June Monseigneur Duparc came very close to publicly condemning the new political group: [The FRDF] "still believes, even after the Pope's letter, that only democracy can bring the reign of pure justice . . . instead of sincerely following the Church in the restoration of the Christian community . . . [it] preaches fraternity ending in class war . . . [and] boasts independence from bishops and the Pope. . . . I am obliged to say that this party is still full of the Sillon's ideas."[102]

Several weeks later the president of the FRDF, Pierre Trémintin, met with the bishop and used the opportunity to stave off official condemnation of the movement.[103] During the meeting, Monseigneur Duparc expressed his reservations regarding the FRDF's commitment to democracy, which, he claimed disturbed the Vatican, particularly the cardinal Merry del Val. Despite his "monarchist preferences," he assured Trémintin that he had no intention of condemning the FRDF as a political organization, but argued in favor of Catholic unity. Trémintin concluded that the FRDF would have to remain on guard by taking into account the "episcopal mentality that is clearly unfavorable to our political ideas and our actions. He treats us like suspects."[104]

Despite opposition from the ecclesiastical hierarchy and from representatives of right- and left-wing political groups in Finistère, the newly formed FRDF continued to have significant success in local as well as national elections by steering a careful course between right-wing Catholics and leftist anticlerical republicans. It captured two new seats in the department by 1919. In 1923, the prefect of Finistère reported that the silloniste party had an enormous amount of support in the department among all social groups and was "active, unified, well organized," and in continual contact with the electorate through "tenacious propaganda."[105] He regarded it as the most significant party in the department, and though it had strong support from among the lower clergy, was not merely a Catholic party dedicated to the defense of religious interests: "Catholic, it rallies former conservatives . . . very reduced in number and apparently forgetful

---

[101] *Progrès du Finistère*, 12 April 1913.

[102] *Progrès du Finistère*, 21 June 1913.

[103] A.D. Finistère, 104 J, Fonds Trémintin, "Entretien avec Monseigneur Duparc, Chatel-Guyon," 4 July 1913, submitted to Monseigneur Fauvel by letter, 24 November 1964.

[104] Ibid.

[105] A.D. Finistère, 1M133, monthly report, 4 February 1924.

of past discords . . . republican, it gathers a number of republican voices, especially from among the regime's neophytes; social, to an extreme, and even . . . to the point of demagoguery" it gathers those who "do not dare to associate themselves with socialist violence or with the forceful blows of revolution."[106] In short, the Fédération des républicains démocrates du Finistère mobilized the electorate of Finistère along new political lines, and these lines did not fit easily into the bipartite structure of national politics. It came to represent a *troisième voie* (third way) that increasingly neither local politicians nor the government could ignore.

[106] Ibid.

7

Party-Building: Between the Region and the Nation, 1918–1926

THE FIRST WORLD WAR took an enormous human toll on Brittany, which lost proportionally more soldiers than any other region in France.[1] More than 300,000 Breton conscripts had been mobilized during the war, and many arrived at the western front not knowing a word of French and unable to understand the dialects of their Breton compatriots. The experience of war helped to heal the deep enmities between the clerical and anticlerical factions of the prewar decade throughout France and therefore contributed to a spirit of religious appeasement immediately following the signing of an armistice. The postwar government did not impose the secular laws and the Concordat on the newly acquired provinces of Alsace-Lorraine, and France soon reestablished diplomatic relations with the Vatican. The war, in addition, did more than Jules Ferry's secular primary educational system or the roads and railways built during the early Third Republic to introduce the inhabitants of Lower Brittany to worlds beyond the parish.

In Finistère the "particularism of regions and districts" nonetheless survived among a predominantly rural population attached to "old traditions and personal habits."[2] The spirit of the Sillon also survived, perhaps even better adapted to the new political climate in France because sillonistes distanced themselves from the religious divisions of the prewar period. Shortly after the signing of the armistice the Fédération des républicains démocrates du Finistère organized its first congress in August 1919, establishing the political council for the group: Pierre Trémintin, president; Paul Simon, vice-president; Francis Bellec, E. Berest, and Saik Ar Gall; Dr. Vrouc'h from Plomodiern in southern Finistère; Adolphe Le Goaziou, a bookseller from Quimper; and Fournis, a lawyer from Quimperlé.[3]

Many former sillonistes who belonged to the newly created Fédération des républicains démocrates du Finistère occupied positions in local gov-

---

[1] It is estimated that the five departments comprising Brittany lost a total of 120,000 soldiers. Skol Vreiz, *Histoire de la Bretagne et des pays celtiques de 1914 à nos jours*, Vol. 5: *La Bretagne au XX siècle* (Rennes, 1983), p. 24.

[2] A.D. Finistère, 1M133, report from the prefect of Finistère to the minister of the interior, 4 February 1924.

[3] *Le Petit Démocrate du Finistère*, October 1919.

ernment in the north and the south, which later served as stepping stones for national office. Trémintin was the first silloniste to be elected at the local level in 1904 by becoming the mayor of Plouescat, a commune in the ceinture dorée of northern Finistère, at the age of twenty-eight.[4] In 1912, Paul Simon became municipal councillor of the city of Brest and deputy in 1913. In 1919, Pierre Mocaër assumed the position of conseiller général of the tiny island of Ouessant after defeating his anticlerical republican adversary.[5] According to government officials, these successes could be attributed to the fact that the silloniste party was the most active and well-organized political group in the department in the immediate postwar period.[6]

The history of the Fédération des républicains démocrates du Finistère, which was largely instrumental in founding in 1924 the first national mass-based Christian Democratic party in France, the Parti Démocrate Populaire, demonstrates that the silloniste party became a major political force in Finistère that effected political alliances with the Right and the Left, without being subsumed by either. Silloniste deputies elected from Finistère in 1919 were able, moreover, to form an alliance with republican groups on the national level by becoming members of the *republicains de gauche* in the Chamber of Deputies in 1919, while attempting to steer an independent course between parties of Left and Right at the local level. The electorate came to be mobilized on other than religious lines by the FRDF, and the results of national elections reflected the further democratization of the political process.[7] At the same time the FRDF took a lead in pressuring the leaders of the powerful Office Central de Landerneau to formulate new social policies, and in creating a bridge between the locality and the nation consolidated a new political identity for the region.

War and "National Union"

Shortly after the Treaty of Versailles was signed in June 1919, the wartime government headed by Georges Clemenceau scheduled legislative elections for November of the same year. The government introduced a new elec-

---

[4] A.D. Finistère, 3M380.

[5] *Le Citoyen*, 20 December 1919.

[6] A.D. Finistère, 1M133, report from the prefect of Finistère to the minister of the interior, 4 February 1924.

[7] One scholar has claimed that despite the "deep inroads" made by silloniste ideas in Finistère, the primacy of the religious issue dug an unbridgeable chasm between the Left and the Right, which made it "impossible" for sillonistes to ally with groups on the Left who "shared their views on social and economic questions" in the interwar period. The sillonistes in her view therefore failed to become an effective political force in the department. Berger, *Peasants Against Politics*, pp. 49, 52.

toral procedure, the *scrutin de liste*, which established large multimember electoral districts that generally corresponded to the perimeters of the department, replacing small single-member constituencies associated with the prewar *scrutin d'arrondissement*. The scrutin de liste encouraged the formation of electoral alliances because in the case in which no party achieved an absolute majority, legislative seats were assigned according to a quotient based on the number of votes each list and each candidate on the list obtained. Because the scrutin de liste forbade runoffs, it therefore avoided the frequent behind-the-scenes political bartering associated with the scrutin d'arrondissement and the runoff election. Moderate republicans and conservatives, who by and large favored the scrutin de liste, argued that the new procedure would better represent the preferences of the French electorate, which would vote for political programs rather than personalities.[8] Some conservatives and republicans, however, clearly hoped that this new form of proportional representation would work in favor of moderate and conservative groups and guard against the overrepresentation of socialists from "red" pockets of the country.[9]

In preparation for the November 1919 elections, moderate republicans and conservative groups effected a new electoral alliance in the form of the Bloc National predicated on national reconciliation, on the economic and military regeneration of France, and, most important, on preventing the spread of Bolshevism. To cement such an alliance republicans and conservatives were forced to bury the religious hatchet of the prewar decade. To this effect, the Bloc National affirmed that the "secular state must reconcile itself with the rights and liberties of all citizens whatever their beliefs." This vague statement affirmed the principle of a secular state but demonstrated a desire to appease Catholic voters. The Bloc National was repudiated by intransigent Catholics, however, who could not accept the principle of secularization and who tended to support extreme right-wing groups such as the Action Française. Diehard anticlerical Radicals found it equally difficult to tolerate an alliance based on any form of Catholic appeasement and withdrew their support in some areas of France just prior to the November election.

In Finistère, Radicals, *progressistes* (moderate republicans), sillonistes,

[8] Daniélou, a moderate republican who stood for reelection in Finistère in 1919, told an audience of supporters that under the new electoral procedure candidates would be less likely to have to defend themselves from attacks on their private lives and "questions of personality would be put to one side: Today one votes for a complete list of candidates in the department as a whole and for a program." A.D. Finistère, 3M316, report by the commissaire of police in Quimper to the prefect, 6 November 1919.

[9] Electoral history seemed to confirm this view. In 1885, the only election under the early Third Republic that implemented the scrutin de liste marked a victory for the conservative Right who united against a fragmented and divided Left.

and conservatives, like their counterparts in other parts of France, sought to create a single republican list "in face of the Bolshevik danger."[10] Negotiations between the various republican and other groups in Finistère broke down, however, when Georges Le Bail, the anticlerical Radical deputy of the second electoral district of Quimper, openly objected to the candidacy of Alain de Guébriant, who was a wealthy noble landowner and mayor of Saint-Pol-de-Léon, on the grounds that public opinion would not accept both names on the same list. Le Bail's *Le Citoyen*, Finistère's Radical newspaper, blamed the conservative party for being largely responsible for driving a wedge between the Radical party and other republican groups in Finistère. The Radical party, led by Georges Le Bail, therefore created an alternative anticlerical list (the Liste de Concentration Républicaine), consisting of intransigent Radicals and independent socialists. Paul Simon and a number of moderate republicans in the department accused Le Bail of constructing a "closed republic," to which only he gave access.[11]

Conservative Catholics,[12] moderate republicans, and members of the Fédération des républicains démocrates du Finistère thus drew up their own electoral list (Liste Républicain et Démocratique d'Union Nationale), which adhered to the principles of the Bloc National.

This conservative/silloniste electoral coalition consisted of four members of the silloniste party—Paul Simon, Pierre Trémintin, Jean Jadé, and Victor Balanant—who were among the youngest candidates to stand for national election in France. Simon, the only silloniste candidate holding national office, was thirty-three, Trémintin forty-three, Balanant thirty-one, and Jadé twenty-nine. Jadé, Trémintin, and Simon had trained as lawyers, and Balanant, president of the veterans' association in Finistère, was an arsenal worker in Brest and the son of a carpenter. The other candidacies were divided between moderate republicans and conservatives,[13] some of whom were political veterans.[14] Only two candidates,

[10] *Dépêche de Brest*, 30 October 1919, p. 1.

[11] A.D. Finistère, 3M316, report by the commissaire de police in Quimper, 6 November 1919.

[12] The conservative Catholic "party" in Finistère was referred to as the "Liberal party" in the interwar period because it consisted of former members of the Action Libérale Populaire.

[13] Alain de Guébriant stood as candidate even though it had first been rumored that his son, Hervé de Guébriant, president of Office Central, might do so. A.D. Finistère, 3M316, report by the subprefect of Morlaix, 28 August 1919. Hervé de Guébriant criticized Georges Le Bail at a public meeting in Saint-Pol-de-Léon for not accepting his father's candidacy. Georges Le Bail replied that he wanted the republic to survive and did not want it to have the same fate as the Second Republic. A.D. Finistère, 3M316, report by the commissaire de police, Saint-Pol-de-Léon, 6 November 1919.

[14] Corentin Guyho, a retired magistrate, had been deputy, as had Daniélou, publicist and mayor of Locronan. Both men were moderate republicans.

conservative Laurent Boucher and moderate republican Vincent Inizan,[15] were peasant landowners. The anticlerical republican list contained no candidates engaged in an agricultural occupation.

The Bloc National triumphed in the postwar elections in France as a whole, forming a chamber that was dominated by moderate republicans. In Finistère the 1919 elections also constituted a resounding victory for the electoral coalition forged by sillonistes and a defeat for the old-style anticlerical Radical party of the prewar period. The Radical party lost three seats and the sillonistes, including two political newcomers Victor Balanant and Jean Jadé, took their place. Paul Simon was reelected for a third term. The socialists also gained one seat. Part of the FRDF success can be attributed to the fact that it won new support in areas of southern Finistère, which had previously voted for anticlerical republicans. Moreover, as no staunchly conservative candidate was elected in the department, the electorate of Finistère clearly rejected the the traditional Right on the list of the Union Nationale and showed its preference instead for sillonistes and moderate republicans, much to the chagrin of the conservative wing of the electoral coalition.

The anticlerical Radical party had tried to mobilize voters by pointing to the clerical threat and lost areas to both socialist candidates and sillonistes. Much of the success of silloniste candidates and moderates on the list of Union Nationale can be linked to its effective organization and a clearly enunciated political program that sought to avoid religious issues.

The FRDF's program, incorporated into the platform of the Union Nationale, elaborated on the principles contained in the 1911 program but specifically focused on postwar problems affecting Finistère. A renewed attention to regionalism and decentralization was inherent in the federation's program after the war. The FRDF's additions to its 1911 program set out in greater detail proposals to decentralize government institutions by arguing in favor of abolishing the department and creating larger regions that would have budgetary autonomy and represent professional interests in parliament. As in 1911, the issues of regional and cultural defense were at the top of the FRDF's agenda, but by 1919 they became an integral and sharply honed part of the group's program. In contrast to existing regionalist groups, which sought a solution to the region's problems in autonomy and in the vaguely defined dreams of a preindustrial past, the FRDF declared itself in favor of economic integration and development and the fostering of regional identity through the maintenance of regional lan-

---

[15] Inizan had sympathies for the newly created FRDF. He was a farmer and had obtained a secondary education and frequently contributed articles to the *Dépêche de Brest*, the *Courrier du Finistère*, and *L'Ouest Eclair*. A.D. Finistère, 3M316, electoral notes.

guages within the primary and secondary school systems. The FRDF defended regional culture and decentralization in practical rather than emotive terms, however: Budgetary rather than political independence, for example, would assure a more efficient tax system and a more equitable distribution of taxes.

Both Trémintin and Mocaër came out in favor of the propagation of the Breton language, but each did so in the interests of the larger French nation. In 1920, Trémintin spoke in terms of developing knowledge of the Breton language for "the greatest good of our compatriots and in the higher interests of *French culture* [emphasis in the original]."[16] Several months later, Pierre Mocaër, perhaps one of the most ardent supporters of the regionalist cause among the postwar sillonistes, declared, "what we want is the development of Brittany through the agency of Breton interests and know-how. . . . If this means hankering after isolation we plainly declare that we formally oppose that; on the contrary, we want to intensify the relationships between a self-conscious and developed Brittany of which we dream and the other regions of France."[17]

FRDF attention to the regionalist cause must in part be seen in the context of the postwar proliferation of a number of regionalist and autonomist groups that sought to direct local attention to the economic underdevelopment of the region as well as to a set of ethnic nationalist claims. These groups included La Jeunesse de Bretagne, which ultimately became the Parti Autonomiste Breton in 1927, alongside older groups like the Union Régionaliste Bretonne established before the war. Whereas the Parti Autonomiste Bretonne increasingly used the experience of the First World War to justify demands for independence, the sillonistes used Breton casualties as evidence of Breton loyalty to France and to illustrate Brittany's unique contribution to the national community. Indeed, the First World War marked a fundamental turning point in social Catholic articulation of national identity in Lower Brittany. If social Catholics attempted to reconcile the claims of the nation with those of the region before the war, the direct and acute experience of that trauma was used by sillonistes and the government of the Bloc National alike to forge a new national consensus.

The memory of war came to be commemorated in countless Breton towns and villages through the erection of monuments to the dead. These monuments, often draped with French flags, bore the inscription: "La

---

[16] Regretting that he could not take part in two events devoted to the cause of Breton culture, he argued that although the events did not have the same program they had the same goal: "l'enseignement méthodique, littéraire et artistique du Breton pour le plus grand bien de nos compatriotes et dans l'intérêt supérieur de la culture française," *Mouez Ar Vro* (La voix du pays), 30 August 1920, p. 4.

[17] Ibid., 4 December 1920, p. 4.

commune de . . . à ses enfants morts pour la France."[18] Although it can be argued that the commemoration of the dead was a "secular cult,"[19] the iconography of the large number of monuments built during the interwar period in Brittany combined religious symbols with the depiction of the fallen soldier. The *monument aux morts* in the commune of Pouldreuzic (arrondissement of Quimper), which had a population of 2,286 in 1911, is a case in point: It depicts two soldiers, one fallen, before a freestanding calvaire and bears the inscription, "Aux enfants de Pouldreuzic morts pour la France." Commemoration of the war dead was grafted onto Brittany's cult of the dead and onto traditional religious observances, but these commemorations also ironically came to symbolize both Brittany's martyrdom and its ties to France.

   In a region that had more veterans and casualties than virtually any other in France, the FRDF advocated strict adherence to the principle of reparations and war indemnity as well as the maintenance of a strong military. Indeed, it was over a nationalist foreign policy that the Fédération parted ways with a now pacifist Marc Sangnier and his newly formed Jeune République in 1919.[20] Wounded war veterans Victor Balanant and Jean Jadé assumed a stridently nationalist stance, which may, in fact, have won them seats in parliament. The FRDF made explicit and direct appeals to the returning *poilus* by participating in a number of veterans groups that formed in the department immediately after the war. This nationalism, which defined itself against the experience of the First World War, was used as a rallying cry in Finistère, even as the FRDF elaborated its regionalist program in its 1919 manifesto. Like no other political grouping in Finistère, the silloniste party used the language of the French nation to commemorate Brittany's sacrifice during the war and assert its regional claims to the Breton language.

   If the FRDF claimed to represent interests of veterans and the nation as members of a "national union," it did not dwell on the problem of the relationship between Church and state in 1919. As self-declared democrats dedicated to the principle of liberty, the FRDF merely called for liberty of conscience.[21] The 1919 program focused instead on the necessity of far-reaching political and social reform. The FRDF declared itself an ardently

---

[18] Antoine Prost, "Les monuments aux morts: Culte républicain? culte civique? culte patriotique," in *Les Lieux de mémoire*, Vol. 1: *La république*, ed. Pierre Nora (Paris, 1984), pp. 195–225.

[19] Ibid., p. 221.

[20] Biton, *La Démocratie chrétienne*, p. 58, and Prélot, "Les démocrates d'inspiration chrétienne," pp. 533–59.

[21] Fonds Trémintin, A.D. Finistère, 104J, Fédération des républicains démocrates du Finistère, programme de 1911, 1919, p. 1.

republican supporter of parliamentary government; it opposed any proposal to weaken the power of the parliament and to strengthen the execu-
tive. The FRDF's solution to the seeming paralysis of the parliament—its
inability to carry through legislation decisively—would be solved by "a
truly universal suffrage" through the introduction of "the vote of women
and the 'vote familiale.'"[22] The federation's political interest in female
suffrage—the issue is entirely absent from the 1911 program—was a reflection of new efforts to organize and mobilize women, though women did
not occupy any positions of leadership in the interwar period. In short, this
interest was probably more strategic than real, but it shaped the inclusion-
ary nation that the FRDF sought to define in the post–World War I
period.[23]

The social program of the FRDF reflected the organization's sulloniste
origins. It supported a graduated income tax and the limited intervention
of the state to solve the three major social problems afflicting postwar
Finistère: tuberculosis, alcoholism, and unsanitary housing conditions. In
response to the growing insecurity among tenants in the countryside, it
proposed legislation that would guarantee the tenant an indemnity for
improvements made on the land he rented when the lease was terminated.
It also proposed a system of low-income housing. True to its social Catholic
origins, the FRDF stressed, however, the necessity of strengthening corporate professional institutions in the form of unions and cooperatives. Former sillonistes associated with the FRDF were largely responsible for creating a number of consumer cooperatives throughout the department of
Finistère: La Bretonne in Saint-Pol-de-Léon, La Léonarde in Plabennec, Le
Nord-Finistère in Morlaix, and La Fraternelle in Quimper.[24] Trémintin
headed a departmental committee, founded in 1908, to coordinate the
development of low-income housing.

The sillonistes' affirmation of religious neutrality and acceptance of the
principle of the secular state clearly irritated the ecclesiastical hierarchy in
Finistère. And the failure of the conservative Right to achieve electoral
success resulted in new fissures between sillonistes and conservatives, who,
after the elections of 1919, increasingly attacked the FRDF's left-wing
social positions. Ultimately both conservatives and Radicals began to com-

[22] Ibid., p. 7.

[23] "Fils de 1789, nous déclarons la dictature du prolétariat aussi odieuse que toute autre, et
restons fidèlement attachés au principe du Souvraineté Nationale. Seule elle peut réaliser,
dans la liberté et la justice, la solidarité des classes, seule elle crée un pouvoir exécutif
conscient de sa force et de sa responsabilité, travaillant au bien général sous le contrôle d'un
Parlement, libre, lui aussi, parce que dégagé des entraves d'une administration napoléonienne
et appuyé sur des régions concentrant autour d'elles les forces vives de la Nation." Ibid.

[24] *Le Petit Breton*, July 22, 1923. Saik Ar Gall founded La Leonarde in Plabennec in 1919.
By 1920, it had ten offices; a year later it had 477 shareholders, and two years later 650
shareholders. In 1923, a cooperative bank was founded in Morlaix.

pete unsuccessfully with the FRDF in local elections in the department. In 1921, a government official observed that members of the silloniste party had aspired to "become, it is said, the only organization of the future."[25] Three years later the prefect of Finistère claimed in 1924 that "a fact of a permanent order dominates . . . the general situation . . . that is the existence of a party peculiar to it [Finistère], the 'républicain démocrate,' commonly called the 'silloniste party'. . . . Silloniste, anti-silloniste, there you will see the political criterion [dividing] political groups in Finistère."[26]

Between the Right and the Left, 1919–1924

The FRDF, Catholic conservatives, and anticlerical republicans entered into a number of electoral scuffles as all parties jockeyed for positions in local government between 1920 and 1924. Sillonistes won important victories between 1919 and 1924 against their adversaries on the Right, and, more important perhaps, against their adversaries on the Left, in areas previously dominated by anticlerical republicans.

In local elections where sillonistes faced Radicals and conservative Catholics, they steadfastly avoided campaigning on religious issues, attempting to steer a course between the Catholic Right and the anticlerical Left. As a result, Georges Le Bail, deputy and leader of the anticlerical Radical party in Finistère, accused the FRDF of being a "political race without tradition or ancestors." Sillonistes responded by insisting that it was possible to be Catholic and republican and that even certain Radical Socialists now believed that the "politics of division and discord practiced by their party before 1914 had hurt France."[27] Indeed, even before the onset of the First World War Robert Cornilleau had stated the case to Le Bail in the following terms: "Between you, the Old Radical, the republican patriot, the out-of-date doctrinaire of a party that will die because it no longer has a doctrine, and us, the young democrats, as you call us—and we are proud of this title— . . . there are two conceptions of the Republic. . . . It is true . . . that we are republicans, that is in your eyes a *heresy*. Your secular republicanism is a sort of political dogmatism . . . an unconscious clericalism in reverse. . . . Our presence in the republic is a scandal to you. That troubles you, as if it marks the failure of your ideal and the end of your system."[28]

[25] A.N. F⁷12983, report by the commissaire spécial des chemins de fer to the directeur de la Sûreté Nationale, 30 April 1921.

[26] A.D. Finistère, 1M133, 4 February 1924 prefect report.

[27] *Le Démocrate*, 7 June 1914.

[28] Ibid.

The FRDF's attempts to suppress the religious question paid off in electoral terms. In 1921, Georges Le Bail, Radical deputy of Finistère and conseiller général of Plogastel-St.-Germain in southern Finistère faced serious opposition for the first time in many years from a well-to-do peasant landholder and long-time municipal councillor, Jean Henaff, who identified himself as a *républicain démocrate*. Jean Henaff was vigorously supported by local sections of the FRDF and by *Le Petit Breton*, the silloniste weekly founded in 1919. The sixty-two-year-old Henaff defeated the leader of the Radical party of Finistère by a narrow margin in an area that had traditionally voted for anticlerical republicans. For Jean Jadé, the young silloniste deputy of Finistère, Le Bail's defeat merely represented the failure of the "old sterile sectarian politics of the *bloc des gauches*" that focused solely on the clerical menace, and it marked the victory of the "peasant" long excluded from power over "a man issued from the Radical bourgeoisie."[29]

One year later Jean Jadé, newly elected as a silloniste deputy from southern Finistère, entered the local electoral fray himself, challenging the Radical senator Fénoux for the seat of conseiller général of the canton of Pont-Croix. Fénoux had represented Pont-Croix for eighteen years. In a three-way electoral race between Jadé, Fénoux, and a socialist candidate, Jadé defeated the Radical senator by 989 votes.[30] Whereas Fénoux appealed primarily to the anticlerical sentiments of the electorate, Jadé focused on the necessity of improving communications in the department through the coordination of the railway lines serving northern and southern Finistère, facilitating access to credit for farmers, and instituting low-income housing projects. The FRDF accused the Radical party of having no social program because it was absorbed by its "anticlerical preoccupations" and "materialistic bourgeois prejudices."[31]

The success of Jean Jadé and Jean Henaff in the cantonal elections in the southern cantons of Pont-Croix and Plogastel-St.-Germain was important to the FRDF because it represented new support for a movement that had initially drawn most of its members and organizational base from northern Finistère. Henaff and Jadé, moreover, displaced seasoned Radical politicians who represented electoral fiefs renowned for their anticlericalism and growing religious indifference. The number of churchgoers declined significantly in these areas in the interwar period just as the clerical party associated with the Sillon began to gain electoral ground,[32] an indica-

[29] *Le Petit Breton*, 17 July 1921.

[30] A total of 5,021 voted in the cantonal election. A.D. Finistère, 3M355, and *Le Petit Breton*, 21 May 1922.

[31] *Le Petit Breton*, 7 January 1923.

[32] In Plogastel-St. Germain the number of pascalisants declined from 90 percent in 1909 to 70 percent in 1954, and even fewer parishioners (57 percent) attended Sunday mass. In Pont Croix the percentage of pascalisants dropped from 96 percent in 1909 to 72 percent in 1954,

tion that sillonistes were not voted in solely because of their Catholic sympathies.

The enmity between conservative and republican Catholics ran deeper than the hostility between anticlerical Radicals and sillonistes. Conservative Catholics and the ecclesiastical hierarchy in Finistère accused sillonistes of undermining the principle of Catholic unity. The depth of this rancor was evident in the election of Paul Simon from the second electoral district of Brest in 1913, and it surfaced again in early 1922.

In 1922, Laurent Boucher, the conservative conseiller général of the canton of Ploudiry, died; his seat was thus left vacant in the Conseil Général. His son, Marcel Boucher, immediately announced his candidacy by declaring himself to be a "sincere republican" and a "committed Catholic."[33] Paul Simon, silloniste deputy of Finistère, declared his candidacy a month later, and the conservative Catholic weekly Le Progrès and abbé Madec's Le Militant roundly accused Simon of bowing to political opportunism and sowing divisions among Catholics, which would only aid the cause of anticlerical republicans.[34] Simon argued that as deputy of Finistère he could achieve more for the canton than an individual with purely local ties. Le Militant nonetheless declared Simon's candidacy "regrettable."[35]

To the surprise of many, Simon failed in the election, garnering only 344 votes whereas his adversary was elected with 607 of the 1,149 votes cast. He did not have the local popular support that Boucher, a peasant landowner, had, but more important Simon was portrayed by his opponent and the conservative Catholic press as a "collectivist." The Progrès reproduced a portion of a speech given by a silloniste at a celebration honoring the cooperative society La Fraternelle in Quimper: "I do not say that the cooperative creates fraternity, but it is an opportunity for individuals to divide their goods in common."[36] The Progrès warned the electors of Ploudiry to vote against such quasi-socialist theories.

Bolstered by their success in the cantonal election of 1922 in Ploudiry

---

with only 53 percent attending Sunday mass in 1954. Lambert, Catholicisme et société dans l'Ouest 1: 60, and Lagrée, Catholicisme et société dans l'Ouest 2: 55.

[33] Le Militant, 7 January 1922.

[34] Abbé Madec was born in Plounéour Ménez in northern Finistère in 1879 and was affectionately called "Madec Social." He was an ardent regionalist and social Catholic who had participated actively in the cours d'oeuvres at the seminary in Quimper. He was a member of the Sillon before its condemnation in 1910 and founded a weekly newspaper in Brest before the war entitled La Quinzaine Ouvrière. Fighting on the western front during the war, he was decorated for valor. After the war he distanced himself from former members of the Sillon; he placed Catholic interests before political questions and often criticized the FRDF in Le Militant, which was founded in 1912.

[35] Le Militant, 7 January 1922.

[36] Le Progrès du Finistère, 7 January 1922.

after a series of electoral defeats beginning in 1913 at the hands of sillonistes in Finistère, the conservative Catholic press began to argue that
there was no place for the FRDF in the department and that it was an "error
for its leaders to believe that the numerous electors who sent them to the
Chamber in the last legislative elections wanted to condone the political
and social program of the democratic republicans before all else."[37]
Georges Le Bail's Radical weekly, Le Citoyen, ironically shared in the
Right's assessment of the FRDF; the paper indicated that the sillonistes
were despised by the "whites" and the "reds," both of whom vehemently
attacked this new political "hybrid."

> The democratic republicans are hybrids, like the mule, for example, born of a
> union between a horse and an ass. The coupling of clericalism and demagoguery
> has given birth to a singular product, to this half-breed political race that will not
> last. In our country, there can be only two political parties: the red and the white.
> I call reds all those who want laicization and the social Republic. I call whites all
> those who have put their free will in the hands of priests who are irreconcilable
> enemies of democracy born of the revolution of 1789 and who have sworn to lead
> us back into slavery. Between the two parties, conciliation is impossible. The
> struggle will be eternal.[38]

The FRDF's steadfast attempt to avoid religious issues made it increasingly difficult to forge electoral alliances with either the anticlerical republican left or the conservative Right. Although the prefect argued that
the group would probably be called "to play an important role in the next
legislative elections of 1924," that role seemed uncertain.[39]

The Legislative Election of 1924

One month before the May 1924 legislative elections, Le Finistère, a republican weekly, announced that the order of the day for republicans in
Finistère should be "Down with the Sillon!"[40] Le Finistère launched a
personal attack on sillonistes in the department: "The electoral battle in
the department is not one that is solely concerned with programs and
doctrines. . . . It is a question of whether Finistère would like to continue
to be represented in Parliament by the adepts of the Sillon, and if by their
noisy and odious methods of bluff and exaggerated publicity" electors

[37] Ibid., 14 January 1922.
[38] Le Citoyen, 14 January 1922.
[39] A.D. Finistère, 3M355, report by the prefect of Finistère, 14 May 1922.
[40] Le Finistère, 19 April 1924, p. 1. "Beat the Sillon and its disingenuous politics which
dishonors all parties in Finistère."

would prefer men "fulfilling their mandate with much less noise, and much more conscience."[41]

Both the major anticlerical republican newspaper *Le Finistère* and Le Bail's Radical *Le Citoyen* set out to discredit the Sillon in the eyes of the Left and the Right. *Le Finistère* reminded Catholic voters that they had voted for sillonistes allegedly to defend their "essential demands," but once the sillonistes arrived in the Chamber of Deputies, they declared themselves partisans of the "secular state" and began fraternizing with the Protestant pastor Soulier.[42] The newspaper informed republican voters that the sillonistes were nothing less than socialists in religious garb.[43]

Conservatives showed no signs of coming to the defense of the sillonistes. The prefect of Finistère informed his superiors two months before the legislative election of 1924 that it would be impossible to predict whether conservatives and sillonistes would renew their electoral alliance of 1919. According to the prefect, the bishop would probably press for renewing the electoral coalition as a "marriage of reason" to promote a single list of "Catholic and Breton" candidates.[44]

This prediction was in fact fulfilled when an electoral alliance between conservatives and sillonistes was sealed one month before the election. These wary and sparring partners were joined by an unlikely third party, the Fédération des Groupements Industriels et Commerciaux, to form a common electoral list. The Fédération des Groupements Industriels et Commerciaux represented the professional interests of regional commerce and industry in Finistère and traditionally endorsed anticlerical republicans and Radicals. When the federation met in Morlaix in April to discuss the position the group would assume in the election, the 102 delegates present voted unanimously to oppose the Cartel des Gauches, an electoral alliance between socialists and Radicals that was in the process of being formed at the national level on the eve of the election.[45] They agreed to open negotiations with conservatives and sillonistes. The resulting electoral list joined three factions: Louis Coic, Louis Rivière, and Auguste Artur, representing the Groupements Industriels et Commerciaux; Paul Simon, Jean Jadé, Victor Balanant, Vincent Inizan, and Pierre Trémintin, representing the FRDF; and Jacques Quiennec, a lawyer, and two peasant landowners, Mathurin Thomas and Louis Henry, representing conservatives. Thomas was the president of the agricultural syndicate of Daoulas

---

[41] *Le Finistère*, 26 April 1924.

[42] Ibid.

[43] Ibid.

[44] A.D. Finistère, 1M133, report by the prefect, 5 March 1924.

[45] Fédération des Groupements Industriels et Commerciaux, Bulletin mensuelle, May 1924.

and vice-president of the Office Central et de l'Union des Syndicats Agricoles du Finistère.[46]

This new alliance faced a divided anticlerical Left, which consisted of
anticlerical Radical Republicans, Socialists, and Communists because a
cartel of Radicals and Socialists effected at the national level was never
formed in Finistère. Anticlerical republican groups attempted to make
Church-State issues a central electoral focus by capitalizing on differences
in silloniste and conservative ranks concerning the issue of proportional
funding for state and Catholic schools. These differences did indeed make
it difficult for the silloniste coalition to formulate a clear statement regarding the coalition's political position vis-à-vis "the secular state." Pierre
Trémintin declared at a meeting in Scaër, for example, that he was opposed
to state funding of private confessional schools, whereas at the same meeting Mathurin Thomas stated that he supported it.[47]

Nonetheless, the results of the 1924 elections demonstrated that electoral tactics employed by the anticlerical republican Left were largely unsuccessful. Whereas Georges Le Bail won 50,380 votes and Boullioux
Laffont 50,751 in 1919,[48] in 1924, they won 47,511 and 45,993 votes,
respectively.[49] These declines may in part be explained by the fact that two
more lists—the Communist and an alternative republican—were presented to the electorate in Finistère, but the additional lists had no effect on
the number of votes cast for silloniste candidates. In 1919, Paul Simon won
61,579 votes and Balanant 61,319.[50] In 1924, these deputies won 66,241
and 66,397, respectively.[51] Veteran Radical Georges Le Bail and moderate
republican Bouilloux-Laffont were reelected, but the Radical coalition did
not gain any new seats and actually lost electoral support, particularly in
southern Finistère. All the silloniste deputies retained their seats, and a
fifth, Pierre Trémintin, joined them. No candidate associated with the
Fédération des Groupements Industriels et Commerciaux was elected, and
of the three conservative candidates only Louis Henry succeeded. The
1924 election was a clear victory for the silloniste list, which held six of the
department's eleven seats, but more particularly for the FRDF. The coalition gained 5,582 more votes than they had in 1919, and many of these
gains were made in formerly Radical and Radical-Socialist enclaves in

---

[46] The "ban on participation in party politics" was not as effective as Suzanne Berger
implies, and she acknowledges that "one leader" [Mathurin Thomas] ran for political office.
Berger, *Peasants Against Politics*, p. 74.

[47] *La Dépêche de Brest*, 6 May 1924.

[48] A.D. Finistère, 3M316.

[49] A.D. Finistère, 3M320.

[50] A.D. Finistère, 3M316.

[51] A.D. Finistère, 3M320.

southern Finistère.[52] The sillonistes gained 2,355 votes in the arrondissement of Quimper alone and 733 votes in the arrondissement of Quimperlé.[53] The list also drew new support in the anticlerical communes of Lanmeur and Plouigneau in the arrondissement of Morlaix in northern Finistère. Of the 153,961 votes cast the silloniste coalition won a total of 65,864 votes; the anticlerical republican list, 44,670; the Socialist party, 31,217; and Communist, 4,480.[54]

Le Citoyen, the Radical weekly founded by Georges Le Bail, attributed the electoral losses of the traditional Left to "fear of the reds" among bourgeois republicans and to the effectiveness of the social Catholic press in Finistère, notably *L'Ouest Eclair*, the regional daily published in Rennes, and *Le Petit Breton*.[55] *Le Citoyen* called for the creation of a republican regional daily that would "fight a battle of ideas" and contribute to the "political and social education of the people."[56] *Le Citoyen* recognized the lack of unity and organization among the anticlerical republican parties. The bishop of Quimper, according to *Le Citoyen*, was able to bridge differences between sillonistes and conservatives and had a time-honored political organization in the form of the parish clergy.[57]

There is no doubt the FRDF benefited from an effective and coordinated political network that contrasted with the purely electoral initiatives of both conservative and Radical groups in the department and from an active press. Shortly after the first postwar congress of the FRDF in 1919, militants organized political sections in northern and southern Finistère on a permanent basis, even though it must be said that these sections predominated in the north.[58] Conservative parties still relied on infrequent political meetings by invitation only, and the Radical party used ad hoc committees during election times.

The FRDF had, moreover, the support of two of the most widely read newspapers in the department: *Le Courrier du Finistère* and *Le Petit Breton*, which the FRDF had first launched as a monthly publication entitled *Le Petit Démocrate du Finistère* before it became the weekly *Le Petit Breton* in October 1920. *Le Petit Breton* claimed in 1921 that it had

---

[52] The silloniste coalition lost some electoral support in northern Finistère in the cantons of Landerneau and Brest, where the Communists and Socialists gained new ground. *Le Petit Breton*, "Après la victoire du 11 mai," by Pierre Trémintin, p. 1.

[53] *Le Petit Breton*, "Après les élections," 31 May 1924, p. 2.

[54] 3M320, A.D. Finistère.

[55] According to *Le Citoyen*, these newspapers "inoculated credulous electors with the virus of their evil suggestions and self-interested calumnies." *Le Citoyen*, 22 May 1924.

[56] Ibid.

[57] Ibid.

[58] In 1919, there were eight sections in northern Finistère—three in Brest alone—and three in the south. *Le Petit Démocrate du Finistère*, October 1919.

the second largest circulation in the department.[59] The prefecture of Quimper ranked *Le Petit Breton* third in the department in 1924 with a circulation of 17,000.[60] The republican *Dépêche de Brest* ranked first with a circulation of 40,000 and the Catholic *Courrier du Finistère* second with a circulation of 27,300.[61] By contrast, the *Progrès* had a circulation of 5,000, and Georges Le Bail's *Le Citoyen* had 1,500.[62]

The FRDF worked closely with local commercial and agricultural associations and drew up a program that had been translated into a number of legislative proposals in the 1920s. The silloniste deputies from Finistère assumed positions on a number of parliamentary commissions, which facilitated this effort. Jean Jadé became a member of the merchant marine commission. Simon and Balanant became members of the navy commission, and Inizan a member of the customs commission and the parliamentary commission that oversaw the reintegration of Alsace-Lorraine.

The FRDF focused on four principal issues in the legislative chamber and in the Conseil Général: (1) the coordination of railway lines in the department and the reduction in railway tariffs for the transport of agricultural products; (2) the creation of credit institutions to enable tenant farmers to acquire land and the creation of indemnities for farmers who improved the value of the land they tilled at the termination of the lease; (3) financial allocations for large families; and (4) the creation of a system of bilingual education.

The silloniste deputies from Finistère formulated a number of legislative proposals directed toward improving the opportunities for tenants and peasant landowners in an area dominated by the small family farm. They supported legislation to provide indemnities for the large families that were numerous in Lower Brittany.[63] On 18 February 1923, several deputies, including Defos du Rau, Jadé, and Balanant proposed a bill that would give tenant farmers indemnities on the termination of a lease, provided they could demonstrate that they improved their land. Although this bill ultimately failed to pass the legislative assemblies, along with a bill that extended the term of leases in 1928, expectations raised by these proposals encouraged the largest agricultural union in the department to address

[59] *Le Petit Breton*, 2 January 1921.

[60] A.D. Finistère, 1M133 [1924], "Presse—Département du Finistère."

[61] Ibid. Louis Elegoet found that in the commune of Saint-Méen in northern Finistère the *Dépêche de Brest* was read rarely in the interwar period. The local population generally bought the weekly editions of either the *Courrier du Finistère* or *Le Petit Breton*. L. Elegoet, *Saint-Méen*, p. 269.

[62] A.D. Finistère, 1M133, "Presse—Département du Finistère" [1924].

[63] In 1922, Jean Henaff, the new conseiller général of Plogastel-St. Germain proposed such a measure in the Conseil Général of Finistère, which was approved. *Le Petit Breton*, 7 May 1922.

itself to the issue. In 1926 the Office Central de Landerneau voluntarily set up a commission of tenant farmers and landowners to adjudicate disputes over leases, drafted a model lease that provided indemnification for value added to farms by improvements, and extended the term of leases to at least nine years instead of three to six, as had been the standard term.[64]

Pierre Tremintin was president of the departmental office of low-income housing in Finistère and sponsored a number of credit institutions, including "La Familiale" in Brest, which were responsible for building 175 single-family homes in Quimper.[65] When a law providing funds for low-income housing was passed in December 1922, the Chamber of Deputies added an article to the bill, at the request of social Catholic deputies, to make provisions for reserving space in new projects for large families.[66]

The FRDF continued to defend vigorously regional economic and cultural interests without calling the political claims of the nation into question. Pierre Mocaër, conseiller général of Ouessant, became a particularly ardent advocate of the economic development of the Breton peninsula through measures that would improve the transportation system in the area, reduce tariffs, and give regional councils a larger voice in regional planning. In 1919, he founded, along with regionalists of various political persuasions, including socialist Emile Masson and royalist Marquis d'Estourbeillon, a bilingual journal devoted to "Breton action," entitled *Buhez Breiz* (The Life of Brittany), of which he became editor-in-chief.[67] *Buhez Breiz* advocated enlarging the authority of conseils généraux throughout France in deciding how funds should be allocated locally because they would be in a better position to make such judgments. It demanded, in addition, that no functionary or government officer be named to a rural area in Brittany without demonstrating a sufficient knowledge of Breton and that these functionaries should be responsible to local elected assemblies rather than to the central government. *Buhez Breiz* and the FRDF staunchly supported the unification of railway lines in Finistère. The northern and southern parts of the peninsula were served by two railway lines, one owned by the state and the other by a private concern. The lack of coordination between the two lines, according to the FRDF, hampered the commercial and industrial development of the peninsula. On 17 December 1920, through the efforts of social Catholic deputies, the Chamber of

---

[64] Berger, *Peasants Against Politics*, pp. 106–7.

[65] *Journal Officiel*, 3 July 1928, pp. 2211–12.

[66] A.D. Finistère, Fonds Trémintin, letter from Pierre Trémintin to the minister of health, 16 February 1923.

[67] In 1930, Mocaër founded a second journal and regionalist organization, both of which were entitled *Adsao* (renewal), devoted to the economic renewal of Brittany. *Adsao* served as a lobby in Finistère.

Deputies voted to reorganize the railway system in the country as a whole in response to similiar complaints in a number of regions in France.

The goal of social Catholic regionalists in Finistère was to encourage the material development of the region without sacrificing local traditions and values.[68] From 1919 to the outbreak of the Second World War the FRDF advocated the introduction of a bilingual educational system in Brittany and argued that schools should be adapted to local conditions. In 1919, *Buhez Breiz* called for the immediate introduction of Breton in primary schools where it was to be, in part, employed as a means of teaching French and advocated a curriculum that would incorporate one hour of Breton history and geography each week, preferably taught in the Breton language. Mocaër submitted a number of proposals in favor of bilingual education to the Conseil Général in Finistère in the 1920s, and these proposals were carried to the Chamber of Deputies by Pierre Trémintin and Vincent Inizan. Mocaër proposed in the Conseil Général that Breton be placed on the same footing as other languages in the baccalauréat and called for the expansion of Celtic studies at the university level.

The FRDF represented the regional concerns of a predominantly rural electorate as well as small-business commercial interests. Its program was not a simple reduction of national political concerns and issues, but it was adapted to local conditions in a way that the Radical program frequently was not. Its protection of regional interests and local culture, however, had little in common with the sentimental regionalism of the Right, which wanted to restore a "traditional" society that had long since disappeared.

The legislative election of 1924 ultimately demonstrated that the FRDF's support was not confined to the devout cantons of northern Finistère, and it bore witness to the effectiveness of the FRDF's political organization. In eleven years the political representation of the FRDF had increased from one deputy to five, but these silloniste deputies faced a very different legislative chamber in Paris.

The Cartel des Gauches and the Formation of the Parti Démocrate Populaire, 1924–1926

In contrast to Finistère, anticlerical republicans and socialists had managed to smooth over their profound differences prior to the 1924 elections at the national level and formed a cartel des gauches that dominated the

---

[68] "We want to assure the birth of a Brittany where materially and morally there will be a better life for all Bretons, where factories will not be . . . prisons, where farms will not be damp hovels . . . where schools will not be places where one teaches children to despise their country and where they are punished for speaking their own language." *Buhez Breiz*, January 1919, p. 4.

new chamber. Once in power, however, the sharp divisions between socialists and Radicals on social and economic issues again became evident. The only question on which both seemed to agree was religious policy. Both the socialists and Radicals were rabidly anticlerical and firmly believed that the 1919 chamber had made too many concessions to Catholics.

The ministry, headed by the Radical Edouard Herriot, began to implement new anticlerical legislation. Ironically, however, this legislation coincided with new papal initiatives that were intended to make peace with the Republic. In February 1922, Pope Pius XI replaced his intransigent predecessor and began, once again, to reconsider the problem of reconciling Catholics to republican institutions in France. He assumed a more guarded position toward the antirepublican Action Française, which had been supported by the ecclesiastical hierarchy during the tenure of Pius X.[69] One of Herriot's first moves was to withdraw France's diplomatic representation at the Vatican that had been reestablished through a parliamentary vote in November 1920, even though the Vatican had just approved the formation of religious associations in accordance with the laws on separation. In addition, the Herriot government extended the secular laws governing religious associations and education to Alsace-Lorraine despite the fact that the previous legislative chamber had voted to maintain the concordat in the newly acquired provinces indefinitely.

These measures met with stiff resistance in Alsace-Lorraine and in Brittany, particularly after the government attempted to ban the use of regional languages and patois from primary schools in 1925. There was no single confessional party in France to mobilize the resistance to the new anticlerical assault by the Radical-Socialist ministry of Herriot. Catholic voters were divided between a variety of parties and groups including the Action Française and Jeune République. Catholics very rapidly founded action groups, however. In August 1924, several of these groups organized meetings to protest the abrogation of the Concordat in Alsace Lorraine. In Finistère, the ecclesiastical hierarchy and Catholic action groups organized mass demonstrations to oppose the anticlerical measures of the Herriot government.[70] The largest in the early years of the Herriot ministry was held in Quimper and in Le Folgoët on 7–8 December 1924 where demonstrators gathered to show support for their compatriots in Alsace-Lorraine, protest the rupture of diplomatic relations with the Vatican, and defend Catholic private education.[71] The newly elected silloniste deputies of

[69] Paul, *The Second Ralliement*, pp. 100–147.

[70] An association was formed in Landerneau on 18 September 1924 to defend the "civic rights and liberties of members of the clergy," recalling the great resistance of 1902 in the department. A.D. Finistère, 1M191, 25 September 1924.

[71] Brittany and Alsace were not the only regions to experience unrest. Twenty-five thousand demonstrators turned out in Laval for a similar demonstration, sixty thousand in

Finistère, Jadé and Trémintin, attended and spoke to an audience of 15,000 in Quimper, according to official estimates, and 25,000, according to the *Courrier du Finistère*.[72] On the following day in Le Folgoët in northern Finistère the Church organized a similar event that was attended by 25,000, according to official estimates, and 55,000, according to the *Courrier du Finistère*.[73] In the prefect's estimation, the clergy and the leaders of the democratic republicans directed "this clerical campaign," by "enlisting the peasantry who follow the orders given to them."[74]

Shortly after the December mass demonstration in Finistère, a Ligue de la Défense et l'Action Catholique, modeled after the Union Catholique of 1911, was formed in the diocese of Quimper. Similar organizations were created in other parts of France. In February 1925, eighty-two such groups joined to form the Fédération Nationale Catholique (FNC) under the leadership of General de Castelnau. Commandant Vannier became the secular leader of Action Catholique in Finistère. The goal of the FNC was to protect the interests of religion, family, society and national patrimony, and it declared its independence from any particular political group.[75]

In Finistère a number of prominent sillonistes became members of the FNC. Sillonistes exploited, through Action Catholique and their own political groups, the political blunders of the Herriot ministry and argued that his policies represented nothing more than statist Jacobinism whose aim was to destroy regional traditions and values. They argued that the Radicals had no coherent social or economic program. The sharp decline in the value of the franc and the inability of Herriot's ministry to stabilize the currency seemed to confirm this assessment two years later. By 1926, the prefect of Finistère reported that a certain "malaise and incertitude" was evident in the Léon where the local population became disillusioned not with the republican regime per se, but with the parliament.[76]

Between 1924 and 1926, as in 1902, the parliament focused most of its attention and energies on ridding France of a clerical menace. Consequently, the sillonistes found it difficult during these years to avoid the religious question. However, they tended to present themselves as a party defending not Catholic interests, but regional interests. This became particularly evident when the Cartel's local language policy was implemented by Minister of Education Anatole de Monzie in 1925.

Angers, and ten thousand in Verdun. *Ligue de Défense et l'Action Catholique, Bulletin mensuelle*, 15 April 1925, p. 9.

[72] A.D. Finistère, 1M191, report by the prefect to the président du Conseil and minister of foreign affairs, 9 December 1924.

[73] Ibid.

[74] Ibid.

[75] *Ligue de la Défense et l'Action Catholique, Bulletin mensuelle*, 15 April 1925, no. 2, p. 31.

[76] A.D. Finistère, 1M133, report by the prefect, 20 February 1926.

In the course of a visit to the Breton Pavillion at the Exhibit of Decorative Arts in July 1925, de Monzie declared that the teaching of patois was unwarranted. Shortly thereafter, he issued a circular forbidding the use of local idioms, including Breton, Provençal, Basque, and Flemish in primary schools (4 August 1925). In doing so, he went further than Emile Combes who banned the use of Breton in religious instruction in 1902. Silloniste deputies and local representatives in the Conseil Général had not only encouraged the use of Breton in primary education but also advocated a bilingual educational system. Pierre Mocaër, conseiller général of the island of Ouessant, had submitted a number of resolutions between 1919 and 1924 in support of bilingual education, and Vincent Inizan and Pierre Trémintin had argued in favor of such proposals in the Chamber of Deputies in December 1921 and 1924, respectively.

In September 1925, Vincent Inizan, republican deputy of Finistère, wrote an open letter to the minister of education that was published in *l'Ouest Eclair* and *Le Petit Breton*, condemning the circular. He argued that Breton was a language in its own right, not patois, and that Bretons were loyal supporters of the nation and the republic.[77] He pointed out that de Monzie's predecessor Léon Bérard favored the use of regional languages in primary schools.[78] In October 1925, Pierre Mocaër voiced his own protest in the Conseil Général in Finistère and presented a summary of his views to Pierre Trémintin. He argued that the use of Breton would in fact only facilitate the rational instruction of the French language and that many state school teachers on the extreme left of the political spectrum favored the use of Breton in primary schools.[79] Pierre Trémintin, an early leader of the FRDF in Finistère, seconded Inizan and argued that Breton was not a bastardized language as French was: "Breton is the direct heir to Celtic, spoken by the conquerors of Europe before the Christian era."[80] He

[77] The growing autonomist movement in Alsace made calls for the preservation of regional languages suspect. Trémintin claimed in 1925 in the Chamber of Deputies that there were many "ardent regionalists" in Brittany but that he belonged to those groups that "will never be separatist." *Journal Officiel*, 5 December 1925, p. 4317.

[78] Quoted in Inizan's open letter to the minister of public instruction, *Le Petit Breton*, 20 September 1925. Bérard in fact originated from a region where Basque was commonly used.

[79] A.D. Finistère, Fonds Trémintin, 104J141, "La Langue Bretonne & M. De Monzie" by Pierre Mocaër [1925]. In the 1930s a bipartisan organization supporting bilingual education, Union pour l'enseignement du Breton or Ar Brezoneg er Skol, was formed largely with the active participation of the democratic republicans of Finistère. Abbé Desgranges, a social Catholic, presented a bill on bilingual education that drew support from most communes in Lower Brittany in 1938. Ar Brezoneg er Skol, *Enseigner le breton, exigence bretonne: la campagne et les efforts d'A.B.E.S. Un programme minimum. Le rapport Desgranges. Textes et documents* (Rennes, 1938).

[80] A.D. Finistère, Fonds Trémintin, 104J141, draft letter to De Monzie. In making this claim, Trémintin drew on a theory of language originating in the sixteenth century, if not before, which identified Celtic as the universal, primordial language spoken in Europe's distant past.

argued, moreover, that "Bretons have become French" and, if they have entered into the French community, it is with all of their intellectual and moral baggage: "*Brittany can only really be French in a Breton way* [my emphasis], and her 250,000 children killed during the war attests that this is not the worst [way]."[81] As in 1902, the social Catholic party in Finistère was unequivocally associated with the defense of regional culture and traditions in contrast to Georges Le Bail and other prominent anti-clerical republican politicians who were associated with Herriot's Radical ministry.

Several months before the fall of Herriot's ministry, the Ligue de la Défense et l'Action Catholique and the Fédération Nationale Catholique organized a second mass demonstration in Finistère that was attended by 35,000 to 40,000 people by official estimates, and by 100,000, according to the organizers. The demonstration that took place in Landerneau on 28 February 1926 protested the government's religious and language policies.[82] Silloniste deputies played a prominent role in the demonstration, that faced a hostile counterdemonstration organized by the Comité de Défense Laïque. The Radical deputy of Finistère Georges Le Bail spoke to a crowd of 3,500 to 4,000.[83]

This demonstration, however, marked the last mass mobilization of Catholic defense in Finistère during the Third Republic. In turn, the last great anticlerical campaign of the Third Republic came to an end with the fall of Herriot's ministry in 1926 owing to the decline in the value of the franc and the country's worsening financial situation. The Republic encountered threats of a new kind in the form of the antirepublican and antiparliamentary leagues of the 1930s, and, this time, the Vatican was often on the side of the government in the condemnation of such groups.[84]

Despite the fact that the FRDF opposed the anticlerical policies of Herriot's government and rallied to support the deputies of Alsace-Lorraine in their resistance to imposing the laical laws of the Third Republic, it did not attempt to create a national "Catholic" party or place the religious question above all other issues. Indeed, during the tenure of the Herriot cabinet the FRDF helped to found the first lasting nonconfessional republican political party of Christian Democratic inspiration: the Parti Démocrate Populaire (PDP).[85]

---

[81] A.D. Finistère, Fonds Trémintin, 104J141.

[82] A.N. F⁷13219, report by the commissaire spécial to the directeur de la Sûreté Nationale, 1 March 1926.

[83] Ibid.

[84] The Vatican condemned Action Française on 24 December 1926. Paul, *The Second Ralliement*, pp. 148–85. Also see Arnal, *Ambivalent Alliance*, pp. 123–45.

[85] For an exhaustive treatment of the origins of the PDP and its role in French politics, see Delbreuil, "Le Parti Démocrate Populaire." Members of the party, unfortunately, destroyed the PDP's archives and dossiers in 1940 to prevent them from being seized by the Germans.

The PDP was born several months after Herriot came to power in 1924. On 15–16 November, 300 delegates from social Catholic organizations as diverse as the FRDF, the Federation of the Seine, and the Catholic trade union Confédération Française des Travailleurs Chrétiens met to discuss the creation of a new political party, not simply to defend the rights of Catholics but to fulfill a social and political program that the traditional parties of Left and Right did not embody.[86] Eleven deputies from the new legislative chamber attended the meeting, including the sillonistes from Finistère, Victor Balanant, Jean Jadé, Pierre Trémintin, and Paul Simon; Canon Louis and Louis Mayer of Moselle; Camille Bilger and Joseph Brom of the Haut-Rhin; Thomas Selz and Michel Walter of the Bas-Rhin; and Auguste Champetier de Ribes of the Basses-Pyrénées. The appellation *républicains démocrates* used by a number of social Catholic political federations was dropped in favor of *démocrates populaires*.[87] The adoption of the term *populaire* revealed the influence of the Italian theorist Don Sturzo and perhaps of the Italian PPI (Parti Populaire Italien). The new PDP elected party officers including Dr. Georges Thibout, former deputy of the Seine, president; Emmanuel Desgrees du Lou, vice-president and political director of *L'Ouest Eclair*; Paul Simon, vice-president; Joseph Zamanski, social Catholic industrialist, treasurer; Jean Raymond-Laurent, an instructor at the Collège des Sciences Sociales, general party secretary; and Robert Cornilleau, editor-in-chief of the Parisian-based *Le Petit Démocrate*, political secretary.

The program of the PDP, like that of the FRDF, reflected both the democratic and intransigent traditions of social Catholicism, defining its own variety of "popular" or corporate democracy against both the "individualist democracy" of "Jacobin radicalism" and the "statist democracy" propagated by Marxist socialism.[88] Popular Democrats, according to Raymond-Laurent, recognized the necessity of "intermediary groups" between the state and the individual in the form of professional organizations, the family, and the region. For this reason, they advocated administrative decentralization and the representation of corporate professional interests in the Conseil d'Etat. The social program of the PDP mirrored the measures introduced by the members of the FRDF in parliament, including indemnity to tenant farmers for land improvements on termination of a lease and creation of low-income housing projects.

The PDP's religious policy was, like that of its progenitor, the FRDF, somewhat ambiguous. The PDP advocated the restoration of religious peace but reserved the right to try to change the laical laws of the early Third Republic. It affirmed the "secular State," which it defined as a state

[86] Delourme, *Trente-cinq années de la politique religieuse*, pp. 259–60.
[87] Mayeur, *La vie politique sous la Troisième République*, pp. 303–05.
[88] Raymond-Laurent, *Le Parti Démocrate Populaire*, p. 4.

impartial to different forms of religion in a nation where a unity of belief was impossible, but it claimed that the secular state should not be confused with "laicism."[89] To this extent the PDP declared itself an advocate of Catholic interests in a way the FRDF had not, but it remained independent of the ecclesiastical hierarchy.

The PDP was organized on a federative basis and represented the interests of rural France, but more particularly the small family farm as well as the small entrepreneur and shopkeeper. Fourteen deputies in the 1924 legislative chamber became members of the party—the eleven who attended the November meeting that led to the PDP's formation, along with deputies Edmond Petitfils of the Ardennes, Armand Le Douarec of Ille-et-Vilaine, and Pierre Lamazou-Betbeder of the Basses-Pyrénées.

The Parti Démocrate Populaire was the culmination of a number of attempts during the early Third Republic to create a lasting democratic party of Christian inspiration, which, in the words of abbé Gayraud, did not "require of its members a profession of Catholic faith."[90]

During the two years of the Herriot ministry, the PDP lent support to Catholic action groups such as the FNC, but it was not subsumed by them. Two years after the fall of Herriot's ministry, the PDP increased its representation to twenty in the Chamber of Deputies in the legislative elections of 1928, despite the return of the scrutin d'arrondissement. Champetier de Ribes, PDP deputy from the Basse-Pyrénees became minister of finance during the Tardieu cabinets.[91] The PDP enjoyed new favor in the Vatican, which applauded the party's success in the 1928 elections, though the party remained independent of the clerical hierarchy. The PDP continued to bask in this support through the 1930s, and conservative Catholics who had looked to organizations such as Action Française for leadership now found little sympathy for their political proclivities in Rome.

The PDP, which became a mass-based party with a highly developed and effective political organization, nonetheless was a regionally based party during the interwar period. It drew its members—the peasantry and petite bourgeosie—from the peripheral, ethnically distinct areas of the Pyrenees, Alsace, and Brittany, which may in part be explained by the fact that it became the only alternative to the reactionary counterrevolutionary right that wished to return to an idealized conception of the Old Regime and the anticlerical Left that, in the Jacobin tradition, sought to eradicate regional

[89] Raymond-Laurent, *Le Parti Démocrate Populaire, 1924–1944*, p. 17.

[90] Quoted in Biton, *La démocratie chrétienne dans la politique française*, p. 141. The Christian Democratic party formed in Reims in 1896 was dissolved owing to a changing tide in Rome, and the Action Libérale Populaire that was founded in 1901 began to disintegrate after only several years of existence. The PDP by contrast became a permanent part of the French political landscape from 1924 until the Second World War.

[91] Mayeur, *La vie politique sous la Troisième République*, p. 305.

and cultural institutions and values. The PDP also provided an alternative to the autonomist and separatist organizations, that advocated secession from the French nation.[92]

The political successes of the FRDF and the PDP in Finistère dissipated, however, in the 1930s as the alliance between agriculture and small business, on which the FRDF had originally been based, eroded with a worsening economy that increasingly pitted town against country. Nonetheless, despite the increasing polarization of politics and the PDP's regional base in the interwar years, the party served as a training ground for the founders of the postwar Mouvement Républicain Populaire (MRP), which became one of the largest parties in France during the Fourth Republic. These founders included Georges Bidault, who became president of the National Council of the Resistance during the War after the death of Jean Moulin; Germaine Peyroles, MRP deputy of Seine-et-Oise; and Germaine Poinso-Chapuis, MRP deputy of Marseilles who became minister of public health and population, one of the first women to achieve a major ministerial post in the postwar period.[93] Following the Second World War, the MRP quickly became firmly implanted in Finistère, which can in large part be attributed to a long tradition of social Catholicism in the department.

In mobilizing a coalition of town and country along new lines in the interwar period, the Center-Left silloniste party in Finistère ultimately succeeded in challenging the traditional bipartite divisions in French politics. It refused to make the Church-state conflict a central issue in a region where religion traditionally defined political affiliation. It contributed to changes in local political practices by drawing on new social groups for leadership rather than on traditional elites and gained broad-based support in anticlerical bastions within the department that had formerly voted for Radical politicians. In an area where the electorate had to choose between an anticlerical "jacobin" Left in the form of the Radical and Socialist parties and an antirepublican Right, the FRDF and ultimately the PDP provided alternatives to regional groups who were committed to the Republic but refused either to compromise local interests or to abandon cultural traditions and values. Finally, in refusing to conflate cultural and national identity, for good or for ill, they ultimately forged a new republican political identity on the borders of France.

[92] Representatives of the PDP in Finistère clearly repudiated the autonomist movement and separatism, which led to bitter reprisals among supporters of these movements. In a 1924 speech at the Causerie of Paris Pierre Trémintin condemned separatism but supported regional languages. Abbé Perrot, a leader of a Breton Catholic cultural organization, Bleun Brug, condemned his position.

[93] See Irving, *Christian Democracy in France*, pp. 19–105.

8

Religion, Identity, and the Nation

> It is certainly futile to try to reduce France to
> *one* discourse, *one* equation, *one* formula, *one*
> image or *one* myth.
> (*Fernand Braudel*)

BETWEEN THE nineteenth and twentieth centuries, economic change, the communications revolution, state-sponsored mass educational institutions, and the experience of war transformed the face of Lower Breton society. Ever larger numbers of Bretons emigrated to Paris and abroad to return only infrequently to a region that never became wholly absorbed into the dominant secular culture of the French capital. Indeed, it is impossible to trace a linear path by which political and cultural attitudes at the center replaced "traditional" beliefs and political practices.[1] Nonetheless the inhabitants of Lower Brittany did come to share in a common, national political culture. The turmoil engendered by the republican state's effort to impose its conception of a secular, unitary nation at the periphery through education and cultural policies designed to eradicate regional cultural difference served as a catalyst for the political acculturation of the region by stimulating an awareness of the relationship between the national politics and local problems and issues.

Indeed, the political struggle between the Church and the state was one of the major conflicts of nineteenth-century France.[2] This conflict was in part rooted in the French Revolution, which shaped modern political alignments by allegedly separating a "democratic, lay [anticlerical] Left" from a "Catholic [clerical], hierarchical Right."[3] French electoral sociolo-

---

[1] As Hobsbawm has recently argued, "men and women did not choose collective identification as they chose shoes, knowing that one could only put on one pair at a time." Hobsbawm, *Nations and Nationalism since 1870*, p. 123.

[2] See Theodore Zeldin's general assessment of the dimensions of this conflict in "Were There Two Frances?" in *Conflicts in French Society*, pp. 9–11. Also see James F. Macmillan, "Religion and Politics in Modern France," *Historical Journal* 12 (1982): 1021–27.

[3] These definitions were originally formulated by André Siegfried, the founder of French electoral sociology, to describe the political temperaments of modern France. He identified religion as an important predictor of political behavior. Siegfried, *Tableau politique de la France de l'Ouest*, pp. 192–94, 496–506. One exception to this rule is Berenson's *Populist Religion and Left-Wing Politics in France*.

gists and historians, as well as nineteenth-century French bureaucrats themselves, have used religion as a predictor of voting patterns, generally associating right-wing areas with highly practicing areas and left-wing areas with areas of religious indifference in part because since the French Revolution the Church was allied politically and ideologically with the Right. In the western department of the Sarthe, one could observe a clear geographical boundary dividing these two irreconcilable political factions; one embraced as a political ideal a secular republican nation, and the other a Catholic, hierarchically ordered nation rooted in France's prerevolutionary past.[4] Indeed, some scholars have pointed to the continued persistence of regional voting patterns and religious differences, which have been attributed to family patterns and structures or alternatively to modes of production.[5]

Although historians and contemporary observers have long recognized the importance of the clerical/anticlerical struggle in national politics, only recently have they illuminated the extent to which it shaped political alignments in provincial France. Popular anticlericalism and conflicts between Catholics and Protestants in southern France, for example, have been shown to have contributed to the meteoric rise of an anticlerical Left in the early nineteenth century in a former royalist enclave where "currents of popular religious feeling discontented with Catholicism were soon diverted into the democratic movement."[6]

The role that religion played in the political integration of areas of France that remained predominantly Catholic has hardly been explored, though electoral sociologists and historians have argued that fervent Catholicism generally coincided with right-wing voting behavior. The religious history of the Upper Breton department of Ille-et-Vilaine and the southern Massif Central in the nineteenth century indicates,[7] however, that the relationship between religion and politics cannot be so easily reduced to equating re-

---

[4] Bois, *Paysans de l'Ouest*.

[5] See, e.g., Le Bras and Todd, *L'invention de la France*. For critiques of this approach, see Jean-René Tréanton, "Faut-il exhumer Le Play? ou les héritiers abusifs," *Revue française de la sociologie* 25 (July–September 1984): 458–83, and Hugues Lagrange and Sebastien Roché, "Types familiaux et géographie politique en France," *Revue française de la science politique* 38 (December 1988): 941–64. Also see William Brustein, *The Social Origins of Political Regionalism: France 1849–1981* (Berkeley, 1988), and Ted Margadant's critique of Brustein in *French Politics and Society* 8, no. 3 (Summer 1990): 97–104.

[6] Agulhon, *The Republic in the Village*, pp. 111, 101–4; Berenson, *Populist Religion and Left-Wing Politics in France*; Margadant, *French Peasants in Revolt*, pp. 142–43, 146–47, 150–51. Margadant shows how "religion easily became the symbolic issue around which national loyalties were grafted onto local faction" (p. 150). Here Protestantism and dechristianization are associated with republicanism and Catholicism with legitimism (pp. 150–51).

[7] Lagrée, *Mentalités, religion et histoire en Haute Bretagne*, and Jones, *Politics and Rural Society*.

ligious fervor with the political dominance of the Right and religious indifference with the preponderance of the Left.[8] In the diocese of Rennes the geography of the "blues," supporters of the revolution, did not in fact correspond with areas of religious indifference. This finding has led Michel Lagrée to formulate the concepts of *christianisme bleu* and *christianisme blanc* to describe the relationship between political and religious behavior in the area.[9] The existence of christianisme bleu indicates that the "spirit of faith" and the "spirit of progress" were not contradictory:[10] The progress of republican ideas in the region coincided with a process of "declericalization," rather than with the "dechristianization" of the diocese.[11] Similarly, in the Massif Central, religion was not a reliable indicator of political affiliation toward the end of the nineteenth century.

The history of the Lower Breton department of Finistère from 1890 to the 1920s illustrates the pitfalls of explaining political behavior in terms of religious belief and provides one of the clearest examples of the importance of the Church-state conflict in contributing to the emergence of a national consciousness at the periphery. Moreover, it demonstrates that the creation of the nation in the peninsula did not necessarily lead to the repudiation or disappearance of collective regional or religious cultural identities. Local politics had been dominated by traditional elites until the 1890s. Finistère had undergone significant economic change that resulted in expanding local markets and economic opportunities from the 1820s to the 1870s. These changes increasingly afforded the peasant greater economic independence and contact with other worlds, but they did not in themselves lead to a heightened awareness of national politics. They provided the conditions that enabled the peasantry to repudiate their former lords. The implementation of the republican government's anticlerical legislation during the early Third Republic and the Ralliement destroyed the political consensus in the region. Rather than strengthening the Left in Finistère, social antagonism and the new social agenda of the lower clergy drove a wedge between the clergy and the nobility, thereby dividing authorities that formerly spoke the same language.[12] The political conflict that ensued contributed to factionalized politics, which ultimately led to the democratization of local political behavior. In addition, this conflict gave rise to a

---

[8] Tony Judt has suggested that "a sympathy for the right" may have helped to "prolong a practising faith which conservative ideology so fervently espoused," but he warns against using religion as a key to understanding voting behavior. Judt, *Socialism in Provence*, pp. 176, 248.

[9] Lagrée, *Mentalités, religion et histoire en Haute Bretagne*, pp. 73–91.

[10] Ibid., p. 91.

[11] Ibid., p. 90.

[12] Eugen Weber has emphasized the sociopolitical importance of religious conflict in setting "lord against lord and priest against priest, dividing authorities" that were "natural to heed." Weber, "Comment la Politique Vint aux Paysans," p. 367.

new political phenomenon that has had a profound impact on local politics in Lower Brittany: social Catholicism.

Social Catholicism was first introduced to the department of Finistère by the lower clergy of northern Finistère in the late 1880s. The spirit of Rerum Novarum already existed in the department before the actual promulgation of the encyclical in 1891. It represented an early attempt by the lower clergy to maintain the faith by ministering to the material as well as spiritual needs of their parishioners. Unlike their counterparts in most other regions of France, the parish clergy of Finistère later heeded the Pope's call for Catholics to rally to the Republic. This decision was predicated on the social antagonism between former political allies—the nobility and the parish clergy—that became evident to even the casual observer. In the 1880s and 1890s the lower clergy of Finistère, who were largely recruited from among the Lower Breton peasantry, increasingly came into conflict with the nobility over questions of political strategy and social policy. The clergy's decision to rally to the Republic won them the enmity of the local nobility whose political leadership in the department was challenged by the clergy's conversion to the Republic. The clergy came to realize that defending the social influence of the nobility was incompatible with defending the Church because such defense ignored the social problems in modern society as well as the democratic movement afoot in France. The clergy entered the electoral fray with a vengeance by using old tactics of political persuasion as well as modern electoral methods, which included public meetings, the press, and local organization. The introduction of such practices marked the end of the political hegemony of local notables. Their disappearance contributed to the decline of royalism, and republican ideas, albeit defined and shaped by their new clerical supporters, gained ground. In Finistère, unlike Ille-et-Vilaine, the progress of republican ideas coincided with neither declericalization nor dechristianization. Both the lay school and the clergy in the highly clericalized culture of Lower Brittany introduced the Republic to a people who initially seemed indifferent to its appeals in the name of a broader national community. The parish clergy, who had long served as cultural brokers in the peninsula, now acted as independent political brokers representing the interests of the parish in the capital.

These clerical neophytes of the Republic were sharply criticized by the anticlerical Left and the Catholic Right who declared that the clergy in essence forced their ideals on unwilling subjects through their time-tested methods of coercion, including refusal to grant absolution, ostracism, and the confessional. The clergy's withdrawal from overt participation in the movement owing to a change in Vatican policy in 1903 did not lead to the movement's decline, however, an indication that its implantation in the region could not simply be attributed to clerical influence. A new lay leadership that frequently came into conflict with the ecclesiastical hierarchy, which accused the movement of sowing social discord, breathed new life into the movement between 1902 and 1911. Moreover, the ministry of Père Combes gave it fresh momentum even in anticlerical bastions. Combes's application of the Law on Associations and his language policy, which came to be associated with the anticlerical Left, alienated many rural voters in Finistère and made them sharply aware of the relationship between the national government and local institutions and issues. The mass resistance of 1902 worked to the advantage of the nascent social Catholic movement, which became identified with the resistance and the protection of regional interests and values. The movement, however, did not defend "traditional" society in the hands of a clerico-aristocratic elite. Rather, it attempted to protect local institutions, such as schools managed by the Breton order of the Filles du Saint-Esprit, that had become integral parts of parish culture only during the early Third Republic. What began as a movement of religious defense and social reform now became a movement of regional defense.

The growing hostility of the Catholic Church and the ecclesiastical hierarchy toward the social Catholic movement resulted in the condemnation of one its most progressive elements. The condemnation of the Sillon in 1910 did not, however, herald the disappearance of the movement's political wing. In 1911, the members of the disbanded Sillon in Finistère and its sympathizers formed a political organization, the Fédération des républicains démocrates du Finistère, that dominated local electoral politics in the interwar period. As the Right and the Left organized their campaigns and strategies around the religious question and the Church-state conflict in the postwar period, the FRDF pointed to regional inequities in the formulation of national policy, economic development, and social reform. It became the beneficiary of the "politics of religion," which consumed the Right and the Left, and both lost electoral ground to the movement. Indeed, the veteran Radical deputy of Finistère, Georges Le Bail, became so preoccupied with the religious issue that he ignored the interests of the peasantry he represented.[13] The FRDF steered clear of the religious issue between 1919 and 1924, and it even went so far as to affirm the legitimacy of the "secular state." The rural electorate of Finistère clearly distinguished between the silloniste party and the Right in casting their ballots for the new party in the interwar period.

Historians have long accepted the republican appraisal of the silloniste party as white owing to its Catholic origins, in spite of the progressive social and political positions assumed by its representatives, but the tradi-

---

[13] Burguière, *Bretons de Plozévet*, p. 231. Also see Capitan, "Enquête pluridisciplinaire sur Plozévet."

tional Right, not the FRDF, was subsumed in electoral alliances. The nobility, finding refuge in politically neutral agricultural syndicalism, of which the Office Central was the most successful example, gradually disappeared from public office.

The social Catholic movement of the 1890s and its heir the FRDF introduced new electoral practices—public meetings, political fanfare, an active press, and tight-knit local political organizations—that definitively transformed the issues as well as the style of electoral politics in Lower Brittany. Voters were wooed and harangued rather than bribed and cajoled. The FRDF nationalized local issues and conflicts, but ironically much of its success can be attributed to its adaptation to local conditions in a region where the wholesale imposition of the state's ideas, values, and political categories was resisted. Indeed, many political skirmishes and wars of words during this period concerned a fundamentally contested, dualistic articulation of "nation" issuing from the French Revolution. By increasingly conflating cultural and national identity as a result of the conflicts engendered by the secularization of French primary education, the republican state called regional allegiances into question. The social Catholic movement in its political form represented a local response to these encroachments by the state, as local groups refused to renounce religious or regional identities while pledging allegiance to a differently defined republican nation.

Religious conflict served as a catalyst for a distinct pattern of nation formation on the borderlands of France. Religious dissension did not necessarily move the electorate into the traditional ideological camps of the secular left or Catholic right. It transformed patterns of clientage, divided rural elites, democratized the rules of local politics, and forcefully and swiftly demonstrated to men and women in the provinces the relationship between national political events and local problems and issues. Although the inhabitants of lower Brittany were loath to accept many anticlerical cultural policies of the Third Republic that were considered necessary in Paris for the acceptance of the republican nation, Bretons clearly embraced the democratic political culture on which the republican nation rested.

The history of Finistère during the early Third Republic offers a model of integration that challenges center-outward approaches to nation formation at the periphery. The political acculturation of Finistère was effected through local cultural institutions and political organizations rather than the transference of urban ideologies and national organizations from Paris to provincial France. The Sillon, a social Catholic movement formed in Paris, did become an important force in Finistère, but it was grafted on a preexisting social Catholic movement, adapted to local conditions, and was itself shaped by social Catholic leaders in the peninsula.

The Lower Breton pattern of political integration opposes those patterns presented by historians influenced by modernization theory;[14] they have argued that socioeconomic change, urbanization, education, and new forms of market organization associated with the emergence of industrial capitalism gradually transformed peasant society—traditional forms of sociability, production, and communal life—and paved the way for the periphery's entry into the modern world through the diffusion of urban values.

The history of Finistère might lead one to conclude that certain regions have never become integrated into the political life of the French nation;[15] indeed, rural elites consciously designed forms of organization to insure that this continued to be so. One should not, however, conclude from the history of Lower Brittany that the region failed to become politicized because local issues and political organizations did not precisely reflect national political issues and categories. In other words, the advent of modern politics in the countryside should not simply be equated with the transference of national political labels and parties from the center to the periphery. The history of social Catholicism in Finistère indicates that the integration of rural France was in some cases effected through the activity of home-grown political movements rather than those spawned in Paris.

Indeed, opposing views that deny this perspective on the political integration of provincial France may in fact be a function of a conception of politics that must see modern political behavior at the local level as an image in miniature of the Parisian political stage. This conception implies that "politics" is confined to issues of state and to ideologies defined by its servants as well as its enemies. According to this conception, the process of acculturation presupposes a shared understanding of the principal political problems in the nation as a whole but, more important, shared views regarding their resolution.

This unidimensional conception of politics that distinguishes between the purely local and national, however, does not specifically address an issue at the heart of the political acculturation of provincial France: the structural process by which old elites come to be replaced by a new

[14] See C. E. Black, *The Dynamics of Modernization: A Study in Comparative History* (New York, 1966), and Samuel Huntington, *Political Order in Changing Societies* (New Haven, 1968), and for a critique of these theories, see D. C. Tipps, "Modernization Theory and the Comparative Studies of Societies: A Critical Perspective," *Comparative Studies in Society and History* 15 (1973): 199–226.

[15] Karnoouh, "La démocratie impossible," pp. 24–56; L. Levi-Strauss, "Pouvoir municipal et parenté dans un village bourgignon," *Annales, économies, sociétés, et civilisations* 30, no. 1 (January–February 1975): 149–59; J. Jolas and F. Zonabend, "Cousinage, voisinage," *Archives d'ethnologie française* 11 (1970): 169–80; C. Pelras, "Goulien, commune rurale du Cap Sizun (Finistère): étude d'ethnologie globale," *Bulletin et mémoires de la société d'anthropologie de Paris* 10 (1966): 520–25; Berger, *Peasants Against Politics*; F. Elegoet, "Prêtres, nobles et paysans en Léon," pp. 39–90.

democratic leadership and the extent to which the political system comes to be perceived and used as an instrument to promote local interests. The political acculturation of Lower Brittany must be understood in terms of what Daniel Halévy described more than fifty years ago as the end of the notables. During the early Third Republic, a clerico-aristocratic elite was replaced in Finistère, as in other parts of France, by a new notability of doctors, lawyers, and notaries and a new working class of arsenal workers and peasants. The replacement of a noble ruling elite in municipal and national office by its social inferiors in many remote regions of France represents a qualitative change in the political perceptions of the peasantry, indicating that they had come of age as citizens.

This study suggests, then, that despite the emergence of new information and transportation systems, the commercialization of agriculture, the dissemination of new ideas and national organizations emanating from the center, certain areas did not unreservedly adopt the values exported by Paris but rather created new cultural and political forms grounded in local tradition.[16] In Finistère, these new forms challenged elites and the traditional political categories predicated on the Left/Right dichotomy and transformed local political practices. The social Catholic movement defended the regional identity of the area it came to represent in Paris, and, in so doing, defined the republican nation at the periphery in new terms.

To what extent can the Lower Breton model of national integration be generalized to other parts of France or indeed to other parts of Europe? It is difficult to make generalizations of any kind on the basis of a regional study owing to both variations in land tenure, topography, language, and cultural traditions in areas as diverse as Alsace, Poitou, Gascogne, Flanders, or Bourbonnais in France and different national experiences outside France.[17] The history of Finistère may provide an interpretive key, however, to patterns of nation formation in areas where religious practices persisted.

Outside the Breton peninsula, in other predominantly Catholic regions of France, the Church-state conflict similarly contributed to the "political edification of populations not accessible to ideological argument in other

[16] This was true of not only politics but also economic and family structures. In the Loire valley, for example, certain types of subsistence agriculture were adapted to the introduction of new market forces. Dallas, *The Imperfect Peasant Economy*, p. 5. Dallas argues that the peasant communities of the Loire valley did not follow an expected pattern of profit maximization by abandoning traditional forms of subsistence agriculture. He realized that his study was not to be one of the "gradual assimilation of rural communities into a larger, more complex society, but rather how they managed to maintain their own particular forms of cultural identity" (ibid.). Also see Rogers, *Shaping Modern Times in Rural France*.

[17] No one expressed this better than Gordon Wright who has argued that "rural France is almost infinitely diverse, and almost any generalization about the peasantry becomes partially false as soon as it is formulated." Wright, *Rural Revolution in France*, p. v.

terms,"[18] but the political outcome was in many cases quite different and depended on clerical structures and economic relationships between the region and the state. In the barren highlands of the southern Massif Central, populated by a largely illiterate peasant population, the "guerilla warfare between church and state" during the early Third Republic "forced upon the peasantry . . . a *prise de conscience* unlike anything it had experienced since 1789."[19] As in Lower Brittany, the peasantry was highly devout, and the Church served as a cultural integrator in an area of dispersed habitat. The introduction of the ballot box in the southern Massif Central in 1848 coincided with a popular religious revival, and the ballot was initially enlisted to serve the interests of the Catholic church and to resist incursions by the state in local affairs.[20] In 1885, the clerical party won stunning successes, as in Finistère, by capitalizing on the religious issue and the agricultural depression. By 1893, however, the predominantly Catholic electorate trudged to the polls to vote for anticlerical republican candidates. This dramatic change in political conviction was apparently tactical rather than ideological. In a region where the Church and the local populace were much poorer and more financially dependent on the state than in Brittany, the peasant learned to "serve both God and mammon as incarnated in the 'milch cow' state."[21] The state provided jobs and government subsidies that the region could ill afford to lose. That the Ralliement and social Catholicism gained little ground in the area can in part be explained in terms of clerical structures. The ecclesiastical hierarchy, which had greater moral and financial control over its parish clergy than its counterpart in Finistère, was intransigent. The alliance between the clergy and the nobility remained strong. But the failure of the clerico-aristocratic elite to respond to the material needs of the peasantry and to adapt to the conditions of modern electoral politics insured its political decline.

The history of the politics of the Kulturkampf and the formation of the Center party in Germany provide the historian of France with an interesting parallel to the relationship between religion and nation formation in parts of Catholic France. Scholars have recently shown how the Kulturkampf of the 1870s in Germany mobilized the Catholic populations to create a united political Catholicism devoted to Catholic and regional interests.[22] The Center party was created to represent German Catholics, a

---

[18] Weber, "Comment la Politique Vint aux Paysans," p. 359.

[19] Jones, *Politics and Rural Society*, p. 305.

[20] "In clericalism, the upland peasantry found refuge from the encroaching power of the state." Ibid., p. 5.

[21] Ibid., p. 305.

[22] Sperber, *Popular Catholicism in Nineteenth-Century Germany*, p. 286. Sperber argues, however, that the mobilization of Catholics was predicated on the religious revival that characterized the previous quarter century.

minority facing the discriminatory and anticlerical policies of the newly formed Reich. Indeed, out of the Kulturkampf the Catholic Center party emerged as an influential force in German politics, although there were regional variations in its leadership and character. In Rhineland-Westphalia, political Catholicism was directed by the clergy, and its success represented a clerical triumph more than in the areas of southern and southwestern Germany, where the Center party mobilized the electorate on economic issues, including protection of the guild system and agricultural tariffs.[23] In Württemberg, the Center party remained almost exclusively a party of Catholics, but in the 1890s it moved, as did the silloniste party, away from being a predominantly confessional and clerical party.[24] The Center party consistently defended agricultural interests and small business, and, as in Finistère, by "addressing itself to peasant and petty-bourgeois grievances" the party "acquired and consolidated its mass base."[25]

Although there are striking similarities between the role that the Church-state struggle played in mobilizing Catholic voters and in creating new political organizations in the form of the Center party in Germany and various social Catholic political groupings in France, the differences between the two cases are equally apparent. A unified political Catholic movement did not emerge in France as in Germany, the existence of the Parti Démocrate Populaire, the first lasting party of Christian Democratic inspiration, notwithstanding. Attempts to create a Catholic party on the German model failed because political divisions among Catholics were too great to surmount. For this reason the Action Libérale Populaire disintegrated soon after it was founded in 1901. One can perhaps attribute the relative cohesiveness and longevity of the Center party in Germany to the fact that Catholicism was a minority religion in the Empire. The Center party focused much of its attention on fighting the discriminatory policies of the Empire, which affected all Catholics. Indeed the "parity question" and the slogan "out of the Tower" were central to the party's platform and assured unity even when conflict arose in the party's ranks.[26]

The geography of the social Catholic movement suggests that it may have served functions similar to the Center party in Germany. Centrist social Catholic political groups and the Parti Démocrate Populaire had

[23] Ibid., pp. 290–91.

[24] Blackbourn, *Class, Religion, and Local Politics in Wilhelmine Germany*, p. 234.

[25] Ibid., p. 234. Sperber has warned against reducing religion to an "epiphenomenon of economic interests" and argues that in the Catholic cities of the Rhine Valley or in the mixed areas of the Ruhr, "social issues when explicitly expressed were often harmful to the Catholic cause . . . but when subsumed under religious questions had a powerful attractive force." Sperber, *Political Catholicism in Nineteenth-Century Germany*, pp. 287, 295. Jean-Marie Mayeur suggests, however, that it is unlikely that parties predicated simply on religious defense would last. Mayeur, *Des partis catholiques à la démocratie chrétienne*, p. 10.

[26] Ronald J. Ross, *Beleaguered Tower: The Dilemma of Political Catholicism in Wilhelmine Germany* (Notre Dame, 1976).

their strongest support in the interwar period in peripheral, ethnically distinct areas, including Brittany, the Basque region, and Alsace,[27] which contained large numbers of practicing Catholics and which were perhaps the least integrated into the dominant secular national culture of the Third French Republic. In each of these regions autonomist and regionalist organizations emerged alongside the social Catholic movement during the early Third Republic.[28] Social Catholicism represented the interests of minority groups, whose loyalty was in doubt in the case of Alsace or whose traditions were ridiculed in the case of Brittany. Religion did act as a vehicle of cultural resistance in the lower Breton context, but it did not become an instrument through which to express alternative national claims on a mass basis. Indeed, the successful implantation of a democratic strand of Social Catholicism in the lower Breton peninsula in a period of intense political conflict and its continued vitality into the Fourth Republic severely limited mass support for autonomist and ethnic nationalist movements. The Parti Démocrate Populaire and the Mouvement Républicain Populaire provided one of the few alternatives to autonomist and separatist groups who advocated secession, and it represented an indigenous attempt to bridge the Republican nation with the region.[29] The social Catholic movement supplanted autonomist initiatives by becoming a party identified with the protection of regional interests that advocated a decentralist rather than a separatist solution to the regional question. In contesting the secular, unitary conception of the republican nation, the inhabitants of Lower Brittany strove to construct an alternative conception of the Republic. In so doing, they reconciled their identities as Catholics and Bretons with the claims of a larger France.

[27] Prélot, "Les démocrates d'inspiration chrétienne," p. 545.

[28] One of the first movements of this kind, Union Régionaliste Bretonne, was formed in 1898 in Morlaix (Finistère) under the leadership of largely aristocratic patrons. The membership consisted of 25 percent noble landowners, 17 percent clergy, 1 percent liberal professions, and 11 percent commerçants. No peasants were represented in the organization. Commission "Histoire" de Skol Vreizh, Histoire de la Bretagne et des pays celtiques de 1789 à 1914, 4: 268. In 1905, a priest from Finistère, abbé Jean Marie Perrot, founded Bleun Brug, an organization that combined religious and cultural defense. Poisson, L'abbé Jean-Marie Perrot. In 1911, two new groups, one regionalist, the Fédération Régionaliste Bretonne, and one separatist, Parti Nationaliste Breton, were formed.

[29] Zeldin makes this argument for Alsace: the "main result of the republic's hostility [to regional claims] was that Alsace Lorraine became largely 'Christian democrat' and 'Centre.'" Zeldin, France 1848–1945, p. 82.

Selected Bibliography

Archival Sources

Archives Nationales, Paris

SERIES BB (JUSTICE)

BB³⁰1679 Religious Associations, Morlaix
BB³⁰1680 Religous Associations, Quimperlé, Saint-Pol-de-Léon

SERIES C (NATIONAL ASSEMBLIES)

C4491 Chamber of Deputies, elections, 1885–1889, Finistère
C4822 Chamber of Deputies, elections, 1889–1893, Finistère
C4986 Chamber of Deputies, elections, 1893–1898, Finistère
C5353 Chamber of Deputies, elections, 1898–1902, Finistère
C6072–73 Chamber of Deputies, elections, 1902–1906, Finistère
C6325–27 Chamber of Deputies, elections, 1906–1910, Finistère
C6593–95 Chamber of Deputies, elections, 1910–1914, Finistère

SERIES F⁷ (POLICE)

F⁷6780 Reports, political situation, Dordogne-Jura, 1829–1835
F⁷12477–79 Catholic congresses, regional assemblies, associations, and circles, 1872–1901
F⁷12480 Union Nationale, 1895–1905
F⁷12481 Catholic electoral action in Paris and the provinces, 1895–1904
F⁷12482–84 Catholic congresses
F⁷12486 Catholic demonstrations, sermons, public and private meetings, religious festivals
F⁷12541 Legislative elections, 1902, Ain-Finistère
F⁷12544 Legislative elections, 1906, Ain-Finistère
F⁷12547 Municipal elections, 1904, Ain-Jura
F⁷12715 Application of the 1 July 1901 Law on Associations and Separation of Church and State; resistance to these measures
F⁷12719 Nationalists: general information; Action Libérale Populaire, 1898–1910
F⁷12738 Reports by commissaires spéciaux on departments, 1924–1928
F⁷12878 Action Libérale Populaire, 1902–1912
F⁷12983–84 Miscellaneous reports on departments, 1919–1939
F⁷13219 Fédération Nationale Catholique
F⁷13626–28 General notes and press clippings on agricultural movements, 1904–1936

SERIES F¹⁸ (PRESS)

F¹⁸456 Press, Finistère

SERIES F⁹ (RELIGIOUS AFFAIRS)

F¹⁹1973 Separation of Church and State: clerical attitudes and implementation by department, 1905–1906

F¹⁹2381 Personnel: statistics, year XIII to 1891

F¹⁹2564 Personnel: archbishops, bishops, dossiers by diocese, Quimper

F¹⁹2653 Personnel: curés, desservants, vicaires, statistics, year X to 1896

F¹⁹2655 Desservants: removibility, 1839–1881

F¹⁹3004–6 Personnel: curés by diocese, Quimper

F¹⁹5503 Use of dialects in religious instruction—Breton, 1891–1906

F¹⁹5582 Festivals and Public Ceremonies, 1884–1903

F¹⁹5610 Police: reports and notes on the clergy's attitudes toward Carlism

F¹⁹5613 Reports on the political orientation of the clergy, 1891–1910

F¹⁹5617 Elections: clerical influence, 1876–1886

F¹⁹5618 General elections, 1889

F¹⁹5619 Municipal elections, 1892 and 1896; general elections, 1893; Election of abbé Hippolyte Gayraud to Finistère, 1897

F¹⁹5620 General elections, 1898

F¹⁹5621–22 General elections, 1902

F¹⁹5631 Religious Associations, Christian Democracy (1896)

F¹⁹5633 *Oeuvres sociales*, Sillon, 1904–1906

F¹⁹5637 Secular activity among priests: practice of medical and pharmaceutical services, 1805–1901

F¹⁹5649 Catholic processions

F¹⁹5651 Sillon, caisses rurales

F¹⁹5656 Miscellaneous: catechism, emblems, elections of 1910; use of dialects in religious instruction

F¹⁹5927 Role of clergy in elections, 1880–1905

F¹⁹5979 Religious affairs, miscellaneous, Finistère

F¹⁹6068–69 Clerical politicians and miscellaneous reports on clergy

F¹⁹6079 Application of the Law on Associations in Finistère

F¹⁹6116 Clerical salaries, Year XI–1881

F¹⁹6117 Clerical salaries: the issue of augmentation, 1819–1874

F¹⁹6118 Clerical salaries: desservants and vicaires, 1809–1888

F¹⁹6131 Clerical salaries: circulars and correspondence, 1882–1905

F¹⁹6157 Curés and desservants, diocese of Quimper

F¹⁹6651–54 Fiches of clerical personnel by diocese, Quimper

F¹⁹6268–69 Preparation and execution of laws and decrees, 1901–1905; unauthorized religious associations formed since 1901

Archives Départementales du Finistère, Quimper and Brest

SERIES J (SPECIAL ACQUISITIONS)

3J33–34 Various canticles and catechisms printed in Breton and French, nineteenth–twentieth centuries

25J Fonds Soudry

104J Fonds Trémintin

SERIES M (ADMINISTRATION)

1M132 Prefect reports, 1857–1909

1M133 Prefect reports, 1910–

1M134 Subprefect reports, Brest, 1830–1935
1M135 Subprefect reports, Châteaulin, 1831–1936
1M136 Subprefect reports, Morlaix, 1831–1936
1M137 Subprefect reports, Quimperlé, 1830–1924
1M140 Police reports, 1861–1938
1M141 Police reports, 1880–1928
1M142 Police reports, Douarnenez, 1862–1924
1M143 Police reports, Pont l'Abbé, 1862–1924
1M144 Police reports, Quimper, 1889–1936
1M145–46 Miscellaneous police reports, 1814–1934
1M156 Economic activity, reports, Year XIII–1939
1M170 Surveillance of royalist opposition; notes on functionaries and parliamentarians, 1857–1940
1M180–89 Surveillance of public opinion, 1870–1940
1M190 Public meetings, 1881–1913
1M191 Catholic demonstration in Quimper, 7 December 1924
1M192 Catholic demonstration in Landerneau, 28 February 1926
1M197–98 Press, 1884–1912, 1919–1940
1M200–201 Religious affairs, demonstrations, information on priests, Catholic parties
1M228 Political parties: Free Masonry, 1887–1888; Sillon, 1905–1923; Parti Démocrate Populaire, 1921–1939; Action Libérale Populaire, 1887–1939
1M230 Peasant movements, reports and posters
1M481 Correspondence, reports, petitions regarding the education law of 1879, 1878–1929

SERIES 3M (ELECTIONS)
3M289 Legislative elections of 1893
3M290 By-election of 21 January 1894, second district of Morlaix
3M291 By-election of 24 January 1897, third district of Brest
3M293 By-election of August 1897, third district of Brest
3M294 Legislative elections of 1898
3M297–98 Legislative elections of 1902
3M300–301 Legislative elections of 1906
3M304–5 Legislative elections of 1910
3M311 By-election of 30 March 1913, second district of Brest
3M312–15 Legislative elections of 1914
3M316–17 Legislative elections of 1919
3M319–20 Legislative elections of 1924
3M355 Conseil Général
3M380 Cantonal elections, 1904
3M381 Conseil Général, general information
3M396 Cantonal elections of 8 January 1922, Ploudiry
3M429 Municipal elections, reports, 1870–1940

SERIES 4M (POLICE)
4M129 Commissariat of Police, Morlaix: Miscellaneous reports, 1899–1901
4M161 Commissariat of Police, Quimper: Reports on meetings, demonstrations, and miscellaneous correspondence, 1905–1939

4M173 Cantonal elections, 1907–1922

4M175 Miscellaneous information regarding legislative election, 1924

4M177 Surveillance of private political meetings, 1919–1939

4M183 "La Masse du Combat des Paysans"

4M194 Incidents of religious and educational conflict

SERIES 6M (POPULATION, ECONOMIC AFFAIRS, STATISTICS)

6M881 Report on emigration from Finistère (1926)

6M990 Annual statistics for the department, 1885–1938

6M994–1023 Annual agricultural statistics by arrondissement and canton, 1853–1932

SERIES 7M (AGRICULTURE)

7M78 Agricultural *syndicats*, 1909

7M746 Cultivation of flax and hemp: Statistics and information, year X to 1921

7M747 Linen manufacture

7M748 Agricultural labor force: emigration, family allocations, departmental commission

7M254 Agriculture: correspondence, statistics, reports, 1812–1937

7M256 Potatoes: reports, export, 1813–1936

7M259 Agricultural land use, 1810–1837

7M261–62 Miscellaneous reports on agricultural production

7M267 Agricultural inquiry of 1929

7M288 Agricultural syndicats

SERIES S (TRANSPORT)

4S134 Statistics, tonnage from ports

SERIES T (EDUCATION AND CULTURAL AFFAIRS)

1T68 Instruction of Breton language: Correspondence, reports, 1822–1938

1T75 Primary Education: Opposition to lay education, 1905–1937

1T78 Catechism in public schools, 1879, 1891, 1924

2T29–45 Departmental press, 1841–1940

2T56–61 Periodicals published in Finistère, 1810–1845

SERIES V (RELIGIOUS AFFAIRS)

1V39–40 Police générale des cultes, 1875–1894; Catholic congress in Landerneau, 1896; Diocesan synod in Quimper, 1902

1V42 Catholic associations and groups: Catholic circles, 1886–1887; Assumptionist committees, 1899; Jeunesse Catholique Bretonne, Quimper congress, 1906

1V48 Missions, pilgrimages, 1881–1903

1V49 Processions, 1872–1903

1V50 Quêtes (public collections), 1871–1907

1V56 Instruction of catechism in school, electoral catechisms, use of Breton, 1887–1904

1V57–63 [Unauthorized] use of Breton in religious instruction

1V64–70 Political activity and attitudes among the clergy during elections, suspension of salaries
1V84–86 Dossiers of the bishops of Quimper
1V665 Budgets, 1897–1911
1V1109–1242 Religious congregations: Application of the Law of 1 July Law on Associations

SERIES Z (SUBPREFECTURES)
1Z–5Z Unclassified documents and reports, subprefectures of Brest, Châteaulin, Morlaix, Quimper, Quimperlé

Direction Départementale de l'Agriculture du Finistère, Quimper

Direction des Services Agricoles—Département du Finistère. "Monographie agricole du Finistère, 1929." Typescript.

Archives de l'Evêché de Quimper et Léon, Quimper

3F "Questionnaire pour la visite canonique." Diocese of Quimper, 1909.
2H310–13 Fonds du Grand Séminaire à Quimper. Sécretariat de la Conférence des Cours d'Oeuvres, 1885–1908

Bibliothèque Nationale, Paris

MSS 3342 Nouvelles acquisitions françaises, chansons bretonnes
Yn 1–512 Chansons bretonnes sur feuilles volantes

French Government Publications

Ministère de l'Agriculture. *La petite propriété rurale. Enquêtes monographiques (1908–1909)*. Paris: Imprimerie Nationale, 1909.
_____. *Statistique agricole de la France: Résultats généraux de l'enquête décennale de 1862*. Strasbourg: Imprimerie Administrative Berger-Levrault, 1868.
_____. *Statistique agricole de la France: Résultats généraux de l'enquête décennale de 1882*. Nancy: Imprimerie Administrative Berger-Levrault, 1887.
_____. *Statistique agricole de la France: Résultats généraux de l'enquête décennale de 1892*. Paris: Imprimerie Nationale, 1897.
Ministère de l'Agriculture, du Commerce et des Travaux Publics. *Agriculture: Résultats généraux de l'enquête décennale de 1862*. Strasbourg: Imprimerie Administrative Berger-Levrault, 1868.
_____. *Enquête agricole. Deuxième série: Troisième Circonscription*. Paris: Imprimerie Impériale, 1868.

Newspapers and Almanacs

Action Libérale de Quimper, 1902–1906
Adsao! 1930–1933
L'Ajonc, 1904–1910

Almanach ann den Honest
Almanach de Léon et de Cornouaille: Gallek ha Brezonek
Almanach républicain électoral illustré
Ann Hader
Buhez Breiz, 1919–1924
Bulletin de la Fédération des Groupements Industriels du Finistère, 1924
Bulletin de la Ligue de Défense et d'Action Catholique, 1925–1926
Bulletin de l'Office Central et l'Union Régionale des Syndicats Agricoles du Finistère, 1919–1926
Bulletin des syndicats agricoles de la Basse Bretagne, 1892–1914
Le Citoyen, 1906–1926
La Cocarde
Le Courrier du Finistère, 1892–1926
Le Démocrate de Brest, 1912
La Dépêche de Brest, 1890–1926
L'Echo Paroissial de Brest, 1900–1911
L'Etoile de la Mer, 1895–1901
Le Finistère, 1890–1926
L'Indépendent du Sud Finistère, 1906–1908
Le Militant, 1912–1914, 1919–1924
Mouez Ar Vro, 1919–1921
Le Petit Breton, 1920–1926
Le Petit Démocrate du Finistère, 1919–1920
Le Progrès du Finistère, 1907–1926
La Quinzaine ouvrière de Relecq Kerhuon, 1907–1912
Le Républicain démocrate, 1914
La Résistance de Morlaix, 1890–1926
La Semaine religieuse du diocèse de Quimper et Léon, 1890–1926
L'Univers, 1897

Contemporary Printed Material

Allignol, C. *De l'état actuel du clergé en France et en particulier des curés ruraux appelés desservants*. Paris: N.p., 1839.

D' Angeville, Adolphe. *Essai sur la statistique de la population française considerée sous quelques-uns de ses rappports physiques et moraux*. Paris: n. p., 1836. Reprint, Hague: Mouton and Maison des Sciences de l'Homme, 1969.

Augé-Laribé, Michel. *L'évolution de la France agricole*. Paris: A. Colin, 1912.

Barrès, Maurice. *Les lézardes sur la maison*. 4th ed. Paris: Sansot, 1904.

_____. *Scènes et doctrines du nationalisme*. Paris: Plon, 1925.

_____. *L'oeuvre de Maurice Barrès*. Vols. 4 and 5. Paris, 1965.

Baudrillart, Henri. *Les populations agricoles de la France*. Vol. 1: *Normandie et Bretagne*. Paris: Hachette, 1885.

Bertillon, Jacques. *Le dépopulation de la France: ses conséquences, ses causes, mesures à prendre pour la combattre* Paris: Alcan, 1911.

Cambry, Jacques. *Voyage dans le Finistère ou état de ce départment en 1794 et 1795*. 3 vols. Paris: Librairie du Cercle Social, 1799.

Chevalier, Louis. *Statistique agricole du Finistère*. Quimper: A. Jaoucn, 1893.

Choleau, Jean. *La condition actuelle des serviteurs ruraux bretons.* Vannes: La-folye, 1907.

_____. *Expansion bretonne au XIXe siècle.* Paris: Champion, 1922.

Combes, Emile. *Mon ministère, 1902–1905.* Paris: Plon, 1956.

Corgne, Eugène. *Histoire du collège de Lesneven (1833–1914).* Brest: Imprimerie du "Courrier du Finistère," 1922.

De Jésus, Anne. *Istor Breiz ou histoire populaire de la Bretagne par une fille du Saint-Esprit.* 4th ed. Brest: n.p., 1893.

Delourme, Paul. *Trente-cinq années de la politique religieuse ou l'histoire de "l'Ouest Eclair."* Paris: Fustier, n.d.

Dupin, Charles. *Forces productives et commerciales de la France.* 2 vols. Brussels: Jobard, 1828.

Dupont, Joseph. *Une contrebrochure à propos de l'amovibilité des desservants.* Paris: n. p., 1865.

_____. *Tribulations du desservant.* Aisne: Retheuil, 1870.

de Gailhard-Bancel, Hyacinthe. *Les syndicats agricoles aux champs et au parlement, 1884–1924.* Paris: Spes, 1930.

Gayraud, Hippolyte. *Questions du jour: Politiques, sociales, religieuses, philosophiques.* Paris: Bloud & Barral, 1897.

_____. *Les démocrates chrétiens: Doctrine et programme.* Paris: Lecoffre, 1899.

_____. *La république et la paix religieuse.* Paris: Perrin, 1900.

_____. *Un catholique peut-il être socialiste?* Paris: Bloud & Gay, 1904.

_____. *La loi de séparation et le pape Pie X.* Paris: Bloud & Gay, 1906.

Goyen, F. *Expulsées.* Quimper: de Kerangal, 1903.

Kerviler, René. *La Bretagne pendant la Révolution.* Rennes: F. Simon, 1912.

Le Bail, Albert. *l'agriculture dans un département français: Le Finistère agricole, étude d'économie rurale.* Angers: Société française d'imprimerie d'Angers,

Le Bail, Albert. *l'agriculture dans un département français: Le Finistère agricole, étude d'économie rurale.* Angers: Société française d'imprimerie d'Angers, 1925.

Le Bail, Georges. *Une élection législative de 1906 (miettes électorales), mémoires,* Giard & E. Brière, 1913.

Le Bourhis, Francis. *Etude sur la culture et les salaires agricoles en Haute-Cornouaille.* Rennes: Fr. Simon, 1908.

Le Roux, Sylvère. *Conférences sur la crise agricole dans la région Nord-Finistère.* Brest: L. Evain-Roger, 1885.

Maurras, Charles. *L'idée de la décentralisation.* Paris: Revue encyclopédique, 1898.

_____. *Enquête sur la monarchie.* Paris: Nouvelle Librairie Nationale, 1924.

_____. *Oeuvres capitales.* Vols. 2 and 3. Paris: Flammarion, 1954.

Mocaër, Pierre. *La question bretonne: régionalisme et nationalisme.* Lorient: Le Bayon-Roger, 1916.

Morand, Maurice Emile. *De la production et du commerce des primeurs dans le pays de Léon (Finistère).* Rennes: Imprimeries Réunies, 1932.

Picard, Yves. *L'ouvrier agricole de Saint-Pol-de-Léon.* Brest: Imprimerie e la Dépêche, 1924.

Picaud, Ernest. *De la culture des primeurs dans les communes de Plougastel-Daoulas, Saint-Pol-de-Léon, Roscoff.* Rennes: n. p., 1912.

De Pierrefeu, Guy. *Le clergé fin-de-siècle.* Paris: Dentu, 1896.

Pottier, Paul. *Les prolétaires dans le clergé français*. Paris: Davy, 1899.

Raymond-Laurent, Jean. *Manuel politique et social: Le programme des républicaines démocrates*. Paris: Spes, 1924.

———. *Le parti démocrate populaire: Ses origines, son organisation, son action, son programme, ses statuts*. Paris: Editions P.D.P., 1927.

———. *Le parti démocrate populaire 1924–1944: La politique intérieure et extérieure de la France, 1919–1939*. Le Mans: Imprimerie Commerciale, 1965.

———. *Le parti démocrate populaire: Ce qu'il est—ce qu'il veut*. Paris: Editions P.D.P., n.d.

———. *Pour sortir de la crise: Le plan démocrate populaire*. Paris: Editions P.D.P., n.d.

Renan, Ernest. *Qu'est-ce q'une nation?: conférence faite en Sorbonne, le 11 Mars 1882*. Paris: Calmann-Lévy, 1882.

———. *Souvenirs d'enfance et de la jeunesse*. Paris: Calmann-Levy, 1912.

———. "What is a Nation?" In *Nation and Narration*. Edited by Homi Bhahba. Translated by Martin Thom. New York: Routledge, 1990.

Souvestre, Emile. *Les derniers Bretons*. Paris: Michel Lévy, 1858.

Vallaux, Camille. *La Basse-Bretagne: Etude de géographie humaine*. Paris, 1906. Reprint, Geneva: Slatkine, 1980.

Young, Arthur. *Travels in France and Italy during the Years, 1787, 1788, and 1789*. London: Dent, 1922.

———. *Voyages in France during the Years 1787, 1788, and 1789*, ed. Constantia Maxwell. Cambridge, 1929.

Secondary Sources

Achard, Pierre. "History and the Politics of Language in France: A Review Essay." *History Workshop Journal* 10 (Autumn 1980): 175–83.

Agulhon, Maurice. "Vues nouvelles sur la France rurale au 19ᵉ siècle." In *Irlande et France XVIIIᵉ–XXᵉ siècles: Pour une histoire rurale comparée*, edited by L. M. Cullen and François Furet. Paris: Editions de l'Ecole des Hautes Etudes en Sciences Sociales, 1980.

———. *The Republic in the Village: The People of the Var from the French Revolution to the Second Republic*. Translated by Janet Lloyd. Cambridge: Cambridge University Press, 1982.

Anderson, Benedict. *Imagined Communities: Reflections on the Origin and Spread of Nationalism*. London: Verso, 1983.

Andries, Lise. "Almanacs: Revolutionizing a Traditional Genre." In *Revolution in Print: The Press in France, 1775–1800*, edited by Robert Darnton and Daniel Roche. Berkeley: University of California Press, 1989.

Armengaud, André. "Enseignement et langues régionales au XIXe siècle: l'exemple du sud-ouest toulousain." In *Régions et régionalisme en France du XVIII siècle à nos jours*, edited by Christian Gras and Georges Livet, pp. 265–72. Paris: Presses Universitaires de France, 1977.

Arnal, Oscar L. "The Nature and Success of Breton Christian Democracy: Example of *l'Ouest Eclair*." *Catholic Historical Review* 68 (April 1982): 226–48.

———. *Ambivalent Alliance: The Catholic Church and the Action Française 1899–1939*. Pittsburgh: University of Pittsburgh Press, 1985.

Aupest-Conduche, Dominique, et al. *Histoire religieuse de la Bretagne*. Chambry: C.L.D., 1980.

Auspitz, Katherine. *The Radical Bourgeoisie: The Ligue de l'Enseignement and the Origins of the Third Republic, 1866–1885*. Cambridge: Cambridge University Press, 1982.

Badone, Ellen. *The Appointed Hour: Death, Worldview, and Social Change in Brittany*. Berkeley: University of California Press, 1989.

Baker, Keith. *Inventing the French Revolution: Essays in French Political Culture*. Cambridge: Cambridge University Press, 1990.

Barbier, Emmanuel. *Histoire du catholicisme libéral et du catholicisme social en France du concile de Vatican à l'avènement de Benoît XV*. Vols. 3 and 4. Bordeaux: Cadoret, 1924.

Barnard, F. M. "National Culture and Political Legitimacy: Herder and Rousseau." *Journal of the History of Ideas* 44 (April–June 1983): 231–53.

Barral, Pierre. *Les agrariens de Méline à Pisani*. Cahiers de la Fondation Nationale des Sciences Politiques, no. 164. Paris: A. Colin, 1968.

———. "Les syndicats bretons de cultivateurs cultivants." *Le Mouvement Social*, no. 67 (April–June 1969): 147–61.

Barrows, Susanna. "After the Commune: Alcoholism, Temperance, and Literature in the Early Third Republic." In *Consciousness and Class Experience in Nineteenth-Century Europe*, edited by John M. Merriman, pp. 205–18. New York: Holmes and Meier, 1979.

Bedel-Bernard, Marine. "L'enseignement primaire dans le Finistère, 1863–1905." Thèse d'Etat, Ecole Nationale des Chartes, 1981.

Bendix, Reinhard. *Nation-Building and Citizenship*. New York: Wiley, 1964.

Berenson, Edward. *Populist Religion and Left-Wing Politics in France, 1830–1852*. Princeton: Princeton University Press, 1984.

Berger, Suzanne. *Peasants Against Politics: Rural Organization in Brittany, 1911–1967*. Cambridge: Harvard University Press, 1972.

Berthou, Albert. Interview with author. Brest, France, 4 October 1984.

Bertocci, Philip A. *Jules Simon: Republican Anticlericalism and Cultural Politics in France, 1848–1886*. Columbia: University of Missouri Press, 1978.

Biersack, Aletta. "Local Knowledge, Local History: Geertz and Beyond. In *The New Cultural History*, edited by Lynn Hunt, pp. 72–96. Berkeley: University of California Press, 1989.

Biton, Louis. *La démocratie chrétienne dans la politique française: Sa grandeur, ses servitudes*. Angers: H. Siraudeau, n.d.

Blackbourn, David. *Class, Religion and Local Politics in Wilhelmine Germany: The Center Party in Württemberg before 1914*. New Haven: Yale University Press, 1980.

Bois, Paul. *Paysans de l'Ouest: Des structures économiques et sociales aux options politiques depuis l'epoque révolutionnaire dans le Sarthe*. Le Mans: Le Vilaine, 1960.

Boserup, Ester. *Population and Technological Change: A Study of Long-Term Trends*. Chicago: University of Chicago Press, 1981.

Boulard, Fernand. *Essor ou déclin du clergé français?* Paris: Cerf, 1950.

Bowman, Frank Paul. *Le Christ des barricades, 1789–1848.* Paris, Cerf, 1987.

Braudel, Fernand. *L'identité de la France.* 3 vols. Paris: Flammarion, 1988.

Brekilien, Yann. *La vie quotidienne des paysans en Bretagne au XIX siècle.* Paris: Hachette, 1966.

Brugerette, Joseph. *Le prêtre français et la société contemporaine.* Vol. 1: *La restauration catholique, 1851–1871.* Paris: Lethielleux, 1933.

———. *Le prêtre français et la société contemporaine* Vol. 2: *Vers la séparation de l'eglise et de l'état, 1871–1908.* Paris: Lethielleux, 1935.

Burguière, André. *Bretons de Plozévet.* Paris: Flammarion, 1977.

Burns, Michael. *Rural Society and French Politics: Boulangism and the Dreyfus Affair, 1886–1900.* Princeton: Princeton University Press, 1984.

Capitan, Collette. "Enquête pluridisciplinaire sur Plozévet: La vie politique de la Révolution aux lendemains de la Liberation." Archives Départementales du Finistère, Quimper. Typescript, n.d.

Caron, Jeanne. *Le sillon et la démocratie chrétienne, 1894–1910.* Paris: Plon, 1967.

Charpy, Jacques. "Dénombrement de la population des communes du Finistère (1790–1968)." *Bulletin de la société archéologique du Finistère* 99, no. 2 (1972): 849–87.

Chartier, Roger. *Cultural History: Between Practices and Representations.* Translated by Lydia Cochrane. Ithaca: Cornell University Press, l988.

Chaunu, Pierre. *France: Histoire de la sensibilité des français à la France.* Paris: Laffont, 1982.

Cholvy, Gérard. "Enseignement religieux et langues maternelles en France au XIXe siècle." *Revue des langues romanes* 82 (1976): 27–52.

———. "Régionalisme et clergé catholique au XIXe siècle." In *Régions et régionalisme en France du XVIII à nos jours,* edited by Christian Gras and Georges Livet, pp. 187–201. Paris: Presses Universitaires de France, 1977.

Cholvy, Gérard, and Yves-Marie Hilaire. *Histoire religieuse de la France contemporaine.* Vol. 1: *1800–1880.* Toulouse: Privat, 1985.

———. *Histoire religieuse de la France contemporaine.* Vol. 2: *1880–1930.* Toulouse: Privat, 1989.

Chombart de Lauwe, Jean. *Bretagne et pays de la Garonne.* Paris: Presses Universitaires de France, 1946.

Christian, William A., Jr. *Person and God in a Spanish Valley.* Princeton: Princeton University Press, 1989.

Cleary, M. C. *Peasants, Politicians, and Producers: The Organisation of Agriculture in France since 1918.* Cambridge: Cambridge University Press, l989.

Cloître, Marie-Thérèse. "Aspects de la vie politique dans le département du Finistère de 1848 à 1870." *Bulletin de la Société Archéologique du Finistère* 99, no. 2 (1972): 731–802.

———. "Les années 1898–1914 vues par *L'Echo Paroissial de Brest.*" In *Etudes sur la presse en Bretagne aux XIXe et XXe siècles,* edited by Yves Le Gallo. Cahiers de Bretagne Occidentale, no. 3. Landerneau: Cloître, 1981.

Clout, Hugh. "Land-Use Change in Finistère during the Eighteenth and Nineteenth Centuries." *Etudes rurales* 73 (January–March 1979): 69–76.

———. *The Land of France, 1815–1914.* London: Allen and Unwin, 1983.

Collet, Daniel. "La population rurale du Finistère au XIXe siècle (1821–1901)." *Mémoires de la Société d'Histoire et d'Archéologie de Bretagne* 59 (1982): 83–115.

Colley, Linda. "Whose Nation? Class and National Consciousness in Britain, 1750–1830." *Past and Present* 33 (1986): 96–117.

Coornaert, E. "Flamand et français dans l'enseignement en Flandre français des annexations au XXe siècle. *Revue du Nord* 53, no. 209 (1971): 217–21.

Corbin, Alain. *Archaisme et modernité en Limousin au XIXe siècle, 1845–1880.* 2 vols. Paris: M. Rivière, 1975.

Croix, Alain, and Fanch Roudaut, *Les bretons, la mort et Dieu de 1600 nos jours.* Paris: Messidor, 1984.

Dallas, Gregor. *The Imperfect Peasant Economy: The Loire Country, 1800–1914.* Cambridge: Cambridge University Press, 1982.

Daniel, Tanguy. "Religion paysanne et catholicisme romain, analyse d'un phénomène d'acculturation en Basse-Bretagne au milieu du XVIIe siècle." *Bulletin de la Société Archéologique du Finistère* 99, no. 2 (1972): 683–704.

Dansette, Adrian. *Religious History of Modern France: From the Revolution to the Third Republic.* Vols. 1 and 2. Translated by John Dingle. New York: Herder and Herder, 1961.

Davis, Natalie Z. "The Rites of Violence." In *Society and Culture in Early Modern France*, pp. 152–87. Stanford: Stanford University Press, 1976.

De Certeau, Michel. *Une politique de la langue: La révolution française et les patois.* Paris: Gallimard, 1975.

Delbreuil, Jean-Claude. "Le parti démocrate populaire: Des origines au M.R.P." 4 vols. Thèse d'ètat. Université de Paris X—Nanterre, 1984.

Delumeau, Jean, ed. *Histoire de la Bretagne.* Toulouse: Privat, 1969.

Denis, Michel. *L'église et la république en Mayenne, 1896–1906.* Paris: Klincksieck, 1967.

———. *Les royalistes de la Mayenne et le monde moderne, XIXe–XXe siècles.* Paris: Klincksieck, 1977.

Desan, Suzanne. "Redefining Revolutionary Liberty: The Rhetoric of Religious Revival during the French Revolution." *Journal of Modern History* 60, no. 1 (1988): 1–27.

———. "Crowds, Community, and Ritual in the Work of E. P. Thompson and Natalie Davis." In *The New Cultural History*, edited by Lynn Hunt, pp. 47–71. Berkeley: University of California Press, 1989.

———. *Reclaiming the Sacred: Lay Religion and Popular Politics in Revolutionary France.* Ithaca: Cornell University Press, 1990.

Dion, Michel. *L'Etat, l'église et luttes populaires.* Paris: Presses Universitaires de France, 1980.

Duby, Georges, et al., eds. *Histoire de la France rurale.* 4 vols. Paris: Seuil, 1975–1976.

Dupuy, Roger. "Les femmes dans la contre-révolution dans l'ouest." *Bulletin d'histoire économique et sociale de la Révolution française*, année 1979. Paris: Bibliothéque Nationale, 1980. pp. 61–70.

Duroselle, Jean-Baptiste. *Les débuts du catholicisme social en France (1822–1870).* Paris; Presses Universitaires de France, 1951.

Eggs, Eckhard. "Kirche-Sprache-Religion: Zur Role der katholischen Kirche in der Bretagne." *Lendemains*, no. 15 (1979): 57–76.

Elegoet, Fanch. "Prêtres, nobles et paysans en Léon au début du XXe siècle: Notes sur le nationalisme breton, Feiz Ha Breiz, 1900–1914." *Pluriel*, no. 18 (1979): 40–97.

———. *Paysannes de Léon*. Tud Ha Bro, Sociétés Bretonnes, nos. 3–4. Landerneau: Cloître, 1980.

———. *Révoltes paysannes en Bretagne: A l'origine de l'organisation des marchés*. Plabennec: Editions du Léon, 1984.

Elegoet, Louis. *Saint-Méen: Vie et déclin d'une civilisation paroissiale dans le Bas-Léon*. Paris: Anthropos, 1981.

Faury, Jean. *Cléricalisme et anticléricalisme dans le Tarn (1848–1900)*. Toulouse: Université de Toulouse, 1980.

Febvre, Lucien. "Langue et nationalité en France au XVIII siècle." *Revue du synthèse historique* 42 (1926): 19–40.

Fishman, J. A., ed. *Language Problems in Developing Nations*. New York, 1968.

Ford, Caroline. "Religion and the Politics of Cultural Change in Provincial France: The Resistance of 1902 in Lower Brittany." *Journal of Modern History* 62, no. 1 (1990): 1–33.

Furet, François, and Jacques Ozouf, eds. *Reading and Writing in France from Calvin to Jules Ferry*. Cambridge: Cambridge University Press, 1982.

Gargan, Edward T. "The Priestly Culture in Modern France." *Catholic Historical Review* 57 (April 1971): 3–20.

Gasnault-Beis, M. Cl. "Enquête pluridisciplinaire sur Plozévet. Foi et laïcisme: La paroisse de Plozévet à l'époque contemporaine." Archives Départmentales du Finistère. Typescript, n.d.

Geertz, Clifford. *The Interpretation of Cultures: Selected Essays*. New York: Basic Books, 1973.

———. *Local Knowledge: Further Essays in Interpretive Anthropology*. New York: Basic Books, 1983.

Gibson, Ralph. *A Social History of French Catholicism, 1789–1914*. New York: Routledge, 1989.

Gildea, Robert. *Education in Provincial France 1800–1914: A Study of Three Departments*. Oxford: Clarendon Press, 1983.

Girard, Christian. "L'évolution quantitative du clergé diocésain de Quimper, 1803–1968." Mémoire de maîtrise, Université de Rennes, 1968.

Girauden, Daniel. "Chanteurs populaires et production imprimée au XIXe siècle en Basse Bretagne." *Mémoires de la société d'histoire et d'archéologie de Bretagne* 62 (1985): 415–25.

Goardon, Henri. "Moeurs et coutumes du Cap Sizun au début du XXe siècle." *Bulletin de la Société Archéologique du Finistère* 102 (1974): 223–79; 103 (1975): 255–75.

Godechot, Jacques. "Nation, patrie, nationalisme et patriotisme en France au XVIIIe siècle." In *Regards sur l'époque révolutionnaire*, pp. 53–68. Toulouse: Privat, 1980.

Goguel, François. *La politique des partis sous la Troisième République*. Paris: Seuil, 1948.

Goldstein, Jan. "The Hysteria Diagnosis and the Politics of Anticlericalism in Late Nineteenth-Century France." *Journal of Modern History* 54, no. 2 (June 1982): 209–39.

Guin, Yannick. *Histoire de la Bretagne de 1789 à nos jours: Contribution à la critique de l'idéologie nationaliste.* Paris: Maspero, 1982.

Guiomar, Jean-Yves. *L'idéologie nationale: nation, représentation, propriété.* Paris: Champ Libre, 1974.

Helias, Pierre Jakez. *The Horse of Pride: Life in a Breton Village.* Translated by June Guicharnaud. New Haven: Yale University Press, 1978.

Heywood, Colin. "The Role of the French Peasantry in French Industrialization, 1815–1880." *Economic History* 34 (August 1981): 359–76.

Higonnet, Patrice. "The Politics of Linguistic Terrorism and Grammatical Hegemony during the French Revolution." *Social History* 5 (January 1980): 41–69.

Hilaire, Yves-Marie. *Une chrétienté au XIXe siècle: La vie religieuse des populations du diocèse d'Arras (1840–1914).* 2 vols. Villeneuve-d'Ascq: Universitè de Lille III, 1977.

_____, ed. *Matériaux pour l'histoire religieuse du peuple français, XIXe–XXe siècles.* Paris: Presses de la Fondation Nationale des Sciences Politiques, 1987.

Hobsbawm, Eric. *Nations and Nationalism since 1780: Programme, Myth, Reality.* Cambridge: Cambridge University Press, 1990.

Hufton, Olwen. "Women in Revolution, 1789–1796." *Past and Present* 53 (1971): 90–108.

_____. "The Reconstruction of the Church, 1796–1801." In *Beyond the Terror: Essays in Regional and Social History, 1794–1815,* edited by Gywnne Lewis and Colin Lucas, pp. 21–52. Cambridge: Cambridge University Press, 1984.

Hufton, Olwen, and Frank Tallett. "Communities of Women, the Religious Life, and Public Service in 18th-Century France." In *Connecting Spheres: Women in the Western World, 1500 to the Present,* ed. Marilyn Boxer and Jean Quataert, pp. 75–85. Oxford: Oxford University Press, 1987.

Hunt, Lynn. *Politics, Culture, and Class in the French Revolution.* Berkeley: University of California Press, 1984.

Irving, R.E.M. *Christian Democracy in France.* London: George Allen and Unwin, 1973.

Isambert, J. A., and J. P. Terrenoire. *Atlas de la pratique cultuelle des catholiques en France.* Paris: Presses de la Fondation Nationale des Sciences Politiques, 1980.

Jones, Colin. *Charity and Bienfaisance: The Treatment of the Poor in the Montpellier Region, 1740–1815.* Cambridge: Cambridge University Press, 1982.

Jones, P. M. "La république au village in the southern Massif Central." *Historical Journal* 23 (1980): 793–812.

_____. "Political Commitment and Rural Society in the Southern Massif Central." *Europeans Studies Review* 10 (1980): 337–56.

_____. "Parish, Seigneurie and the Community of Inhabitants in Southern Central France during the Eighteenth and Nineteenth Centuries." *Past and Present* 91 (May 1981): 74–108.

_____. *Politics and Rural Society: The Southern Massif Central c. 1750–1880.* Cambridge: Cambridge University Press, 1985.

Judt, Tony. *Socialism in Provence 1871–1914: A Study in the Origins of the Modern French Left*. Cambridge: Cambridge University Press, 1979.

Karnoouh, Claude. "La démocratie impossible: Parenté et politique dans un village lorrain." *Etudes rurales* 52 (1973): 24–56.

Lagrée, Michel. *Catholicisme et société dans l'Ouest, cartes et statistiques*. Vol. 2: *Le XIXᵉ siècle*. Rennes: Université de Haute-Bretagne, n.d.

———. *Mentalités, religion et histoire en Haute Bretagne au XIXᵉᵐᵉ siècle: Le diocèse de Rennes, 1815–1848*. Paris: Klincksieck, 1977.

Lambert, Yves. *Catholicisme et société dans l'Ouest, cartes et statistiques*. Vol. 1: *Le XXᵉ siècle*. Rennes: Université de Haute Bretagne, 1982.

Lancelot, Alain. *Abstentionisme électoral en France*. Paris: A. Colin, 1968.

Langlois, Claude. *Le catholicisme au féminin: les congrégations françaises à supérieure générale au XIX siècle*. Paris, 1984.

Latrielle, A., and René Rémond. *Histoire du catholicisme en France*. Vol. 3: *La période contemporaine*. Paris: Spes, 1962.

Le Bras, Hervé, and Immanuel Todd. *L'invention de la France*. Paris: Livre de Poche, 1986.

Le Gallo, Yves. "Aux sources de l'anticléricalisme en Basse Bretagne: Un recteur sous la IIIe République." *Bulletin de la Société Archéologique du Finistère* 99, no. 2 (1972): 803–48.

———. "Une caste paysanne du Haut-Léon: Les 'Juloded.'" *Mémoires de la Société d'Histoire et d'Archéologie de Bretagne* 59 (1982): 53–82.

Le Goff, T.J.A. *Vannes and Its Region: A Study of Town and Country in Eighteenth-Century France*. Oxford: Oxford University Press, 1981.

Le Guirriec, Patrick. *Paysans, parents, partisans dans les Monts d'Arées*. Brasparts: Beltan, 1988.

McManners, John. *Church and State in France, 1870–1914*. New York: Harper & Row, 1972.

Magraw, Roger. *France, 1815–1914: The Bourgeois Century*. London: Oxford University Press, 1984.

Mallet, Serge. "A propos du syndicalisme agricole finistérien." *Etudes rurales* 8 (January–March 1963): 56–61.

Margadant, Ted W. *French Peasants in Revolt: The Insurrection of 1851*. Princeton: Princeton University Press, 1979.

———. "Tradition and Modernity in Rural France during the Nineteenth Century." *Journal of Modern History* 56 (December 1984): 667–97.

Martin, Benjamin F., Jr. "The Creation of the Action Libérale Populaire: An Example of Party Formation in Third Republic France." *French Historical Studies* 9 (Fall 1976): 660–89.

———. *Count Albert de Mun: Paladin of the Republic*. Chapel Hill: University of North Carolina Press, 1978.

Maurain, Jean. *La politique ecclésiastique du second empire de 1852 à 1869*. Paris: Felix Alcan, 1950.

Mayeur, Jean-Marie. "Le catholicisme social en France à la fin du XIXe siècle." *Mouvement Social*, no. 57 (October–December 1966): 211–16.

———. "Géographie de la résistance aux inventaires février-mars 1906." *Annales, économies, sociétés, civilisations* 21, no. 6 (November–December 1966): 1259–72.

———. *L'abbé Lemire: Un prêtre démocrate, 1853–1928*. Paris: Casterman, 1968.

———. "Catholicisme intransigeant, catholicisme social, démocratie chrétienne." *Annales, économies, sociétés, civilisations* 27, no. 2 (March–April 1972): 483–99.

———. "Démocratie chrétienne et régionalisme." In *Regions et régionalisme en France du XVIII siècle à nos jours*, edited by Christian Gras and Georges Livet. Paris: Presses Universitaires de France, 1977.

———. *Des partis catholiques à la démocratie chrétienne, XIX–XXe siècles*. Paris: A. Colin, 1980.

———, ed. *Libre pensée et religion laique en France de la fin du Second Empire à la fin de la Troisième République*. Strasbourg: Cerdic, 1980.

———. *La vie politique sous la Troisième République, 1870–1940*. Paris: Seuil, 1984.

Mayeur, Jean-Marie, and Madeleine Rébérioux. *The Third Republic from Its Origins to the Great War, 1871–1914*. Translated by J. R. Foster. Cambridge: Cambridge University Press, 1984.

Marcilhacy, Christianne. *Le diocèse d'Orléans au milieu du XIXe siècle: Les hommes et leurs mentalités*. Paris: Sirey, 1964.

Mévellec, F. *Le combat du paysan breton à travers les siècles*. Morlaix: Chez l'Auteur, 1973.

Mitchell, Harvey. "Resistance to the Revolution in Western France." *Past and Present* 63 (May 1974): 94–131.

Morin, Edgar. *Commune en France: La métamorphose de Plodémet*. Paris: Fayard, 1967.

Morineau, Michel. *Les faux semblants d'un démarrage économique en France au XVIII siècle*. Paris: A. Colin, 1971.

Nicolet, Claude. *L'idée républicaine en France: essai d'histoire critique*. Paris: Gallimard, 1982.

Nora, Pierre, ed. *Les lieux de mémoire*. Vol. 2: *Nation*. Paris: Gallimard, 1986.

———. "Nation." In *Critical Dictionary of the French Revolution*, edited by François Furet and Mona Ozouf, pp. 742–52. Translated by Arthur Goldhammer. Cambridge: Harvard University Press, 1989.

Noriel, Gérard. *Le creuset français: histoire de l'immigration français, XIX–XX siecles*. Paris: Seuil, 1988.

Ogès, Louis. *L'agriculture dans le Finistère au milieu du XIXe siècle*. Brest: Imprimerie du "Télégramme," 1949.

Ollivier, Joseph. *Catalogue bibliographique de la chanson populaire bretonne sur feuilles volantes (Léon, Tréguier, Cornouaille)*. Quimper: Le Goaziou, 1942.

Partin, Malcolm P. *Waldeck-Rousseau, Combes, and the Church: The Politics of Anticlericalism, 1899–1905*. Durham: Duke University Press, 1969.

Pascal, Jean. *Les députés bretons de 1789 à 1983*. Paris: Presses Universitaires de France, 1983.

Paul, Harry W. *The Second Ralliement: The Rapprochement between Church and*

State in France in the Twentieth Century. Washington, D.C.: Catholic University Press of America, 1967.

Pérennès, Chanoine H., and R. Cardaliaquet. "Vie de Mgr. Adolphe Duparc, évêque de Quimper et de Léon (1857–1946)." Archives de l'Evêché de Quimper. Typescript, n.d.

Peyre, Henri. *La royauté et les langues provinciales.* Paris: Presses modernes, 1933.

Pilenco, Alexandre. *Les moeurs du suffrage en France (1848–1928).* Paris: Editions de la "Revue Mondiale," 1930.

Poisson, Henri. *L'abbé Jean-Marie Perrot: Fondateur de Bleun Brug (1877–1943).* Rennes: Plihon, 1955.

Poulat, Emile. *Eglise contre la bourgeoisie.* Paris: Casterman, 1977.

Prélot, Marcel. "Les démocrates d'inspiration chrétienne entre les deux guerres (1919–1939)." *La vie intellectuelle* (December 1950): 533–59.

Quémeneur, abbé Francis. "Le Sillon: Morlaix, Landivisiau, Saint-Pol-de-Léon, 1903–1912." Archives de l'Evêché de Quimper. Typescript, n.d.

Quéré, Marie-Thérèse. "L'élection de l'abbé Gayraud dans la troisième circonscription de Brest en 1897." Diplôme d'études supérieures, Université de Paris IV, 1966.

Ramet, Pedro, ed. *Religion and Nationalism in Soviet and East European Politics.* Durham: Duke University Press, 1989.

Raoul, Lucien. *Un siècle du journalisme breton de l'académie celtique à la glorieuse Bretagne des armées.* Le Guilvinec: Le Signor, 1981.

Rapley, Elizabeth. *The Dévotes: Women and the Church in Seventeenth-Century France.* Montreal: McGill University Press, 1989.

Reece, Jack E. *The Bretons Against France: Ethnic Minority Nationalism in Twentieth-Century Brittany.* Chapel Hill: University of North Carolina Press, 1977.

Rémond, René. *Les deux congrès ecclésiastiques de Reims et de Bourges, 1896–1900.* Paris: Sirey, 1964.

Roger, Philippe. "Le débat sur la 'langue révolutionnaire.'" In *La carmagnole des muses: l'homme de lettres et l'artiste dans la révolution,* edited by Jean-Claude Bonnet, pp. 157–84. Paris: A. Colin 1988.

Rogers, Susan Carol. *Shaping Modern Times in Rural France: The Transformation and Reproduction of an Aveyronnais Community.* Princeton: Princeton University Press, 1991.

Roué, Jacques. "Etudes sur la vie paroissiale et religieuse de Lannilis, commune de Léon, du concordat à 1914." Mémoire de maîtrise. Université de Bretagne Occidentale, Brest, 1970.

Sahlins, Peter. "The Nation in the Village: State-Building and Communal Struggles in the Catalan Borderland in the Eighteenth and Nineteenth Centuries." *Journal of Modern History* 60, no. 2 (June 1988): 234–63.

———. *Boundaries: The Making of France and Spain in the Pyrenees.* Berkeley: University of California Press, 1989.

Schlesinger, Philip. "On National Identity: Some Conceptions and Misconceptions Criticized." *Social Science Information* 26 (1987): 219–64.

Sedgewick, Alexander. *The Ralliement in French Politics 1890–1898.* Harvard Historical Studies, vol. 74. Cambridge: Harvard University Press, 1965.

Segalen, Martine. *Love and Power in the Peasant Family: Rural France in the Nineteenth Century.* Chicago: University of Chicago Press, 1983.

———. *Quinze générations de Bas-Bretons: parenté et société dans le pays bigouden Sud, 1720–1980.* Paris: Presses Universitaires de France, 1985.

Siegfried, André. *Tableau politique de la France de l'Ouest sous la Troisième République.* Paris: A. Colin, 1913.

Skol Vreiz, *Histoire de la Bretagne et des pays celtiques.* Vol. 4: *La Bretagne au XIX siècle.* Rennes: Imprimerie Commerciale, 1980.

———. *Histoire de la Bretagne et des pays celtiques.* Vol. 5: *La Bretagne au XX siècle.* Rennes: Imprimerie Commerciale, 1983.

Smith, Bonnie. *Ladies of the Leisure Class: The Bourgeoises of Northern France.* Princeton: Princeton University Press, 1981.

Sperber, Jonathan. *Popular Catholicism in Nineteenth-Century Germany.* Princeton: Princeton University Press, 1984.

Sternhell, Zeev. *Maurice Barrès et le nationalisme français.* Paris: A. Colin, 1972.

Sutherland, Donald. *The Chouans: The Social Origins of Popular Counter-Revolution in Upper Brittany, 1770–1796.* Oxford: Clarendon Press, 1982.

Tackett, Timothy. *Priest and Parish in Eighteenth-Century France: A Social and Political Study of the Curés in the Diocese of Dauphiné, 1750–1791.* Princeton: Princeton University Press, 1977.

———. "The West in France in 1789: The Religious Factor and the Origins of the Counterrevolution." *Journal of Modern History* 54 (December 1982): 715–45.

———. *Religion, Revolution, and Regional Culture in Eighteenth-Century France: The Ecclesiastical Oath of 1791.* Princeton: Princeton University Press, 1986.

———. "Women and Men in Counterrevolution: The Sommières Riot of 1791." *Journal of Modern History* 59 (1987): 680–704.

Talmy, Robert. *Le syndicalisme chrétien en France (1871–1930): Les difficultés et controverses.* Paris: Bloud & Gay, 1965.

Tilly, Charles. "Did the Cake of Custom Break?" In *Consciousness and Class Experience in Nineteenth-Century Europe,* edited by John M. Merriman, pp. 17–44. New York: Holmes and Meier, 1979.

Tréboul, Charles. "Louis Hémon (1844–1914), député et sénateur républicain et la vie politique dans la Cornouaille quimperoise sous la Troisième République." Thése de troisième cycle, Université de Bretagne Occidentale, Brest, 1978.

Weber, Eugen. *Peasants Into Frenchmen: The Modernization of Rural France, 1870–1914.* Stanford: Stanford University Press, 1976.

———. "The Second Republic, Politics and the Peasant." *French Historical Studies* 11 (Fall 1980): 521–50.

———. "Comment la Politique Vint aux Paysans: A Second Look at Peasant Politicization." *American Historical Review* 87 (April 1982): 357–89.

Wilson, Stephen. "Catholic Populism in France at the Time of the Dreyfus Affair: The Union Nationale." *Journal of Contemporary History* 10 (October 1975): 667–705.

Wright, Gordon. *Rural Revolution in France: The Peasantry in the Twentieth Century.* Stanford: Stanford University Press, 1964.

Wright, Vincent. "Religion et politique dans les Basses-Pyrénées pendant la Deuxième République et le Second Empire." *Annales du Midi* 94 (October 1969): 409–42.

Zeldin, Theodore. *France 1848–1945: Politics and Anger*. London: Oxford University Press, 1979.

———, ed. *Conflicts in French Society: Anticlericalism, Education and Morals in the Nineteenth Century*. London: Allen & Unwin, 1970.

Index _____